.095

The Lesbian Issue

The Lesbian Issue
Essays from SIGNS

edited by

Estelle B. Freedman
Barbara C. Gelpi
Susan L. Johnson
Kathleen M. Weston

The University of Chicago Press
Chicago and London

The articles in this volume originally appeared in the Autumn 1982 (Volume 8, number 1), Winter 1983 (Volume 9, number 2), Summer 1984 (Volume 9, number 4), and Autumn 1984 (Volume 10, number 1) issues of *Signs: Journal of Women in Culture and Society.*

The University of Chicago Press, Chicago 60637
The University of Chicago Press, Ltd., London

Library of Congress Cataloging in Publication Data
Main entry under title:

The Lesbian issue.

Includes index.
1. Lesbians—Addresses, essays, lectures. I. Freedman, Estelle B., 1947–   . II. Signs.
HQ75.5.L44   1985   306.7'663   84–16246
ISBN 0-226-26151-4
ISBN 0-226-26152-2 (pbk.)

Contents

Introduction

When *Signs* first began publication in 1975, it, along with other women's studies journals, served as outlet for but also as ratification of feminist scholarship; centering one's scholarly interest on the subject of women—a topic that in earlier years was made to seem trivial or nonexistent or simply inappropriate—now had validity. These adjectives have, in the main, continued to be applied to the study of women whose primary relation is to other women. Such women, and such relationships, have been considered peripheral at best and threatening at worst to the "real"—that is, heterosexual—world and thus unimportant to the humanities and social sciences. If the heterosexual scholar remained uninterested in exploring lesbianism, the lesbian scholar was often in no position to compensate for this silence; for many women in academia, even the hint of a personal life of intimacy with other women remained professionally risky.

For these reasons, when we started planning this collection as a special issue of *Signs* in 1982, we decided that it would be called, simply, "The Lesbian Issue," for we felt that in academia to study a lesbian subject, as to be a lesbian scholar, remained a controversial issue. At the completion of this project in 1984, we were pleased to be able to give recognition to so much exciting new research. Submissions for the issue suggested that lesbian scholarship was flourishing in almost all academic disciplines; of the forty manuscripts considered, one-third were in the field of literature, another third in the social sciences, and a final third in history, anthropology, politics, and theory. To the original ten essays selected for inclusion in the special issue, we have added here five others that have appeared in *Signs* since 1982. These fifteen essays reflect, we suspect, the more thorough development of lesbian studies in literature and history, disciplines that are overrepresented here. We take note as well of the fact that both women and men, homosexuals and heterosexuals, have contributed to this book. We hope that this collection of their current work will serve as a milestone in feminist scholarly recognition of the legitimacy of lesbian studies and its import to a full understanding of women in culture and society.

The essays here, while differing in particular focus, center on two major themes: first, lesbian identity—its historical genesis and its relationship to both lesbian and heterosexual communities—and, second, the survival, in homophobic cultures, of women whose primary relation is to other women. The emphasis of both these themes and their treatment so far in fictional accounts and personal narratives may help to explain why thinking on the subject of lesbianism seems most highly developed in the fields of literature and history. Unquestionably, there is interest in the subject within the social sciences, as Susan Krieger's review essay on lesbian identity and community reveals. But, as Krieger notes, both research method and theory are hampered at present. One of the methodological problems results from many lesbians' decision to remain "in the closet" in the face of society's homophobia—a situation that prevents acquisition of data from a group large enough to make meaningful analysis possible. Another problem lies in the white, middle-class background of most researchers, who lack the contacts necessary to build trust among research populations sufficiently varied in class, ethnicity, and work experiences. More significant, however, is the vacuum in theory, except for historical theory on lesbian identity. Such focus on identity may in fact limit inquiry to those cultures in which lesbian identity and survival *as lesbians* are crucial matters of concern; it may hinder cross-cultural analysis, for example, because it provides inadequate vocabulary for discussion of relationships among Third World women.

The current focus on identity may also lie behind our very limited number of submissions from or about women outside Europe and the United States. The historical evolution of a lesbian identity has in this North Atlantic area been of remarkable significance, but discussion of lesbianism in these terms has relevance only where identity and sexuality are intertwined and where personal identity is itself a cultural value. Evelyn Blackwood's essay on the female cross-gender role among Native American peoples, for example, emphasizes the importance of supplying historical and cultural context in examining an identity that incorporated sexual relations between women but that rested on performance of a social role rather than on sexuality. She concludes that those who categorize the berdache using the standards of Western society fail to comprehend the conditions of sexual equality, the dissociation of gender from physical attributes, and the wide range of options open to women in Native American cultures. A great deal more of such work must be done before we can begin to grasp the scope and significance of woman-centered relationships across different cultures and among different classes. Nonetheless, *The Lesbian Issue*, while necessarily building on previous work in which the theme of identity has been paramount, will, we hope, act as signpost as well as milestone and encourage new research on these and other questions.

The complex topics of both lesbian identity and lesbian survival in themselves, of course, are hardly limiting, as the contributions here demonstrate. For instance, Judith Brown's Archive on the trial of a nun in Renaissance Italy, Martha Vicinus's essay on English schoolgirl crushes on schoolmistresses or other young women, and the Archive of John D'Emilio and Allan Bérubé on changes within U.S. armed forces policies toward lesbians all describe social institutions—convents, boarding schools, the military—that encourage intense relationships among women, thus creating opportunities for assumption of lesbian identity, and yet deny, suppress, and punish expressions that might otherwise encourage movement toward such identity. However, we learn as well that efforts to suppress can also indicate the extent to which lesbianism has become a cultural category, as in the case of the explicit attack on lesbianism by the U.S. armed forces in the 1950s.

The doublethink reflected in these particular situations—the fostering of women's relationships coupled with insistence that sexual expression within them is deviant and unnatural—constitutes historically perhaps the greatest barrier to a woman's untroubled assumption of a lesbian identity. Both Esther Newton's essay on the significance of Radclyffe Hall's *The Well of Loneliness* and Sharon O'Brien's essay on Willa Cather detail the complexity of assuming such identity at a time when homosexuality itself was emerging as a prominent, if stigmatized, feature of North Atlantic culture.

Newton and O'Brien, along with Vicinus, bring new insights to discussions about the role of sexologists such as Richard von Krafft-Ebing and Havelock Ellis in creating modern lesbian identities. More important, however—not only in these three essays but also in Bonnie Zimmerman's review of lesbian personal narratives and in Jean Kennard's article on a lesbian approach to reader-response theory—are women's own strategies for survival and for creating lesbian identity while participating in dominantly heterosexual and often homophobic cultures. Indeed, as Martin Levine and Robin Leonard's report on discrimination against lesbians in the U.S. work force shows, despite the possibilities that now exist for women to assume a lesbian identity, survival in a homophobic workplace can and still does involve passing as heterosexual in order to avoid harassment and eventual dismissal. And, as Lourdes Arguelles and Ruby Rich suggest in their essay on homosexuality in Cuba, gay and lesbian identities can take many covert and overt forms, depending in large part on the material as well as the ideological and cultural conditions within with they develop.

Women writers have also employed various strategies in their struggle to achieve a woman-centered expression that challenges the dominant literary tradition. Susan Gubar shows how women modernists from the 1890s to the 1930s, incuding such writers as Renée Vivien and H. D., attempted to resolve the contradiction between the identity of woman and that of writer through "the dynamic of collaboration with Sappho," invoking the poet of Lesbos to confirm both their artistic and sexual identities. Namascar Shaktini's analysis of *Le corps lesbien* by Monique Wittig considers the threat to women's identity posed by a language system that makes a male-identified subject the focus of all discourse. Wittig accomplishes a restructuring of language that reveals a lesbian subject previously obscured by phallogocentric formulations. Achievement of a language that gives voice to lesbian experiences silenced by patriarchy is also the theme of Susan Friedman's essay on the close connection between the poets H. D. and Adrienne Rich. Friedman explores the way in which Rich's allusions to the work of H. D. in *The Dream of a Common Language* create a virtual dialogue between the poets that illuminates the woman-centered world each (though in differing ways) takes as her ideal.

Where lesbian identity is shared and valued—as it is in the context of lesbian communities discussed by Krieger, lesbian personal narratives reviewed by Zimmerman, and the lesbian auto-repair shop described by Kathleen Weston and Lisa Rofel—other issues surface concerning both relationships and institutions within the community. Krieger explores the complications that arise when we realize that lesbian communities not only affirm but also challenge the individual lesbian's sense of self. Zimmerman details the ways in which the focus on sameness and commonalities in lesbian narratives written before the early 1980s has given way, with the publication of *This Bridge Called My Back* and *Nice Jewish Girls*, to emphasis on difference and diversity among lesbians. Likewise, Weston and Rofel's account of conflicts between workers and owners in a lesbian shop analyzes how class relations emerged there as a consequence of the division of labor and the ownership of property and also were structured by aspects of lesbian identity that bridge the traditional split between public and private spheres. Their essay concludes, however, with an acknowledgment of the potential within such lesbian institutions for nonalienated labor and a continuing redefinition of lesbian identity through group interaction.

In her comment on Kreiger's review essay, Chela Sandoval observes that "class, culture, race, and sex intersect in various ways to produce different kinds of women, lesbians, and lesbian communities." In writing this thought may seem unquestionable, yet in the interactions of life we often lose sight of it, demanding singleness in identity and a unified strategy for survival. As editors it is our hope that *The Lesbian Issue*, while a unity in its commitment to the study of lesbian experience, will both bear witness to and take its place in the long, complex, and varied history of lesbian identity and lesbian survival.

Stanford University

We extend our gratitude to our co-workers, whose skills, energy, and commitment made this volume possible: *Signs* managing editor Clare Novak, intern Sharon Dyer, and associate editors Jane Fishburne Collier, Carol Nagy Jacklin, Nancy Hartsock, Myra Strober, Barrie Thorne, Margery Wolf, and Sylvia Yanagisako. We also thank the many anonymous reviewers who evaluated these articles and the others submitted for "The Lesbian Issue" of *Signs*.

The Mythic Mannish Lesbian:
Radclyffe Hall and the New Woman

Esther Newton

> I hate games! I hate role-playing! It's so ludicrous that
> certain lesbians, who despise men, become the exact rep-
> licas of them! [Anonymous interview in *The Gay Report*,
> ed. Karla Jay and Allen Young]

Because the proposition that lesbianism is an intensified form of female
bonding has become a belief, thinking, acting, or looking like a man
contradicts lesbian feminism's first principle: the lesbian is a "woman-

This essay grew out of an earlier one called "The Mythic Lesbian and the New Woman:
Power, Sexuality and Legitimacy," written with Carroll Smith-Rosenberg and presented by
us at the Berkshire Conference on the History of Women, Vassar College, June 16, 1981. A
revised version of that paper has appeared in French under the title "Le Mythe de la
lesbienne et la femme nouvelle," in *Strategies des femmes* (Paris: Éditions Tierce, 1984). The
French collection is forthcoming in English from Indiana University Press. Smith-
Rosenberg's further use of this material will appear as chap. 9, "The New Woman and the
Mannish Lesbian: Gender Disorder and Social Control," in her book *The New Woman and the
Troubled Man* (New York: Alfred A. Knopf, Inc., in press). Developing the Radclyffe Hall
material independently, I drew conclusions that do not represent Smith-Rosenberg's think-
ing and for which she is in no way responsible. But we worked jointly for two years, and I am
in her debt for all I learned from her as historian and for her unflagging support. I am also
indebted to the members of the Purchase women's studies seminar, particularly Mary
Edwards, Suzanne Kessler, and Louise Yellin, who read drafts and made helpful suggestions, as did David M. Schneider, Carole Vance, Wendy McKenna, and especially Amber
Hollibaugh. I thank the Lesbian Herstory Archives in New York, where I did early research,
and Jan Boney for technical help. And for another kind of insight and support, without
which this paper might never have been written, I thank the women of the B. group.

identified woman."[1] What to do, then, with that figure referred to, in various times and circumstances, as the "mannish lesbian," the "true invert," the "bull dagger," or the "butch"? You see her in old photographs or paintings with legs solidly planted, wearing a top hat and a man's jacket, staring defiantly out of the frame, her hair slicked back or clipped over her ears; or you meet her on the street in T-shirt and boots, squiring a brassily elegant woman on one tattooed arm. She is an embarrassment indeed to a political movement that swears it is the enemy of traditional gender categories and yet validates lesbianism as the ultimate form of femaleness.

Out of sight, out of mind! "Butch and femme are gone," declares one lesbian author, with more hope than truth.[2] But what about those old photographs? Was the mannish lesbian a myth created by "the [male] pornographic mind"[3] or by male sexologists intent on labeling nineteenth-century feminists as deviant? Maybe the old photographs portray a few misguided souls—or perhaps those "premovement" women thought men's ties were pretty and practical?

In the nineteenth century and before, individual women passed as men by dressing and acting like them for a variety of economic, sexual, and adventure-seeking reasons. Many of these women were from the working class.[4] Public, *partial* cross-dressing among bourgeois women was a late nineteenth-century development. Earlier isolated instances of partial cross-dressing seem to have been associated with explicit feminism (e.g., French writer George Sand and American physician Mary Walker), although most nineteenth-century feminists wore traditional women's clothing. From the last years of the century, cross-dressing was increasingly associated with "sexual inversion" by the medical profession. Did the doctors invent or merely describe the mannish lesbian? Either way, what did this mythic figure signify, and to whom? In addressing

1. Two key texts are Radicalesbians, "The Woman Identified Woman," reprinted in *Radical Feminism*, ed. Anne Koedt, Ellen Levine, and Anita Rapone (New York: Quadrangle, 1973), pp. 240–45; and Adrienne Rich, "Compulsory Heterosexuality and Lesbian Existence," *Signs: Journal of Women in Culture and Society* 5, no. 4 (Summer 1980): 631–60. The best analysis of how these ideas have evolved and of their negative consequences for the feminist movement is Alice Echols, "The New Feminism of Yin and Yang," in *Powers of Desire*, ed. Ann Snitow, Christine Stansell, and Sharon Thompson (New York: Monthly Review Press, 1983), pp. 439–59.

2. Sasha Gregory Lewis, *Sunday's Women* (Boston: Beacon Press, 1979), p. 42.

3. Andrea Dworkin, *Pornography and Silence: Culture's Revenge against Nature* (New York: Harper & Row, 1981), p. 219.

4. On passing women, see San Francisco Lesbian and Gay History Project, *"She Even Chewed Tobacco": Passing Women in Nineteenth-Century America* (1983), slide-tape distributed by Iris Films, Box 5353, Berkeley, California 94705; Jonathan Katz, *Gay American History: Lesbians and Gay Men in the U.S.A.* (New York: Thomas Y. Crowell, 1976), pp. 209–80.

these questions, my paper explores and speculates on the historical relationships between lesbianism, feminism, and gender.

One of the central figures in this debate is British author Radclyffe Hall (1880–1943). Without question, the most infamous mannish lesbian, Stephen Gordon, protagonist of *The Well of Loneliness* (1928), was created not by a male pornographer, sexologist, legislator, or novelist but by Hall, herself an "out" and militantly tie-wearing lesbian. And *The Well*, at least until 1970, was *the* lesbian novel.[5] Why is it that *The Well* became famous rather than all the others? Why does this novel make so many lesbian feminists and their allies squirm?[6]

Unable to wish Radclyffe Hall away, sometimes even hoping to reclaim her, our feminist scholars have lectured, excused, or patronized her. Radclyffe Hall, they declare, was an unwitting dupe of the misogynist doctors' attack on feminist romantic friendships. Or, cursed with a pessimistic temperament and brainwashed by Catholicism, Hall parroted society's condemnation of lesbians. The "real" Radclyffe Hall lesbian novel, this argument frequently continues, the one that *ought* to have been famous, is her first, *The Unlit Lamp* (1924). Better yet, Virginia Woolf's *Orlando* (1928) should have been the definitive lesbian novel. Or Natalie Barney's work, or anything but *The Well*.[7]

5. "Most of us lesbians in the 1950s grew up knowing nothing about lesbianism except Stephen Gordon's swagger," admits Blanche Wiesen Cook, herself a critic of Hall; see Cook's " 'Women Alone Stir My Imagination': Lesbianism and the Cultural Tradition," *Signs* 4, no. 4 (Summer 1979): 719–20. Despite Stephen Gordon's aristocratic trappings, her appeal transcended geographic and class barriers. We know that *The Well* was read early on by American lesbians of all classes (personal communication with Liz Kennedy from the Buffalo Oral History Project [1982]; and see Vern Bullough and Bonnie Bullough, "Lesbianism in the 1920s and 1930s: A Newfound Study," *Signs* 2, no. 4 [Summer 1977]: 895–904, esp. 897). *The Well* has been translated into numerous languages. According to Una Troubridge, in the 1960s it was still steadily selling over a hundred thousand copies a year in America alone; Troubridge was still receiving letters of appreciation addressed to Hall almost twenty years after Hall's death (Una Troubridge, *The Life and Death of Radclyffe Hall* [London: Hammond, Hammond & Co., 1961]). Even today, it sells as much as or more than any other lesbian novel, in straight and women's bookstores (personal communication with Amber Hollibaugh [1983], who has worked at Modern Times Bookstore [San Francisco], Djuna Books, and Womanbooks [New York City]).

6. Hall deserves censure for her possible fascist sympathies, but this is not the focus of feminist attacks on her. In any case, such sympathies developed after she wrote *The Well;* see Troubridge, pp. 118–24.

7. For the anti-*Well* approach, see Cook; Lillian Faderman and Ann Williams, "Radclyffe Hall and the Lesbian Image," *Conditions* 1, no. 1 (April 1977): 31–41; Catharine R. Stimpson, "Zero Degree Deviancy: The Lesbian Novel in English," in *Writing and Sexual Difference,* ed. Elizabeth Abel (Chicago: University of Chicago Press, 1982), pp. 243–60; Lillian Faderman, *Surpassing the Love of Men* (New York: William Morrow & Co., 1981), pp. 322–23; Vivian Gornick, "The Whole Radclyffe Hall: A Pioneer Left Behind," *Village Voice* (June 10–16, 1981). Only Inez Martinez, whose approach is quite different from mine, defends Hall: see "The Lesbian Hero Bound: Radclyffe Hall's Portrait of Sapphic Daughters and Their Mothers," *Journal of Homosexuality* 8, nos. 3/4 (Spring/Summer 1983): 127–37.

Heterosexual conservatives condemn *The Well* for defending the lesbian's right to exist; lesbian feminists condemn it for presenting lesbians as different from women in general. But *The Well* has continuing meaning to lesbians because it confronts the stigma of lesbianism—as most lesbians have had to live it. Maybe Natalie Barney, with her fortune and her cast-iron ego, or safely married Virginia Woolf were able to pooh-pooh the patriarchy, but most lesbians have had to face being called or at least feeling like freaks. As the Bowery bum represents all that is most feared and despised about drunkenness, the mannish lesbian, of whom Stephen Gordon is the most famous prototype, has symbolized the stigma of lesbianism and so continues to move a broad range of lesbians.[8] A second reason for *The Well*'s continuing impact, which I will explore briefly at the close of this paper, is that Stephen Gordon articulated a gender orientation with which an important minority of lesbians still actively identify.

By "mannish lesbian" (a term I use because it, rather than the contemporary "butch," belongs to the time period I am studying) I mean a figure who is defined as lesbian *because* her behavior or dress (and usually both) manifest elements designated as exclusively masculine. From about 1900 on, this cross-gender figure became the public symbol of the new social/sexual category "lesbian." Some of our feminist historians deplore the emergence of the mannish lesbian, citing her association with the medical model of pathology. For them, the nineteenth century becomes a kind of lesbian Golden Age, replete with loving, innocent feminist couples.[9] From the perspective of Radclyffe Hall's generation, however, nineteenth-century models may have seemed more confining than liberating. I will argue that Hall and many other feminists like her embraced, sometimes with ambivalence, the image of the mannish lesbian and the discourse of the sexologists about inversion primarily because they desperately wanted to break out of the asexual model of romantic friendship. Two questions emerge from this statement of the problem. First, why did twentieth-century women whose primary social and intimate interest was other women wish their relationships to become explicitly sexual? Second, why did the figure of the mannish lesbian play the central role in this development?

*   *   *

8. Many lesbians' connection to the mannish lesbian was and is painful. The relation of any stigmatized group to the figure that functions as its symbol and stereotype is necessarily ambiguous. Even before lesbian feminism, many lesbians hastened to assure themselves and others that they were not "like that." Lesbians who could pass for straight (because they were married or appeared feminine) often shunned their butch sisters. I have dealt with these concepts at length in *Mother Camp: Female Impersonators in America* (Chicago: University of Chicago Press, 1979); I argue that the effeminate man is the stigma bearer for gay men.

9. See esp. Faderman.

The structure and ideology of the bourgeois woman's gender-segregated world in the nineteenth century have been convincingly described.[10] As British and American women gained access to higher education and the professions, they did so in all-female institutions and in relationships with one another that were intense, passionate, and committed. These romantic friendships characterized the first generation of "New Women"—such as Jane Addams, Charlotte Perkins Gilman, and Mary Wooley—who were born in the 1850s and 1860s, educated in the 1870s and 1880s, and flourished from the 1890s through the First World War. They sought personal and economic independence by rejecting their mothers' domestic roles. The battle to be autonomous was the battle to stay single *and* to separate from the family sphere. Ironically, they turned to romantic friendships as the alternative, replicating the female world of love and commitment in the new institutional settings of colleges and settlement houses.

Whether or not these women touched each other's genitals or had orgasms together, two things seem clear: their relationships were a quasi-legitimate alternative to heterosexual marriage, and the participants did not conceive of them as sexual. Their letters generally do not use the acknowledged sexual language—medical, religious, or pornographic—of the nineteenth century. Nor do the letters exhibit shame, in an era when lust was considered dirty and gross. On the contrary, the first generation had nothing to hide because their passionate outpourings were seen as pure and ennobling.

The bourgeois woman's sexuality proper was confined to its reproductive function; the uterus was its organ. But as for lust, "the major current in Victorian sexual ideology declared that women were passionless and asexual, the passive objects of male sexual desire."[11] Most bourgeois women and men believed that only males and déclassé women were sexual. Sex was seen as phallic, by which I mean that, conceptually, sex could only occur in the presence of an imperial and imperious penis. Working women and women of color's low status as well as their participation in the public sphere deprived them of the feminine purity that protected bourgeois women from males and from deriving sexual pleasure. But what "pure" women did with each other, no matter how good it

10. See Carroll Smith-Rosenberg, "The Female World of Love and Ritual," *Signs* 1, no. 1 (Autumn 1975): 1–30; and Faderman. On the contradictions within the romantic friendship system, see Martha Vicinus, " 'One Life to Stand Beside Me': Emotional Conflicts of First-Generation College Women in England," *Feminist Studies* 8, no. 3 (Fall 1982): 602–28.

11. George Chauncey, Jr., "From Sexual Inversion to Homosexuality: Medicine and the Changing Conceptualization of Female Deviance," *Salmagundi*, nos. 58/59 (Fall 1982–Winter 1983), pp. 114–45, esp. 117. He has reached the same conclusion I have regarding the "necessary" masculinity of the early lesbian persona.

felt, could not be conceived as sexual within the terms of nineteenth-century romantic discourse. Insofar as first-generation feminists were called sexual deviants, it was because they used their minds at the expense of their reproductive organs.

* * *

The second generation of New Women were born in the 1870s and 1880s and came of age during the opening decades of the twentieth century. This was an extraordinarily distinguished group. Among them we count critics of the family and political radicals Margaret Sanger and Crystal Eastman; women drawn to new artistic fields, such as Berenice Abbot and Isadora Duncan; and lesbian writers such as Gertrude Stein, Willa Cather, Margaret Anderson, Natalie Barney, and Radclyffe Hall. For them, autonomy from family was, if not a given, emphatically a right. Hall's first novel, *The Unlit Lamp* (1924; hereafter *The Lamp*) is a sympathetic analysis of the first generation from the perspective of the second. The novel portrays a devouring mother using the kinship claims of the female world to crush her daughter's legitimate bid for autonomy.[12] Hall understands that, for the first generation, economic and social separation from the family and home was the first and necessary condition of freedom.

Joan Ogden is the competent, ambitious daughter of an upper-middle-class family living in an English provincial town. Young Joan is tutored by Elizabeth Rodney, a Cambridge graduate, whose dream is to see Joan escape from Seabourne and become a doctor. But Mrs. Ogden, Joan's hypochondriac mother, wants to keep Joan with her at all costs. When Elizabeth proposes to live with Joan in Cambridge while Joan studies medicine, Mrs. Ogden frustrates their plans by appealing successfully to Joan's guilt. Joan reflects on her wish to leave her mother in first-generation language: "'Good God' she thought bitterly, 'can there be no development of individuality in this world without hurting oneself or someone else?' She clenched her fists. 'I don't care, I don't care! I've a right to my life. . . . I defy precedent'" (pp. 247–48).[13]

But unlike M. Carey Thomas and other successful members of the first generation who used romantic friendships as an alternative to the domestic circle, Joan fails to assert her individuality. Family ties are an "octopus" (which was the novel's original title), squeezing life from the

12. For a related approach, see Carolyn Burke, "Gertrude Stein, the Cone Sisters, and the Puzzle of Female Friendship," in Abel, ed. (n. 7 above), pp. 221–42. Gertrude Stein shared the second generation's frustration with "daughters spending a lifetime in freeing themselves from family fixations" (p. 223).

13. All page numbers cited in the text are from Radclyffe Hall, *The Unlit Lamp* (New York: Dial Press, 1981).

daughters. In contrast, romantic friendship with Elizabeth offers Joan "companionship . . . understanding . . . help in work and play . . . freedom and endeavor" (p. 245). But Mrs. Ogden prevails; Elizabeth finally gives up, marries a wealthy man she does not love, and moves to South Africa. Joan is left to care for her mother as an unpaid nurse and companion.

Hall uses the family in *The Lamp* to symbolize society, the imposition of traditional gender divisions, and the subjugation of female fulfillment to traditional bourgeois norms. The family stands for bourgeois proprieties: proper dress, stifling garden parties, provincial gossip. Colonel Ogden is a stuffy tyrant, Mrs. Ogden the homebound woman. Fearful of alternatives, uncreative and unimaginative, the mother seeks to bind her daughter to an equally banal and confining life.

Conversely, Hall uses a masculinized body and a strong, active mind to symbolize women's rejection of traditional gender divisions and bourgeois values. Joan wants to be a doctor. Her mind is swift, intelligent, her body large, strong, healthy. She and Elizabeth hike on cold winter days, talking about science and a life away from the enclosed world of Seabourne and domesticity. As an adolescent Joan had been "large-boned and tall for her age, lanky as a boy, with a pale face and short black hair" (p. 11). She reminds Elizabeth of a young "colt." After Joan loses her battle for autonomy, however, her body changes, her health deteriorates, her ability to move freely, to see clearly is impeded. At forty-three she is an old woman, given to hysteria and hypochondria: "Constantly assailed by small, annoying symptoms . . . she had grown to dread the pulling up of the blind, because her eyes felt sensitive. . . . If she read now it was novels of the lightest kind, and she really preferred magazines" (p. 268).

Hall does not strongly develop male body and clothing imagery in *The Lamp*. But in a momentous confrontation near the novel's conclusion, masculine clothing is unambiguously used to symbolize assertiveness and modernity. Second-generation women are described as "active, aggressively intelligent women, not at all self-conscious in their tailor-made clothes, not ashamed of their cropped hair; women who did things well, important things . . . smart, neatly put together women, looking like well-bred young men" (p. 284). When two such women see Joan, now faded and failed, they ridicule her old-fashioned appearance: " 'Have you seen that funny old thing with the short gray hair?' '. . . Wasn't she killing? Why moiré ribbon instead of a proper necktie?' '. . . I believe she's what they used to call a New Woman,' said the girl in breeches, with a low laugh. 'Honey, she's a forerunner, a kind of pioneer that's got left behind. I believe she's the beginning of things like me' " (p. 284).

Though gender ambiguity is positively associated with autonomy, there is no explicit discussion of sexuality. Joan tells a male suitor, "I've never been what you'd call in love with a man in my life" (p. 302), without a trace of embarrassment. Joan and Elizabeth's passionate relationship is described in the traditional language of sentiment, never in a language of lust. Sexuality is not the problematic issue for Joan Ogden, nor is her ambition symbolized in sexual terms. *The Lamp* is a novel about autonomy.

*   *   *

For many women of Radclyffe Hall's generation, sexuality—for itself and as a symbol of female autonomy—became a preoccupation. These women were, after all, the "sisters" of D. H. Lawrence and James Joyce. For male novelists, sexologists, and artists rebelling against Victorian values, sexual freedom became the cutting edge of modernism. Bourgeois women like Hall had a different relation to modernist sexual freedom, for in the Victorian terms of the first generation, they had no sexual identity to express. Women of the second generation who wished to join the modernist discourse and be twentieth-century adults needed to radically reconceive themselves.

That most New Women of the first generation resented and feared such a development, I do not doubt. But many women of the second welcomed it, cautiously or with naive enthusiasm. (One has only to think of Virginia Woolf's thrilled participation in Bloomsbury to see what I mean.) They wanted not simply male professions but access to the broader world of male opportunity. They drank, they smoked, they rejected traditional feminine clothing, and lived as expatriates, some-times with disastrous results. But if modernism and the new sex ideas entailed serious contradictions for women, many wrote daring novels and plunged into psychoanalysis and promiscuity anyway. After all, this was what the first generation had won for them—the tenuous right to try out the new ideas and participate in the great social movements of the day.

It was in the first two decades of the twentieth century in Britain, with perhaps a ten-year lag in the United States, that due to both external attack and internal fission the old feminist movement began to split along the heterosexual/homosexual divide that is ancestral to our own. If women were to develop a lustful sexuality, with whom and in what social context were they to express it? The male establishment, of course, wanted women to be lusty with men. A basic tenet of sexual modernism was that "normal" women had at least reactive heterosexual desire.[14] The sex reformers attacked Victorian gender segregation and promoted the new idea of companionate marriage in which both women's and men's heterosexual desires were to be satisfied.[15] Easier association with men

---

14. See Paul Robinson, *The Modernization of Sex* (New York: Harper & Row, 1976), pp. 2, 3, and chap. 1.

15. Christina Simmons, "Companionate Marriage and the Lesbian Threat," *Frontiers* 4, no. 3 (Fall 1979): 54–59.

quickly sexualized the middle-class woman, and by the 1920s the flapper style reflected the sexual ambience of working-class bars and dance halls. The flapper flirted with being "cheap" and "fast," words that had clear sexual reference.

But what about the women who did not become heterosexual, who remained stubbornly committed to intragender intimacy? A poignant example is furnished by Frances Wilder, an obscure second-generation feminist.[16] Wilder had inherited the orthodox first-generation views. In a 1912 letter to the radical *Freewoman*, she advocated self-restraint, denouncing the new morality for encouraging the "same degrading laxity in sex matters which is indulged in by most of the lower animals including man." She herself, aged twenty-seven, had "always practised abstinence" with no adverse effects. But just three years later she was writing desperately to homosexual radical Edward Carpenter: "I have recently read with much interest your book entitled The Intermediate Sex & it has lately dawned on me that I myself belong to that class & I write to ask if there is any way of getting in touch with others of the same temperament" (p. 930). Wilder was aware of the price tag on the new ideas. "The world would say that a physical relationship between two of the same sex is an unspeakable crime," she admits, but gamely reasons that, because of the "economic slavery" of women, "*normal* sex" is "*more* degrading."

The New Woman's social field was opening up, becoming more complex, and potentially more lonely. Thus, along with their desire to be modern, our bourgeois lesbian ancestors had another powerful reason to embrace change. Before they could find one another, they had to become visible, at least to each other. What they needed was a new vocabulary built on the radical idea that women apart from men could have autonomous sexual feeling.

* * *

"I just concluded that I had . . . a dash of the masculine (I have been told more than once that I have a masculine mind . . .)," Frances Wilder had confessed to Carpenter in 1915, explaining her "strong desire to caress & fondle" a female friend.[17] Like most important historical developments, the symbolic fusion of gender reversal and homosexuality was overdetermined. God himself had ordained gender hierarchy and heterosexuality at the Creation. The idea that men who had sex with other men were like women was not new. But in the second half of the nineteenth century, the emerging medical profession gave scientific sanction to tradition; homosexual behavior, the doctors agreed, was both

16. Ruth F. Claus, "Confronting Homosexuality: A Letter from Frances Wilder," *Signs* 2, no. 4 (Summer 1977): 928–33.
17. Ibid., p. 931.

symptom and cause of male effeminacy. The masculine female invert was perhaps an analogous afterthought. Yet the mannish lesbian proved a potent persona to both the second generation of New Women and their antifeminist enemies. I think that her image came to dominate the discourse about female homosexuality, particularly in England and America, for two reasons. First, because sexual desire was not considered inherent in women, the lesbian was thought to have a trapped male soul that phallicized her and endowed her with active lust. Second, gender reversal became a powerful symbol of feminist aspirations, positive for female modernists, negative for males regardless of whether they were conservatives or modernists.[18]

It was Richard von Krafft-Ebing who articulated the fusion of masculinity, feminist aspirations, and lesbianism that became, and largely remains, an article of faith in Anglo-American culture.[19] Krafft-Ebing categorized lesbians into four increasingly deviant and masculine types.[20] The first category of lesbians included women who "did not betray their anomaly by external appearance or by mental [masculine] sexual characteristics." They were, however, responsive to the approaches of women who appeared or acted more masculine. The second classification included women with a "strong preference for male garments." These women were the female analogy of effeminate men. By the third stage "inversion" was "fully developed, the woman [assuming] a definitely masculine role." The fourth state represented "the extreme grade of degenerative homosexuality. The woman of this type," Krafft-Ebing explained, "possesses of the feminine qualities only the genital organs; thought, sentiment, action, even external appearance are those of the man."[21] Not only was the most degenerate lesbian the most masculine, but any gender-crossing or aspiration to male privilege was probably a symptom of lesbianism. In these pathological souls, "The consciousness of being a woman and thus to be deprived of the gay college life, or to be barred out from the military career, produces painful reflections."[22] In fact, lesbianism is a congenital form of lust caused by and manifested in gender reversal, as Krafft-Ebing makes clear in discussing one case:

18. Sandra Gilbert has developed this idea in the context of modernist literature in "Costumes of the Mind: Transvestism as Metaphor in Modern Literature," in Abel, ed. (n. 7 above), pp. 193–220.

19. Chauncey argues that medical opinion began to shift from an exclusive focus on "inversion" as gender reversal to "homosexuality" as deviant sexual orientation in the 1930s. The change has had only limited effect on popular ideology.

20. A similar section on the sexologists was first developed by Smith-Rosenberg in our joint paper and has been worked out further in her forthcoming book (see unnumbered note above).

21. Richard von Krafft-Ebing, *Psychopathia Sexualis*, trans. Franklin S. Klaf (1886; New York: Bell Publishing Co., 1965), pp. 262–64.

22. Ibid., p. 264.

"Even in her earliest childhood she preferred playing at soldiers and other boys' games; she was bold and tom-boyish and tried even to excel her little companions of the other sex. . . . [After puberty] her dreams were of a lascivious nature, only about females, with herself in the role of the man. . . . She was quite conscious of her pathological condition. Masculine features, deep voice, manly gait, without beard, small breasts; cropped her hair short and made the impression of a man in woman's clothes."[23]

Havelock Ellis simplified Krafft-Ebing's four-part typology.[24] He kept the notion of an ascending scale of inversion, beginning with women involved in "passionate friendships" in which "no congenital inversion is usually involved" and ending with the "actively inverted woman." Ellis's discussion of the former was devastating; it turned the value that first-generation feminists had placed on passionate friendships upside down. A "sexual enthusiast,"[25] he saw these "rudimentary sexual relationships" as more symptomatic of female sexual ignorance and repression than of spiritual values. At the same time, his inclusion of such friendships in a discussion of inversion inevitably marked them with the stigma of "abnormality."

When Ellis got to the hard-core inverts, he was confounded by his contradictory beliefs. He wanted to construct the lesbian couple on the heterosexual model, as a "man" and a woman invert. But his antifeminism and reluctance to see active lust in women committed him to fusing inversion and masculinity. What to do with the feminine invert? His solution was an awkward compromise:

> A class of women to be first mentioned . . . is formed by the women to whom the actively inverted woman is most attracted. These women differ in the first place from the normal or average woman in that they are not repelled or disgusted by lover-like advances from persons of their own sex. . . . Their faces may be plain or ill-made but not seldom they possess good figures, a point which is apt to carry more weight with the inverted woman than beauty of face . . . ; they are of strongly affectionate nature . . . and *they are always womanly* [emphasis mine]. One may perhaps say that they are the pick of the women whom the average man would pass by. No doubt this is often the reason why they are open to homosexual advances, but I do not think it is the sole reason. So far as they may be said to constitute a class they seem to possess a genuine, though not precisely sexual, preference for women over men.[26]

23. Ibid., pp. 278–79.

24. Havelock Ellis, "Sexual Inversion in Women," *Alienist and Neurologist* 16 (1895): 141–58.

25. See Robinson (n. 14 above) for a balanced appraisal of Ellis's radicalism in sexual issues vs. his misogyny.

26. Ellis, pp. 147–48.

This extraordinary mix of fantasy, conjecture, and insight totally contradicts Ellis's insistence that "the chief characteristic of the sexually inverted woman is a certain degree of masculinity."[27] No mention is made of "congenital" factors in regard to this "womanly" invert, and like most examples that do not fit pet paradigms, she is dropped. Gender reversal is not always homosexual, Ellis contends, exempting certain "mannish women" who wear men's clothes out of pragmatic motives, but the "actively inverted woman" always has "a more or less distinct trace of masculinity" as "part of an organic instinct."[28] Because of her firm muscles, athletic ability, dislike of feminine occupations, and predilection for male garments, "because the wearer feels more at home in them," the sexually inverted woman, people feel, "ought to have been a man."[29]

Thus the true invert was a being between categories, neither man nor woman, a "third sex" or "trapped soul." Krafft-Ebing, Ellis, and Freud all associated this figure with female lust and with feminist revolt against traditional roles; they were at best ambivalent, at worst horrified, by both.[30] But some second-generation feminists, such as Frances Wilder, Gertrude Stein, and Vita Sackville-West, associated themselves with important aspects of the "third sex" persona. None did so as unconditionally and—this must be said—as bravely as Radclyffe Hall did by making the despised mannish lesbian the hero of *The Well of Loneliness*, which she defended publicly against the British government. Hall's creation, Stephen Gordon, is a double symbol, standing for the New Woman's painful position between traditional political and social categories, and for the lesbian struggle to define and assert an identity.

In *The Well*, Stephen Gordon's parents want a son; when a daughter is born her father names her Stephen and permits her much of the freedom boys enjoy. She grows up resembling her father physically and emotionally, despising feminine pursuits and clothing. In her late teens she rejects a sympathetic male suitor because she has no sexual feeling for him. At twenty she develops a passion for a neighbor's wife, who ultimately betrays Stephen to save her own reputation. In the aftermath, Stephen's mother forces Stephen to leave Morton, the family estate, and Stephen discovers, by reading Krafft-Ebing's *Psychopathia Sexualis* in her dead father's library, that she is an "invert," an identity she instantly but painfully accepts.

27. Ibid., p. 152.
28. Ibid., p. 148.
29. Ibid., p. 153.
30. Freud's analysis was by far the most sophisticated. He rejected the trapped-soul paradigm and distinguished between "choice of object" and "sexual characteristics and sexual attitude of the subject." However, his insights were distorted by his antifeminism and his acceptance of a biological base for gender. See esp. "The Psychogenesis of a Case of Homosexuality in a Woman," in *Freud: Sexuality and the Psychology of Love*, ed. Philip Rieff (New York: Collier Books, 1963), pp. 133–59.

During World War I, Stephen works in an ambulance unit and falls in love with Mary, who is young, innocent, and "normal." On holiday together after the armistice, Stephen is tormented by moral scruples. Hesitant to lure Mary into an outcast life and fearful of rejection, she struggles to remain chaste. But Mary, "no coward and no weakling," forces a confrontation; they become lovers, abandoning themselves to "what can be the most relentless of human emotions," passionate sexual love (p. 312).[31] But life in Paris, where they make a home, becomes increasingly problematic. Stephen's absorption in her writing leaves Mary bored and unhappy. Both hate being excluded from bourgeois heterosexual society. Finally, to release Mary, Stephen pretends to have an affair; Mary reluctantly leaves with Stephen's old suitor, Martin, and Stephen is left alone.

Both *The Lamp* and *The Well* deal with autonomy, power, and legitimacy. In *The Lamp*, the family traps first-generation New Women. But in *The Well*, the female body itself becomes the nemesis of the second generation. Accordingly, the relative importance and resonance of these symbols shift from one novel to the next. In *The Lamp*, the family is realistically drawn and personified in Joan's mother, Mrs. Ogden, who dominates the novel. The family is female, retentive, and destructive. Mrs. Ogden stands for the guilt, respectability, and subjugation of individuality that destroy Joan.

Stephen Gordon must also leave the family to realize herself. But here, the family is aristocratic and romanticized. Instead of crushing Stephen in its embrace, it denies her patriarchal legitimacy solely because she is born female. Though her father gives her his looks, his intelligence, his money, and a boy's name, tragically, she cannot be his true heir. As heroic female, she is inherently illegitimate, only at home in the pages of Krafft-Ebing. Stephen's mother Lady Anna, like Mrs. Ogden, restricts individuality. But the mother is no longer the chief antagonist—the female body is. In *The Lamp*, mother and daughter war over issues of self-fulfillment; in *The Well*, over issues of gender and, ultimately, sexuality.

Even newborn, Stephen's body is mythically masculine: "Narrow-hipped and wide shouldered" (p. 13). She grows and her body becomes "splendid," "supple," "quick"; she can "fence like a man"; she discovers "her body for a thing to be cherished . . . since its strength could rejoice her" (p. 58). But as she matures, her delight degenerates into angst. She is denied male privilege, of course, in spite of her masculine body. But her physical self is also fleshly symbol of the femininity Stephen categorically rejects. Her body is not and cannot be male; yet it is not traditionally female. Between genders and thus illegitimate, it represents Every New

---

31. All page numbers cited in the text are from Radclyffe Hall, *The Well of Loneliness* (New York: Pocket Books, 1950).

Woman, stifled after World War I by a changed political climate and reinforced gender stereotypes. But Hall also uses a body between genders to symbolize the "inverted" sexuality Stephen can neither disavow nor satisfy. Finding herself "no match" for a male rival, the adolescent Stephen begins to hate herself. In one of Hall's most moving passages Stephen expresses this hatred as alienation from her body:

> That night she stared at herself in the glass; and even as she did so, she hated her body with its muscular shoulders, its small compact breasts, and its slender flanks of an athlete. All her life she must drag this body of hers like a monstrous fetter imposed on her spirit. This strangely ardent yet sterile body. . . . She longed to maim it, for it made her feel cruel: it was so white, so strong and so self-sufficient; yet withal so poor and unhappy a thing that her eyes filled with tears and her hate turned to pity. She began to grieve over it, touching her breasts with pitiful fingers, stroking her shoulders, letting her hands slip along her straight thighs—Oh, poor and most desolate body! [P. 187]

Stephen's difference from Joan Ogden, her overt sexuality, is also represented by cross-dressing. But if male writers used cross-dressing to symbolize and castigate a world upside down, while Virginia Woolf and other female modernists used it to express "gleeful skepticism" toward gender categories,[32] Stephen's cross-dressing asserts a series of agonizing estrangements. Stephen is alienated from Lady Anna as the New Woman often was from her own mother, as the lesbian was, increasingly, from heterosexual women. Unlike Orlando, Stephen is trapped in history; she cannot declare gender an irrelevant game. She, like many young women then and now, alternately rebels against her mother's vision of womanhood and blames herself for her failure to live up to it. Preferring suits from her father's tailor, she sometimes gives in to her mother's demand that she wear "delicate dresses," which she puts on "all wrong." Her mother confirms Stephen's sense of freakishness: "It's my face," Stephen announces, "something's wrong with my face." "Nonsense!" her mother replies, "turning away quickly to hide her expression" (p. 73).

Cross-dressing for Hall is not a masquerade. It stands for the New Woman's rebellion against the male order and, at the same time, for the lesbian's desperate struggle to be and express her true self. Two years exiled from Morton, Stephen, now her own woman with a profession, wears tailored jackets, has nicotine-stained fingers, and keeps her hair cropped "close like a man's."[33] No matter how "wrong" she seems to the world, Stephen herself grows "fond of her hair" (p. 210).

---

32. Gilbert (n. 18 above), p. 206.
33. For the New Woman of the twenties, cutting off traditionally long hair was a daring act with enormous practical and symbolic implications. It was never a neutral act.

The New Woman's modernity and aspiration to male privilege already had been associated with cross-dressing in *The Lamp*. But in *The Well*, Hall, like the sexologists, uses cross-dressing and gender reversal to symbolize lesbian sexuality. Unlike the sexologists, however, Hall makes Stephen the subject and takes her point of view against a hostile world. Though men resented Stephen's "unconscious presumption," Hall defends Stephen's claim to what is, in her fictional universe, the ultimate male privilege: the enjoyment of women's erotic love. The mythic mannish lesbian proposes to usurp the son's place in the Oedipal triangle.[34]

Hall had begun to describe an eroticized mother/daughter relation several years earlier, in *The Lamp*, where presumably the nonsexual framework of the novel as a whole had made it safe:

> The mother and daughter found very little to say to each other; when they were together their endearments were strained like those of people with a guilty secret. . . . Joan knew that they never found what they sought and never would find it now, any more. . . . She wanted to love Mrs. Ogden, she felt empty and disconsolate without that love. She longed to feel the old quick response when her mother bent towards her, the old perpetual romance of her vicinity. She was like a drug-taker from whom all stimulant has been suddenly removed; the craving was unendurable, dangerous alike to body and mind. [P. 75]

In this respect only, *The Lamp* is a "closet" novel. Hall, hiding in the old language, describes what is, I believe, a central component of lesbian sexuality—mother/daughter eroticism.[35] I write "eroticism" because sexual desire is distinct from either "identification" or "bonding." A woman can be close to her mother ("bond," "identify") in many ways and yet eroticize only men. Conversely, one can hate one's mother and have little in common with her, as did Radclyffe Hall, and yet desire her fiercely in the image of other women. In my view, feminist psychology has not yet solved the riddle of sexual orientation.

As bold as Hall was, she could not treat mother/daughter eroticism directly in *The Well*; instead, she turned it inside out. Stephen is strangely uncomfortable with all women, especially with her mother. Lady Anna is not a flesh-and-blood woman who, like Mrs. Ogden, can feel "guiltily

34. My use of Freud's concept indicates my conviction that it does begin to explain sexual desire, at least as it operates in our culture. Hall rejected or ignored Freud, presumably because of the implication, which so many drew from his work, that homosexuality could be "cured" (see Faderman and Williams [n. 7 above], p. 41, n. 11).

35. Ruth-Jean Eisenbud asserts that "primary lesbian choice" occurs at about age three, resulting from the little girl's "precocious eroticism" directed toward a mother who is excluding her ("Early and Later Determinates of Lesbian Choice," *Psychoanalytic Review* 69, no. 1 [Spring 1982]: 85–109, esp. 99). Martinez (n. 7 above), whose theme is the mother/daughter relationship in Hall's two novels, ignores the concept of mother/daughter eroticism, rejecting any relevance of the psychoanalytic model.

happy" when her daugher kisses her, "as if a lover held her" (p. 13). Anna is a servile mother of the patriarchy; her daughter's ambiguous gender and explosive sexuality repel her.[36] Stephen, in turn, rejects her mother's role and values, identifying instead with her father (thereby making herself so unpopular with feminist critics). In Hall's terms, one might say that Stephen is so like her father that she assumes his sexuality.

The Oedipal drama is played out, as it often was for boys of the same class, with the maid standing in for the mother. At seven, Stephen's intense eroticism is awakened by Collins (who, as working-class sex object, never gets a first name), in an episode infused with sexual meaning. Collins is "florid, full-lipped and full-bosomed" (p. 16), which might remind informed readers of Ellis's dictum that the good figure counts more with the "congenital invert" than does a pretty face. When the enchanted child reaches out "a rather uncertain hand . . . to stroke [the maid's] sleeve," Collins exclaims, "What very dirty nails!" (p. 17). The invert's hand is a sexual instrument, but it is polluted. Stephen responds by running to scrub her nails. After this episode, thinking of Collins makes Stephen "go hot down her spine," and when Collins kisses her on impulse, Stephen is dumbfounded by something "vast, that the mind of seven years found no name for" (p. 18). This "vast" thing makes Stephen feel like a boy. She dresses as "young Nelson," causing Collins to say, "Doesn't Miss Stephen look exactly like a boy?" to which Stephen answers, "I must be a boy, 'cause I feel exactly like one." When Collins snubs her she is "deflated," dons the hated girls' clothing, and torments her dolls, "thumping their innocuous faces" (p. 20).[37] The end comes when the child sees the footman roughly kiss Collins on the mouth. In a rage she throws a broken flower pot and hits the footman's cheek. Stephen's sympathetic and protective father resolves the situation by firing the domestics.

For modern readers, by this point in the novel the nature of Stephen's feeling is evident. But writing in 1928, Hall had to go farther. She shows us Sir Phillip reading sexologist Karl Heinrich Ulrichs and making notes in the margins. Later, after her disastrous passion for a scheming American woman, Stephen reads Krafft-Ebing in her dead father's library and recognizes herself as "flawed in the making."

A high price to pay for claiming a sexual identity, yes. But of those who condemn Hall for assuming the sexologists' model of lesbianism I ask, Just how was Hall to make the woman-loving New Woman a sexual being? For example, despite Hall's use of words like "lover" and "passion"

---

36. Hall makes the mother's fear pretty explicit: when Lady Anna says goodnight to adolescent Stephen, she kisses her quickly on the forehead "so that the girl should not wake and kiss back" (p. 83).

37. In another notable minority novel, Toni Morrison's *The Bluest Eye* (New York: Pocket Books, 1972), the black child heroine hates and torments her white doll. In *The Well*, the heroine hates her doll simply because of its femininity.

and her references to "inversion," her lawyer actually defended *The Well* against state censorship by trying to convince the court that "the relations between women described in the book represented a normal friendship." Hall "attacked him furiously for taking this line, which appeared to her to undermine the strength of the convictions with which she had defended the case. His plea seemed to her, as her solicitor commented later, 'the unkindest cut of all' and at their luncheon together she was unable to restrain 'tears of heartbroken anguish.'"[38]

How could the New Woman lay claim to her full sexuality? For bourgeois women, there was no developed female sexual discourse; there were only male discourses—pornographic, literary, and medical—*about* female sexuality. To become avowedly sexual, the New Woman had to enter the male world, either as a heterosexual on male terms (a flapper) or as—or with—a lesbian in male body drag (a butch).

Ideas, metaphors, and symbols can be used for either radical or conservative purposes.[39] By endowing a biological female with a masculine self, Hall both questions the inevitability of patriarchal gender categories *and* assents to it. The mannish lesbian should not exist if gender is natural. Yet Hall makes her the breathing, suffering hero (not the villain or clown) of a novel. Stephen not only survives social condemnation, she also argues her own case. But she sacrifices her legitimacy as a woman and as an aristocrat. The interpersonal cost is high, too: Stephen loses her mother and her lover, Mary. *The Well* explores the self-hatred and doubt involved in defining oneself as a "sexual deviant." For in doing so, the lesbian accepts an invidious distinction between herself and heterosexual women.

Men have used this distinction to condemn lesbians and to intimidate straight women. The fear and antagonism between us has certainly weakened the modern feminist movement. And that is why lesbian feminists (abetted by some straight feminists) are intent on redefining lesbianism as "woman-identification," a model that, not incidentally, puts heterosexual feminists at a disadvantage.[40] Hall's vision of lesbianism as

38. Vera Brittain, *Radclyffe Hall: A Case of Obscenity?* (New York: A. S. Barnes & Co., 1969), p. 92.

39. The sexologists' discourse, itself hostile to women, "also made possible the formation of a 'reverse' discourse: homosexuality began to speak in its own behalf, to demand that its legitimacy or 'naturality' be acknowledged, often in the same vocabulary, using the same categories by which it was medically disqualified" (Michel Foucault, *The History of Sexuality*, vol. 1, *An Introduction* [New York: Vintage Books, 1980], p. 102).

40. Superficially, cultural feminism reunites lesbians and straight women under the banner of "female values." As Echols points out, hostility still surfaces "as it did at the 1979 Women Against Pornography conference where a lesbian separatist called Susan Brownmiller a 'cocksucker.' Brownmiller retaliated by pointing out that her critic 'even dresses like a man'" (Echols [n. 1 above], p. 41).

sexual difference and as masculinity is inimical to lesbian feminist ideology.

Like Hall, I see lesbianism as sexual difference. But her equation of lesbianism with masculinity needs not condemnation, but expansion. To begin with, we need to accept that whatever their ideological purposes, Hall and the sexologists were describing something real. Some people, then and now, experience "gender dysphoria," a strong feeling that one's assigned gender as a man or a woman does not agree with one's sense of self.[41] This is not precisely the same thing as wanting power and male privilege—a well-paid job, abortion on demand, athletic prowess—even though the masculine woman continues to be a symbol of feminist aspirations to the majority outside the movement. Masculinity and femininity are like two different languages. Though each of us knows both, most suppress one system and express only the other.[42] Many lesbians, like Stephen Gordon, are biological females who grow up speaking parts of the "wrong" gender language.

Obviously, the more narrow and rigid gender categories are, the more easily one can feel "out of role." And, of course, if there were no more gender categories, gender dysphoria would disappear (as would feminism). However, feminist critiques of traditional gender categories do not yet resolve gender dysphoria because, first, we have made little impact on the deep structures of gender and, second, it appears that

41. Sexologists often use the concept of "gender dysphoria syndrome" synonymously with "transsexualism" to describe the "pathology" of people who apply for gender reassignment surgery. Of course the effort to describe and treat transsexualism medically has been awkward since gender is a cultural construct, not a biological entity. My broader use of "gender dysphoria" is in agreement with some sexologists who limit the word "transsexual" to people who actually have had surgery to alter their bodies. Gender dysphoria, then, refers to a variety of difficulties in establishing conventional (the doctors say "adequate" or "normal") gender identification; intense pain and conflict over masculinity and femininity is not limited to people who request reassignment surgery. See Jon K. Meyer and John Hoopes, "The Gender Dysphoria Syndromes," *Plastic and Reconstructive Surgery* 54 (October 1974): 447. Female-to-male transsexuals appear to share many similarities with lesbian butches. The most impressive difference is the rejection or acceptance of homosexual identity. Compare *The Well* to the lives described in Ira B. Pauly, "Adult Manifestations of Female Transsexualism," in *Transsexualism and Sex Reassignment*, ed. Richard Green and John Money (Baltimore: Johns Hopkins University Press, 1969), pp. 59–87. Gender dysphoria could very fruitfully be compared with anorexia nervosa, a more socially acceptable and increasingly common female body-image problem. As feminists, we need a much more sophisticated vocabulary to talk about gender. Sexologists are often appallingly conservative, but they also deal with and try to explain important data. See, e.g., John Money and Anke A. Ehrhardt, *Man & Woman, Boy & Girl* (Baltimore: Johns Hopkins University Press, 1972). For a radical scholarly approach, see Suzanne J. Kessler and Wendy McKenna, *Gender: An Ethnomethodological Approach* (New York: John Wiley & Sons, 1978). One of the best recent pieces on gender reversal is Pat Califia, "Gender-Bending: Playing with Roles and Reversals," *Advocate* (September 15, 1983).

42. See Money and Ehrhardt, pp. 18–20.

individual gender identity is established in early childhood. Although gender dysphoria exists in some simple societies,[43] it may be amplified by the same sociohistorical processes—radical changes in the economy, in family structure and function, and in socialization—that have given rise to feminism. Why should we as feminists deplore or deny the existence of masculine women or effeminate men? Are we not against assigning specific psychological or social traits to a particular biology? And should we not support those among us, butches and queens, who still bear the brunt of homophobia?

Hall's association of lesbianism and masculinity needs to be challenged not because it doesn't exist, but because it is not the only possibility. Gender identity and sexual preference are, in fact, two related but separate systems; witness the profusion of gender orientations (which are deeply embedded in race, class, and ethnic experience) to be found in the lesbian community. Many lesbians *are* masculine; most have composite styles; many are emphatically feminine. Stephen Gordon's success eclipsed more esoteric, continental, and feminine images of the lesbian, such as Renée Vivien's decadent or Colette's bisexual. The notion of a feminine lesbian contradicted the congenital theory that many homosexuals in Hall's era espoused to counter demands that they undergo punishing "therapies." Though Stephen's lovers in *The Well* are feminine and though Mary, in effect, seduces Stephen, Hall calls her "normal," that is, heterosexual. Even Havelock Ellis gave the "womanly" lesbian more dignity and definition. As a character, Mary is forgettable and inconsistent, weakening the novel and saddling Hall with an implausible ending in which Stephen "nobly" turns Mary over to a man. In real life, Hall's lover Una Troubridge did not go back to heterosexuality even when Hall, late in her life, took a second lover.

But the existence of a lesbian who did not feel somehow male was apparently unthinkable for Hall. The "womanly" lesbian contradicted the convictions that sexual desire must be male and that a feminine woman's object of desire must be a man. Mary's real story has yet to be told.[44]

Division of Social Science
State University of New York College at Purchase

43. Harriet Whitehead, "The Bow and the Burden Strap: A New Look at Institutionalized Homosexuality in Native North America," in *Sexual Meanings: The Cultural Construction of Gender and Sexuality*, ed. Sherry B. Ortner and Harriet Whitehead (Cambridge: Cambridge University Press, 1981), pp. 80–115.

44. Two impressive beginnings are Joan Nestle, "Butch-Fem Relationships," and Amber Hollibaugh and Cherríe Moraga, "What We're Rollin' Around in Bed With," both in *Heresies 12* 3, no. 4 (1981): 21–24, 58–62. The latter has been reprinted in Snitow, Stansell, and Thompson, eds. (n. 2 above), pp. 394–405.

Sexuality and Gender
in Certain Native American Tribes:
The Case of Cross-Gender Females

Evelyn Blackwood

Ideological concepts of gender and sexuality arise from cultural constructions and vary from culture to culture. The female cross-gender role in
certain Native American tribes constituted an opportunity for women to
assume the male role permanently and to marry women.[1] Its existence
challenges Western assumptions about gender roles. Some feminist anthropologists assume that it is in the nature of sex and gender systems to
create asymmetry in the form of male dominance and female subservience and to enforce corresponding forms of sexual behavior.[2] Because
kinship and marriage are closely tied to gender systems, these social
structures are implicated in the subordination of women. The existence

I am particularly grateful to Naomi Katz, Mina Caulfield, and Carolyn Clark for their
encouragement, support, and suggestions during the development of this article. I would
also like to thank Gilbert Herdt, Paula Gunn Allen, Sue-Ellen Jacobs, Walter Williams, Luis
Kemnitzer, and Ruby Rohrlich for their insightful comments on an earlier version.

1. The term "berdache" is the more common term associated with the cross-gender
role. It was originally applied by Europeans to Native American men who assumed the
female role, and was derived from the Arabic *bardaj*, meaning a boy slave kept for sexual
purposes. I prefer the term "cross-gender," first used by J. M. Carrier, particularly for the
female role. See J. M. Carrier, "Homosexual Behavior in Cross-Cultural Perspective," in
Homosexual Behavior: A Modern Reappraisal, ed. Judd Marmor (New York: Basic Books,
1980), pp. 100–122.

2. Sherry B. Ortner and Harriet Whitehead, eds., *Sexual Meanings: The Cultural
Construction of Gender and Sexuality* (Cambridge: Cambridge University Press, 1981); Gayle
Rubin, "The Traffic in Women: Notes on the 'Political Economy' of Sex," in *Toward an
Anthropology of Women*, ed. Rayna R. Reiter (New York: Monthly Review Press, 1975), pp.
157–210.

Reprinted from *Signs: Journal of Women in Culture and Society* 10, no. 1 (Autumn 1984):
27–42.

of the female cross-gender role, however, points to the inadequacies of such a view and helps to clarify the nature of sex and gender systems.

This study closely examines the female cross-gender role as it existed historically in several Native American tribes, primarily in western North America and the Plains. It focuses on western tribes that shared a basically egalitarian mode of production in precolonial times,[3] and for which sufficient data on the female role exist. Although there were cultural differences among these groups, prior to the colonial period they all had subsistence-level economies that had not developed significant forms of wealth or rank. These tribes include the Kaska of the Yukon Territory, the Klamath of southern Oregon, and the Mohave, Maricopa, and Cocopa of the Colorado River area in the Southwest. The Plains tribes, by contrast, are noteworthy for the relative absence of the female cross-gender role. Conditions affecting the tribes of the Plains varied from those of the western tribes, and thus analysis of historical-cultural contexts will serve to illuminate the differing constraints on sex and gender systems in these two areas.

Ethnographic literature has perpetuated some misconceptions about the cross-gender role. Informants frequently describe the institution in negative terms, stating that berdache were despised and ridiculed. But ethnographers collected much of the data in this century; it is based on informants' memories of the mid- to late 1800s. During this period the cross-gender institution was disappearing rapidly. Thus, twentieth-century informants do not accurately represent the institution in the precontact period. Alfred Kroeber found that "while the [berdache] institution was in full bloom, the Caucasian attitude was one of repugnance and condemnation. This attitude . . . made subsequent personality inquiry difficult, the later berdache leading repressed or disguised lives."[4] Informants' statements to later ethnographers or hostile white officials were far different from the actual attitude toward the role that prevailed in the precolonial period. An analysis of the cross-gender role in its

---

3. Much feminist debate has focused on whether male dominance is universal, or whether societies with egalitarian relations exist. For a more comprehensive discussion of egalitarian societies, see Mina Davis Caulfield, "Equality, Sex and Mode of Production," in *Social Inequality: Comparative and Developmental Approaches*, ed. Gerald D. Berreman (New York: Academic Press, 1981), pp. 201–19; Mona Etienne and Eleanor Leacock, eds., *Women and Colonization: Anthropological Perspectives* (New York: J. F. Bergin, 1980); Eleanor Burke Leacock, *Myths of Male Dominance: Collected Articles on Women Cross-Culturally* (New York: Monthly Review Press, 1981); Karen Sacks, *Sisters and Wives: The Past and Future of Sexual Inequality* (Westport, Conn.: Greenwood Press, 1979); Rayna R. Reiter, ed., *Toward an Anthropology of Women* (New York: Monthly Review Press, 1975); and Eleanor Burke Leacock and Nancy O. Lurie, eds., *North American Indians in Historical Perspective* (New York: Random House, 1971).

4. Alfred L. Kroeber, "Psychosis or Social Sanction," *Character and Personality* 8, no. 3 (1940): 204–15, quote on p. 209.

proper historical context brings to light the integral nature of its relationship to the larger community.

Cultural Significance of the Female Cross-Gender Role

Most anthropological work on the cross-gender role has focused on the male berdache, with little recognition given to the female cross-gender role. Part of the problem has been the much smaller data base available for a study of the female role. Yet anthropologists have overlooked even the available data. This oversight has led to the current misconception that the cross-gender role was not feasible for women. Harriet Whitehead, in a comprehensive article on the berdache, states that, given the small number of cross-gender females, "the gender-crossed status was more fully instituted for males than for females."[5] Charles Callender and Lee Kochems, in a well-researched article, base their analysis of the role predominantly on the male berdache.[6] Evidence from thirty-three Native American tribes indicates that the cross-gender role for women was as viable an institution as was the male berdache role.[7]

The Native American cross-gender role confounded Western concepts of gender. Cross-gender individuals typically acted, sat, dressed, talked like, and did the work of the other sex. Early Western observers described the berdache as half male and half female, but such a description attests only to their inability to accept a male in a female role or vice versa. In the great majority of reported cases of berdache, they assumed the social role of the other sex, not of both sexes.[8] Contemporary theorists, such as Callender and Kochems and Whitehead, resist the idea of a complete social role reclassification because they equate gender with biological sex. Native gender categories contradict such definitions.

---

5. Harriet Whitehead, "The Bow and the Burden Strap: A New Look at Institutionalized Homosexuality in Native North America," in Ortner and Whitehead, eds. (n. 2 above), pp. 80–115, quote on p. 86.

6. Charles Callender and Lee M. Kochems, "The North American Berdache," *Current Anthropology* 24, no. 4 (1983): 443–56.

7. These tribes by area are as follows: Subarctic—Ingalik, Kaska; Northwest—Bella Coola, Haisla, Lillooet, Nootka, Okanagon, Queets, Quinault; California/Oregon—Achomawi, Atsugewi, Klamath, Shasta, Wintu, Wiyot, Yokuts, Yuki; Southwest—Apache, Cocopa, Maricopa, Mohave, Navajo, Papago, Pima, Yuma; Great Basin—Ute, Southern Ute, Shoshoni, Southern Paiute, Northern Paiute; Plains—Blackfoot, Crow, Kutenai.

8. See S. C. Simms, "Crow Indian Hermaphrodites," *American Anthropologist* 5, no. 3 (1903): 580–81; Alfred L. Kroeber, "The Arapaho," *American Museum of Natural History Bulletin* 18, no. 1 (1902): 1–150; Royal B. Hassrick, *The Sioux: Life and Customs of a Warrior Society* (Norman: University of Oklahoma Press, 1964); Ronald L. Olson, *The Quinault Indians* (Seattle: University of Washington Press, 1936); Ruth Murray Underhill, *Social Organization of the Papago Indians* (1939; reprint, New York: AMS Press, 1969).

Although the details of the cross-gender females' lives are scant in the ethnographic literature, a basic pattern emerges from the data on the western tribes. Recognition and cultural validation of the female cross-gender role varied slightly from tribe to tribe, although the social role was the same. Among the Southwestern tribes, dream experience was an important ritual aspect of life and provided success, leadership, and special skills for those who sought it. All cross-gender individuals in these tribes dreamed about their role change. The Mohave *hwame* dreamed of becoming cross-gender while still in the womb.[9] The Maricopa *kwiraxame* dreamed too much as a child and so changed her sex.[10] No information is available for the development of the female cross-gender role (*tw!nnaek*) among the Klamath. It was most likely similar to the male adolescent transformative experience, which was accomplished through fasting or diving.[11] Dreaming provided an avenue to special powers and also provided sanction for the use of those powers. In the same way, dreams about the cross-gender role provided impetus and community sanction for assumption of the role.

The female candidate for cross-gender status displayed an interest in the male role during childhood. A girl avoided learning female tasks. Instead, as in the case of the Cocopa *warrhameh*, she played with boys and made bows and arrows with which to hunt birds and rabbits.[12] The Mohave *hwame* "[threw] away their dolls and metates, and [refused] to shred bark or perform other feminine tasks."[13] Adults, acknowledging the interests of such girls, taught them the same skills the boys learned. Among the Kaska, a family that had all female children and desired a son to hunt for them would select a daughter (probably the one who showed the most inclination) to be "like a man." When she was five, the parents tied the dried ovaries of a bear to her belt to wear for life as protection against conception.[14] Though in different tribes the socializing processes varied, girls achieved the cross-gender role in each instance through accepted cultural channels.

Upon reaching puberty, the time when girls were considered ready for marriage, the cross-gender female was unable to fulfill her obligations

9. George Devereux, "Institutionalized Homosexuality of the Mohave Indians," *Human Biology* 9, no. 4 (1937): 498–527.

10. Leslie Spier, *Yuman Tribes of the Gila River* (Chicago: University of Chicago Press, 1933).

11. Leslie Spier, *Klamath Ethnography*, University of California Publications in American Archaeology and Ethnology, vol. 30 (Berkeley: University of California Press, 1930).

12. E. W. Gifford, *The Cocopa*, University of California Publications in American Archaeology and Ethnology, vol. 31, no. 5 (Berkeley: University of California Press, 1933).

13. Devereux (n. 9 above), p. 503.

14. John J. Honigmann, *The Kaska Indians: An Ethnographic Reconstruction*, Yale University Publications in Anthropology, no. 51 (New Haven, Conn.: Yale University Press, 1954), p. 130.

and duties as a woman in marriage, having learned the tasks assigned to men. Nonmarriageable status could have presented a disadvantage both to herself and to her kin, who would be called upon to support her in her later years. But a role transfer allowed her to enter the marriage market for a wife with whom she could establish a household. The Mohave publicly acknowledged the new status of the woman by performing an initiation ceremony. Following this ceremony she assumed a name befitting a person of the male sex and was given marriage rights.[15] At puberty, the Cocopa *warrhameh* dressed her hair in the male style and had her nose pierced like the men, instead of receiving a chin tattoo like other women.[16] These public rites validated the cross-gender identity, signifying to the community that the woman was to be treated as a man.

In adult life cross-gender females performed the duties of the male gender role. Their tasks included hunting, trapping, cultivating crops, and fighting in battles. For example, the Cocopa *warrhameh* established households like men and fought in battle.[17] The Kaska cross-gender female "dressed in masculine attire, did male allocated tasks, often developing great strength and usually becoming an outstanding hunter."[18] The Mohave *hwame* were known as excellent providers, hunting for meat, working in the fields, and caring for the children of their wives.[19] Cross-gender females also adhered to male ritual obligations. A Klamath *tw!nnaek* observed the usual mourning when her long-time female partner died, wearing a bark belt as did a man.[20] Mohave *hwame* were said to be powerful shamans, in this case especially good at curing venereal disease.[21] Many other cross-gender females were considered powerful spiritually, but most were not shamans, even in the Southwest. Cross-gender females did not bear children once they took up the male role. Their kin considered them nonreproductive and accepted the loss of their childbearing potential, placing a woman's individual interests and abilities above her value as a reproducer.[22]

In most cases ethnographers do not discuss the ability of cross-gender females to maintain the fiction of their maleness. Whitehead suggests that women were barred from crossing over unless they were, or at least pretended to be, deficient physically.[23] However, despite some reports that cross-gender women in the Southwest had muscular builds, unde-

15. Devereux (n. 9 above), pp. 508–9.
16. Gifford (n. 12 above).
17. Ibid., p. 294.
18. Honigmann (n. 14 above), p. 130.
19. Devereux (n. 9 above).
20. Spier, *Klamath Ethnography* (n. 11 above), p. 53.
21. Devereux (n. 9 above).
22. Ibid.; Gifford (n. 12 above); Honigmann (n. 14 above).
23. Whitehead (n. 5 above), pp. 92–93.

veloped secondary sexual characteristics, and sporadic or absent menstruation,[24] convincing physical evidence is noticeably lacking. In fact, the Mohave *hwame* kept a husband's taboos with regard to her menstruating or pregnant wife and ignored her own menses.[25] That such may have been the case in other tribes as well is borne out by the practice of the Ingalik cross-gender female. Among the Alaskan Ingalik, the *kashim* was the center of men's activities and the place for male-only sweat baths. The cross-gender female participated in the activities of the *kashim*, and the men were said not to perceive her true sex.[26] Cornelius Osgood suggests that she was able to hide her sex, but, as with the Mohave, the people probably ignored her physical sex in favor of her chosen role. Through this social fiction, then, cross-gender females dismissed the physiological functions of women and claimed an identity based on their performance of a social role.

Gender Equality

Women's ability to assume the cross-gender role arose from the particular conditions of kinship and gender in these tribes. The egalitarian relations of the sexes were predicated on the cooperation of autonomous individuals who had control of their productive activities. In these tribes women owned and distributed the articles they produced, and they had equal voice in matters affecting kin and community. Economic strategies depended on collective activity. Lineages or individuals had no formal authority; the whole group made decisions by consensus. People of both sexes could achieve positions of leadership through skill, wisdom, and spiritual power. Ultimately, neither women nor men had an inferior role but rather had power in those spheres of activity specific to their sex.[27]

24. C. Daryll Forde, *Ethnography of the Yuma Indians*, University of California Publications in American Archaeology and Ethnology, vol. 28, no. 4 (Berkeley: University of California Press, 1931), p. 157; Gifford (n. 12 above), p. 294; Devereux (n. 9 above), p. 510.

25. Devereux (n. 9 above), p. 515.

26. Cornelius Osgood, *Ingalik Social Culture*, Yale University Publications in Anthropology, no. 53 (New Haven, Conn.: Yale University Press, 1958).

27. Based on ethnographic data in Honigmann (n. 14 above); Gifford (n. 12 above); Leslie Spier, *Cultural Relations of the Gila and Colorado River Tribes*, Yale University Publications in Anthropology, no. 3 (New Haven, Conn.: Yale University Press, 1936), *Klamath Ethnography* (n. 11 above), and *Yuman Tribes* (n. 10 above); Theodore Stern, *The Klamath Tribe* (Seattle: University of Washington Press, 1966); Alfred L. Kroeber, *Mohave Indians: Report on Aboriginal Territory and Occupancy of the Mohave Tribe*, ed. David Horr (New York: Garland Publishing, 1974), and *Handbook of the Indians of California*, Bureau of American Ethnology Bulletin no. 78 (Washington, D.C.: Government Printing Office, 1925); William H. Kelly, *Cocopa Ethnography*, Anthropological Papers of the University of Arizona, no. 29 (Tucson: University of Arizona Press, 1977); Lorraine M. Sherer, *The Clan System of the Fort Mohave Indians* (Los Angeles: Historical Society of Southern California, 1965).

Among these tribes, gender roles involved the performance of a particular set of duties. Most occupations necessary to the functioning of the group were defined as either male or female tasks. A typical division of labor allocated responsibilities for gathering, food preparation, child rearing, basket weaving, and making clothes to women, while men hunted, made weapons, and built canoes and houses. The allocation of separate tasks to each sex established a system of reciprocity that assured the interdependence of the sexes. Because neither set of tasks was valued more highly than the other, neither sex predominated.

Gender-assigned tasks overlapped considerably among these people. Many individuals engaged in activities that were also performed by the other sex without incurring disfavor. The small game and fish that Kaska and Klamath women hunted on a regular basis were an important contribution to the survival of the band. Some Klamath women made canoes, usually a man's task, and older men helped women with food preparation.[28] In the Colorado River area, both men and women collected tule pollen.[29] Engaging in such activities did not make a woman masculine or a man feminine because, although distinct spheres of male and female production existed, a wide range of tasks was acceptable for both sexes. Because there was no need to maintain gender inequalities, notions of power and prestige did not circumscribe the roles. Without strict gender definitions, it was then possible for some Native American women to take up the male role permanently without threatening the gender system.

Another factor in creating the possibility of the cross-gender role for women was the nature of the kinship system. Kinship was not based on hierarchical relations between men and women; it was organized in the interest of both sexes. Each sex had something to gain by forming kin ties through marriage,[30] because of the mutual assistance and economic security marital relations provided.[31] Marriage also created an alliance between two families, thereby broadening the network of kin on whom an individual could rely. Thus, marriage promoted security in a subsistence-level economy.

The marriage customs of these tribes reflected the egalitarian nature of their kinship system. Since status and property were unimportant, marriage arrangements did not involve any transfer of wealth or rank

28. Julie Cruikshank, *Athapaskan Women: Lives and Legends* (Ottawa: National Museums of Canada, 1979); Spier, *Klamath Ethnography* (n. 11 above).

29. Gifford (n. 12 above).

30. The five tribes discussed here varied in forms of kinship, but this variation did not have a significant effect on the relations between the sexes. Lacking rank or wealth, kinship groups were not the focus of power or authority, hence whether a tribe was matrilineal or patrilineal was not as important as the overall relationship with kin on either side.

31. John J. Honigmann, *Culture and Ethos of Kaska Society*, Yale University Publications in Anthropology, no. 40 (New Haven, Conn.: Yale University Press, 1949), and *Kaska Indians* (n. 14 above).

through the female. The small marriage gifts that were exchanged served as tokens of the woman's worth in the marriage relationship.[32] Furthermore, because of the unimportance of property or rank, individuals often had a series of marriages, rather than one permanent relationship; divorce was relatively easy and frequent for both women and men.[33] Marriages in these tribes became more permanent only when couples had children. Women were not forced to remain in a marriage, and either partner had the right to dissolve an unhappy or unproductive relationship.

This egalitarian kinship system had important ramifications for the cross-gender female. A daughter's marriage was not essential for maintenance of family rank; that is, a woman's family did not lose wealth if she abandoned her role as daughter. As a social male, she had marriage rights through which she could establish a household and contribute to the subsistence of the group. Additionally, because of the frequency of divorce, it was possible for a married cross-gender female to raise children. Evidence of cross-gender females caring for their wives' offspring is available only for the Mohave *hwame*. Women in other tribes, however, could also have brought children into a cross-gender marriage, since at least younger offspring typically went with the mother in a divorce.[34] A cross-gender woman might acquire children through marriage to a pregnant woman, or possibly through her wife's extramarital relationships with men. Cross-gender couples probably also adopted children, a practice common among heterosexual couples in many tribes.

Details from the Mohave help to illuminate the cross-gender parent/ child relationship. The Mohave believed that the paternity of an unborn child changed if the pregnant woman had sex with another partner; thus, the cross-gender female claimed any child her wife might be carrying when they married. George Devereux states that such children retained the clan affiliation of the previous father.[35] But the clan structure of the Mohave was not strongly organized and possessed no formal authority or ceremonial functions.[36] The significant relationships were those developed through residence with kin. Thus, children raised in a cross-gender household established strong ties with those parents. The investment of parental care was reciprocated when these children became adults. In this way the cross-gender female remained a part of the network of kin through marriage.

32. Spier, *Klamath Ethnography* (n. 11 above); J. A. Teit, "Field Notes on the Tahltan and Kaska Indians: 1912–15," *Anthropologica* 3, no. 1 (1956): 39–171; Kroeber, *Handbook* (n. 27 above); Gifford (n. 12 above).

33. Kelly (n. 27 above); Spier, *Klamath Ethnography* (n. 11 above).

34. Kelly (n. 27 above).

35. Devereux (n. 9 above), p. 514.

36. Kelly (n. 27 above); Forde (n. 24 above).

Sexual Relations in the Cross-Gender Role

Sexual behavior was part of the relationship between cross-gender female and the women they married. Although the cross-gender female was a social male, Native Americans did not consider her sexual activity an imitation of heterosexual behavior. Her sexual behavior was recognized as lesbian—that is, as female homosexuality. The Mohave were aware of a range of sexual activities between the cross-gender female and her partner—activities that were possible only between two physiological females. Devereux recorded a Mohave term that referred specifically to the lesbian love-making of the *hwame* and her partner.[37] The Native American acceptance of lesbian behavior among cross-gender females did not depend on the presence of a male role-playing person; their acceptance derived instead from their concept of sexuality.

Native American beliefs about sexuality are reflected in the marriage system. Theorists such as Gayle Rubin have implicated marriage as one of the mechanisms that enforce and define women's sexuality. According to Rubin, the division of labor "can . . . be seen as a taboo against sexual arrangements other than those containing at least one man and one woman, thereby enjoining heterosexual marriage."[38] Yet in certain Native American tribes other sexual behavior, both heterosexual and homosexual, was available and permissible within and outside of marriage. Homosexual behavior occurred in contexts within which neither individual was cross-gender nor were such individuals seen as expressing cross-gender behavior.[39] Premarital and extramarital sexual relations were also permissible.[40] Furthermore, through the cross-gender role, women could marry one another. Sexuality clearly was not restricted by the institution of marriage.

Native American ideology disassociated sexual behavior from concepts of male and female gender roles and was not concerned with the identity of the sexual partner. The status of the cross-gender female's partner is telling in this respect. She was always a traditional female; that is, two cross-gender females did not marry. Thus, a woman could follow the traditional female gender role, yet marry and make love with another woman without being stigmatized by such behavior. Even though she was the partner of a cross-gender female, she was not considered homosexual or cross-gender. If the relationship ended in divorce, heterosexual marriage was still an option for the exwife. The traditional female gender role did not restrict her choice of marital/sexual partners. Consequently,

37. Devereux (n. 9 above), pp. 514–15.
38. Rubin (n. 2 above), p. 178.
39. See Forde (n. 24 above), p. 157; Honigmann, *Kaska Indians* (n. 14 above), p. 127.
40. Spier, *Klamath Ethnography* (n. 11 above), and *Yuman Tribes* (n. 10 above); Kroeber, *Handbook* (n. 27 above).

individuals possessed a gender identity, but not a corresponding sexual identity, and thus were allowed several sexual options. Sexuality itself was not embedded in Native American gender ideology.

Women on the Plains

The conditions that supported the development and continuation of the cross-gender role among certain western tribes were not replicated among the Plains tribes. Evidence of cross-gender females there is scant while reports of male berdache are numerous. Whitehead suggests that the absence of cross-gender females resulted from the weakness of the cross-gender institution for women.[41] A more plausible explanation involves the particular historical conditions that differentiate the Plains tribes from the western tribes. Yet it is precisely these conditions that make accurate interpretation of women's roles and the female cross-gender role much more difficult for the Plains tribes.

The Plains Indian culture of nomadic buffalo hunting and frequent warfare did not develop until the late eighteenth and early nineteenth centuries as tribes moved west in response to the expansion and development of colonial America. The new mode of life represented for many tribes a tremendous shift from an originally settled and horticultural or hunting and gathering life-style. With the introduction of the horse and gun, the growth of the fur trade, and pressure from westward-moving white settlers, tribes from the east and north were displaced onto the Plains in the late 1700s.[42] As the importance of hide trade with Euro-Americans increased in the early 1800s, it altered the mode of production among Plains tribes. Increased wealth and authority were accessible through trade and warfare. Individual males were able to achieve greater dominance while women's social and economic autonomy declined.[43] With the growing importance of hides for trade, men who were successful hunters required additional wives to handle the tanning. Their increasing loss of control in this productive sphere downgraded woman's status and tied her to marital demands. Recent work on the Plains tribes, however, indicates that this process was not consistent; women maintained a degree of autonomy and power not previously acknowledged.[44]

41. Whitehead (n. 5 above), p. 86.
42. Gene Weltfish, "The Plains Indians: Their Continuity in History and Their Indian Identity," in Leacock and Lurie, eds. (n. 3 above).
43. Leacock and Lurie, eds. (n. 3 above); Alan Klein, "The Political-Economy of Gender: A 19th Century Plains Indian Case Study," in *The Hidden Half: Studies of Plains Indian Women*, ed. Patricia Albers and Beatrice Medicine (Washington, D.C.: University Press of America, 1983), pp. 143–73.
44. See Albers and Medicine, eds.

Early ethnographic descriptions of Plains Indian women were based on a Western gender ideology that was contradicted by actual female behavior. Although traditional Plains culture valued quiet, productive, nonpromiscuous women, this was only one side of the coin. There was actually a variability in female roles that can only be attributed to women's continued autonomy. Beatrice Medicine provides an excellent discussion of the various roles open to women among the Blackfoot and Lakota. Such roles included the "manly-hearted woman," the "crazy woman" (who was sexually promiscuous), the Sun Dance woman, and the chief woman or favorite wife.[45] According to Ruth Landes, Lakota women served in tribal government and were sometimes appointed marshalls to handle problems among women. Most Plains tribes had women warriors who accompanied war parties for limited purposes on certain occasions, such as avenging the death of kin, and who received warrior honors for their deeds.[46] As Medicine states, "These varied role categories . . . suggest that the idealized behavior of women was not as rigidly defined and followed as has been supposed."[47]

The presence of a variety of socially approved roles also suggests that these were normative patterns of behavior for women that need not be construed as "contrary" to their gender role. Warrior women were not a counterpart of the male berdache, nor were they considered cross-gender.[48] Ethnographers' attributions of masculinity to such behavior seem to be a product of Western beliefs about the rigid dichotomization of gender roles and the nature of suitable pursuits for women. That men simply accepted females as warriors and were not threatened by such behavior contradicts the notion that such women were even temporarily assuming the male role.[49] The men's acceptance was based on recognition of the women warriors' capabilities as women.

There were individual Plains women in the nineteenth century whose behavior throughout their lives exemplified a cross-gender role. They did not always cross-dress, but, like Woman Chief of the Crow, neither did they participate in female activities. They took wives to handle their households and were highly successful in hunting and raiding activities. They were also considered very powerful. Of these women, the Kutenai cross-gender woman always dressed in male attire and was re-

45. Beatrice Medicine, " 'Warrior Women'—Sex Role Alternatives for Plains Indian Women," in Albers and Medicine, eds., pp. 267–80; see also Oscar Lewis, "Manly-Hearted Women among the North Piegan," *American Anthropologist* 43, no. 2 (1941): 173–87.

46. Ruth Landes, *The Mystic Lake Sioux* (Madison: University of Wisconsin Press, 1968).

47. Medicine, p. 272.

48. Sue-Ellen Jacobs, "The Berdache," in *Cultural Diversity and Homosexuality*, ed. Stephen Murray (New York: Irvington Press, in press); Medicine, p. 269.

49. On male acceptance of women warriors, see Landes.

nowned for her exploits as warrior and mediator and guide for white traders. Running Eagle of the Blackfoot lived as a warrior and married a young widow. Woman Chief became the head of her father's lodge when he died and achieved the third highest rank among the Crow. She took four wives.[50] Particularly since no records of earlier cross-gender women have been found, these few examples seem to constitute individual exceptions. What then was the status of the female cross-gender role among Plains tribes?

Part of the difficulty with answering this question stems from the nature of the data itself. Nineteenth-century observers rarely recorded information on Plains Indian women, "considering them too insignificant to merit special treatment."[51] These observers knew few women and only the more successful males. "Those who did become known were women who had acted as go-betweens for the whites and Indians,"[52] such as the Kutenai cross-gender female. Running Eagle and Woman Chief were also exceptional enough to be noticed by white traders. Except for the Kutenai woman, none of the women are identified as berdache in nineteenth-century reports, although all were cross-gender. Observers seem to have been unable to recognize the female cross-gender role. Indeed, no nineteenth-century reports mention cross-gender females among even the western tribes, although later ethnographers found ample evidence of the role.

Ethnographers had no solid evidence of the female cross-gender role among Plains Indians. Several factors may help to explain this discrepancy. White contact with Plains tribes came earlier than with the western tribes and was more disruptive. The last cross-gender females seem to have disappeared among Plains tribes by the mid-nineteenth century, while in the Southwest this did not occur until the end of the century, much closer to the time when ethnographers began to collect data. Discrepancies also arise in informants' stories. The Kutenai denied the existence of cross-gender females among them, in contradiction with earlier evidence, and yet willingly claimed that such women lived among the Flathead and Blackfoot.[53] The Arapaho told Alfred Kroeber that the

50. Edwin Thompson Denig, *Of the Crow Nation*, ed. John C. Ewers, Smithsonian Institution, Bureau of American Ethnology, Bulletin no. 151, Anthropology Papers no. 33 (Washington, D.C.: Government Printing Office, 1953), and *Five Indian Tribes of the Upper Missouri*, ed. John C. Ewers (Norman: University of Oklahoma Press, 1961); Claude E. Schaeffer, "The Kutenai Female Berdache: Courier, Guide, Prophetess, and Warrior," *Ethnohistory* 12, no. 3 (1965): 193–236.

51. Patricia Albers, "Introduction: New Perspectives on Plains Indian Women," in Albers and Medicine, eds. (n. 43 above), pp. 1–26, quote on p. 3.

52. Katherine Weist, "Beasts of Burden and Menial Slaves: Nineteenth Century Observations of Northern Plains Indian Women," in Albers and Medicine, eds. (n. 43 above), pp. 29–52, quote on p. 39.

53. Harry H. Turney-High, *Ethnography of the Kutenai*, Memoirs of the American Anthropological Association, no. 56 (1941; reprint, New York: Kraus Reprint, 1969), and

Lakota had female berdache, but there is no corroborating evidence from the Lakota themselves.[54] Informants were clearly reticent or unwilling to discuss cross-gender women. In her article on Native American lesbians, Paula Gunn Allen suggests that such information was suppressed by the elders of the tribes.[55] Most information on Plains Indian women was transmitted from elder tribesmen to white male ethnographers. But men were excluded from knowledge of much of women's behavior;[56] in this way much of the data on cross-gender females may have been lost.

The record of Plains cross-gender females remains limited. Certain social conditions may have contributed to the small number of women who assumed the role in the nineteenth century. During the 1800s the practice of taking additional wives increased with the men's need for female labor. This phenomenon may have limited women's choice of occupation. The pressures to marry may have barred women from a role that required success in male tasks only. The practice of sororal polygyny particularly would have put subtle pressures on families to assure that each daughter learned the traditional female role. Indeed, there were said to be no unmarried women among the Lakota.[57] Furthermore, given the constant state of warfare and loss of able-bodied men, the tribes were under pressure merely to survive. Such conditions in the 1800s discouraged women from abandoning their reproductive abilities through the cross-gender role. In fact, among the Lakota, women who insisted on leading men's lives were ostracized from the group and forced to wander by themselves.[58] Knowledge of the female cross-gender role may have persisted, but those few who actually lived out the role were exceptions in a changing environment.

The Demise of the Cross-Gender Role

By the late nineteenth century the female cross-gender role had all but disappeared among Native Americans. Its final demise was related to a change in the construction of sexuality and gender in these tribes. The dominant ideology of Western culture, with its belief in the inferior

The Flathead Indians of Montana, Memoirs of the American Anthropological Association, no. 48 (1937; reprint, New York: Kraus Reprint, 1969).

54. Kroeber, "The Arapaho" (n. 8 above), p. 19.

55. Paula Gunn Allen, "Beloved Women: Lesbians in American Indian Cultures," *Conditions: Seven* 3, no. 1 (1981): 67–87.

56. Alice Kehoe, "The Shackles of Tradition," in Albers and Medicine, eds. (n. 43 above), pp. 53–73.

57. Hassrick (n. 8 above).

58. Jeannette Mirsky, "The Dakota," in *Cooperation and Competition among Primitive Peoples*, ed. Margaret Mead (Boston: Beacon Press, 1961), p. 417.

nature of the female role and its insistence on heterosexuality, began to replace traditional Native American gender systems.

Ideological pressures of white culture encouraged Native American peoples to reject the validity of the cross-gender role and to invoke notions of "proper" sexuality that supported men's possession of sexual rights to women. Communities expressed disapproval by berating the cross-gender female for not being a "real man" and not being properly equipped to satisfy her wife sexually. In effect, variations in sexual behavior that had previously been acceptable were now repudiated in favor of heterosexual practices. Furthermore, the identity of the sexual partner became an important aspect of sexual behavior.

The life of the last cross-gender female among the Mohave, Sahaykwisa, provides a clear example of this process. According to Devereux, "Sahaykwisa . . . was born toward the middle of the last century and killed . . . at the age of 45. Sahaykwisa had at a certain time a very pretty wife. Other men desired the woman and tried to lure her away from the *hwame*." The men teased Sahaykwisa in a derogatory manner, suggesting that her love-making was unsatisfactory to her wife in comparison to that of a "real man." They ridiculed her wife and said, "Why do you want a transvestite for your husband who has no penis and pokes you with the finger?"[59] Such derision went beyond usual joking behavior until finally Sahaykwisa was raped by a man who was angered because his wife left him for Sahaykwisa. The community no longer validated the cross-gender role, and Sahaykwisa herself eventually abandoned it, only to be killed later as a witch. By accusing the cross-gender female of sexual inadequacy, men of the tribe claimed in effect that they had sole rights to women's sexuality, and that sexuality was appropriate only between men and women.

Conclusion

In attempting to fit the Native American cross-gender role into Western categories, anthropologists have disregarded the ways in which the institution represents native categories of behavior. Western interpretations dichotomize the gender roles for each sex, which results from erroneous assumptions about, first, the connection between biology and gender, and, second, the nature of gender roles. Callender and Kochems state, "The transformation of a berdache was not a complete shift from his or her *biological* gender to the opposite one, but rather an approximation of the latter in some of its social aspects."[60] They imply that anatomy

59. Devereux (n. 9 above), p. 523.
60. Callender and Kochems (n. 6 above), p. 453 (italics mine).

circumscribed the berdache's ability to function in the gender role of the other sex. Whitehead finds the anatomical factor particularly telling for women, who were supposedly unable to succeed in the male role unless deficient physically as females.[61] These theorists, by claiming a mixed gender status for the berdache, confuse a social role with a physical identity that remained unchanged for the cross-gender individual.

Knowing the true sex of the berdache, Native Americans accepted them on the basis of their social attributes; physiological sex was not relevant to the gender role. The Mohave, for example, did not focus on the biological sex of the berdache. Nonberdache were said to "feel toward their possible transvestite mate as they would feel toward a true woman, [or] man."[62] In response to a newly initiated berdache, the Yuma "began to feel toward him as to a woman."[63] These tribes concurred in the social fiction of the cross-gender role despite the obvious physical differences, indicating the unimportance of biological sex to the gender role.[64]

Assumptions regarding the hierarchical nature of Native American gender relations have created serious problems in the analysis of the female cross-gender role. Whitehead claims that few females could have been cross-gender because she assumes the asymmetrical nature of gender relations.[65] In cultures with an egalitarian mode of production, however, gender does not create an imbalance between the sexes. In the western North American tribes discussed above, neither gender roles nor sexuality were associated with an ideology of male dominance. Women were not barred from the cross-gender role by rigid gender definitions; instead, they filled the role successfully. Although cross-gender roles are not limited to egalitarian societies, the historical conditions of nonegalitarian societies, in which increasing restrictions are placed on women's productive and reproductive activities, strongly discourage them from taking on the cross-gender role.

Anthropologists' classification of gender roles as dichotomous has served to obscure the nature of the Native American cross-gender role. For Whitehead, the male berdache is "less than a full man" but "more than a mere woman,"[66] suggesting a mixed gender role combining elements of both the male and the female. Similarly, Callender and Kochems

61. Whitehead (n. 5 above), p. 92.
62. Devereux (n. 9 above), p. 501.
63. Forde (n. 24 above), p. 157.
64. Data on the Navajo *nadle* are not included in this article because the Navajo conception of the berdache was atypical. The *nadle* was considered a hermaphrodite by the Navajo—i.e., of both sexes physically—and therefore did not actually exemplify a cross-gender role. See W. W. Hill, "The Status of the Hermaphrodite and Transvestite in Navaho Culture," *American Anthropologist* 37, no. 2 (1935): 273–79.
65. Whitehead (n. 5 above), p. 86.
66. Ibid., p. 89.

suggest that the berdache formed an intermediate gender status.[67] Native conceptualizations of gender, particularly in the egalitarian tribes, do not contain an invariable opposition of two roles. The Western ideology of feminine and masculine traits actually has little in common with these Native American gender systems, within which exist large areas of over-lapping tasks.

The idea of a mixed gender role is particularly geared to the male berdache and assumes the existence of a limited traditional female role. Such a concept does not account for the wide range of behaviors possible for both the male and female gender roles. By contrast the term cross-gender defines the role as a set of behaviors typifying the attributes of the other sex, but not limited to an exact duplication of either role. Attributes of the male berdache that are not typical of the female role—for example, certain ritual activities—do not indicate a mixed gender category. These activities are specialized tasks that arise from the spiritual power of the cross-gender individual.

The term "cross-gender," however, is not without its problems. Sue-Ellen Jacobs suggests that a person who from birth or early childhood fills this variant role may not be "crossing" a gender boundary. She prefers the term "third gender" because, as among the Tewa, the berdache role may not fit either a male or female gender category but is conceived instead as another gender.[68] Kay Martin and Barbara Voorheis also explore the possibility of more than two genders.[69] Certainly the last word has not been spoken about a role that has confounded researchers for at least one hundred years. But it is imperative to develop an analysis of variant gender roles based on the historical conditions that faced particular tribes since gender systems vary in different cultures and change as modes of production change.

Department of Anthropology
San Francisco State University

67. Callender and Kochems (n. 6 above), p. 454.

68. Sue-Ellen Jacobs, personal communication, 1983, and "Comment on Callender and Kochems," *Current Anthropology* 24, no. 4 (1983): 459–60.

69. M. Kay Martin and Barbara Voorheis, *Female of the Species* (New York: Columbia University Press, 1975).

Distance and Desire:
English Boarding-School Friendships

Martha Vicinus

Recovering lost lesbians of the past and establishing bases for self-definition have been to this point the chief concerns of lesbian historiography.[1] The vexed question of when and why single-sex genital contact became labeled deviant has absorbed much energy. Scholars have concentrated, for example, on such issues as whether the famous sexologists of the late nineteenth and early twentieth centuries were detrimental or helpful to women's single-sex friendships.[2] Some, following the lead of the British historian Jeffrey Weeks, have argued that labeling has enabled women to identify themselves, to seek out companions, and to form conscious subcultures, such as those created in Paris and Berlin between

An earlier version of this essay was presented at the "Among Men, among Women" Conference, University of Amsterdam, June 22–26, 1983. I am indebted to the participants of this conference for many helpful suggestions; the enthusiastic sharing of work and information made this international conference an especially happy and memorable experience. I am grateful to Estelle Freedman, Bea Nergaard, and Ann Scott for their comments and criticisms. Research for this essay was made possible by a grant from the American Council of Learned Societies and the John Simon Guggenheim Foundation; I wish to thank them for their timely assistance.

1. For a discussion of lesbian historiography in the context of the history of sexuality, see my review essay, "Sexuality and Power: A Review of Current Work in the History of Sexuality," *Feminist Studies* 8 (Spring 1982): 147–51; see also Estelle Freedman, "Sexuality in Nineteenth-Century America: Behavior, Ideology and Politics," *Reviews in American History* 10, no. 4 (1982): 196–215.

2. See George Chauncey, Jr., "From Sexual Inversion to Homosexuality: Medicine and the Changing Conceptualization of Female Deviance," *Salmagundi* 58/59 (Fall 1982–Winter 1983): 114–46.

Reprinted from *Signs: Journal of Women in Culture and Society* 9, no. 4 (Summer 1984): 600–622.

the wars.[3] Others, however, have seen the work of sexologists such as Richard von Krafft-Ebing, Havelock Ellis, and Cesare Lombroso as effecting a blight on romantic friendships, leading to their "morbidification." According to these critics, the medical world's labeling of women's friendships as deviant had a wholly pernicious effect on women.[4] A major difficulty these historians have faced is that of dating: exactly when did the theories of the medical men become well known among the general public? What impact did this knowledge have? When precisely did public disapproval of women's friendships begin? These questions have led to premature and exaggerated claims for several different time frames. They have, moreover, left lesbian history overly concerned with external labeling, rather than with the consideration of what homoerotic friendships were like and how they were a part of and apart from general social attitudes toward women as private and public beings.

In this essay I examine one aspect of the most widely known of women's friendships, the adolescent crush, during the late nineteenth and early twentieth centuries. I am concerned with its social origins, its various phases, and its impact on both the younger woman and the older recipient of her love. Although a good deal has been written about the "morbidification" of these friendships, their benefits and liabilities for both girls and women have largely been assumed. Neither the ingredients that make up an intense friendship nor its impact on the participants may have changed over time, but I believe that beginning in the late nineteenth century we find a different conjunction of public demands and private needs; these will be explored here. Boarding-school life during a period when women were pioneering new public roles and professional occupations especially encouraged an idealized love for an older, publicly successful woman. I cannot from my evidence answer the

3. Jeffrey Weeks, *Coming Out: Homosexual Politics in Britain from the Nineteenth Century to the Present* (London: Quartet Books, 1977), pp. 101–11; Gayle Rubin's introduction to Renée Vivien's *A Woman Appeared to Me*, trans. Jeannette Foster (Reno, Nev.: Naiad Press, 1976).

4. See Lillian Faderman, "The Morbidification of Love between Women by 19th-Century Sexologists," *Journal of Homosexuality* 4, no. 1 (1978): 73–90, and *Surpassing the Love of Men: Romantic Friendship and Love between Women from the Renaissance to the Present* (New York: William Morrow & Co., 1981), which generally values romantic friendships over the lesbian "underworld" and minimizes the issue of sexuality in romantic friendships. Using rather limited evidence, Nancy Sahli argues that after 1875 "smashing" (same-sex crushes) became suspect: "Smashing: Women's Relationships before the Fall," *Chrysalis* 8 (Summer 1979): 17–27. Sahli has been used uncritically by Marjorie Houspian Dobkin in her edition of the early journals and letters of M. Carey Thomas, *The Making of a Feminist* (Kent, Ohio: Kent State University Press, 1979); and by Adrienne Rich, "Compulsory Heterosexuality and Lesbian Existence," *Signs: Journal of Women in Culture and Society* 5, no. 4 (Summer 1980): 631–60. For a more subtle analysis of the impact of the sexologists, see Carroll Smith-Rosenberg, "The Body Politic: Abortion, Deviance and the Sexualization of Language," in *The New Woman and the Troubled Man* (New York: Alfred A. Knopf, Inc., in press).

question of precisely how sexually aware the participants were in these "new" crushes, but surely some were, while others were not. Although a religious vocabulary effectively masked personal desires, a woman who loved another girl or woman always spoke of this love in terms that replicated heterosexual love. The strong emphasis on the power of the emotions suggests an understanding of what we would now label as sexual desire; commentators would probably not have argued so forcefully for the control of these emotions if they had not recognized their sexual source. Indeed, self-control became a key means of expressing love within the boarding-school world, and herein lies the core of my analysis.

* * *

Women's homoerotic friendships require specific preconditions to flourish. As Lillian Faderman has documented, women need to be minimally freed from the constraints of family and kinship (although friendships between cousins were common).[5] Familial responsibilities and economic dependence meant that few women before 1870 in Europe or America could hope to live with a beloved woman. Many might have wished to flee the world with a special friend, following the example of Sarah Ponsonby and Eleanor Butler, who eloped in 1778. The "Ladies of Llangollen" lived on a small stipend from their families, but they were a rare exception at that time. Far more common were lifetime friendships formed during the school years, in which neither woman ever lived with her beloved. By the late eighteenth century, with the expansion of boarding schools, increasing numbers of middle- and upper-class girls in England and the United States had opportunities to form close ties with someone of their own sex. Much evidence has been uncovered about friendships of great emotional intensity formed among schoolgirls. Both families and schools encouraged these close bonds. As one nineteenth-century guide explained, "Perhaps not even her acceptance of a lover is a more important era in the life of a young girl than her first serious choice of a friend."[6] Yet these same advisors also repeatedly warned parents about the excessive affections of girls. From the very beginning a tension

5. Faderman, *Surpassing the Love of Men,* pp. 85–102, discusses the various psychological and social reasons why romantic friendships were accepted and flourished during the eighteenth century; she deals only indirectly with economic factors, but see pp. 184–89. See also Carroll Smith-Rosenberg, "The Female World of Love and Ritual: Relations between Women in Nineteenth-Century America," *Signs* 1, no. 1 (Autumn 1975): 19–27; William R. Taylor and Christopher Lasch, "Two 'Kindred Spirits': Sorority and Family in New England, 1839–1846," *New England Quarterly* 36, no. 1 (1963): 23–41.

6. Matilda Pullan, *Maternal Counsels to a Daughter* (London: Darton & Co., 1855), p. 192, quoted in Deborah Gorham, *The Victorian Girl and the Feminine Ideal* (Bloomington: Indiana University Press, 1982), p. 113.

surfaced between the desirability of forming close friendships and fears of their superseding family duties. In the words of Elizabeth Sewell, "When romantic friendship puts itself forward as having a claim above those ties which God has formed by nature, it becomes the source of untold misery to all who are connected with it."[7] Friendships, therefore, frequently became the arena in which a young woman fought for independence from her family.

These early relationships were necessarily conducted under the eye of one's family, although they often originated at boarding school or at a relative's home, or even at a church function. During the second half of the nineteenth century, however, the course of such friendships changed as the experiences of adolescent girls in boarding schools changed. The small, family-style schools where middle-class girls had been sent for a few years to learn social skills and a little French and music gradually gave way to schools of two hundred or more girls, with graded learning, organized sports, regular examinations, and trained teachers.[8] These reforms, begun in the 1850s, accelerated rapidly during the last thirty years of the century, so that by 1900 such schools and colleges became the model for middle- and upper-class girls' education in England and America.

The founding of large girls' boarding schools and colleges that were attuned to the needs of an expanding industrial and imperialist economy created a new set of psychological demands for the adolescent. These new institutions changed an emphasis on private duty and renunciation into a more publicly oriented ethic of service and discipline. Students were trained to enter the public worlds of teaching, medicine, philanthropy, and community service and to relate to others on the basis of shared professional concerns or principles rather than personal feelings. The enclosed, private world of women's domestic space, replicated in the old-fashioned boarding schools, was changed into a more public domain, where greater autonomy and individualism were encouraged. A girl was expected to take responsibility for her actions and to recognize their consequences for others. She was to become an autonomous and controlled being within the larger public world of the school, in preparation for the atomized world of industrial capitalism. At the same time, this new individuality was supposed to find expression through the corporate life

7. Elizabeth M. Sewell, *Principles of Education, Drawn from Nature & Revelation, & Applied to Female Education in the Upper Classes* (New York: Appleton, 1871), p. 335.

8. See my forthcoming book, *Independent Women: Work and Community for Single Women in England, 1850–1920* (Chicago: University of Chicago Press, in press). See also Joyce Senders Pedersen, "Schoolmistresses and Headmistresses: Elites and Education in Nineteenth-Century England," *Journal of British Studies* 15, no. 1 (1975): 135–62, and "The Reform of Women's Secondary and Higher Education: Institutional Changes and Social Values in Mid and Late Victorian England," *History of Education Quarterly* 19, no. 1 (1979): 61–91.

and values of the school. Her self-development was redefined as part of a public ethos instead of being circumscribed by her family.

The effect of this increased emphasis on self-control and public life was twofold. On the one hand, girls had a greater sense of freedom and independence. On the other hand, the desire for closeness, for a special, cherished friend, was enhanced. If one's daily life demanded a public mask, a carefully cultivated sense of duty toward the group, then one found refuge—and an assertion of selfhood—through personal friendships. Under these circumstances friendships between girls and young women of roughly the same age continued to flourish. But the very distance between people and the emphasis on self-control encouraged the intense and erotically charged crush on an older and more experienced student or teacher as a girl's most significant emotional experience. Although similarly strong and complex emotions may have been felt by those involved, both the psychic and public structures of this relationship differed from the well-established model of adolescent friendship between girls of the same age. Questions of public power, authority, and control were central to relationships between women of differing ages, just as they were central to the new schools' ideology.

The adolescent crush was so common in the late nineteenth and early twentieth centuries that it was known by many different slang words besides "crush": "rave," "spoon," "pash" (for passion), "smash," "gonage" (for gone on), or "flame." But the particular form it took and general social attitudes toward it were rooted in a specific historical period and social class. The phenomenon of "smashing" in the new women's colleges of New England was identical in its nature to the English schoolgirls' raves. In both cases middle- and upper-class young women and adolescent girls were placed in single-sex communities with a strong reforming ethos. Women leaders were pioneering new roles for their students and were under great external pressure to demonstrate the viability of their institutions. At the same time, the students were eager to prove themselves worthy of the new institutions. A rave simultaneously satisfied the desire for intimacy and individuality, independence and loyalty.

Greater self-development depended on greater self-control, greater distance from others. Sexual and emotional satisfaction was shifted away from familial models and toward individual discipline. The control of one's personal feelings meant self-respect and power for Victorian women, who had for so long been considered incapable of reason. Bodily self-control became a means of knowing oneself; self-realization subsumed the fulfillment of physical desire. Love itself was not displaced, but focused on a distant object, while nonfulfillment—sacrifice—became the source of personal satisfaction.[9] The emotions were concentrated on a

9. I am indebted to my colleague John Kucich, who shared his own work and discussed the ideas in this paragraph with me.

distant, inaccessible, but admired student or teacher; differences in age and authority encouraged and intensified desire. The loved one became the object of a desire that found its expression through symbolic acts rather than actual physical closeness or even friendship in an ordinary sense of daily contact and conversation. Distance was a means of deepening a pleasure, which was experienced as the more fulfilling because nonsexual. Indeed, genital sexual fulfillment would have meant a failure of self-discipline and, therefore, of self-identity.

Although the ravee might not have been aware of the sexual roots of her passion, the older rave usually recognized some aspects of it; she described love, however, in emotional rather than sexual terms, emphasizing the idealistic feelings it aroused. For her the satisfactions of self-control came from knowing one could channel one's almost overpowering emotions into a higher cause, whether religion, the school, or the general betterment of women. The New Woman disliked uncontrolled emotions as much as did conservative advisers such as Elizabeth Sewell. She consecrated love on the altar of public duty. Soon after she had opened the doors of her new college in 1882, Constance Maynard happily recorded her pleasure at the admiration of an attractive student who intended to become a missionary. She sought to establish the ideal balance of personal love and higher duty with her:

> I told her how the capacity for loving always meant the capacity for suffering, & how I should expect the utmost self-control from her; I should expect it continuously, I said, & never say Thank you, for I belonged to the cause, the object, not to the individual, & all Students must be alike to me. And then, coming closer yet, I told her that self-control was not needed for the sake of appearances only, but for our own two selves, for real love, "the best thing in all the world" could be a terribly weakening power . . . suppose when she was sad or in perplexity she only came to me for help, instead of going *there* beside her little white bed, would that not be a step downward? . . . In spite of the glow that seemed to fill her, she seemed fully to see how the cause must come before the single individual, & we both agreed that a denial such as this enforced upon one part of our nature, was a sort of genuine satisfaction to another part, to the love of order, of justice, of doing something great & public.[10]

Maynard's advice catches exactly the combination of loving through self-discipline, of satisfaction through the suppression of desire, that characterized the late nineteenth- and early twentieth-century rave.

Almost inevitably the adolescent girl was brought into collision with

10. Autobiography of Constance Maynard, Westfield College Archives, London, sec. 44 [1882], pp. 19–20. Maynard copied large sections of her diary directly into her autobiography.

her mother and her family because she found at school a whole new set of older women to admire and love at a time when she was necessarily loosening her ties with her family. The system of fostering friendships between girls of different ages and of encouraging school loyalties led to an increase in family tensions. The more astute headmistresses attempted to link the new values they were encouraging, as well as the new emotions, to family relations. Lucy Soulsby warned her students to "see how natural and loving [your Mother's] jealousy is, and spare it by constant tact— instead of being a martyr, feel that it is *she*, and not *you*, who is ill-used." Desire was to be transformed into "discipline and self-denial, so as to develop all the possibilities of nobleness. . . ." Nonfulfillment was a key to improving one's passionate attachment, for, as Soulsby cautioned, "outside, self-chosen affections burn all the stronger for repression and self-restraint; while home ones burn stronger for each act of attention to them and expression of them."[11] She suggested that love for both family and friend could be strengthened if a girl postponed visiting her friend in order to spend time with her family. Opposites—family duty and personal pleasure—could be brought together through iron discipline, which would yield a double reward. One did not give up love but used it to further self-knowledge and self-control. The proper use of friendship could actually enhance the development of personal autonomy—so important for the New Woman—without loss of family ties.

In boarding school, as opposed to day school, a girl could indulge in her rave unimpeded by her mother's jealousy. The system she found there, indeed, overtly encouraged a kind of surrogate mothering that could often turn into a rave. Although the girls' schools never had the boys' system of fagging (i.e., younger boys acting as servants for older boys), relationships between young women of differing ages were institutionalized through a system of "mothering." An older girl was assigned to "mother" a new girl, to teach her the norms of the school. This relation was designed to foster school as opposed to family loyalty. A woman who attended the Godolphin School in the 1870s remembered, "The older girls had to 'mother' a small one. I think I must have 'mothered' the lot, for my nickname was 'Grannie.' "[12] The new student could worship an all-knowing older girl, who, in turn, received her first taste of power. Inequality of power and of knowledge aided in maintaining the necessary distance; yet, at the same time, it encouraged self-discipline on the part of both girls.

Raves thrived on two apparently contradictory elements—public affirmation and secrecy. Public affirmation came through the continual

11. L. H. M. Soulsby, "Friendship and Love," in *Stray Thoughts for Girls* (London: Longmans, Green, 1910), pp. 172, 176.

12. Alice Pain Barton, quoted in Mary Alice Douglas and C. R. Ash, eds., *The Godolphin School, 1726–1926* (London: Longmans, 1928), p. 31.

discussion in school of favorite students and teachers. But secrecy helped to confirm and heighten private pleasure. Fantasies of service and sacrifice were fostered by the very emotional distance between the lover and the loved one. For most young girls emotions focused on either the head girl or the games captain or a favorite young teacher—all remote, yet familiar and publicly admired figures. These persons could be seen daily, yet rarely in private, and even more rarely in any kind of intimate setting. Such situations encouraged a life lived largely through symbolic acts and symbolic conversations.

The thrills of being "gone on" someone could be discussed endlessly among peers, adding delicious excitement to the routine of the school. Boarding school encouraged a kind of public voyeurism, with admiring girls dissecting the clothes, conversation, and appearance of a favorite. Theodora Benson remembered, "What endless discussions of tactics and strategy we used to hold after supper!" Unaffected herself, she enjoyed passing out advice to her "afflicted friends," even though they rarely took it.[13] Girls made public their most private desires not only because of group encouragement, but also because through talking they could make real impossible fantasies. Moreover, even the most trivial act of homage—helping the loved one put on her coat or cleaning the blackboard—could gain emotional significance through later conversations with other girls. Self-fulfillment came through the endless articulation of each newly aroused feeling, each action, each hope, before an admiring audience.

But secrecy was far more important, for it reinforced self-control. Every girl had her special, secret acts of homage, special ways of betraying her own desires to herself and her rave. Within the limited and confined world of the boarding school, certain acts took on important symbolic significance. The most common form of devotion was to make the beloved's bed or to buy her flowers or candy.[14] Every act became freighted with a sense of self-abnegation. At Cheltenham a ravee indignantly claimed that she could fill her rave's hot-water bottle better than her rival could.[15] These acts of service never involved physical contact but were a means of penetrating the private space of the loved one, of entering her room and secretly making it more attractive. One's presence was then felt by one's absence. Every ravee hoped that her good offices might be noticed, even as she did her work in secret.

An essential pleasure for those who loved a remote figure was the very distance itself, which gave room, paradoxically, for an enriched consciousness of self. Without gratification, countless fantasies could be

13. Theodora Benson, "Hot-Water Bottle Love," in *The Old School*, ed. Graham Greene (London: Jonathan Cape, 1934), p. 40.

14. See Dorothy Eva deZouche, *Roedean School, 1885–1955* (Brighton, 1955), p. 37; Rachel Davis, *Four Miss Pinkertons* (London: Williams & Moorgate, 1936), p. 71.

15. Benson, p. 40.

constructed, a seemingly continuous web of self-examination, self-inspection, self-fulfillment. In the autobiographical tale by Dorothy Strachey Bussy, *Olivia*, the main character felt "a curious repugnance, a terror of getting *too* near" her beloved French teacher at Les Avons, lest mundane facts interrupt the rich emotional life she enjoyed within herself. She especially savored the moment before she entered Mlle. Julie's room: "It seemed an almost superhuman effort to open it. It wasn't exactly fear that stopped me. No, but a kind of religious awe. The next step was too grave, too portentous to be taken without preparation—the step which was to abolish absence. All one's fortitude, all one's powers, must be summoned and concentrated to enable one to endure that overwhelming change. She is behind that door. The door will open and I shall be in her presence."[16] A love such as Olivia's was passionately self-involved, for it opened a wide range of emotions to be experienced in solitude, especially nights when she listened to Mlle. Julie's footsteps in the corridor, hoping she would stop and give her a good-night kiss.

After a ravee had received some sign from her rave that feelings might be reciprocated, moments of greater intimacy were sought, though not necessarily in private, for secrecy could be created in the public domain of the school. The two lovers found means of speaking silently to each other, of sharing words and thoughts that could not be, and would not be, talked about in the general strategy sessions among peers. The secret sharing of a private world in a public place became a major source of pleasure; it affirmed the love, while never removing it from the realm of self-discipline. Indeed, self-control itself was heightened and embraced as a source of pleasure by the very creation of private understandings. Olivia felt certain of Mlle. Julie's love after hearing her read a poem to the class: "It was to me she was reading. I knew it. Yes, I understood, but no one else did. Once more the sense of profound intimacy, that communion beyond the power of words or caresses to bestow, gathered me to her heart. I was with her, beside her, for ever close to her, in that infinitely lovely, infinitely distant star, which shed its mingled rays of sorrow, affection and renouncement on the dark world below."[17] The distance between the lover and the loved one was bridged not through consummation but rather through a unity of sorrow and self-sacrifice.

The rave flourished on a paradox of fulfillment through unrequited love. Had Olivia and Mlle. Julie come too close, they might have found the

---

16. Olivia [Dorothy Strachey Bussy], *Olivia* (London: Hogarth Press, 1949), pp. 59–60. Bussy wrote *Olivia* in 1933 at the age of sixty-four but did not actively seek a publisher until after World War II. The events described occurred in the early 1880s, at "Les Ruches," Marie Souvestre's school outside Paris. See Michael Holroyd, *Lytton Strachey: A Critical Biography* (New York: Holt, Rinehart, & Winston, 1967), 1: 34–41.

17. Olivia, p. 82.

tensions of love unsupportable. So much of the emotional life of a ravee centered on a world of fantasy, out of time and place, on some "infinitely lovely, infinitely distant star." Only there could the love remain safe and unchanged. And yet the very act of falling in love precipitated a crisis of identity in which the ravee moved inexorably toward an increased self-awareness. This new stage, however, involved a kind of reentry into the temporal world, where love had to face the reality of daily life and its buffetings. Later critics have noted the very temporary nature of an adolescent crush and claimed that it was a preamble to heterosexual love, educating a girl emotionally.

It should be seen, rather, as a love based on a temporary condition of isolation, seeming powerlessness, and a willingness to devote oneself entirely to so new and overwhelming an experience. Only rarely did the older woman begin a rave. Even as a ravee felt she might be Echo to her great love, in reality, much of her love was self-created. By her adoration she initiated a response; the distance between herself and her rave then gave her an opportunity, through fantasy, to echo her own love, to examine and reexamine its different facets. Many women, including Bussy (speaking in the voice of Olivia), appear to have found a more complete love as an adolescent than they were ever to find with a man, possibly because they found that the male ego continually demanded that a woman be Echo to its needs and desires, whereas a woman permitted the full range of self-expression, enabling the youthful lover to be both Narcissus and Echo, creator and respondent.

However much a ravee might sustain her love on slight indications of favor and her own imagination, she still hoped that her homage might be repaid by another symbolic act, a vital reward that temporarily bridged the distance between the girl and her beloved. An admired teacher or prefect was ordinarily given social permission to kiss all the younger students. Every night Penelope Lawrence, head of Roedean, kissed each girl in her house good-night; Saturdays she kissed the whole school. She might have used this moment to check each child, but the hurried, physically active, and overfull days of the students hardly suggest such sensitivity on the part of school administrators. More probably she was incorporating an aspect of family life into the residential houses in order to encourage a family atmosphere.[18] Olive Willis, when she started Downe House in the early twentieth century, shed the innumerable regulations she had hated as a student at Roedean, but she kept the symbolic good-night kiss.[19] Such a gesture was so drained of its meaning that it became a means of distancing intimacy, of reminding girls of how far they actually were from home. Yet for the couple involved, on special occasions the kiss

18. Davis, p. 62.
19. Anne Ridler, *Olive Willis and Downe House: An Adventure in Education* (London: John Murray, 1967), p. 32.

was reinvested with meaning, carrying overtones of transitory fulfillment. A virtually meaningless social gesture regained its original meaning and became a private, yet public, expression of love. The mother-daughter moment became a special act of kindness by the loved one, promising untold, unrealizable, future happiness.[20]

Raves existed at boarding schools in a delicate balance between privacy and publicity, self-discipline and uncontrolled feeling, timelessness and the school calendar. Mockery or jealousy could momentarily tip a ravee into the depths of depression and yet also leave her feeling more loyal and trustful of her love. At Roedean during Rachel Davis's time, school raves so dominated that the head, Penelope Lawrence, decided to have the games captain speak before the entire school on the subject. Her short lecture condemning such "sickening *nonsense*" left the students temporarily chastened, but her admirers loved her even more for her courage. Davis shrewdly diagnosed why gonages dominated at Roedean: "It can hardly be called a disease unless it reaches a feverish and inflamed condition. Unfortunately this is nearly always brought about by the clumsy fingers of the unloving, which, in school, as well as outside, must always interfere with what they do not understand. In truth the world has always been afraid of love, and until it can be made to realise that here is the one thing that is right and beautiful in all its shapes, persecution followed by distortion is bound to carry on its work."[21] On the fateful night when the games captain spoke, Davis herself was caught in the "clumsy fingers of the unloving." Those in authority were never alone in their desire to control the uncontrollable. A particularly nasty housemate held up to ridicule Davis's own rave for an older girl. By puncturing the idealism of others she could win attention. Yet the very vulnerability implicit in being gone on someone increased the deliciousness of the feelings. To be mocked for love was another means of self-sacrifice, of demonstrating one's love. To suffer both inwardly and publicly gave both the young girl and her rave greater importance—and fulfillment. And Davis was rewarded on that dreadful night by a special good-night kiss from her beloved prefect.

* * *

Our understanding of raves is incomplete without an examination of the recipients of so much admiration. Since most of the attention not only

20. The most famous example of the importance of the good-night kiss is in the film *Mädchen in Uniform* (1931), where the girls all eagerly wait each night for their favorite teacher, Fräulein von Bernbourg, to come and kiss them good-night. For an analysis of the anti-Nazi lesbianism of the film, see B. Ruby Rich's "*Maedchen in Uniform:* From Repressive Tolerance to Erotic Liberation," *Jump Cut* 24/25 (March 1981): 44–50.

21. Davis, p. 68.

of the sexologists but also of memoirs and autobiographies has focused on the ravee, it is difficult to find the same kind of detailed descriptions about the feelings and responses of the older teacher or student. What evidence we have suggests that they reacted in a variety of ways, sometimes trying to downplay the emotions that they had fanned, sometimes using them to enhance their own self-image publicly and privately, and sometimes channeling them into school loyalty. When the feelings expressed by a younger student or teacher were reciprocated, the rave became an opportunity for mutual spiritual growth under the leadership of the older woman. In the 1870s and 1880s this often meant an evangelical awakening to God's love through a shared earthly love. For a later generation of teachers specific religious commitment had gradually become a generalized sense of duty, public and vaguely Christian. Fulfillment for these older women came through the satisfactions of a spiritual responsibility that matched the idealism of the younger girl.[22]

A rave, however, also offered many concrete advantages, in addition to the more commonly emphasized spiritual benefits. In addition to providing support in a strange environment, an older student frequently tutored her ravee in difficult subjects. Sometimes this could become a mixed benefit, if either let her feelings overcome her ability to concentrate, yet this also deepened the pleasure of the shared time.[23] Teachers were in a position to help with the careers of their protégées. Many older women urged young girls to seize the new opportunities opening up for women and to enter new occupations. M. Carey Thomas's favorite teacher, Miss Slocum, for example, took her aside and told her that she had particular talents as a scholar: "Minnie, I wish I had the chance you girls have—it is too late for me to begin to study now—all I can do is to give you what thoughts I have and help you all I can and then send you out to do what I might have done."[24] Miss Slocum helped Thomas to convince her parents to let her go on to Cornell to study and generally advised her during her early career. This support—a combination of practical information, moral advice, and personal affection—was extremely common. Grace Hadow was given permission to return to school as a pupil-teacher because she so loved her headmistress; with the head's help she went on to university and a distinguished career as an educational

22. A similar pattern of spiritual leadership and homoerotic emotions can be found in accounts of the boys' public schools, although there was also much greater concern about masturbation. See David Newsome, *Godliness and Good Learning: Four Studies on a Victorian Ideal* (London: John Murray, 1961), pp. 79–91; J. R. de S. Honey, *Tom Brown's Universe: The Development of the English Public School in the Nineteenth Century* (New York: Quadrangle, 1977), pp. 167–96; Jonathan Gathorne-Hardy, *The Public School Phenomenon, 597–1977* (London: Hodder & Stoughton, 1977), pp. 156–80.

23. M. Carey Thomas admitted in her journal both at boarding school and at Cornell University that too much of her study time had been taken up thinking about her current "smash" (see Dobkin, ed. [n. 4 above], pp. 90, 117–19).

24. Ibid., p. 92.

reformer.[25] Similar examples are recorded in numerous autobiographies and biographies of famous women.[26]

Many teachers felt an almost awesome sense of responsibility for their protégées, watching over their spiritual well-being with greater care than many mothers. In the late 1870s, for example, Maynard fell in love with a series of admiring students at St. Leonards School. Concerned about balancing the public, academic standards of the new school with her own high sense of Christian mission, she sought a resolution by concentrating on the moral welfare of her favorites. Erotic and maternal love were subsumed under religious duty. Thus, she could write in her diary, "Looking at Katherine, all the mother in me wakes & I think how tender I would be of letting any evil in on a mind such as that, so quick of apprehension yet at present so lovely so sensitive so pure."[27] Maynard's concerns, interestingly, focused on evil thoughts rather than on any possible evil actions or temptations that might assail her favorite. The student was caught in a particular moment of adolescence, in an innocence that by definition must pass, negating Maynard's efforts at protection. The potential for disappointment and failure rested not simply in the possible changes on the part of the student but also in Maynard's own attitude toward her.

Reading aloud, exchanges of letters, and private talks took on the same symbolic importance for the older woman that bed making and flower giving had for the ravees. Some of Mlle. Julie's happiest moments were reading French classics with her favorite students. Private talks, of course, offered intimacy without the loss of distance, for the teacher retained her privileged position of moral instructor. Minor sins, school infractions, and spiritual struggles could be discussed at great length, encouraging a self-examination that became grounds for further intimacies, confessions, and avowals to do better. Maynard, for example, made it a habit to pray with her current favorite as often as possible. Passion was transferred to a spiritual realm, which made it more acceptable, more manageable, and yet also more satisfying.

Letters were an especially important means of communication, as they helped to bridge the distance between the rave and ravee. Shy students who feared to speak directly with someone they loved could pour out their affection in letters. In turn, teachers who were anxious about their public, professional role could break their silence through letters of

25. Helena Deneke, *Grace Hadow* (London: Oxford University Press, 1946), pp. 18–21.

26. See, e.g., Eleanor Roosevelt's grateful appreciation of Mlle. Souvestre, who took her on tour through Europe when she was sixteen (Roosevelt was a student at Allenswood and had classes with both Mlle. Souvestre and Dorothy Strachey [Bussy]); see *The Autobiography of Eleanor Roosevelt* (New York: Harper & Bros., 1958), pp. 29–32.

27. Diary of Constance Maynard, July 14, 1878, Westfield College Archives, London.

advice, consolation, and love. Letter writing, however, also reveals the ways in which school life differed from home life for the ravee. Many girls begged their raves to write to them during the holidays, to give them advice while they were away from school and in the midst of what they saw as "worldly" temptations. School seemed to make possible a loftier ideal of living, which included both love for a teacher and service to a wider community, whereas at home a young girl often felt confined by the husband-hunting social round and the petty duties of stepping and fetching for various members of the family. Constance Maynard became deeply involved in the spiritual life of another student, Mary Tait, after Katherine left St. Leonards. The adolescent Mary found her home life to be "distasteful or a bore" and hated her family obligations. Maynard wrote to her exhorting her to greater self-discipline. The correspondence gave them both a sense of moving out of the mundane and into the rarefied atmosphere of spiritual strivings. Maynard noted in her diary that, just before the end of the Christmas holidays, Mary wrote, "You can't think how delicious it is to know you are pleased. It is awfully severe sometimes to do what is right, but I always think of you & it becomes quite easy to do it."[28] Maynard, in turn, prayed for Mary, carrying her letters with her "as a secret unaccountable source of gladness of heart."[29] The discipline Constance imposed on Mary was one of obedience to her family as well as to her teachers, so that at least temporarily the rave improved her general attitude toward her elders, as all the authorities hoped it would.

But after the holidays Mary began to wilt under the pressures exerted by Constance. When she was reprimanded for a poor effort on her Drawing exam, Mary wrote back, "I was not aware that Drawing was a subject of such extreme importance. . . . I *am* indifferent to everything, except that you should not take everything I do so much to heart." Constance was heartbroken, interpreting her rejection not as stemming from the fickleness of an admittedly spoiled girl but, instead, as involving the loss of a soul. She wrote in her diary, "Oh, Mary, Mary, I loved you, *loved*—do you know what that means? . . . Oh my child my child, are you lost to me indeed? and I was the link through which you were dimly feeling after a higher life—are you lost to that too?"[30] Mary had sought to overturn the discipline of her family life, but she was then unwilling to embrace another new discipline, which Constance's love demanded of her. She escaped into her circle of adolescent friends, leaving Constance as forlorn as any rejected mother—or lover. Idealized self-control and

28. Quoted by Maynard, ibid., February 9, 1879.
29. Ibid., April 12, 1879.
30. Ibid.

spiritual seeking did not satisfy Mary, but Constance based much of her emotional life on this combination.[31]

Maynard's misery and confusion over Mary's rejection raises the issue of the power differential in school friendships and their transitory nature. Maynard, an inexperienced and unhappy teacher, hoped through her love of individual students to overcome her discipline problems and to find emotional fulfillment. But she failed to consider an inevitable teacher-student dilemma: the teacher is static, remaining in one spot, growing older but not altering in her or his role, while the student is in flux, bound to leave at a certain time, and is expected to flower and grow in the larger world. At school Mary Tait was experimenting and testing new emotions, ideas, and needs before she "came out" in society, while Maynard was learning to reconcile herself to a new, possibly permanent occupation and residence. The very temporary nature of her relationship with Mary gave it an urgency, if not desperation, that the girl sensed and rejected.[32]

Although the older woman had the greater power initially over the younger, she also had the most to lose in admitting her love. She gained most by keeping the relationship distant, by fostering self-control within herself and the ravee. When she bridged the inequality between them, she risked not only rejection but also the loss of spiritual leadership. Many teachers, like Maynard, found themselves brought under the sway of a younger student by their love for her.[33] Indeed, the emotional center of the relationship almost inevitably shifted to the ravee as soon as the attraction between the two women had been acknowledged because so much emphasis was placed on her spiritual growth. The older woman was in a position of self-sacrifice, giving moral guidance and personal love. But her sexuality could undermine the authority lent by distance, leading to a closeness that revealed the young girl's power over her. The implications were frightening, for they brought to the surface conflicting needs for power, autonomy, sexual expression, and spirituality. The ravee might prefer to retreat back to her former distance, her untouched fantasies, or she might use the love she had aroused to extend her emotional power and to explore her sexuality. The relationship could then only go forward to further intimacy.

Constance Maynard's friendship with Mary Tait was typical in many ways of those experienced by the new generation of professional single

---

31. See my article, " 'One Life to Stand beside Me': Emotional Conflicts of First-Generation College Women in England," *Feminist Studies* 8, no. 3 (Fall 1982): 602–28.

32. I am indebted to Lawrence Senelick for reminding me of this crucial element in all teacher-student relationships, erotic or otherwise.

33. A similar pattern is described for male homosexual love in a boys' public school by T. C. Worsley in *Flannelled Fool: A Slice of Life in the Thirties* (London: Alan Ross, 1967), pp. 122–24.

women who sought careers in the reformed girls' schools of the last thirty years of the nineteenth century. A devout Evangelical, Constance interpreted earthly love as a sign of God's love—and of a privileged duty. Not only was she involved with a favorite student at St. Leonards, but she was herself in a similar unequal, adoring relationship with her headmistress, Louisa Lumsden. The private and public inequality of power within the school made it easy for Constance to see her relationships in terms of the traditional family. She and Louisa both referred to their life together as a "marriage," in which Constance was expected to play the role of the submissive wife. Louisa was head and "husband" of the school, while Constance "mothered" the students. In this context Mary Tait was their wayward daughter, to be disciplined through love. Louisa had intervened for Constance, forcing Mary Tait to apologize for rudely rebuffing Constance; the incident strengthened her love for her vulnerable "wife." The transference of sexual tensions into the language of the family (and sexual love into the language of religion) left Constance, and many like her, without an appropriate vocabulary to describe and analyze their emotions. Indeed, these metaphors helped to conceal the physical basis of so much of their love. Although Constance could admit her loves to herself, she always saw them in emotional rather than physical terms.[34]

Passion such as Constance felt for so many of her students could not always be kept on the spiritual level; its very expression was rooted in earthly acts of love, however mediated by a spiritual vocabulary. Some students, indeed, could not contain themselves. In 1883, when Maynard was in charge of her own college, she was confronted by a hysterical student who could no longer hold back "the hopeless, perfectly self-controlled love which had evidently brought her into this state." On the doctor's advice, Maynard coaxed the deranged student into her room and away from the other students. She then had to lie down with her on her bed, which gave the girl the opportunity to grasp her tightly and to declare that they were now married. In "solemn tones" she insisted, "We are two no longer. I am part of you & you are part of me. I know all your thoughts by instinct. We can never be separated. Two souls for one forever."[35] The next day the girl was quickly taken away and returned to her family for care, and Maynard lost sight of her. Suddenly freed from parental restraints, the girl appears to have become unbalanced, although

---

34. In her autobiography (n. 10 above) Maynard, at seventy-seven, evaluated her life's work for women's education and commented, "The whole was spoiled & devastated by love, by what psycho-analysts call by highly disagreeable names, such as 'the thwarted sex instinct,' " and later, "It is all very well to call [my] loneliness 'sex feeling,' but I can honestly say my thoughts never strayed to a man" (sec. 44 [1882], p. 3; sec. 50 [1887], p. 172). Maynard appears never to have linked her passionate love of women with sex, which she defined narrowly as heterosexuality.

35. Ibid., sec. 44 [1883], pp. 23–24.

her expressions of passionate love never went beyond a parody of love making. However much a rave depended on the imagination of the ravee, virtually every girl wished for some sign that she had been singled out for special attention. As Maynard's preference for another student became obvious, the girl may have lost hope. Hysteria became a way of breaking through to her beloved teacher; when mad she could relinquish self-control and permit herself to act out the full expression of her love. Maynard, however, never felt that her declarations of love were anything more than the product of insanity, bearing no relation to the "sweet converse" she enjoyed with her favorite.

To judge from one fictionalized account, students were not always alone in their inability or unwillingness to place limits on their homoerotic love. In *Olivia* Mlle. Julie's "marriage" to Mlle. Cara could not tolerate the strains of adolescent adoration, and so the school was broken up. In the midst of this messy "divorce," Mlle. Cara died by what appeared to be suicide. Olivia's deeply idealistic love for Mlle. Julie provided meager comfort in the days that followed. Mlle. Julie's farewell to her beloved Olivia, just before going into exile, warned against and praised lesbian love:

> "It has been a struggle all my life—but I have always been victorious—I was proud of my victory." And then her voice changed, broke, deepened, softened, became a murmur: "I wonder now whether defeat wouldn't have been better for us all—as well as sweeter." Another long pause. She turned now and looked at me, and smiled. "You, Olivia, will never be victorious, but if you are defeated—" how she looked at me! "when you are defeated—" she looked at me in a way that made my heart stand still and the blood rush to my face, to my forehead, till I seemed wrapped in flame.[36]

Mlle. Julie, Olivia, and the others involved in the tragedy of Les Avons school recognized and gloried in the sexual roots of their spiritual love, even though they also insisted on containing it through self-control.

But *Olivia* is a fictionalized autobiography. Writing fifty years after the events, in the mid-1930s, Bussy portrayed her love for Mlle. Souvestre as wholly spiritual, even though she admitted its sexual undercurrent, and assumed her teacher's greater self-awareness. What Bussy remembered and what she knew or felt at the time must remain two different things. Moreover, she appears to have added the tragic finale, for no published evidence exists that Marie Souvestre's lover committed suicide; Mlle. Souvestre did not close her school but transferred it to Allenswood, near London, where Bussy was hired to teach Shakespeare. Perhaps Bussy revenged herself on the past by such a reordering of events,

36. Olivia (n. 16 above), p. 102.

although she thereby continued the stereotype of the doomed lesbian relationship established by Radclyffe Hall's *Well of Loneliness* (1928). Bussy never thought of her love as deviant, but she interpreted victory as suppression, not expression. Yet her book—dedicated to the memory of Virginia Woolf—is a poignant tribute to an enduring love that was never replicated with the same strength, beauty, or power.

*   *   *

Olivia's year of love was a time when she found that "I first became conscious of myself, of love and pleasure, of death and pain, and when every reaction to them was as unexpected, as amazing, as *involuntary* as the experience itself."[37] Ravee, rave—and headmistress—all agreed that raves were in part involuntary and therefore especially difficult to banish. Those in authority, like previous generations, focused efforts on channeling them into areas they could more easily control. Sara Burstall, an early head of the Manchester High School for Girls, explained in a textbook on English girls' schools that romantic friendship "should be recognised, allowed for, regulated, controlled, and made a help and not a hindrance to moral development. . . . A woman's life is, moreover, largely concerned with emotion; to suppress this will be injurious, to allow it to develop slowly and harmlessly, in respect or even reverence for someone who is older and presumably wiser than the girl herself, is not injurious and may be helpful."[38] Burstall defined homoerotic friendships in terms of woman's traditional sphere, as the familiar preamble to marriage. Lilian Faithfull, a second-generation headmistress, emphasized subordinating raves to the needs of the school. During the early years of the twentieth century, she advised her students to cure their raves by sharing their friend with everyone they knew. Girls were advised that, if their emotional attachment did not improve their work, play, and "general power of helping others," it should be "root[ed] out with unhesitating courage and unwavering will."[39] She even admitted to having cured herself in this manner. Ironically, her actions may have encouraged raves since they flourished on public discussion. More effective, possibly, was public ridicule. Olive Willis, headmistress of Downe House, had a teacher write a satirical play about raves when she found them too popular for her taste. Her comic rendition of the love-sick admirer shamed her students into recognizing what she saw as their immaturity.[40]

37. Ibid., p. 9.
38. Sara Burstall, *English High Schools for Girls* (London: Longmans, 1907), pp. 160–61.
39. Lilian Faithfull, *You and I: Saturday Talks at Cheltenham* (London: Chatto & Windus, 1928), p. 121.
40. Ridler (n. 19 above), pp. 97–98.

In all these cases the headmistress did not simplistically label their students' behavior as deviant. Rather, they saw raves as a phase many adolescent girls underwent, which was unfortunately contagious in the confined world of a school and which could be contained, if not driven away, by hearty exposure to adult discipline. In effect, the rave was simply part of the growing-up process with which a teacher or headmistress had to deal. Well into the twentieth century educational texts and etiquette books focus on how best to control the girls' emotions so as to make their raves part of their moral development. Belief in the asexuality of girls persisted in schools, along with many other notions about women's innate nature; common sense and clearly articulated values, it was assumed, would cure virtually every problem. But this attitude left the authorities with little understanding of the profoundly disruptive nature of raves. For the ravee, love was a means of self-assertion that could become as destructive as Olivia's love for Mlle. Julie. By the middle of the nineteenth century male educators appear to have become fixated by fears of masturbation among their boys, minimizing the strong spiritual element in male raves.[41] Women, however, did the opposite, exaggerating the spiritual characteristics and neglecting the sexual. This failure to deal adequately with the sexual and emotional underpinnings of the rave left women teachers especially vulnerable to alternative analyses of what they interpreted as a controllable phase.

Women educators, etiquette-book writers, and other advice givers for over a century spoke the same language when discussing romantic friendships. Whether they focused on same-age friendships or on raves, they all agreed that time spent in such relationships could be important spiritually and emotionally for those involved but that participants should guard against extremes. This single discourse held as long as appropriate female roles were clearly defined both within the world of women and in the larger middle- and upper-class society.[42] But one of the natural results of the new educators' emphasis on careers for women, public responsibilities, and professional behavior was a blurring of the clear distinctions between the domestic, female world and the male, public world. As women gained a voice in the public sphere, their single-sex institutions came under attack. Their schools, settlement houses, and political orga-

41. See Gathorne-Hardy (n. 22 above), pp. 79–93, 144–56.
42. I am obviously ignoring here an important but entirely separate discourse, that of the so-called sexual underworld, which would include women who cross-dressed as well as the libertine and the prostitute. This world is just now beginning to be investigated through police records and scandal sheets; the problems of interpretation and identification are obvious. For an initial exploration of cross-dressing among women, see the San Francisco Lesbian and Gay History Project, *"She Even Chewed Tobacco": Passing Women in Nineteenth-Century America* (1983), slide-tape distributed by Iris Films, Box 5353, Berkeley, California 94705; Jonathan Katz, *Gay American History: Lesbians and Gay Men in the U.S.A.* (New York: Thomas Y. Crowell, 1976), pp. 209–79.

nizations were often the home bases of reforming women and so were obvious targets for those who feared change. Friendships between teachers were stigmatized as abnormal, and raves were attacked as permanently distorting. At the height of the militant suffrage campaign a conservative journalist, Ethel Colquhoun, "regretted that the influence of mothers has been so largely superseded nowadays by the female celibate pedagogue."[43]

The attack by journalists in the popular media appears to have remained intermittent and closely linked to the public visibility of women. But a second alternative discourse began as early as the mid-1880s, when pioneering sexologists began to publish their elaborate taxonomies of sexual behavior in medical journals and other publications with a very limited distribution.[44] Rather than the emotional love that concerned women educators, this medical discourse described seemingly involuntary (and uncontrollable) sexual behavior that conflicted with approved social roles. Early definitions of lesbians all included descriptions of women engaged in so-called male behavior. When women appeared to be stepping outside their preconceived social role, they were pigeonholed as sexually variant, a label that was easy for journalists to use during periods of feminist militancy. But the sexologists were also concerned about the psychological roots of sexual behavior and were convinced that the powerful emotions felt by Olivia could be defined as either congenital, temporary (due to her youth), or acquired (by living in a single-sex institution). Thus, Havelock Ellis could explain,

> While there is an unquestionable sexual element in the "flame" relationship, this cannot be regarded as an absolute expression of real congenital perversion of the sex-instinct. The frequency of the phenomena, as well as the fact that, on leaving college to enter social life, the girl usually ceases to feel these emotions, are sufficient to show the absence of congenital abnormality. . . . We find here, in solution together, the physiological element of incipient sexuality, the psychical element of the tenderness natural to this age and sex, the element of occasion offered by the environment, and the social element with its nascent altruism.[45]

43. Ethel Colquhoun, "Modern Feminism and Sex-Antagonism," *Quarterly Review* 219 (1913): 155.

44. Havelock Ellis's first edition of *Sexual Inversion* (London: Wilson & McMillan, 1897), e.g., was impounded by the English police as pornography after the sale of the third copy; they were particularly anxious to bring his bookseller to trial because of his anarchist connections. Distribution of the book was extremely limited in Great Britain; his multivolume *Studies in the Psychology of Sex* (New York: F. A. Davis Co., 1901) has never been published there to this day. See Phyllis Grosskurth, *Havelock Ellis: A Biography* (New York: Alfred A. Knopf, Inc., 1980), pp. 180–204.

45. Havelock Ellis, "Appendix B: The School-Friendships of Girls," in *Studies in the Psychology of Sex* (New York: Random House, 1936), 1:375.

Ellis described in "scientific" language exactly the same elements that educators had found in the raves they attempted to control. But unlike them, he did not issue calls to personal duty, nor did he worry about the future moral development of girls. The medical men saw themselves as neutral, scientific recorders of existing and past sexual behavior. Ellis, in particular, prided himself on his efforts to remove sexuality from the realm of moral and social judgments. The route between Ellis, at least, and the labeling of schoolgirl friendships as deviant was extremely circuitous.

Raves, not surprisingly, did not significantly change after they had been labeled by the sexologists. Since more and more girls were going to secondary schools and joining such organizations as the Girl Guides, opportunities to know and love older women actually increased during the first thirty years of the twentieth century. These years were the heyday of the schoolgirl story, when millions of copies of Angela Brazil's novels were sold, not to mention those of her countless imitators. In many of her stories same-age girls become fast friends, share secrets and sweets, and love an admired older student or teacher. Inspired by loyalty to her and to their school, they learn to discipline their natural high spirits and are able to serve their school in an unexpected emergency.[46] Raves were a familiar part of the schoolgirl story. Adult fiction set in a school or college also frequently included a rave as an accepted, but minor, episode.[47] Although writers such as D. H. Lawrence and Clemence Dane portrayed raves negatively as early as World War I, they were by no means the majority among writers. Meanwhile, passionately admiring friendships appear to have continued through the 1940s and 1950s, essentially unchanged in character, in single-sex institutions and organizations.[48]

For many years at least two separate discourses continued side by side, touching only occasionally through, for example, the private correspondence of the Bloomsbury intelligentsia, or novels such as Dane's *Regiment of Women* (1917), or in response to a specific scandal or feminist (unfeminine) public behavior.[49] The years leading up to and following

46. Gillian Freeman, *The Schoolgirl Ethic: The Life and Work of Angela Brazil* (London: Allen Lane, 1976); Mary Cadogan and Patricia Craig, *You're a Brick, Angela! A New Look at Girls' Fiction from 1839 to 1975* (London: Victor Gollancz, 1976).

47. See, e.g., Colette's *Claudine* series, Rosamond Lehman's *Dusty Answer*, Josephine Tey's *Miss Pym Disposes*, Antonia White's *Frost in May*, not to mention numerous novels without settings in schools or colleges, such as Virginia Woolf's *Orlando*.

48. On American women's organizations, see Leila J. Rupp, " 'Imagine My Surprise': Women's Relationships in Historical Perspective," *Frontiers* 5, no. 3 (Fall 1980): 61–70.

49. See Holroyd (n. 16 above); Quentin Bell, *Virginia Woolf: A Biography*, 2 vols. (London: Hogarth Press, 1972); Robert Skidelsky, *John Maynard Keynes: Hopes Betrayed, 1883–1920* (London: Macmillan Co., 1983). See also Winifred Ashton [Clemence Dane], *Regiment of Women* (London: William Heinemann, 1917). For attacks on the militant suffrage movement, see Sir Almroth Wright, *The Unexpurgated Case against Women's Suffrage* (Lon-

World War I need to be studied in far greater depth if we are to understand the process whereby women's friendships, and specifically adolescent crushes, came to be seen as dangerous. Certainly by the time Radclyffe Hall published *Well of Loneliness* in 1928, many educators, journalists, politicians, and writers were actively discussing and reinterpreting women's sexuality, including their homosexuality. In 1921, for example, an attempt to amend the Criminal Law Amendment Act to make lesbianism (like male homosexuality) illegal was defeated on the grounds that women might learn something they knew nothing about.[50] The public discourse on sexuality had clearly altered by the 1920s, but we have yet to unravel the complex historical elements that brought about these changes.

The question is not whether the sexologists were pernicious or beneficial to women's romantic friendships and raves but, rather, when and why these two discourses came first to impinge on each other and then one discourse to replace the other.[51] The answers to these questions must remain tentative at this stage, especially given our limited sources and knowledge. A major contribution of the sexologists, and perhaps one reason why they came to be accepted, was their vocabulary, which made it possible to describe the complex connections among spirituality, sexuality, and personal emotions. Those who, like M. Carey Thomas and Constance Maynard (both of whom lived into the 1930s), were without a language of sexuality remained insulated from the medical discourse. But the lack of an appropriate language, or even an inappropriate one, could be as debilitating, as silencing, as any external labeling. Dorothy Strachey Bussy, looking back over fifty years, could see clearly the sexual nature of her love for Mlle. Souvestre, but at the time she may have had no means of understanding her passion. Only in the 1930s did she have the language to describe the emotions that had whirled through her during that fateful year. She could then crystallize the delicate balance of distance and desire, sacrifice and fulfillment, that made a rave so intoxicating: "Love has always been the chief business of my life . . . But at that time I was innocent, with the innocence of ignorance. I didn't know what was hap-

don: Constable, 1913); Walter Heape, *Sex Antagonism* (London: Constable, 1913); Herbert J. Claiborne, "Hypertrichosis [excessive hair growth] in Women: Its Relation to Bisexuality (Hermaphroditism): With Remarks on Bisexuality in Animals, Especially Man," *New York Medical Journal* 99 (1914): 1178–84 (I am indebted to George Chauncey, Jr., for this citation).

50. Jeffrey Weeks, *Sex, Politics and Society: The Regulation of Sexuality since 1800* (London: Longman, 1981), p. 105. See also pp. 114–17 and 164–67, and Weeks, *Coming Out* (n. 3 above), pp. 87–111, for an outline of the changes in attitudes toward sexuality during these crucial years.

51. George Chauncey, Jr. (n. 2 above), warns against attributing "inordinate power to [medical] ideology as an autonomous social force" (p. 115).

pening to me. I didn't know what had happened to anybody. I was without consciousness, that is to say, more utterly absorbed than was ever possible again. For after that first time there was always part of me standing aside, comparing, analyzing, objecting: 'Is this real? Is this sincere?' "[52]

Department of English
University of Michigan, Ann Arbor

52. Olivia (n. 16 above), p. 31.

"The Thing Not Named":
Willa Cather as a Lesbian Writer

Sharon O'Brien

> Whatever is felt upon the page without being specifically
> named there—that, one might say, is created. It is the
> inexplicable presence of the thing not named, of the
> overtone divined by the ear but not heard by it, the verbal
> mood, the emotional aura of the fact or the thing or the
> deed, that gives high quality to the novel or the drama, as
> well as to poetry itself. [WILLA CATHER]

In her often-quoted essay on the craft of fiction, "The Novel Démeublé,"[1]
Willa Cather asks her readers to consider the importance of an unnamed,
absent presence in the literary text. Whereas phrases like "overtone,"
"verbal mood," and "emotional aura" suggest ineffable realms of experience and feeling—complex or barely sensed signifieds for which there
exists no precise verbal signifier—Cather's startling phrase "the thing not
named" has another connotation: an aspect of experience possessing a
name that the writer does not, or cannot, employ. A sophisticated novelist
well read in fin de siècle literature, Cather must have been aware of the

I have been working on Willa Cather for some years now but could not have written
this article without the insights I have gained from the feminist scholarship that informs my
interpretation of Cather's letters to Louise Pound. I am grateful also to friends and col-
leagues who have nurtured or influenced my work on Cather: William Curtin, Janice
Radway, Annette Niemtzow, John Sears, Mary Kelley, Miles Orvell, Lonna Malmsheimer,
Ellen Rosenman, Glenda Hobbs, and Margaret Garrett. I thank the National Endowment
for the Humanities for funding a year to work on the book of which this article is a part: *Willa
Sibert Cather: A Literary Biography* (in manuscript).
    1. Willa Cather, "The Novel Démeublé," in *Not under Forty* (New York: Alfred A.
Knopf, Inc., 1922), pp. 43–51.

Reprinted from *Signs: Journal of Women in Culture and Society* 9, no. 4 (Summer 1984):
576–599.

similarity between the phrase she made central to her literary aesthetic and the phrase used as evidence in Oscar Wilde's trial: "the Love that dared not speak its name."[2] Certainly the most prominent absence and the most unspoken love in her work are the emotional bonds between women that were central to her life. From one perspective, Cather in "The Novel Démeublé" is the modernist writer endorsing allusive, suggestive art and inviting the reader's participation in the creation of literary meaning. But from another, she is the lesbian writer forced to disguise or to conceal the emotional source of her fiction, reassuring herself that the reader fills the absence in the text by intuiting the subterranean, unwritten subtext.

That Willa Cather was a lesbian writer should not be an unexamined assumption, however, but a conclusion reached after considering questions of definition, evidence, and interpretation.[3] To be addressed first is a controversial question in lesbian and feminist criticism, What is a lesbian writer? The two major sections of the essay follow: an assessment of the historical and biographical evidence for Cather's lesbianism and an exploration of how her need to camouflage and conceal her sexual identity as the "thing not named" affected her fiction.

Defining "Lesbian Writer"

In the last few years the importance to feminist criticism of defining both "lesbian" and "lesbian writer" has been addressed, although no conclusions have been reached. For good reason, genital sexual experience with women has been the least-used criterion. As several critics have observed, to adopt such a definition requires the unearthing of "proof" we do not think necessary in defining writers as heterosexual—proof, moreover, that is usually unavailable. And even if it were, to define

2. In a comment on Wilde's trial written in 1895, Cather described his "sins of the body" as "small" in comparison with his sin against art but nevertheless judged him "deservedly" imprisoned. While her opinion may show the influence of her Nebraska readership, Cather expresses the same difficulty with naming that she later described in "The Novel Démeublé": "I did not know whether to give the name of the author of [Wilde's "Helas"] or not, for he has made even his name impossible" (Bernice Slote, ed., *The Kingdom of Art: Willa Cather's First Principles and Critical Statements, 1893–96* [Lincoln: University of Nebraska Press, 1966], pp. 391–92; hereafter cited in parentheses in the text as *KA*).

3. Jane Rule included a chapter on Cather in *Lesbian Images* (New York: Doubleday & Co., 1975), pp. 74–87. More recently Deborah Lambert described Cather as a "lesbian who could not, or did not, acknowledge her homosexuality," in "The Defeat of a Hero: Autonomy and Sexuality in *My Ántonia*," *American Literature* 53, no. 4 (January 1982): 676–90, esp. 676. Phyllis Robinson is less forthright—in part continuing the genteel tradition of Cather's previous biographers by never applying the word "lesbian" directly to Cather—although she does discuss Cather's romantic attachments (*Willa: The Life of Willa Cather* [New York: Doubleday & Co., 1983], esp. pp. 57–62).

lesbianism in narrowly sexual terms ignores the possibility that a woman who never consciously experienced or acted on sexual desire for another woman might possess a lesbian identity more broadly construed (for example, defined to include primary emotional bonding with women) and assumes a rigid separation between the sexual and the nonsexual, certainly an inadequate view of human experience.[4]

Two major approaches to definition extend the meaning of lesbianism beyond the sexual, narrowly conceived. The formulation of the first that has received the most attention is Adrienne Rich's frequently quoted definition of the "lesbian continuum." Rich intends the term "to include a range—through each woman's life and throughout history—of woman-identified experience; not simply the fact that a woman has had or consciously desired genital experience with another woman." Blanche Cook also makes genital sexuality secondary by defining lesbians as "women who love women, who choose women to nurture and support and to create a living environment in which to work creatively and independently."[5]

For critics who need precise methodological tools, the problem with Rich's and Cook's definitions is their over-inclusiveness. We might want to distinguish, for example, between women who defined themselves as lesbian and women who did not.[6] Such definitions also blur important distinctions among women's experiences in varying cultures or historical periods, such as the eighteenth and nineteenth centuries when romantic female friendships were normative, the modern period (beginning roughly in the last two decades of the nineteenth century) when lesbianism became a cultural category ideologically linked with deviance, and the period since the women's movement of the late 1960s when lesbian feminists defined their own experience and identity and increasingly found in marginality the source for a radical critique of patriarchal and heterosexual institutions.

In answer to these difficulties, Ann Ferguson offers a historically grounded statement in which self-identification as lesbian is an essential component of personal identity. If "lesbian" is to be a cognitive and

4. Cather's letters to close friends such as Elizabeth Sergeant, Zoë Akins, and Dorothy Canfield, located at the University of Virginia Library, the Huntington Library, and the University of Vermont Library, respectively, do not refer explicitly to erotic or physical attraction; they do, however, reveal the emotional intensity Cather channeled into her relationships with women.

5. Adrienne Rich, "Compulsory Heterosexuality and Lesbian Existence," *Signs: Journal of Women in Culture and Society* 5, no. 4 (Summer 1980): 631–60, esp. 648; Blanche W. Cook, " 'Women Alone Stir My Imagination': Lesbianism and the Cultural Tradition," *Signs* 4, no. 4 (Summer 1979): 718–39, esp. 738.

6. For a fuller discussion of such problems, see Bonnie Zimmerman, "What Has Never Been: An Overview of Lesbian Feminist Literary Criticism," *Feminist Studies* 7, no. 3 (Fall 1981): 451–75, esp. 456.

emotional category for an individual woman—a prerequisite for self-identification—"lesbianism" must be a concept in her social environment: "A person cannot be said to have a sexual identity unless there is in his or her historical period and cultural environment a community of others who think of themselves as having the sexual identity in question." According to Ferguson, then, a lesbian is a "woman who has sexual and erotic-emotional ties primarily with women" or who "sees herself as centrally involved with a community" of such women and who is a "self-identified lesbian." This identity is possible only in the modern period, since, according to Ferguson, "there was no lesbian community in which to ground a sense of self before the twentieth century."[7]

Although I think that Ferguson's dates need to be questioned—as we will see, Willa Cather possessed a lesbian "sense of self" in the late nineteenth century—I find Ferguson's more limited and precise definition useful for understanding the complex relationships among self, culture, and text in the late nineteenth century when "lesbian" was emerging as both a social category and a personal identity. Because the concept "lesbian" existed in the culture when Willa Cather began to write, the creative process meant something different for her than it did for an earlier writer like Sarah Orne Jewett—just as the act of writing for Jane Rule or Rita Mae Brown, who can write directly of lesbian relationships if they wish, is different from what it was for either Cather or Jewett.[8]

In adopting this historically linked definition, we must also address the equation made between lesbianism and the culturally imposed concept of deviance. To do so is neither to perpetuate an oppression we want to reject nor to require an acceptance of deviance as a component of lesbian identity. We need, however, to explore the interplay between the cultural definition of lesbianism and the writer's self-definition, as well as to examine the writer's individual experience and understanding of lesbianism, before we can understand the relationship between sexual identity and creative expression in the modern period. In order to explain, for example, why Gertrude Stein devised a code for expressing lesbian experience, creating different names for emotional and sexual realms that Cather left unnamed, we need to question whether these literary contemporaries experienced lesbian identity differently.[9]

7. Ann Ferguson, "Patriarchy, Sexual Identity, and the Sexual Revolution," Signs 7, no. 1 (Autumn 1981): 159–72, esp. 165.

8. For a different view, see Josephine Donovan's "The Unpublished Love Poems of Sarah Orne Jewett," Frontiers: A Journal of Women Studies 4, no. 3 (1978): 26–31.

9. On Stein's use of coding, see Catharine Stimpson, "The Mind, the Body, and Gertrude Stein," Critical Inquiry 3, no. 3 (Spring 1977): 489–506; Elizabeth Fifer, "Is Flesh Advisable: The Interior Theater of Gertrude Stein," Signs 4, no. 3 (Spring 1979): 472–83; Richard Bridgman, Gertrude Stein in Pieces (New York: Oxford University Press, 1970); Linda Simon, The Biography of Alice B. Toklas (Garden City, N.Y.: Doubleday & Co., 1977).

In deciding whether to define Willa Cather as a lesbian writer and then in determining her individual experience of lesbianism, we cannot use silence—her failure to weave the emotional threads central to her life directly into her fiction—as a clear basis for deduction. Deborah Lambert's point that Cather "could not, or did not, acknowledge her homosexuality" either in the public sphere or in her writing does not mean that Cather did not acknowledge it to herself; moreover, Cather's reticence in itself does not tell us how she experienced lesbian identity.[10] A problem for critics interested in these questions has been the scarcity of biographical data. Cather's destruction of her letters to Isabelle McClung, however suggestive this may be of a romantic attachment, removes the evidence for it. Fortunately, an important collection of letters from Cather to Louise Pound, her fellow student at the University of Nebraska in the 1890s, has recently become available for examination. Filled with unguarded emotional expression and schoolgirl self-dramatization—in sharp contrast to Cather's later reticence—these love letters are central to establishing her sexual identity.

"Unnatural" Friendship

Writing her college friend and fellow novelist Dorothy Canfield in 1921, Cather characterized her undergraduate years as a tempestuous, passionate era when she was continually being overwhelmed by emotional storms.[11] The storm center of the early 1890s was Louise Pound. Three years ahead of Cather at the university, Louise was the fabled "New Woman" of the 1890s, the decade when the college woman, the sportswoman, and the professional woman symbolized female emancipation. A brilliant student, outstanding athlete, and campus leader, Louise earned a master's degree from the University of Nebraska in 1895 and gained her doctorate from the University of Heidelberg, where she passed her exams in two instead of the usual seven semesters. Returning to Lincoln as professor of English, she went on to a distinguished career as philologist and folklorist and eventually conquered another patriarchal academic bastion when she became the first woman president of the Modern Language Association. That triumph was only surpassed when she was the first woman elected to the Nebraska Sports Hall of Fame.[12]

When Willa Cather arrived in Lincoln in 1890 dressed as William Cather, her opposite-sex twin, she was signifying, among other things, her contempt for the masses of ordinary women who devoted themselves

10. Lambert, p. 676.
11. Willa Cather to Dorothy Canfield, April 8, 1921, Dorothy Canfield Papers, University of Vermont Library, Burlington, Vermont.
12. Louise Pound Papers, Nebraska Historical Society, Lincoln, Nebraska.

to respectable domesticity, the world of "babies and salads" she later ridiculed in a satirical short story, "Tommy the Unsentimental" (1896).[13]

While Cather was defining herself against the culturally prescribed feminine identity and role, Louise Pound was encouraging other women to develop skills and interests the cult of domesticity suppressed. She managed the women's basketball team and helped to organize a women's military company, which "drilled with the heavy Springfield rifles of the '80s and made a record at target practice."[14] Louise did not reject the external signs of womanhood as the means of combatting female oppression; while Cather was sporting cropped hair and mannish dress, Louise's college photograph reveals a delicate-featured young woman with long red hair gracefully swept up in a bun, wearing a dress with fashionable leg-of-mutton sleeves and a gold necklace. Drawn together by their shared interest in the arts, the two young women collaborated in the fall of 1891 as associate editors of *The Lasso*, the college literary magazine, and acted together in the drama society. In December 1892 Cather had a prominent role in "A Perjured Padulion," a five-act satire on university life written by Louise.

Despite her loudly proclaimed contempt for the average woman, during her college years Cather was a rapt admirer of female beauty. In a column for the *Lincoln Journal* she lavishly praised the portraits she discovered at a local art exhibit—aesthetic constructions of idealized femininity. "It is a privilege and a blessing to be alone with three such divine femininities for half an hour," she wrote, "for they are made beautiful and are not constantly doing and saying things to spoil it all." One portrait in particular entranced her: "What simplicity and elegance. How the slenderness of the waist, the pose of the head, the carriage, the firmness of the flesh . . . combine to suggest that innate aristocratic refinement which should be the outcome of wealth and culture."[15] This "divine" femininity resembles the women to whom Cather was attracted in life and art: her dress-conscious, handsome Southern mother, the well-born Isabelle McClung, and her fiction's lost ladies—Marian Forrester, Myra Henshawe, Sapphira Colbert. There is also a hint of Louise Pound, the beautiful daughter of a prominent Lincoln family, and Cather may have been drawn to her, as to other women in her life, because she combined Virginia Cather's elegance and refinement with social, cultural, and intellectual sophistication. Whatever the reasons, Willa Cather fell in love with

13. Virginia Faulkner, ed., *Willa Cather's Collected Short Fiction, 1892–1912* (Lincoln: University of Nebraska Press, 1965), pp. 473–82.

14. Roscoe Pound, "My Sister Louise," *Omaha World-Herald Magazine* (July 21, 1957), p. 2.

15. William Curtin, ed., *The World and the Parish: Willa Cather's Articles and Reviews, 1893–1902*, 2 vols. (Lincoln: University of Nebraska Press, 1970), 1:124–25; hereafter cited in parentheses in the text as *WP*.

Louise Pound. Some of Cather's Nebraska classmates recalled her as an assertive, outspoken, rebellious loner who "had no friends and wanted none," but in two intense, self-revealing letters to Louise she abandoned her public pose and revealed a private self (or perhaps a persona dramatized for Louise's benefit): the beseeching lover, infatuated, insecure, and melodramatic.[16]

Writing Louise just before leaving Lincoln for Red Cloud in June, 1892, Cather revealed both her infatuation and her insecurity. She had seen Louise at a party and had neglected to tell her friend how beautiful she looked in her new gown; Cather went on to praise the wearer's beauty, adopting the same stance she assumed in the art gallery as worshiper of female perfection. She had enjoyed making a young man who was also admiring Louise feel envious, and she wrote of the care that she had devoted to choosing her parting gift to Louise: an edition of FitzGerald's *Rubáiyát of Omar Khayyam*. Then Cather confessed the emotional conflicts plaguing her. She described how strange it felt that she would not be seeing Louise for a while and admitted to being jealous of her other friends (presumably women). Cather had not realized her feelings were so strong; it was irrational that she should feel this way, she knew, when three years before she had never seen Louise and three years later . . . —Cather did not finish her sentence, evidently envisioning the diminishment or end of the friendship. It was not right that three years should make any difference, but she knew that they would; she supposed the two of them would laugh at their youthful intensity some day as other women did, but that thought made her feel terrible. It would be better to hate each other than to laugh, she thought. It was so unfair that feminine friendship should be unnatural, but she agreed with Miss De Pue (a classmate) that it was. Cather ended the letter apologizing for her silliness and hoping that Louise would pardon her. She signed it "William."[17]

Over a year later Cather was still totally preoccupied with Louise. She wrote Mariel Gere, a mutual friend and Cather's romantic confidante, a brief, straightforward letter promising to try to speak of Louise no more than once a day if Mariel came down to Red Cloud for a visit. At the same time she wrote a long, histrionic letter to Louise, pleading for proof of

16. Reminiscences of Cather's classmates appear in James Shively, ed., *Writings from Willa Cather's Campus Years* (Lincoln: University of Nebraska Press, 1950), pp. 120–42, esp. p. 135. To examine the Pound letters at Duke University Library, scholars must obtain permission from the library and the university. Because of testamentary restrictions, however, Cather's letters cannot be quoted but must be paraphrased. In a letter thanking me for informing her of the existence of the Pound Collection, Doris Grumbach, now working on a biography of Cather, concurred with my view that these letters are the key documents in establishing Cather's sexual identity (November 22, 1982).

17. Willa Cather to Louise Pound, June 15, 1892, Pound Collection, Duke University Library, Durham, North Carolina.

affection, relief from suicidal despair, and a visit to Red Cloud. In opening she portrayed herself as plunged into depression without knowing
why; the rest of the letter makes it clear that her low spirits were connected with her doubts about Louise's love and commitment. The promise of a visit from Mariel and her two sisters was her only relief from
misery. Evidently trying to spark Louise's jealousy, Cather told her that
she planned to have a wonderful time with the Geres, even though, she
also acknowledged, their visit would be second best. Wasn't there a chance
Louise could come? She might persuade the Geres to wait. She knew that
Louise would either dispel or intensify her terrible sadness, and she
risked rejection because she was so anxious to see her; only Louise could
relieve her sense of worthlessness. Cather then injected a melodramatic
note: if Louise did come to Red Cloud, she might as well bring a pistol and
deliver a miserable soul from its earthly torment.[18] Perhaps Louise's
decision not to visit signified the cooling of her feelings. In any case, this
diminishment and, finally, a break occurred. Despite Cather's bravado,
she was deeply hurt.[19]

How are we to interpret these letters as psychological and biographical documents? Examining only Cather's revelation of feeling, we can
term them love letters. Louise is the all-powerful being who controls
Cather's emotions, making her blissful or miserable as she offers or
withdraws affection. The range of emotion Cather expresses—jealousy,
worshipful admiration, insecurity, self-condemnation, depression—
further reveals a turbulent, passionate attachment. In contrast, the tone
Cather adopts when writing Mariel, while friendly, close, and intimate,
lacks the instability, intensity, and melodrama of the Pound letters.[20]

The question remains whether these love letters reveal a lesbian
attachment. There is no suggestion that Cather and Louise were lovers
physically as well as emotionally, although Cather was enraptured with
her friend's beauty and enjoyed besting male rivals. But a crucial reference signifies that this was a lesbian relationship according to the definition I am using here. When Cather told Louise that, while it was unfair
that feminine friendship should be unnatural, she nonetheless agreed
with Miss De Pue that it was, she betrayed a self-conscious awareness,

18. Willa Cather to Mariel Gere, June 30, 1893, Nebraska Historical Society, Lincoln,
Nebraska; Cather to L. Pound, June 29, 1893.
19. In a letter to Dorothy Canfield, Cather's first biographer E. K. Brown acknowledged that ending the relationship with Louise and the Pound family caused Cather
emotional trauma: "I know a good deal about the quarrel with the Pounds, but so far have
decided against including any mention of it. I have somehow to suggest the emotional
disturbance it caused Miss Cather, which was very intense, as some of the letters show. I think
I can do that without going into the events" (E. K. Brown Papers, Beineke Library, Yale
University, New Haven, Connecticut).
20. Cather to Gere, June 30, 1893.

shared by her community, that women's friendships constituted a special category not sanctioned by the dominant culture. Cather did not use the word "lesbian" to describe her love for Louise; the word was not yet in common usage in the 1890s and we would not expect her to employ such terminology in a love letter in any case.[21] But her interpretation and experience of her love for Louise—and hence her view of herself—was mediated and structured by a cultural category that defined female friendships like theirs as deviant. Cather's response to that definition is complex, however; on the one hand, she challenges the ideological yoking of same-sex friendships with deviance by terming it "unfair," while, on the other, she reveals her acceptance of conventional wisdom by agreeing, however reluctantly, with its accuracy.

Cather's self-conscious awareness that her involvement with Louise placed her in a suspect category of women friends sharply distinguishes her from women who enjoyed romantic same-sex friendships earlier in the century. As Carroll Smith-Rosenberg, Nancy Cott, and Lillian Faderman have shown, close, caring, sensual, and passionate attachments between women were commonplace and accepted in early and mid-nineteenth-century America when women created their own nurturing world of "love and ritual" in a sexually polarized society.[22] Their society encouraged the development of these bonds without specifically naming them; thus a woman who loved other women did not have to make her attraction to such intimacies central to her self-definition. Since the ideology of passionlessness, to use Nancy Cott's term, constructed women as nonsexual beings, they could participate in tender, even sensual bonds without viewing their love as sexual.[23] Lesbianism was not a category for organizing and defining women's emotional and sexual experience in their world; hence, women of this historical period did not possess lesbian identities according to the definition used here.

A member of this earlier generation, Sarah Orne Jewett—Cather's friend and literary mentor in the early 1900s—experienced her love for women in a social/historical context different from that of her younger

21. As Catharine Stimpson observes, the "first citation for lesbianism as a female passion in *The Shorter Oxford English Dictionary* is 1908, for 'sapphism' 1890" ("Zero Degree Deviancy: The Lesbian Novel in English," *Critical Inquiry* 8, no. 2 [Winter 1981]: 363–79, esp. 365).

22. The phrase is from Carroll Smith-Rosenberg's now classic article "The Female World of Love and Ritual: Relations between Women in Nineteenth-Century America," *Signs* 1, no. 1 (Autumn 1975): 1–29. See also Nancy Cott, *The Bonds of Womanhood: "Woman's Sphere" in New England, 1780–1835* (New Haven, Conn.: Yale University Press, 1977), pp. 160–96; Lillian Faderman, *Surpassing the Love of Men: Romantic Friendships between Women from the Renaissance to the Present* (New York: William A. Morrow & Co., 1981), pp. 157–77.

23. See Nancy Cott, "Passionlessness: An Interpretation of Victorian Sexual Ideology, 1790–1850," *Signs* 4, no. 2 (Winter 1978): 219–36, esp. 233.

colleague. Women were also the center of Jewett's emotional world.[24] Her "Boston marriage" with Annie Fields, whose Charles Street home she shared for part of each year, was her most important bond. The two women nurtured each other emotionally and professionally, and when Jewett returned to her South Berwick home for her yearly visit, she wrote to Annie almost daily. "Here I am at the desk again," Jewett begins a typical letter, "all as natural as can be and writing . . . to you with so much love."[25] Jewett is assured of a mutual, enduring affection, and unlike Cather, she views this attachment, like her return to Maine, as "all as natural as can be." Jewett's other friendships, which ranged from the adolescent girl's romantic infatuations to the mature writer's treasured companionships with other New England literary women, were similarly regarded as natural by Jewett's social community and hence by herself.

Because public definitions of a form of intimacy had begun to change in the twenty-five years separating Cather's young womanhood from Jewett's, the younger woman's most private realms of personal experience—love, sexuality, identity, self-concept—were altered. Cather's view of her college attachment to Louise as unnatural correlates with the recent work of Nancy Sahli and Lillian Faderman, who chart an important and gradual shift in the social definition of female intimacies during the last decades of the century, as the concept of lesbianism, linked with perversion and deviance, emerged in the medical literature and to some extent in individual consciousness. The innocent female world of loving friendship in which Jewett and Fields established their Boston marriage was crumbling by the 1890s, now viewed by historians as "a crucial transitional period in the conceptualization and social experience of homosexual relations" in both America and Great Britain.[26] Whereas earlier in the century women's friendships were consistent with their dependent status, the affection between women who were in a number of different ways declaring their equality—or, even more unsettling, their similarity—to men threatened the social, moral, and sexual order. The creation in scientific and medical literature of a category of "deviance" then served as a means of social control as well as of boundary setting.

24. Glenda Hobbs, "Pure and Passionate: Female Friendship in Sarah Orne Jewett's 'Martha's Lady,' " *Studies in Short Fiction* 17, no. 1 (Winter 1980): 21–29.

25. Quoted in Faderman, p. 201. For a fuller discussion of Jewett's views and experience of friendship, see Hobbs; Donovan (n. 8 above).

26. George Chauncey, Jr., "From Sexual Inversion to Homosexuality: Medicine and the Changing Conceptualization of Female Deviance," *Salmagundi*, nos. 58–59 (Fall 1982/Winter 1983), pp. 114–46, esp. p. 114. Nancy Sahli also describes this transition in the conceptualization of female friendships in "Smashing: Women's Relationships before the Fall," *Chrysalis*, no. 8 (1979), pp. 17–27, esp. 25. See also Faderman; and articles in this book: Esther Newton, "The Mythic Mannish Lesbian: Radclyffe Hall and the New Woman," and Martha Vicinus, "Distance and Desire: English Boarding-School Friendships."

Of course the medical literature did not, by itself, create and define homosexual identities that people then "uncritically internalized"; the production of homosexual identities, as George Chauncey points out, is a "complex dialectic between social conditions, ideology, and consciousness."[27] The medical literature itself responded to social changes already under way, and consciousness could be altered without exposure to Krafft-Ebing or Havelock Ellis. In 1895, Ruth Ashmore—a popular writer whose columns in the *Ladies' Home Journal* Willa Cather read—warned female readers against forming exclusive romantic bonds with other young women. "I like a girl to have many girl-friends; I do not like her to have a girl-sweetheart," Ashmore cautioned. Such infatuations were "silly" and short-lived and might have disastrous long-term effects, she cautioned, for a girl who squandered her love on other girls might not have enough left for "Prince Charming when he comes to claim his bride."[28]

Placed in their social and historical context, Willa Cather's letters to Louise Pound reveal the effect that the categorizing of female friendship as lesbian and deviant had on her experience of love for women. Unlike Jewett, she could not write unconflicted, unselfconsciously affectionate or passionate letters to a woman she loved. In a review commenting on Christina Rosetti's "Goblin Market," a poem in which some twentieth-century readers discern a lesbian subtext,[29] Cather referred to the "loathsomeness of our own folly in those we love" as the moral she drew from Rossetti's enigmatic tale of sexual temptation, fall, and redemption (*WP*, 1:42–47). The self-condemnation suggested by "loathsomeness" does not typify Cather's perception of herself and her emotional nature, however; as her letters to Louise reveal, she also objected to the categorization of female friendship as unnatural. In order to understand Cather's individual experience of lesbianism, then, we cannot extrapolate from social ideology to consciousness. What did it mean for her to adopt an "unnatural" identity? To what extent did she internalize, reject, redefine, or enjoy the emerging identification of homosexuality with deviance?

Shaped Imaginings

"The books we read when we were children shaped our lives," wrote Willa Cather, "at least they shaped our imaginings, and it is with our

27. Chauncey, p. 115.
28. Ruth Ashmore, *Side Talks with Girls* (New York, 1895), pp. 122–23. Cather had read Ashmore's advice columns in the *Ladies' Home Journal;* for her critique of the "shining literary light," see *KA* (n. 2 above), pp. 187–89.
29. See Sandra Gilbert and Susan Gubar, *The Madwoman in the Attic: The Woman Writer and the Nineteenth-Century Literary Imagination* (New Haven, Conn.: Yale University Press, 1979), pp. 564–75.

imaginings that we live" (*WP*, 2:852). Cather's childhood imaginings of herself and her future were shaped by her readings in epic, myth, and romantic adventure fiction like *Treasure Island*. Identifying with the male heroes who possessed the autonomy and power she wanted for herself, Cather did not at first grasp what she later termed the "hateful distinction" between boys' and girls' reading: The "fact that I was a girl never damaged my ambitions to be a pope or an emperor" (*WP*, 1:337, 368). But when she reached adolescence, Cather recognized her miscalculation and so decided to become the hero of her own life story by transforming herself into William Cather, Jr. Cather's male impersonation was only the most extreme sign of her adolescent rebellion; she also shocked Red Cloud's bourgeoisie with her interest in vivisection and dissection. The adolescent girl's attraction to a rebellious posture thus anticipates her acceptance of an identity linked with "unnaturalness" a few years later; she was already a self-proclaimed rebel when she met Louise. In addition, since lesbianism was frequently associated, as Chauncey notes, with "inversion," a young woman who had defiantly adopted male dress and name in adolescence might well have been more aware that her attraction to other women was "deviant" than one who was strongly female identified.

During her college years Cather passed through what she later called her "Bohemian" phase, a period of unorthodox behavior she ultimately repudiated when she became less interested in opposing herself to convention. Scornful of piety and prudery—feminine vices in her opinion—when she heard that a friend had sent a copy of Alphonse Daudet's shocking novel *Sapho* to a religiously minded young woman, she told Mariel Gere that this pious maiden would doubtless soon join her in corruption.[30] As drama reviewer for the Lincoln papers Cather frequented the alternative world of the theater; she developed crushes on several actresses whom she treated to champagne and found herself frequently impoverished because she could not refuse their requests for loans. Whether or not her actress friends were self-identified lesbians, they challenged conventional sex roles by choosing a profession Victorians considered of doubtful respectability, and among them Cather could even see women who had theatrical license to flaunt sexual "inversion" and take male parts on the stage just as she was doing in life. And there were other subgroups: the small but select "bevy of admiring students" impressed by her atheism, the young women who also read questionable French fiction.[31] Participation in these alternative social worlds showed Cather's willingness to adopt a role of difference, if not

30. See Cather to Gere, July 11, 1891, Nebraska Historical Society, Lincoln, where Cather ironically refers to her attempt to keep Mariel from reading *Sapho* as her one Christian effort.

31. See Shively, ed. (n. 16 above), p. 133.

"deviance"; and the members of what were—in Victorian America— relatively avant-garde groups would have been among the first to be aware of the conceptualization of homosexuality.

Cather's reading was another, perhaps even more important, means for achieving a consciousness of "unnatural" sexuality. If her imaginings of powerful destinies were shaped by childhood reading in epic and romance, her fantasies in the 1890s of love and sexuality came from non-American literatures that addressed sexual matters far more frankly than was possible in William Dean Howells's America, where fiction was expected to be, as Cather bitingly phrased it, a "young ladies' illusion-preserver" (*KA*, p. 281). In her columns for the Lincoln, and later the Pittsburgh, papers Cather commented, often approvingly, on a wide range of fin de siècle writers, including Swinburne, Rossetti, Wilde, Fitz-Gerald, Baudelaire, and Verlaine, demonstrating her familiarity with the decadence, ennui, and sometimes perverse eroticism characterizing this literature.

Cather's ability to read both Greek and French admitted her to a literary world where homosexual attachments were portrayed with a freedom unknown even in Oscar Wilde's England.[32] In Sappho she found a poet who celebrated the delights and agonies of love between women. Cather read Sappho during her college years and in 1907 wrote "The Star Dial," a poem revealing her identification with this literary and sexual foremother as she assumes Sappho's voice: "All my pillows hot with turning, / All my weary maids asleep; / Every star in heaven was burning / For the tryst you did not keep. / . . . Never fear that I shall chide thee / For the wasted stars of night, / So thine arms will come and hide me / From the dawn's unwelcome light." Evidently Sappho's poetry formed a bond between Cather and Louise, for Cather refers to her verse in one of the letters; understandably the two young women were drawn to this poet of "love and maidens" where they found their own experience of romantic love mirrored.[33] French literature, particularly that of the southern regions of France, was Cather's passion during her college years and throughout her life. For her a warm, sensuous land bathed in light, Provence was linked in her imagination with the southern Mediterranean world—North Africa, Italy, Greece, Turkey, and Persia. French writers like Gautier and Flaubert imbibed the "oriental feeling" of these exotic lands and conveyed it in fiction that "palpitate[d] with heat, like a line of sand hills in the South that dances and vibrates in the yellow glare of noon." A land where the "great passions" were "never wholly conven-

32. Cather began to learn French only in her third year at Lincoln, but some of the literature, particularly the novels, was available to her earlier through translations.

33. "The Star Dial" appeared in *McClure's* 30 (December 1907): 202. Cather prefaced the poem with an epigraph from Sappho (in Greek). The reference to Sappho as the poet of "love and maidens" occurs in *WP* (n. 15 above), 2:584.

tionalized," France to Cather was the symbolic location of the Other, the sign for everything repressed or feared in commercial, puritanical northern climes: it was the decadent, liberated realm of the senses (*KA*, p. 138).

In addition to palpitating sand hills and spice-laden breezes, nineteenth-century French fiction offered Cather a direct portrayal of sexual "inversion" and lesbian desire. As George Stambolian and Elaine Marks have observed, French writers have often exploited the "value of homosexuality as a transgression" in order to question social boundaries and sexual constructions.[34] Some of the French writers Cather read were both attracted and repelled by the figure of the lesbian or the androgynous woman, in part inspired by George Sand, whose portrait Cather eventually enshrined in her New York apartment. Two novels that gripped Cather's imagination in the 1890s featured such heroines: Gautier's *Mademoiselle de Maupin* and Daudet's *Sapho*. In Gautier's novel Cather found a cross-dressing, bisexual heroine who seduces both a male and a female lover, a character who became the "prototype of the lesbian in literature for decades afterward," while in *Sapho*—a cult item among Cather's Lincoln friends and the only novel frequently mentioned in the letters—she encountered the more characteristic association of the lesbian with the evil, perverse temptress.[35] In commenting on the source of *Sapho*'s power, Cather evidently found language an inadequate resource. The novel "involves shades and semitones and complex motives," she wrote, "the struggling birth of things and burnt-out ghosts of things that it baffles psychology to name" (*WP*, 2:688). Her statement interestingly anticipates the language she used in articulating her literary aesthestic in "The Novel Démeublé."

Structuring and mirroring her experience of self and friendship, these literary corollaries to emotions and desires bestowed an ambiguous gift. In Sappho's "broken fragments" Cather found an intense celebration of female sensuality, the power, joy, and despair of romantic love, and a goddess presiding over a female world of love and eroticism (in that "one wonderful hymn to Aphrodite") (*WP*, 1:147). But whereas the sexual love of women was "all as natural" as could be in Sappho's poetry, in French literature Cather encountered the lesbian viewed through male eyes: an enticing but threatening figure associated with artificiality, perversity, and cruelty, she was the femme fatale's deadly sister. Such books presented the male construction of woman as Other, an embodiment of erotic power whose autonomy made her "unnatural" since, paradoxically, she did not conform to the socially constructed feminine identity and role.

34. George Stambolian and Elaine Marks, "Introduction," in *Homosexualities and French Literature*, ed. George Stambolian and Elaine Marks (Ithaca, N.Y.: Cornell University Press, 1979), p. 26.
35. Faderman (n. 22 above), p. 266.

Cather's arrival at a lesbian identity by the 1890s, then, resulted from several psychological and social processes. Her adolescent male impersonation signified her attraction to a rebellious posture and may have predisposed her to respond to the emerging identification between lesbianism and sexual "inversion"; her membership in unconventional Lincoln subgroups gave her social communities that rejected or questioned dominant Victorian values; her reading in fin de siècle, Greek, and French literatures introduced her to the "Oriental" world of hedonism and unconventional passions and gave her differing images of the lesbian. That Cather's construction of a lesbian identity was complex and even contradictory, moreover, is suggested by the letters. Attracted to a "deviant" identity because she delighted in opposing herself to bourgeois, philistine culture, Cather did not fully or uncritically internalize the emotionally crippling definition of lesbianism as "sick" or "perverse" and challenged the social construction of female friendship as unnatural. And yet simultaneously she could not help accepting it. Her ambivalence did not fully dissipate in later years. After the affair with Louise ended she found more stable, nurturing relationships, first with Isabelle McClung and then with Edith Lewis; they offered her, to use Blanche Cook's phrase, a "living environment in which to work creatively and independently." Yet she could never declare her lesbianism publicly. Becoming more conservative and private as her fame increased, Cather shunned overt political activity and refused to align herself with feminism. And in her fiction she never wrote directly of the attachments between women that constituted the emotional center of her life. However "natural" they may finally have seemed to her, Cather knew she could not name them to a twentieth-century audience. By 1911, the year before Cather published her first novel (*Alexander's Bridge*), Annie Fields was being urged by her editor to eliminate the more intimate correspondence from her collection of Jewett's letters; he did not want people reading these passages "wrong."[36]

The Unwritable and the Unnamed

Writing of the differing artistic powers possessed by two actresses, Cather attributed the source of one to "disclosure," the other to "concealment" (*KA*, p. 119). Given her inability to portray women's love for women in her fiction, we might assume that concealment alone characterizes her creative imagination, but "The Novel Démeublé"'s reference to the "inexplicable presence" of the thing she could not name suggests we

36. For a discussion of Mark DeWolfe Howe's editorial suggestions and restrictions, see Donovan (n. 8 above).

might find disclosure in her fiction as well. What impact did Cather's lesbianism have on her fiction?

The contrast between Cather and Jewett is useful in answering this question. Both women found relationships with other women central in their lives, yet only Jewett was free to explore them openly in her work. Many of Jewett's stories focus on heartfelt moments of closeness when her reserved New England countrywomen let down emotional barriers, while her book-length works *Deephaven* and *The Country of the Pointed Firs* have close female friendships at the structural, thematic, and emotional center: the romantic adolescent companionship shared by Kate and Helen in *Deephaven* and the slowly developing, more profound bond between the narrator and Mrs. Todd in *Country*. Moreover, in writing of passionate friendships, as she did in "Martha's Lady," Jewett felt no need to cast one character as male when she presented a friendship marked by sensuality as well as spiritual and emotional intensity. Nor did Jewett view the attachment between Martha and Helena as a stage through which the two women would pass; their love endures through forty years of separation and the story ends with their reunion.[37]

Writing Jewett to praise the aesthetic and emotional power of "Martha's Lady," her friend Sarah Whitman selected for special recognition the phrase "It seemed like yesterday that Helena Vernon had gone away, and it was more than forty years." That wording, Whitman thought, made "that swift appeal to the imagination which only genius can make and to which the whole human heart responds." Jewett's reply remarkably anticipated Cather's statement of her aesthetic theory in "The Novel Démeublé": "You bring something to the reading of a story that the story would go very lame without; it is those unwritable things that the story holds in its heart . . . that make the true soul of it, and these must be understood. . . . In France there is such a code, such recognitions, such richness of allusions."[38]

It might be assumed that Jewett was referring to a "code" writers could use for naming what was culturally unnameable—lesbian relationships—as Gertrude Stein did later. But such an interpretation posits Jewett's self-conscious awareness of lesbian identity and her consequent need to disguise socially unacceptable emotions, a view contradicted both by her unselfconscious love letters to women friends and by the love affair that "Martha's Lady" frankly describes. I agree with Glenda Hobbs, who finds it "more likely" that Jewett was hoping for "an improved reciprocal communication between author and reader, so she could be assured that readers would appreciate the depth of Martha's love."[39] The "unwritable

37. See Hobbs (n. 24 above).

38. Sarah Orne Jewett to Sarah Whitman, n.d., in *Letters of Sarah Orne Jewett*, ed. Annie Fields (Boston: Houghton Mifflin Co., 1911), pp. 112–13.

39. Hobbs, p. 26.

things" to which Jewett refers are then those ineffable, inexpressible psychological and emotional nuances that cannot be expressed in language, or at least in English, a language Jewett considered less attuned to the subtleties of feeling than was French. In order to understand her "unwritable things," Jewett implies as she continues her letter to Whitman, the reader needs not a codebook for deciphering lesbian references but the empathic ability to project herself into Martha and to sense the "unwritable things" hidden "between the lines": "I thought that most of us had begun to grow in just such a way as she [Martha] did, and so could read joyfully between the lines of her plain story, but I wonder if most people will not call her a dull story."

That Jewett's "unwritable things" differ from Cather's "thing not named" is suggested by the continuity only Jewett experienced between emotional life and creative expression. Writing in her diary, a private text where the social pressures to make female intimacies "unwritable"—if they existed—should have been minimal, Jewett also referred to her inability to use language adequately to convey her deep love for a woman friend. "How I wish I could *do* something for you to show that I love you Kate!" she wrote. "When I try to talk about it the only words I can think of, seem such weak silly meaningless ones, just the same ones which people use when they do not mean half that I do!"[40] A member of a linguistic community, Jewett inevitably had to use the same words that other people did; and yet she felt she possessed more emotional intensity than did other speakers. Limited to and by a common language, how could she express herself? This was her dilemma, I think, not the lesbian writer's need to conceal the socially unacceptable. Unlike Cather, Jewett did not have to camouflage her emotional attachments when she moved from private to public genres. Whether the intended audience was herself in her diary, a close friend in a letter, or her reading public in her fiction, she devoted herself to exploring the female world of love and ritual.

That Jewett's experience of female intimacies as "natural" led her to aesthetic choices different from Cather's is demonstrated in an important letter of literacy advice in which she gently chided her younger friend for using a male narrator to express love for a woman in "On the Gull's Road" (1908). Why had Cather adopted a male disguise, Jewett wondered: "The lover is as well done as he could be when a woman writes in the man's character—it must always, I believe, be something of a masquerade. I think it is safer to write about him as you did about the others, and not try to be he! And you could almost have done it as your self—a woman could love her in the same protecting way."[41]

Because Jewett was responding to a problem she thought solely

---

40. Quoted in Donovan, p. 30.
41. Jewett to Cather, November 27, 1908, in Fields, ed. (n. 38 above), pp. 246–47.

literary, her solution was technical: she equated the alternative of changing point of view with changing gender. Cather could either "write about
him as [she] did about the others"—from the outside, that is, by employing third- rather than first-person narration—or she could employ a
female narrator, drawing on her own emotional experience. Jewett was
offering Cather the aesthetic possibilities possessed by a woman writer
whose love for women was normative; evidently she could not see the
social and psychological forces restricting Cather's literary choices in
1908. If we consider "On the Gull's Road" in more detail, however, we can
see why Cather could not "have done it as [her] self" and why she
continued to ignore Jewett's literary advice.

Like *My Ántonia*, "On the Gull's Road" is retrospectively narrated by a
man who recalls a lost lady. During an Atlantic crossing twenty years ago,
he confides, he had fallen in love with a beautiful woman named Alexandra Ebbling. Unsatisfied in a loveless marriage to a brutal, domineering
man, she returns his devotion but leaves him at the voyage's end: she has a
fatal illness and wants to spare him the pain of seeing her die. The dying
woman does leave him something, however—a box of mementos containing a faded magnolia blossom, two sea shells, and a lock of her reddish-
gold hair. The story ends in the present; sitting by the fire, our narrator
savors his memories and keepsakes, including the sensuous lock of hair, a
living symbol of his lost lady. The imagery of the gifts suggests Cather's
intention to imply a sexual attachment, as does her association of Alexandra with the sea, an overwhelming erotic and maternal presence in the
story. A sea goddess, an Aphrodite linked with sea shells, warm Mediterranean waters (Cather's "oriental" setting), and gleaming hair that
"curls and undulates with the tide," Alexandra is a compelling sexual
force, and the sea imagery the narrator uses to describe her influence
becomes one with the inexorable waves of desire.[42]

The literary techniques Cather employs in "On the Gull's Road"
anticipate those she uses to express the "thing not named" in her later
fiction. Sexuality is displaced into the landscape (here the sea, though the
land in most of her writing) and into feminine images like the box, the
hair, and the sea shells; mythic allusions provide a lesbian subtext (Alexandra is associated with Aphrodite, whom Cather further associated with
Sappho and her "wonderful hymn" to the goddess); and the male mask
allows Cather to explore a woman's passion for another woman. Jewett
was on to something in criticizing the narrator: although cast as male, his
gender is left so indeterminate that it seems quite possible a woman could
have loved her just as well, as Jewett thought, because a woman was loving

42. Faulkner, ed. (n. 13 above), pp. 79–94. Cather wrote the story shortly after
crossing the Atlantic with Isabelle McClung and meeting Sarah Orne Jewett, so these two
women may have in part contributed to the portrait of Alexandra Ebbling.

her. The story's framing device in which a bachelor sits by the fire in his study and reflects on a lost love recalls another storyteller whose name revealed that he had something to hide: Miles Coverdale, the untrustworthy narrator of *The Blithedale Romance*. That Cather's Coverdale has something to hide is signified by the absence rather than the presence of a name, however; despite their intimacy, Alexandra never mentions his name in conversation, and the one time we would expect her to use it—in her farewell letter—she addresses him as "My Friend." His namelessness both reinforces his indeterminate gender and suggests Cather's inability to name the love inspiring the story, the emotional "aura" unnamed on the page.

The Inexplicable Presence

Never following Jewett's literary advice, Cather continued her masquerade: her lovers remained heterosexual, her narrators—enraptured by sensual and maternal women—male. Such disguise and displacement raises several interpretive problems. Lambert introduces one when she associates Cather's lesbianism with male identification; like many of Cather's readers, she finds her guilty of "denying her womanhood" and celebrating "male activity and institutions" in novels like *My Ántonia* and *Death Comes for the Archbishop*.[43] But these male narrators and centers of consciousness were literary strategies, and her need to conceal lesbianism should not automatically be equated with a desire to deny womanhood. Nor should we conflate Cather's adolescent male impersonation with the writer's fondness for male narrators, an association that has led some critics to assume that Cather's male identification persisted in adult life. By the time she devoted herself fully to the writing of fiction, a commitment she made with *O Pioneers!* (1913), Cather had confronted and transcended the social forces contributing to her William Cather masquerade, having untangled "male" and "female" from their social definitions and reconciled womanhood with literary vocation.[44]

Some continuity does exist, however, between the psychological forces that prompted Cather to become William in adolescence and Jim

43. Lambert (n. 3 above), pp. 677, 680. See also Carolyn G. Heilbrun, *Reinventing Womanhood* (New York: W. W. Norton & Co., 1979), pp. 79–81; Phyllis Rose, "The Point of View Was Masculine," *New York Times Book Review* (September 11, 1983), p. 15.

44. See my article, "Mothers, Daughters, and the 'Art Necessity': Willa Cather and the Creative Process," in *American Novelists Revisited: Essays in Feminist Criticism*, ed. Fritz Fleishmann (Boston: G. K. Hall & Co., 1982), pp. 269–98. I have also discussed Willa Cather's adolescent male impersonation in "Tomboyism and Adolescent Conflict: Three Nineteenth-Century Case Studies," in *Woman's Being, Woman's Place: Female Identity and Vocation in American History*, ed. Mary Kelley (Boston: G. K. Hall & Co., 1979), pp. 351–72.

Burden in adulthood. Feminist psychoanalytic theory as developed by Nancy Chodorow can help us to discern the unconscious processes at work in both her adolescent and her literary masquerade. As Chodorow points out, in adolescence the female child engages in a "replay" of oedipal issues and engages in a family drama that includes both mother and father; her "turn" to the father reflects the ambivalence and tensions in the mother-daughter bond, demonstrating the daughter's need to reject the mother, to separate from her, and to continue to seek her love.[45] Cather's adolescent playacting, which reflected these paradoxical motives as well as her rejection of an oppressive social role, was a drama of identity as well as sexuality. Her transformation into William Cather both anticipates her lesbianism in suggesting her refusal to abandon her mother as a love object and simultaneously reflects her struggle to define herself as separate from her mother.

One important early story—"The Burglar's Christmas" (1896)—reveals that the same psychodynamics arising from the mother-daughter relationship contributed to her use of male narrators or centers of consciousness to confront maternal or erotic figures. In this aesthestically crude but psychologically fascinating story, Cather uses a male persona (William) to portray the search for the mother/lover. This bizarre tale of the prodigal son—a thief who enters a strange house and unknowingly invades his mother's bedroom—reveals the psychological conflicts central to the mother-daughter, not the mother-son, bond. The terrifying declaration of sameness and identity with which the sensuous mother greets the son ("I have lived all your life before you. You have never had an impulse that I have not known") betrays the preoedipal issues of fusion, sameness, and mutual identification experienced most intensely by mothers and daughters.[46] Cather's use of a male persona in this apprentice work can then be viewed as a defense reflecting her need to define ego boundaries by placing the barrier of gender between herself and the female presence that offered gratification and nurturance but also threatened to obliterate a separate identity.

Thus Willa Cather's use of male narrators and centers of consciousness, although connected with her lesbianism, does not, in my view, signify her acceptance of patriarchal values or her continuing male identification. In part these were strategic personae necessitated by social pressures that required of Cather, if she wrote of the "thing not named," not to name it; in part, they were unconscious defenses against the irresistible pull of the mother/lover toward an undifferentiated state

45. Nancy Chodorow, "Oedipal Resolution and Adolescent Replay," in *The Reproduction of Mothering: Psychoanalysis and the Sociology of Gender* (Berkeley: University of California Press, 1978), pp. 130–40.

46. Faulkner, ed. (n. 13 above), pp. 557–66.

where there is no separation between self and other. Cather needed protection against such terrors, which she often, as in "On the Gull's Road," conveyed through images of drowning. To be sure, Cather never completely freed herself from male constructions of femininity—not a surprising failure in a woman whose youthful imagination was structured so strongly by male writers. Cather's portrayal of erotic and sensual women like Lena Lingard and Marian Forrester particularly reflects male stereotypes; it was more difficult for her to separate women's sexual power from male representations of it than to separate female creative power from maleness. Nevertheless, Cather did revise some male stereotypes of women: Ántonia Shimerda, viewed by some as an archetypal Earth Mother, is a storyteller who pours her creativity into narrative as well as into nurturing.

And the puzzling shift some critics have noted in Cather's fiction from autonomous, powerful women heroes in *O Pioneers!* and *The Song of the Lark* to weaker, romantic women and male perceivers in later novels does not, I think, demonstrate the lesbian writer's increasing adoption of patriarchal values or her intensifying male identification. The strong women heroes into whom Cather projected herself in her early novels reflect her reconciliation of female identity and artistic vocation. After *The Song of the Lark* she did not revert to the patriarchal constructions of male and female identity from which she had so laboriously escaped, but she did suffer the loss of Isabelle McClung, who married in 1917. This grief was an important source for Cather's subsequent stories of romantic love, disappointment, and loss. In writing of heroic protagonists engaged in creative endeavor, as she did in her first novels, Cather concentrated on female characters, but as her imagination became increasingly preoccupied with her lost ladies she had to resort to male masks, her "covers" for a lesbian sensibility. That Cather did not become increasingly male identified is indicated by an important fictional pattern that emerged in later years when she began to explore mother-daughter relationships openly; to do so she used female protagonists in *My Mortal Enemy*, the autobiographical "Old Mrs. Harris" and "The Best Years," and *Sapphira and the Slave Girl*. Her mother's death in 1931 both inspired and freed the daughter to address this subject, and since it was possible to "name" mother-daughter attachments, Cather could explore the psychological and emotional dynamics of female-female bonds without casting one of the actors as male.

In addition to requiring us to distinguish carefully between male personae and male identification, Cather's lesbianism raises other interpretive problems we must now begin to address, puzzling and perhaps ultimately unanswerable issues of meaning and authorial intention. We need to ask an unusual question of her fiction, When is a male character not a male character? Noting that Cather uses male masks is important, but on what grounds do we assume that a male character is not "really" male but female? To argue that most of her male characters engaged in love affairs are not male at all, as some of Cather's readers have done, is to question the writer's ability to transcend self, gender, and sexuality by adopting other selves; it is also to assume that, because Cather was lesbian, she was encoding a lesbian attachment whenever she was writing of heterosexual love—a rigid and reductive view of her fiction. We need to distinguish between thinly disguised "cover" figures whose gender is contradicted in some way by the text and male characters whom Cather created by drawing, in part, on herself.

Viewing Cather's portrayal of heterosexual passion as an encoded transcription of lesbian love posits that the overt, written text conceals a subtext that is the "real" story Cather would have written had she been able. In some of her fiction—"On the Gull's Road," for example—this theory seems plausible, although it does ignore Cather's unconscious motivations for creating male characters as defenses against fusion with a maternal presence. However, in more complex works like *O Pioneers!* the relationship between heterosexual cover story/lesbian subtext becomes more complicated. In the lovers' subplot, for instance, it is possible that Cather was writing two stories simultaneously—a heterosexual and a homosexual story—just as she projected herself into both male and female characters. The heterosexual cover story is not then invariably the false one, the lesbian subtext the real; rather, authorial intention and meaning may oscillate between the two and thus be indeterminate. The spatial metaphor that best captures this pattern is the continual interplay between figure and ground rather than a hierarchical opposition between surface and hidden, overt and covert, secondary and privileged meaning. And there is another possibility: that Cather intended, at times, to write only of heterosexual love, and in *O Pioneers!* projected her resentment of sexual rivals and faithless women into the lovers' bloody destruction.

We should also consider how the lesbianism Cather could not express directly enriched as well as circumscribed her fiction. In writing of lesbian literature, Bonnie Zimmerman has speculated that it may characteristically present "unrequited longing, a longing of almost cosmic totality because the love object is denied not by circumstance or chance, but by necessity."[47] Both stories like "The Burglar's Christmas" and "On the Gull's Road" and mature novels like *My Ántonia* and *A Lost Lady*, inspired by such unrequited longing, suggest the contributions, as well as the restrictions, lesbianism gave to Cather's fiction. Whereas Jewett's "Martha's Lady" was a story of reunion, Cather's romantic tales are characteristically ones of separation and loss; the gain occurs only in time as the narrator recreates his lost lady in memory and imagination, a pattern

47. Zimmerman (n. 6 above), p. 470.

suggesting the role Cather's lesbianism played in a creative process where loss inspired the urge to regain the lost connection in art. When Jim changes the title of his story from *Ántonia* to *My Ántonia*, like Cather he simultaneously declares subjectivity and possession.[48] Cather's inability to write directly from lesbian experience may have also contributed to the most powerful presence in her fiction: the land. If Cather had been free to write openly of erotic and romantic love between women, we might have been deprived of her sexually and emotionally charged descriptions of the landscapes that stirred her—the Divide, the Southwest. These female presences are far more important in her fiction than Jewett's rocky Maine coast was in hers; so much energy is displaced onto the landscape that it becomes a character in its own right.[49]

Finally we must question whether Cather's lesbianism contributed to her fiction the allusive, suggestive quality we associate with modernism: the aesthetic of indirection she espoused in "The Novel Démeublé" suggests at once the lesbian writer forced to conceal and the twentieth-century writer aware of both the inadequacies and the possibilities of language. Even though she was not a self-conscious modernist, because she could not tell the truth directly, she was, at times, forced to tell it slant, and the resulting creative tension between expression and suppression, revealing and concealing, produced fiction that is subtle, richly symbolic, and ambiguous, enriched by the repressed, the hidden, and the covert. Earlier readers both praised and dismissed Cather for her simplicity and conservatism, but in the last decade critics have begun to discover the complexity beneath the apparent surface of simplicity and the resonance of her seemingly transparent, luminous prose. We can hope that a full rereading of Cather's fiction from a feminist perspective will lead to a revaluing of her work. If so, we may be faced with the irony that the necessity both to disclose and to conceal lesbianism contributed to the pleasure Cather found in the creative process and helped her to create sophisticated fiction that may ultimately grant her a higher place in the American literary canon than the one she now occupies.

Had Willa Cather been free to write openly of lesbian relationships, she might not have been able to write of something else. As we begin to explore the richness of this fiction produced by a lesbian writer, we need to examine the dialectic between what is named and what is not, rather than assuming that what is not named is the "real" text, the one Cather would have written in a different social environment. Cather loved to don disguises in life as well as in fiction. Her male impersonation was followed by subtler and more varied forms of camouflage: she employed a variety

---

48. Willa Cather, *My Ántonia* (Boston: Houghton Mifflin Co., 1918), p. ix.

49. In an unpublished manuscript I read after completing this article, Judith Fetterley develops an argument along similar lines.

of pseudonyms in her early work; she created a myth of origins, claiming that she was named for an uncle who died in the Civil War. These real-life costumes revealed as well as concealed the self. Similarly, the surface texts Cather chose to create simultaneously offered her the pleasures of disclosure and concealment. In developing new interpretive strategies for reading Cather's fiction, we would thus do well to become the readers she asked for in "The Novel Démeublé," sensitive to the creative interplay between the written and the unwritten, the named and the unnamed, the tone and the overtone.

Department of English
Dickinson College

Sapphistries

Susan Gubar

```
        ] called you
        ] filled your mouth with plenty
        ] girls, fine gifts
        ] lovesong, the keen-toned harp
        ] an old woman's flesh
        ] hair that used to be black
        ] knees will not hold
        ] stand like dappled fawns
            ] but what could I do?
        ] no longer able to begin again
            ] rosy armed Dawn
                ] bearing to the ends of the earth
                    ] nevertheless seized
                    ] the cherished wife
                    ] withering is common to all
                ] may that girl come and be my lover
I have loved all graceful things [            ] and this
Eros has given me, beauty and the light of the sun.
```

[SAPPHO, in *Archilocos Sappho Alkman*, trans. Guy Davenport]

I am indebted throughout this paper to Sandra M. Gilbert. My title comes from Pat Califia's book on lesbian sexuality, *Sapphistry* (Tallahassee, Fla.: Naiad Press, 1980), and from Jane Marcus's paper on Virginia Woolf, delivered at the 1981 English Institute and reprinted as "Liberty, Sorority, Misogyny" in *The Representation of Women in Fiction*, ed. Carolyn B. Heilbrun and Margaret R. Higonnet (Baltimore: John Hopkins University Press, 1983), esp. pp. 81 and 87. Finally, I have profited from the generous advice of Elyse Blankely, Don Gray, Donna Hollenberg, Dori Katz, Lawrence Lipking, Susan Friedman, and Dolores Rosenblum.

Reprinted from *Signs: Journal of Women in Culture and Society* 10, no. 1 (Autumn 1984): 43–62.

From the poems by Katherine Philips, "the English Sappho," celebrating female friendship to the provocative blank page under the entry for Sappho in Monique Wittig and Sande Zeig's *Lesbian Peoples Material for a Dictionary* (1979), from Elizabeth Barrett Browning's translations and Christina Rossetti's variations to recent publications like Sidney Abott and Barbara Love's *Sappho Was a Right-On Woman* (1972) and Pat Califia's *Sapphistry* (1980), the person and poetics of Sappho have haunted the female imagination.[1] Since the late nineteenth century, of course, the words we use to describe female homosexuality derive from the poet of Lesbos, although the 1971 edition of the *Oxford English Dictionary* actually defines "Sapphism" as "unnatural sexual relations between women" and "Lesbian rule" as "a mason's rule made of lead. . . ." In a manner that might have surprised the lexicographers, however, doubtless because of a flood of male-authored classical scholarship and decadent poetry at the turn of the century, Sappho influenced women writing in the early decades of the twentieth century. Just when translators of Sappho were beginning to honor her choice of a female pronoun for her beloved and classicists were disputing the legends and facts about her life,[2] Sappho's status as a female precursor empowered a number of female modernists to collaborate in exuberant linguistic experiments.

Like "Michael Fields" (pen name of Katherine Bradley and Edith Cooper), whose volume of Sapphics were entitled *Long Ago*, Isadora Duncan viewed Sappho as a legendary survivor from a paradise lost long ago; while Edna St. Vincent Millay identified her as a love-lost suicide, Sara Teasdale idealized Sappho as a mother-poet crooning to her daughter Cleis, Elizabeth Robbins meditated on a Sappho who is "the nursing mother of intellectually free women," and Isak Dinesen associated her with prostitution.[3] Despite their differences, however, all evince the same

1. The indispensable background for the lesbian tradition in literature is Lillian Faderman, *Surpassing the Love of Men* (New York: William Morrow, 1981); see esp. pp. 69–71 on Katherine Philips (see Katherine Philips, "To My Most Excellent Lucasia: On Our Friendship," *Poems* [London, 1697], p. 107). Significantly, Elizabeth Barrett Browning's only mention of a female precursor in "A Vision of Poets" is Sappho (see lines 318–21), and Christina Rossetti's "Sappho" (1846) and "What Sappho Would Have Said Had Her Leap Cured Instead Of Killing Her" (1848) were excised from her collected work by William Michael Rossetti (see Gwynneth Hatton, "Edition of the Unpublished Poems of Christina Rossetti" [Master's essay, Oxford University, 1955]).

2. The poet Anne Winters, of Berkeley, Calif., describes the shift from T. W. Higginson's male pronouns (1871) to J. A. Symonds's female pronouns (1873) in an unpublished paper.

3. [Katherine Bradley and Edith Cooper], *Long Ago* (London: G. Bell & Sons, 1889); Isadora Duncan, *My Life* (1927; reprint ed., New York: Liveright, 1955), pp. 58 and 116–22; Edna St. Vincent Millay, "Sappho Crosses the Dark River into Hades," *Collected Lyrics* (New York: Harper & Bros., 1939), pp. 293–94; Sara Teasdale, "To Cleis (The Daughter of Sappho)," *Helen of Troy and Other Poems* (New York: Macmillan, 1928), pp. 88–89; Elizabeth

desire to recover Sappho that impels Virginia Woolf's women's studies collective in her 1921 short story, "A Society."[4] When the members of this Society of Outsiders evaluate the world of culture created by men, they discover one Professor Hobkin's edition of Sappho which is primarily devoted to a defense of Sappho's chastity. As Jane Marcus has shown, Hobkin's gynecological obsession with "some implement which looks remarkably like a hairpin" dramatizes Woolf's recognition that exceptional women like Sappho have been used not for but against the nurturing of a female literary tradition.[5] One year before writing "A Society," moreover, Woolf discerned in Desmond MacCarthy's newspaper article on the paucity of women's poetry precisely the sentence her society would read in the newspaper: "'Since Sappho there has been no female of first rate.'" In a letter of rebuttal, Woolf claimed that "external restraints" have inhibited the growth of women's literary history after Sappho, for Sappho lived in a time that accorded "social and domestic freedom" to women who were "highly educated and accustomed to express their sentiments." The conditions that make possible the birth of Sappho are first, artistic predecessors; second, membership in a group where art is freely discussed and practiced; and third, freedom of action and experience: "Perhaps in Lesbos," Woolf speculates, "but never since have these conditions been the lot of women."[6]

Significantly, however, some of Woolf's contemporaries were in the process of recovering the artistic freedom they, too, associated with this classical literary foremother who evaded masculine definitions and therefore freed them from the anxiety of authorship suffered by so many women writers.[7] As if to illustrate the problem creativity continued to pose for twentieth-century women artists, as late as 1944 Edith Sitwell complained that "women's poetry, with the exception of Sappho" and a few poems of Christina Rossetti and Emily Dickinson, "is *simply awful*—incom-

---

Robbins, *Ancilla's Share* (1924; reprint ed., Westport, Conn.: Hyperion, 1976), p. 125; Isak Dinesen, *Out of Africa* (1936; reprint ed., New York: Random House, 1965), p. 316. David M. Robinson discusses Teasdale's "Phaon and the Leucadian Leap" in *Sappho and Her Influence* (New York: Cooper Square, 1963), pp. 227–28. Emily Stipes Watts analyzes the use of Sappho in nineteenth-century American poetry by women: *The Poetry of American Women from 1632 to 1945* (Austin: University of Texas Press, 1977), pp. 75–82.

4. Virginia Woolf, "A Society," in *Monday or Tuesday* (New York: Harcourt, Brace, 1921).

5. Jane Marcus, "Liberty, Sorority, Misogyny," in *The Representation of Women in Fiction*, ed. Carolyn Heilbrun and Margaret R. Higonnet (Baltimore: Johns Hopkins University Press, 1983), p. 87.

6. See "Affable Hawk's" review of Arnold Bennet's *Our Women* and Otto Weininger's *Sex and Character* in *The New Statesman* (London, October 9, 1920) and Virginia Woolf's exchange with him.

7. Sandra M. Gilbert and I analyze the anxiety of authorship in *The Madwoman in the Attic* (New Haven, Conn.: Yale University Press, 1979), pp. 45–92.

petent, floppy, whining, arch, trivial, self-pitying."[8] Whether the woman poet confronted no poetic tradition of her own or a tradition only of what Sitwell termed "ghastly wallowing," she suffered isolation and feelings of inferiority. Like so many women writers, both Woolf and Sitwell mulled over the inadequacy of their classical education, specifically the inadequacy of their knowledge of Greek, which made it difficult for them to be what Woolf called Sappho, "an inheritor as well as an originator."[9] Yet, in order to become originators inheriting Sappho's poetic genius, both Woolf and Sitwell would have certainly agreed with Willa Cather that, "If of all the lost riches we could have one master restored to us, . . . the choice of the world would be for the lost nine books of Sappho," for "those broken fragments have burned themselves into the consciousness of the world like fire."[10] To be sure, male writers from Catullus to Lawrence Durrell also turned to Sappho, thereby providing women artists with a prism through which to view their only classical precursor.[11] But, as Louise Bogan has explained, women readers search for the lost fragments of Sappho "less with the care and eagerness of the scholar looking for bits of shattered human art, than with the hungry eyes of the treasure hunter, looking for some last grain of a destroyed jewel."[12]

Sappho represents, then, all the lost women of genius in literary history, especially all the lesbian artists whose work has been destroyed, sanitized, or heterosexualized in an attempt to evade what Elaine Marks identifies as "lesbian intertextuality."[13] Antithetically, the effort to recover Sappho illustrates how twentieth-century women poets try to solve the problem of poetic isolation and imputed inferiority. For the woman poet who experiences herself as inadequate or inadequately nurtured by a nonexistent or degraded literary matrilineage, for the lesbian poet who looks in vain for a native lesbian poetic tradition, Sappho is a very special precursor. Precisely because so many of her original Greek texts were destroyed, the modern woman poet could write "for" or "as" Sappho and

8. Dame Edith Sitwell, *Selected Letters: 1919–1964*, ed. John Lehmann and Derek Parker (New York: Vanguard, 1979), p. 116.

9. Virginia Woolf, *A Room of One's Own* (1929; reprint ed., New York: Harcourt, Brace & World, 1957), p. 113.

10. Willa Cather, "Three Women Poets" (1895), reprinted in *The World and the Parish: Willa Cather's Articles and Reviews, 1883–1902* (Lincoln: University of Nebraska, 1970), p. 147.

11. Lawrence Lipking in "Sappho Descending: Abandonment through the Ages" (Evanston, Ill.: Northwestern University, n.d.) examines how male and female poets interpret Sappho's "Second Ode."

12. Louise Bogan, *A Poet's Alphabet: Reflections on the Literary Art and Vocation*, ed. Robert Phelps and Ruth Limmer (New York: McGraw-Hill, 1970), p. 429.

13. Elaine Marks, "Lesbian Intertextuality," in *Homosexualities and French Literature*, ed. George Stambolian and Elaine Marks (Ithaca, N.Y.: Cornell University Press, 1979), pp. 353–77.

thereby invent a classical inheritance of her own. In other words, such a writer is not infected by Sappho's stature with a Bloomian "anxiety of influence" because her ancient precursor is paradoxically in need of a contemporary collaborator,[14] or so the poetry of Renée Vivien and H. D. seems to suggest. What Sandra Gilbert would call a "fantasy precursor" or what I would term a "fantastic collaboration" simultaneously heals the anxiety of authorship and links these two women poets to an empowering literary history they could create in their own image.

Sappho's preeminence provides Vivien and H. D. with evidence that the woman who is a poet need not experience herself as a contradiction in terms, that the woman who achieves the confessional lyricism of Sappho will take her place apart from but also beside a poet like Homer. Through the dynamics of their collaboration with Sappho, feminist modernists like Renée Vivien and H. D. present themselves as breaking not only with patriarchal literary tradition, but also with nineteenth-century female literary history. Replacing the schizophrenic doubling Sandra Gilbert and I have traced throughout Victorian women's literature with euphoric coupling in which the other is bound to the self as a lover, such poets also offer divergent interpretations of what lesbianism means as an imaginative force. The fantastic collaborations Vivien and H. D. enact through their reinventions of Sappho's verse are not unrelated to the eroticized female relationships that quite literally empowered them to write. By recovering a female precursor of classical stature, moreover, Vivien and H. D. could mythologize the primacy of women's literary language. Whether the recovery of Sappho results in a decadent aesthetic, as it does for Vivien, or in a chiseled classicism, as for H. D., it holds out the promise of excavating a long-lost ecstatic lyricism that inscribes female desire as the ancient source of song. Only in the later work of writers like Amy Lowell and Marguerite Yourcenar would the liabilities of such a collaboration be uncovered.

Like Cather, who especially admired Sappho's creation of "the most wonderfully emotional meter in literature," Renée Vivien was fascinated with Sappho's resonant lines that, in Cather's words, "come in like a gasp when feeling flows too swift for speech."[15] But, unlike Cather, Vivien self-consciously dramatized her efforts to regain Sappho's erotic language specifically for lesbians. Curiously, in 1900, Vivien met the woman she would desire and resist all her life: at a theater, Natalie Barney was reading a letter from Liane de Pougy that would be published the next year in her *Idylle saphique*. And, as Elyse Blankely has shown, Sappho's legend continued to provide the scenic background for the stormy relationship Vivien and Barney pursued, as well as being the central symbol

14. Harold Bloom, *The Anxiety of Influence* (New York: Oxford University Press, 1973).
15. Cather (n. 10 above), p. 147.

of their respective arts.[16] Motivated at least in part by her friendship with Pierre Louÿs, the famous author of *Chansons de Bilitis* (1894) and *Aphrodite* (1896), Natalie Barney published *Cinq petits dialogues grecs* in 1902. In 1906 she produced her *Acts d' entr'actes* with Marguerite Moreno playing the leading role of a Sappho who dies not from love of the boatman Phaon, as the followers of Ovid claimed, but because of her desire for a girl promised in marriage.[17] During this same period, after teaching herself Greek, Vivien published *Sapho* (1903), a collection of translations and imitations of Greek fragments that the Anglo-American Vivien composed in French. In 1904, she and Natalie Barney traveled to Mytilene where Vivien eventually purchased a house of her own. In that same year, she published *Une femme m'apparut* ("A woman appeared to me"), a roman à clef that focused on an androgynous avatar and disciple of the poet of Mytilene who argues not only that Phaon is the vulgar invention of low humorists but also that Sappho is the only woman poet of distinction because she did not deign to notice masculine existence, which is "the Unaesthetic par excellence."[18]

In both her poetry and her novel, Vivien appropriates the sadistic Sappho so prevalent in the late nineteenth-century work of Baudelaire and Swinburne.[19] In a setting of voluptuous, "evil" flowers and narcissistic mirrors like those associated with Swinburne's vampiric and suicidal heroine Lesbia Brandon, Vivien's Sappho morbidly sings, "I believe I take from you a bit of your fleeting life when I embrace you"; like Baudelaire, who portrays the sinful delights of Lesbos, Vivien identifies Sappho with Satan, the incarnation of cunning and the antagonist of both God and his poet, Homer.[20] This satanic Sappho is, of course, the same haunted figure Colette perceived in Vivien herself, living shrouded in the scented darkness of fin de siècle decadence, wasting away in a twilight of anorexic

16. Elyse Blankely, "Returning to Mytilene: Renée Vivien and the City of Women," in *Essays in Feminist Literary Criticism*, ed. Susan Squier (Knoxville: University of Tennessee Press, in press). George Wickes, *The Amazon of Letters: The Life and Loves of Natalie Barney* (New York: G. P. Putnam's Sons, 1976); Jean Chalon, *Portrait of a Seductress: The World of Natalie Barney*, trans. Carol Barko (New York: Crown, 1979); and W. G. Rogerts, *Ladies Bountiful* (New York: Harcourt, Brace, & World, 1968).

17. Jeanette Foster, *Sex Variant Women in Literature* (1956; reprint ed., Baltimore: Diana Press, 1975), pp. 154–73. Also see Bertha Harris, "The More Profound Nationality of Their Lesbianism: Lesbian Society in Paris in the 1920's," in *Amazon Expedition* (New York: Times Change Press, 1973), pp. 77–88.

18. Renée Vivien, *A Woman Appeared to Me*, trans. Jeannette H. Foster (1904; reprint ed., Tallahassee, Fla.: Naiad Press, 1979), p. 34.

19. Mario Praz discusses the lesbian femme fatale in *The Romantic Agony*, trans. Angus Davidson (1933; reprint ed., London: Oxford University Press, 1970), pp. 236–40 and 260–61, as does Faderman (n. 1 above), pp. 269–75. See also Foster (n.17 above), pp. 76–80, 104, and 114.

20. A recitation of San Giovanni, Sappho's avatar in *A Woman Appeared to Me*, p. 17; see Gayle Rubin's "Introduction," p. viii.

self-incarceration.[21] But while in her life Vivien clearly did suffer the consequences of such internalization, in her art she tapped the energy of the decadents' alienated lesbian. The unholy excess and implacable cruelty of lesbian desire in Vivien's fiction and poetry—the tormented hair, unappeased breasts, insatiable thighs, and ardent hands of the lovers described by Vivien—uncover the demonic power that drew Baudelaire and Swinburne to the lesbian femme fatale. Indeed, Vivien suggests that the "unnatural" longing of the decadents' Sappho turns the lesbian into a prototypical artist, for her obsession with a beauty that does not exist in nature is part of a satanically ambitious effort against nature to attain the aesthetic par excellence.

Vivien therefore implicitly reveals the centrality of the lesbian in decadent poetry to claim this image for herself. Like Proust, who had declared "Femmes damneés" the "most beautiful [long poem] that Baudelaire had written," Vivien must have been struck by what Proust called the "strange privilege" Baudelaire assigned himself in "Lesbos": "For Lesbos of all men on this earth elected me / To sing the secret of its flowering virgins / And as a child I was admitted to the dark mystery."[22] Swinburne, with less presumption, responded to a friend's critique of his Sappho-persona by explaining, "It is as near as I can come; and no man can come close to her."[23] As if diagnosing his and Baudelaire's efforts to "come close," the Sapphic androgyne of Vivien's novel explains the limits of such voyeuristic masculine fantasies of lesbianism: "Men see in the love of woman for woman only a spice that sharpens the flatness of their regular performance. But when they realize that this cult of grace and delicacy will permit no sharing, no ambiguity, they revolt against the purity of a passion which excludes and scorns them."[24] Vivien implies that Baudelaire, who originally gave the title *Les Lesbiennes* to *Les Fleurs du mal*, and Swinburne, who spoke to "Anactoria" in the accents of a passionately depraved Sappho, were themselves excluded from what she is elected to sing: the secrets, the dark mysteries of Mytilene. She subversively implies, moreover, that the lesbian is the epitome of the decadent and that decadence is fundamentally a lesbian literary tradition.

No wonder, then, that this Anglo-American girl christened Pauline Tarn seems to have renamed herself after the insinuating seductress

21. Colette, *The Pure and the Impure*, trans. Herma Briffault (1932; reprint ed., London: Penguin, 1971), p. 71.

22. Charles Baudelaire, *The Flowers of Evil/Les Fleurs du mal*, ed. Wallace Fowlie (New York: Bantam, 1964), pp. 106–7. I have departed somewhat from this translation. Also see Marcel Proust, "A propos of Baudelaire," in *Baudelaire: A Collection of Critical Essays*, ed. Henri Peyre (Englewood Cliffs, N.J.: Prentice-Hall, 1962), pp. 125–26.

23. Algernon Charles Swinburne, *Selected Poetry and Prose*, ed. John D. Rosenberg (New York: Modern Library, 1968), pp. 328–29. Dolores Klaich sees Vivien as victimized by Swinburnean decadence in *Woman Plus Woman* (New York: Simon & Schuster, 1974), p. 143.

24. Vivien (n. 18 above), p. 36.

Vivien of Arthurian legend: in Tennyson's *Idylls of the King* and Burne-Jones's *The Beguiling of Merlin*, the enchantress Vivien literally steals Merlin's magical book, which contains a powerful charm to enthrall women to men.[25] Like the Arthurian Vivien, Renée Vivien appropriates the male-authored book of power to usurp male authority and to break what Gayle Rubin calls the male monopoly over women.[26] Of course, as critics like Sandia Belgrade and Pamela Annas have noted, when Pauline Tarn renamed herself Renée Vivien she was also effecting a transformation in which she was reborn (re-*née*), even as she was insisting on retaining her maiden name (*née*) and her maidenhood.[27] Like the sinister but sensuous figure in her poem "Viviane," who has "changed her name, her voice, her visage," Vivien is "born anew" ("elle renaît").[28] Just as the Arthurian Vivien casts Merlin in a lifeless spell, just as Vivien's "Viviane" weaves so that "you fall asleep in her eternal arms," Vivien is reborn a lesbian poet; thus she evades heterosexual consummation with *its* vampiric consumption of women, for in her view the penetration of women ensures the perpetuation of patriarchy.

In a number of poems, therefore, Vivien flouts heterosexual homophobia: "You will never know how to tarnish the devotion / Of my passion for the beauty of women"; in others, she praises female virginity as virility: "I shall flee imprint / And soiling stain. / The grasp that strangles, the kiss that infects / And wounds shall I shun."[29] For Vivien, Sapphism, precisely because it is what the decadents called "barren," provides access not to the future of the human species but to the present of the female of the species. "Our love is greater than all loves," Vivien

25. Both of these popular Victorian works of art would have been familiar to Vivien. I am indebted to Elliot Gilbert for my understanding of Tennyson's *Idylls of the King*. Sandra M. Gilbert and I place Vivien's pseudonym in the context of other feminist modernist names of power in "Ceremonies of the Alphabet," in *The Female Autograph*, ed. Domna Stanton (New York: New York Literary Forum, in press).

26. Gayle Rubin's brilliant introduction to *A Woman Appeared to Me* provides an indispensable introduction to Vivien (pp. iii–xx). Nina Auerbach discusses the relationship between the female and the demonic in pre-Raphaelite painting and in Swinburne's poetry in *Woman and the Demon* (Cambridge, Mass.: Harvard University Press, 1982), pp. 74–81 and 104–6.

27. Sandia Belgrade, "Introduction," *At the Sweet Hour of Hand in Hand* (Tallahassee, Fla.: Naiad Press, 1979), p. xv; Pamela Annas, "'Drunk with Chastity': The Poetry of Renée Vivien," in a special issue of *Women's Studies*, ed. Sandra M. Gilbert and Susan Gubar (in press).

28. "Viviane" is translated in *At the Sweet Hour*, pp. 47–49. Unless otherwise indicated, I am using the Naiad Press translations of Vivien's poetry because they are a pioneering achievement which makes possible the teaching and study of Vivien in this country. For those who wish to see the original, a collected *Poèmes de Renée Vivien* has been reprinted in facsimile (1923–24; reprint ed., New York: Arno, 1975).

29. "The Disdain of Sappho," in *The Muse of the Violets*, trans. Margaret Porter and Catherine Kroger (Tallahassee, Fla.: Naiad Press, 1977), p. 46, and "I shall be always a virgin," p. 44.

declares in "Sappho Lives Again," for "we can, when the belt comes undone, / Be at once both lovers and sisters."[30] Similarly, in "Union," Vivien begins, "Our heart is the same in our woman's breast," and she explains, "Our body is made the same"; "we are of the same race"; "I know exactly what pleases you"; "I am you."[31] Because the beloved feels so much like oneself, however, the realization of her separateness is tormenting. Vivien's feelings about Barney's promiscuity, to which Sappho's poems on the loss of Atthis could serve as utterance, underscore this sense of aloneness, allowing Vivien to privilege lesbianism as the preferred eroticism because it raises crucial issues of fusion and identity.[32]

By opening up the relationship of women to eroticism, Vivien admits an influx of jealousy and self-abasement as well as of consolation and pleasure. Sapphic desire implicates the lover in the beloved's abandonment and the rival's competition, both of which complicate the monolithic ideal of sisterhood that informed so much feminist rhetoric in her time: "For Andromeda," Vivien laments in one Sapphic meditation, "the lightning of your kiss," while she herself is left with only "the grave cadences" of Atthis's voice.[33] Even when the beloved is present to the lover, their lovemaking offers paradoxical intimations of their separateness: in "Chanson," for example, Vivien sees in her beloved a "form . . . that leaves me clutching emptiness" and a "smile . . . that one can never clasp."[34] The need to "evoke the fear, the pain and the torment" of such love repeatedly turns Vivien toward Sappho:

> O perfume of Paphos! O Poet! O Priestess!
> Teach us the secret of divine sorrow,
> Teach us longing, the relentless embrace
> Where pleasure weeps, faded among the flowers!
> O languors of Lesbos! Charm of Mytilene!
> Teach us the golden verse stifled only by death,
>   Of your harmonious breath,
>   Inspire us, Sappho![35]

30. "Sappho Lives Again," in *At the Sweet Hour*, pp. 2–4.

31. "Union," in *Muse of the Violets*, p. 73.

32. The best analysis of Sappho's poetry in terms of the "illusion of perfect union, the inevitability of parting," is Eva Stehle Stiger's "Romantic Sensuality, Poetic Sense: A Response to Hallett on Sappho," *Signs* 4, no. 3 (Spring 1979): 465–71. Adrienne Rich addresses the issue of privileging lesbianism as the preferred eroticism in "Compulsory Heterosexuality and Lesbian Existence," *Signs* 5, no. 4 (Summer 1980): 631–60.

33. "For Andromeda, she has a beautiful recompense," in *Muse of the Violets*, p. 36.

34. "Chanson," in *Muse of the Violets*, p. 24; thanks to a gift from Elin Diamond, I have taken the original, "Sonnet," from *Etudes et preludes* (1904; reprint ed., Paris: Regine Deforges, 1976), p. 24.

35. "Invocation," in *Muse of the Violets*, p. 59. The original appears in *Cendres et poussières* (1902; reprint ed., Paris: Regine Deforges, 1977), pp. 2–4.

Vivien's dramatic poems—"La Mort de Psappha" (The death of Sappho), "Atthis délaissée" (Atthis abandoned), and "Dans un verger" (In an orchard)—are elegies mourning not only the death of the poet of fugitive desire but also the death of desire itself.[36] Paradoxically, however, "Sappho Lives Again" in these elegies, reborn as Vivien: "Some of us have preserved the rites / Of burning Lesbos gilded like an altar."[37] Prefaced with fragments of Sappho's, Vivien's French becomes an aspect of the other muted languages of languor in the poetry: the lexicon of scents, the syntax of flowers, the sign language of fingers on flesh, the intonation of swooning voices sighing in broken phrases. While Vivien's French aligns her poetry with the flagrant fragrance of Continental eroticism in the *belle époque* and thereby frees her to speak the unspoken, prefaced with Sapphic phrase, set off with ellipses, her most fragmentary translations seem to attest to a form of aphasia, symptomatic of an ontological or sexual expatriation, for Vivien's French is as foreign to her native English as her homosexuality is to the hegemonic heterosexual idiom. At a loss for words, Vivien signals her exile for Lesbos, her expatriation from a native language of desire.

Two of the finest of Vivien's original poems that equate the recovery of Sappho with the rediscovery of a distant but distinct female country and the translation of the poet carried across the seas and the centuries to this country are "En débarquant à Mytilène" (While landing at Mytilene) and "Vers Lesbos" (Toward Lesbos).[38] In the first, the poet begins with an effort at return: "From the depths of my past, I turn back to you / Mytilene, across the disparate centuries." Similarly, in "Toward Lesbos," she speaks to a beloved on board a ship headed for Mytilene: "You will come," she tells her lover, "your eyes filled with evening and with yesterday." In both poems, fine fragrances fill the air: in the first, the poet brings her love "like a present of aromatics," and in the second "our boat will be full of amber and spices." In both poems the trip to Greece involves dying into a new life; the poet discovers waves, trees, and vines, a place in which to "melt and dissolve." Or again the boat is "frail like a cradle," as the lovers, sleeping through the risks and rites of passage, wonder if they will be able to move to where "we will live tomorrow." Most important, in both poems the Greek island is a place of the female erotic imagination: in the first, Mytilene is quite simply a woman's body rising out of the sea, "golden-flanked Lesbos"; in the second, the lovers on board hear "myste-

36. Although Vivien's verse dramas have not yet been translated into English, they are available in French in *Poèmes de Renée Vivien* (n. 28 above).
37. "Sappho Lives Again," in *At the Sweet Hour*, p. 2, but I have departed from this translation here with the help of Star Howlett.
38. "While landing at Mytilene" and "Toward Lesbos," in *At the Sweet Hour*, pp. 25–26, and 64–65.

rious songs," the intimation of "supreme music," as they approach "the illusionary island."

This utopian yearning for a visionary land and language of female primacy also impelled the American-born poet H. D. The Englishwoman Bryher saved H. D.'s life in 1919 by caring for her through influenza and a difficult childbirth when she had been abandoned both by her husband and by the father of her child; and in 1920 Bryher took H. D. to the Greek islands to recuperate.[39] H. D. describes the events that led to her recovery in the first section of her novel *Palimpsest*: her heroine, Hipparchia, is a translator of Moero, an ancient woman poet whose imagery resembles Sappho's, although Hipparchia has renounced the struggle to recapture Sappho "as savouring of sacrilege."[40] After she is visited by a girl who has memorized all her translations, Hipparchia embarks on the regenerative voyage which taught H. D. that "Greece is not lost" because "Greece is a spirit."[41] Two or three years after her trip with Bryher, H. D. may have visited Lesbos with her mother, an experience she apparently found overwhelming.[42] Yet, while Vivien and H. D. took imaginative and actual passage to Greece in a similar spirit, they excavate two quite different Sapphos: Vivien's Sappho is languorous and tormented, H. D.'s stark and fierce in her commitment to artistic perfection—a shift in attitude that doubtless reflects the translation history of Sappho's texts in this period. Also, unlike Vivien, who exclusively defines Sappho as a satanic lesbian, H. D. is strikingly reticent about the homosexual content of Sappho's verse. Instead, placing Sappho in a Greek context that extends from Homer to Euripides, H. D. explicitly adopts Sappho's texts as anachronistic literary models to remove herself from the contamination of contemporary sentimentality, even as she implicitly demonstrates that lesbianism furnishes her with a refuge from the pain of heterosexuality and with the courage necessary to articulate that pain.

H. D.'s first use of Sappho, "Fragment 113," is an original poem that presents itself as an exploration of Sappho's fragment "Neither honey nor bee for me."[43] Organized around a series of negatives, this poem refrains from assenting to an old desire. "Not honey," the poet reiterates

39. The most recent biography of H. D. is Barbara Guest's *Herself Defined: The Poet H. D. and Her World* (New York: Doubleday, 1984), see pp. 118–20, 123–26. Also see H. D., *Tribute to Freud* (1945–46; reprint ed., New York: McGraw Hill, 1974), p. 49.

40. H. D., *Palimpsest* (1926; reprint ed., Carbondale: Southern Illinois University Press, 1968), p. 129.

41. Ibid., p. 131.

42. Francis Wolle's account of H. D.'s life records such a visit: *A Moravian Heritage* (Boulder, Colo.: Empire Reproductions, 1972), p. 58. However, Barbara Guest argues that there is no other evidence of such a trip (*Herself Defined*, p. 167).

43. H. D., "Fragment 113," in *H. D.: Collected Poems, 1912–1944*, ed. Louis L. Martz (New York: New Directions, 1983), pp. 131–32.

three times in the first stanza, refusing thereby "the sweet / stain on the lips and teeth" as well as "the deep plunge of soft belly." The voluptuous flight of the plundering bee is associated with sweetness and softness. "Not so" would the poet desire, "though rapture blind my eyes, / and hunger crisp, dark and inert, my mouth." Refusing "old desire—old passion—/ old forgetfulness—old pain—," H. D. speculates on a different desire:

> but if you turn again,
> seek strength of arm and throat
> touch as the god;
> neglect the lyre-note;
> knowing that you shall feel,
> about the frame,
> no trembling of the string,
> but heat, more passionate
> of bone and the white shell
> and fiery tempered steel.

Bone, not belly; shell, not lyre; fiery tempered steel instead of the stealings of the plundering bee: as in her essay on Sappho, H. D. finds in Sappho's poems "not heat in the ordinary sense, diffused and comforting," but intensity "as if the brittle crescent-moon gave heat to us, or some splendid, scintillating star turned warm suddenly in our hand like a jewel."[44]

Sappho's imagery—the storm-tossed rose, lily, and poppy; the wind-swept sea garden; the golden Aphrodite—dominates H. D.'s early poetry. The lyricism of both poets is characterized by a yearning intensity expressed through direct address and situated in a liminal landscape.[45] In her notes on Sappho, entitled "The Island," H. D. imagines Sappho as "the island of artistic perfection where the lover of ancient beauty (ship-wrecked in the modern world) may yet find foothold and take breath and gain courage for new ventures and dream of yet unexplored continents and realms of future artistic achievement."[46] Certainly, from H. D.'s earliest imagist verse to her later, longer epics, the Greek island is a place of female artistry. Specifically, from her dramatization in "Callypso" of Odysseus fleeing Calypso's island, to her paradisal vision in *Trilogy* of "the circles and circles of islands / about the lost center-island, Atlantis," to the central section of *Helen in Egypt*, which is situated on Leuke, *l'île blanche*,

44. See H. D.'s "Notes on Sappho," in her manuscript "Notes on Euripides, Pausanius, and Greek Lyric Poets" (1920), Beinecke Library, Yale University.

45. See the excellent discussion of Sappho's poetry in Paul Friedrich's *The Meaning of Aphrodite* (Chicago: University of Chicago Press, 1978), pp. 107–28.

46. H. D., "Notes on Sappho."

H. D. affirms what she proclaims in her last volume, *Hermetic Definition*, that "the island is herself, is her."[47]

Susan Friedman has explained that "Sappho's influence on imagists no doubt helped to validate H. D.'s leadership role in the development of the modern lyric."[48] Just as important, Sappho's Greek fragments furnished H. D. a linguistic model for the poems that would define the imagist aesthetic. "Fragment 113" presents itself as a numbered remnant, a belated version of a mutilated vision, a translation of a lost original. As H. D. knew, Sappho's texts, excavated in 1898 from Egyptian debris, survived as narrow strips torn from mummy wrappings. Her own poems, narrow columns of print with not a few phrases broken off with dashes, meditate on a loss they mediate as the speaker's series of negatives, presumably a response to a prior sentence omitted from the poem, seem to imply that the text has been torn out of an unrecoverable narrative context. H. D.'s lifelong effort to recreate what has been "scattered in the shards / men tread upon"[49] is reflected in her early fascination with Sappho's poetry, as is her recurrent presentation of herself as a translator of unearthed texts that can never be fully restored or understood. Certainly, H. D. uses the runes of Sappho as the fragments she shores up against her own ruin.

"Fragment 113" was published in the volume *Hymen* in 1921. Significantly, in the title piece of this volume, H. D. begins to extend her short lyrics in the direction of narrative. A cluster of poems describes the bride's impending fate, the loss of her virginity, in terms of the plundering bee who "slips / Between the purple flower-lips."[50] In the context of Sappho's "Neither honey nor bee for me," H. D.'s image of the bee's penetration brings to the foreground the silence and isolation of the veiled, white figure of the bride. In addition, as Alicia Ostriker has pointed out, the very title, "Hymen," with its evocation both of female anatomy and of a male god, turns this celebratory sequence into a somber meditation on the predatory pattern of heterosexuality,[51] a pattern explicitly associated with the simultaneity of the bride's marriage and her

47. "Callypso," in Martz, ed. (n. 43 above), pp. 388–96; *Trilogy* (1944; reprint ed., New York: New Directions, 1973), p. 15; *Helen in Egypt* (1961; reprint ed., New York: New Directions, 1974), p. 109; *Hermetic Definition* (New York: New Directions, 1972), p. 29.

48. Susan Friedman, *Psyche Reborn* (Bloomington: Indiana University Press, 1981), p. 10. Adalaide Morris has noted that the existence of women poets like Sappho, Nossis, and Telesilla illuminates H. D.'s attraction to classical literature: "Prospectus for Gender and Genre Session on H. D." (paper presented at the Modern Language Association convention, Los Angeles, 1982). Hugh Kenner describes Pound's use of Sappho in "The Muse in Tatters," *The Pound Era* (Berkeley: University of California Press, 1971), pp. 54–75.

49. H. D., *Trilogy*, p. 36.

50. In Martz, ed. (n. 43 above), p. 109.

51. Alicia Ostriker, "The Poet as Heroine: Learning to Read H. D.," in *Writing Like a Woman* (Ann Arbor: University of Michigan Press, 1983), pp. 7–41.

divorce from the female community. H. D. transforms Sappho's epithalamia into the choruses of girls, maidens, matrons, and priestesses accompanying the silent bride. The stage directions between the lyrics consist of descriptions of musical interludes (flute, harp), of costumes (tunics, baskets), and of the spatial arrangement of figures in their processionals before the temple of Hera. Linking the lyrics together into a liturgy, these italicized prose passages solve the poetic problem H. D. faced as she struggled to extend a minimalist form without losing the intensity she associated with the image. "Hymen" therefore epitomizes the way in which Sappho empowered H. D. to turn eventually toward a reinvention of Homeric epic in *Helen in Egypt*, where she perfected the interrelationships between individual lyrics and a prose gloss that contextualizes them.

Unlike her husband, Richard Aldington, who published a book of voluptuous Sapphic lyrics, *The Love of Myrrhine and Konales* (1926), and unlike Ezra Pound, whose elegaic point in *Lustra* (1917) was that Sappho's fragments could not be reconstituted, H. D. uses the other five meditations on Sapphic fragments that she wrote early in her career to address the contradiction for the woman poet between artistic vocation and female socialization.[52] Heightening this contradictory need for autonomy as a lyricist and dependence as a desiring woman is the sense she has of her own fragility and frigidity; two poems directly confront these complex emotions. In "Fragment 41" ("... thou flittest to Andromeda"), H. D. describes her beloved's betrayal while defending herself against his charges: "I was not asleep," she declares; or "I was not dull and dead." In "Fragment 40" ("Love . . . bitter-sweet"), Sappho's bittersweet love becomes H. D.'s honey and salt, an unnerving blend of tastes that epitomize the grief of love's abandonment.[53] In these two poems, H. D. is "deserted," "outcast," "shattered," "sacrificed," "scorched," "rent," "cut apart," and "slashed open" by her love for a man who is absent or unfaithful. Paradoxically, however, it is precisely the torment of rupture that sparks the poetry of rapture associated by H. D. with Sappho's ecstasy, her ex-stasis, her breaking out of the self into lyric song.[54] In "Fragment 41," the poet discovers her strength in a supremely generous gift, namely, "the love of my lover / for his mistress." Similarly, at the close of "Fragment 40," she admits that "to sing love, / love must first shatter us."

That Eros is "he" in "Fragment 40" and that the poet's lover is in love with "his mistress" in "Fragment 41" unmistakably and—in the Sapphic

---

52. This point is made by both Thomas Burnett Swann, *The Classical World of H. D.* (Lincoln: University of Nebraska Press, 1962), pp. 109–21; and Vincent Quinn, *Hilda Doolittle* (New York: Twayne, 1967), pp. 43–46.

53. In Martz, ed., pp. 173–75 and 181–84.

54. Willis Barnstone discusses Sappho's poetry in *The Poetics of Ecstasy: From Sappho to Borges* (New York: Holmes & Meier, 1983), pp. 29–41.

context—surprisingly mark desire as heterosexual. Why would H. D. invoke the celebrated poet of lesbianism to articulate what Rachel Blau DuPlessis has called her "romantic thralldom" to a series of male mentors?[55] While it is certainly true that H. D. writes obsessively about her desire for the mastery of such men as Pound, Aldington, and Lawrence, her poetry is motivated less by their presence than by their absence. Like her autobiographical prose, which frequently dramatizes her frigidity when she is with these men,[56] H. D.'s revisions of Sapphic fragments articulate her effort to accept the intensity of desire that, transcending the beloved and his inevitable desertion, compels the poet to translate erotic abandonment into poetic abandon. The very number of Sappho's be-loveds—Atthis, Anactoria, Gyrinno, Eranna, Gorgo—implies that her confessional poetry is an occasion for experiencing and expressing "an island, a country, a continent, a planet, a world of emotion" which H. D. considers the "spirit of song."[57] For H. D., then, inspiration and abandon-ment (by men) are inextricably intertwined. Both Sappho and lesbianism function as a refuge for her, a protective respite from heterosexual deprivation, not unlike the maternal deities she celebrates in her later epics.

While Sappho's lyrical evocation of Aphrodite triumphs over the pain and confusion of mortal love, H. D.'s lyrical invocation of Sappho testifies to her own artistic survival, which was in large measure due to the companion who took her to the Hellas she associated with Helen, her mother. Indeed, just as H. D. is empowered to find the strength and integrity to create poetry out of the pain of abandonment by turning to the intensity she associates with Sappho, in her life she survived male rejection by returning to Bryher, a woman who quite literally shared her visions: repeatedly, in the autobiographical prose, H. D. describes not only how Bryher encouraged her to maintain the heretical concentration necessary to sustain the mystical experiences that would inform H.D.'s poetic development but also how Bryher occasionally saw such visions "for" H. D.[58] While Bryher herself is perceived as a brother in a poem like "I Said,"[59] their joy—which cannot be spoken "in a dark land"—puts H. D.

55. Rachel Blau DuPlessis, "Romantic Thralldom in H. D.," *Contemporary Literature* 20, no. 2 (Spring 1979): 178–203.

56. H. D., *HERmione* (New York: New Directions, 1981), p. 73; H. D., *Bid Me to Live* (New York: Grove Press, 1960), pp. 51, 55, and 160; H. D., *Tribute* (n. 39 above), p. 16. D. H. Lawrence captures this "frozen" quality in two of his fictionalized portraits of H. D., the priestess of Isis in *The Man Who Died* and Julia in *Aaron's Rod*.

57. H. D., "Notes on Sappho" (n. 44 above).

58. Adrienne Rich has written about the collaborative vision H. D. shared with Bryher on Corfu in "Conditions for Work," in *Working It Out*, ed. Sara Ruddick and Pamela Daniels (New York: Pantheon, 1977), p. xix. See also H. D., *The Gift* (New York: New Directions, 1982), p. 142, and *Tribute* (n. 39 above), pp. 56 and 130; and the discussion of female friendship in Louise Bernikow, *Among Women* (New York: Crown, 1980), pp. 165–92.

59. In Martz, ed. (n. 43 above), pp. 322–25.

in touch with the prophetic wisdom she associates with Hellas (Helen). If, as Susan Friedman has recently argued, Adrienne Rich was drawn to H. D. because of Rich's "desire to recreate a strong mother-daughter bond through her reading,"[60] H. D. herself accomplished such a task through both Bryher and Sappho.

While the dynamic of collaboration impels the linguistic experimentation of both Renée Vivien and H. D., it is analyzed most consciously by Amy Lowell, a poet who used Sappho's images to celebrate her passionate response to her lifelong companion, Ada Russell.[61] In "The Sisters" (1926), a poem explicitly about literary matrilineage, Lowell explores not only the significance of Sappho as the first female lyricist, but also the problematic limitations of precisely the collaboration with Sappho that Vivien and H. D. attempted to sustain. Sappho is first "remembered" by the author of "The Sisters," as she is by Vivien and H. D., at the moment when she is wondering why there are so few women poets: "There's Sappho, now I wonder what was Sappho."[62] Imagining a conversation with Sappho, Lowell supposes that she could surprise Sappho's reticence by flinging her own to the wind in order to learn how this irrepressibly sensuous "sister" came at the "loveliness of [her] words." For Lowell, as for Vivien and H. D., Sappho (who is neither a "Miss" nor a "Mrs.") embodies the elemental grandeur of "a leaping fire" and of "sea cliffs," in direct opposition to a poet like Mrs. Browning who writes "close-shuttered" and "squeezed in stiff conventions." Unlike the Victorian poetess, who is shut up in the parlor of propriety, once again Sappho represents the physical release of wind, sea, and sun as well as the mental relief from reticence associated with the "tossing off of garments" and with female conversation. Yet, for all her attraction to Sappho, Lowell also implies that the gulf between the ancient tenth muse and the modern woman poet may not be negotiable: Lowell does not actually talk with Sappho; she wishes that she could. Imagining what "one might accomplish" in a conversation with Sappho, speculating on Mrs. Browning speculating on Sappho, Lowell describes the first sister of her "strange, isolated little family" as "a burning birch-tree" who wrote like "a frozen blaze before it broke and fell."

Although both Vivien and H. D. reject Ovid's influential version of Sappho leaping suicidally from the Leucadian Cliff because of her unrequited love for Phaon, both seem to agree with Lowell that the intensity of

60. Susan Friedman, "'I go where I love': An Intertextual Study of H. D. and Adrienne Rich" (in this book), p. 112.

61. In *Tendencies in Modern American Poetry* (New York: Macmillan, 1917) Amy Lowell defended H. D.'s poetry, which she also published in three imagist anthologies. See poems like "A Decade" and "Opal" in *The Complete Poetical Works of Amy Lowell* (Boston: Houghton Mifflin, 1955), pp. 217 and 214.

62. In *Complete Poetical Works*, p. 459.

Sappho's passion presages a fall: Vivien literally starves and poisons herself, and H. D. writes a number of poems—most notably "Oread"[63]—asking to be obliterated on the shore by the oncoming waves. Both therefore illustrate what Lawrence Lipking has recently called the "poetics of abandonment."[64] Just as potentially destructive, Lowell implies, is the strangely isolated situation of a classical poet defined not as a powerful foremother but as a vulnerable sister. From this point of view, the hegemonic position of Sappho in female poetic history privileges personal sincerity and passionate ecstasy as the lyricism perceived to be appropriately "feminine." In the context of lesbian literature, moreover, Sappho's preeminence as a model paradoxically sets up a single standard for writers defining themselves by their sexual difference, a standard that personalizes experiences already painfully privatized. Writing colloquially and conversationally, Lowell concludes "The Sisters" by admitting to Sappho and her descendants, "I cannot write like you. . . ." Indeed, all of her older "sisters" leave her feeling "sad and self-distrustful."

A number of contemporary women writers express this same distrust of Sappho. For every Rita Mae Brown, writing "Sappho's reply" to protect those "who have wept in direct sunlight" with Sappho's voice which "rings down through thousands of years," there is a Muriel Rukeyser who, rejecting Sappho "with her drowned hair trailing along Greek waters," calls out, "Not Sappho, Sacco"; or an Ann Shockley who uncovers the implicit racism of elitist Sapphic cults in "A Meeting of the Sapphic Daughters."[65] Equally suspicious, for various reasons, are poets from Sylvia Plath to Robin Morgan: Plath begins her poem "Lesbos" with the satiric line, "Viciousness in the kitchen!" while Carolyn Kizer begins "Pro Femina" by considering the poetic line, "From Sappho to myself," only to remind herself that it is still "unwomanly" to discuss this subject; Susan Griffin writes marginalia to her poems that condemn them as "too much an imitation of Sappho"; and Robin Morgan exclaims defiantly, "get off my back, Sappho. / I never liked that position, / anyway."[66] Perhaps May Sarton explains Lowell's resistance to Sappho best when, placing Sappho

63. In Martz, ed. (n. 43 above), p. 55.

64. Laurence Lipking, "Aristotle's Sister: A Poetics of Abandonment," *Critical Inquiry* 10, no. 1 (September 1983): 61–81, esp. 75.

65. Rita Mae Brown, "Sappho's Reply," in *Lesbian Poetry*, ed. Elly Bulkin and Joan Larkin (Watertown, Mass.: Persephone Press, 1981), p. 136; Muriel Rukeyser, "Poem out of Childhood," *The Collected Poems of Muriel Rukeyser* (New York: McGraw-Hill, 1982), p. 3; Ann Allen Shockley, "A Meeting of the Sapphic Daughters," *Sinister Wisdom* 9 (Spring 1979): 54–59.

66. Sylvia Plath, "Lesbos," in *Ariel* (New York: Harper & Row, 1965), p. 30; Carolyn Kizer, "Pro Femina," in *Psyche*, ed. Barbara Segnitz and Carol Rainey (New York: Dell, 1973), p. 131; Susan Griffin, "Thoughts on Writing," in *The Writer on Her Work*, ed. Janet Sternburg (New York: Norton, 1980), p. 115; Robin Morgan, *Monster* (New York: Vintage, 1972), p. 73.

in the company of Emily Dickinson and Christina Rossetti, she claims, "Only in the extremity of spirit and the flesh / And in renouncing passion did Sappho come to bless." She thus demonstrates that "something is lost, strained, unforgiven" in the woman poet.[67]

These writers may help to explain why Djuna Barnes, the historian of Natalie Barney's salon in Paris, and Gertrude Stein, the center of her own coterie, only refer to Sappho tangentially, even sardonically, although they were themselves in the process of creating what Lillian Faderman calls "Lesbos in Paris."[68] Like Lowell's, their swerve from Sappho seems less a fear of being obliterated by her power as literary foremother, as it would be if Bloom's "anxiety of influence" were in effect, than a fear that Sappho was herself enmeshed in contradictions that threatened to stunt their own creative development. But it is Marguerite Yourcenar's treatment of Sappho that directly engages Lowell's reservations in order to question the dynamic of collaboration with Sappho. Although Yourcenar does not situate herself in the lesbian literary tradition, she, like most of the writers discussed here, was to become an expatriate. Her prose-poem, "Sappho, or Suicide," concludes *Fires*, a work she wrote in French in 1935, four years before her departure for America with Grace Frick, and some four decades before she became the first woman to be elected to the French Academy. Reversing the immigration pattern of her predecessors, Yourcenar dramatizes the tragic demise of the dream of a separate sphere for women and thereby engages the tradition we have been tracing here—as she would, too, in her first translation work, of Virginia Woolf's *The Waves*.

"Just as in ancient times she was a poetess," Yourcenar's Sappho is an impoverished, graying acrobat, a "star" in the circus, a "magnetic creature, too winged for the ground, too corporal for the sky."[69] Because she cannot hold her lovers' bodies very long in "this abstract space bordered on all sides by trapeze bars" (p. 117) and because she is fated to worship in her female lovers "what she has not been" (p. 118), she loses Attys, only to fall in love with a Phaon who seems like a "bronze and golden god" (p. 125). Just at this point of thralldom, she begins to neglect "the discipline of her demanding profession" (p. 125) and, after seeing Phaon dressed up to impersonate Attys, she discovers that he "is nothing more than a stand-in for the beautiful nymph" (p. 126). Sappho's final act can only be

67. May Sarton, "My Sisters, O My Sisters," in *Selected Poems of May Sarton* (New York: Norton, 1978), pp. 192–93.

68. Faderman (n. 1 above), pp. 70–72. Djuna Barnes, in her *Ladies Almanack* (1928; reprint ed., New York: Harper & Row, 1972), invokes "a peep of No-Doubting Sappho, blinked from the Stews of Secret Greek Broth, and some Rennet of Lesbos" in one of its potent portions (pp. 71–72).

69. Marguerite Yourcenar, *Fires*, trans. Dori Katz (1963; reprint ed., New York: Farrar Straus Giroux, 1981), p. 116. Subsequent page references appear parenthetically in the text.

to search above the spotlight in the highest reaches of the arena's canopy for "a place to fall." Climbing the rope of her "celestial scaffold" (p. 127) high above what Sylvia Plath would call in "Lady Lazarus" the "peanut-crunching crowd," Yourcenar's Sappho must make her art itself a form of suicide: unable to lose her balance, "no matter how she tries" (p. 128), she dives, "arms spread as if to grasp half of infinity" (p. 129). Yet "those failing at life run the risk of missing their suicide," and she is ultimately pulled from the mesh nets "streaming with sweat like a drowning woman pulled from the sea" (p. 129).

While such a summary hardly catches the subtle brilliance of Yourcenar's lyrical meditation, it does illustrate how she insists on the lonely isolation of the woman artist who can neither break nor keep "the pact that binds us to the earth" (p. 116). For Yourcenar, clearly, this aerial artist, this light princess with a heavy heart, is a divided creature. Finally, then, Sappho falls not only from lesbianism into heterosexuality, but from the fluid and supple women who were her "sky companion[s]" (p. 117) to the unfortunate girl to whom she can only offer a maternal and tender "form of despair" (p. 121) and ultimately to the "weight of her own sex" (p. 126) when she knows herself to be captivated by a man who infiltrates the image of Attys. As it does so often, the revision of Sappho's story here provides a vision of lesbianism. Like Djuna Barnes in *Nightwood* (1936), Yourcenar sets her fable in the "international world of pleasure-seekers between the wars" (p. xii) to explore the disintegration of the lesbian community, implying that lesbianism can degenerate when it replicates the hierarchy implicit in heterosexual relationships. Her title, "Sappho, or Suicide"—with its ambiguous "or"—seems to assume on the one hand that the woman writer must choose either suicide or a lifeline to Sappho, her personal "sky companion," who is destined to be revived and retrieved over and over again; on the other hand, Sappho's second name may be suicide, for the writer who invokes Sappho's fame may be collaborating with the enemy: she may be destined to associate the grace and daring of her art with the anguish of a fated, if not fatal, eroticism. In either case, by the 1930s, the dream of recovering Mytilene had degenerated for Yourcenar into a circus act. She sees lesbianism as an artful and courageous but doomed effort to defy the laws of gravity.

Yet in *Fires* Yourcenar describes that effort in a mode that preserves the utopian grandeur of the lesbian aesthetic project in the modernist period. For, like her soaring acrobatic Sappho, the writers in this tradition were clearly attempting a radical redefinition of the barren grounds of heterosexual culture in general and of a male-dominated literary history in particular. Their two forms of collaboration—writing "for" the admired precursor and/or writing "for" the beloved other—challenge assumptions about the autonomy/authority of the author and the singularity of the subject: to use the language of Gertrude Stein, the writer who analyzed most fully the mechanisms of her own collaboration with Alice B. Toklas, to be "one" is to know oneself as "two."[70] The act of writing cannot be said to originate from a single source, these writers seem to suggest—as Amy Lowell does, too, when she entitles her sequence of Sapphic poems "Two Speak Together."[71]

Early twentieth-century lesbian poets had to reach back into antiquity to find a literary foremother, whose texts had been falsified by classical legends and partially obliterated by patristic injunctions. Clearly they were empowered to do so by the formation of autonomous female communities that the friendships of nineteenth-century women poets could only adumbrate. It is a striking biographical contrast, the shift from the seclusion of Emily Dickinson or the familial sisterhood of Christina Rossetti or the married life of Elizabeth Barrett Browning, to the bonding between women that we find in the erotic unions and female friendships of Vivien, H. D., Lowell, and Yourcenar, and also of Cather, Sitwell, Woolf, and Barnes. In other words, even as it situates itself on the margins, at the edge, of patriarchal culture, the lesbian tradition may serve as a paradigmatic solution to the problem creativity posed to nineteenth-century women artists.

Finally, then, the sapphistries of Vivien, H. D., Lowell, and Yourcenar demonstrate how feminist modernists found—if only fleetingly—what Woolf had thought lost in Lesbos: artistic predecessors, membership in a group where art is freely discussed and practiced, and freedom of action and experience. Living, all but one of them, *ex patria*, outside of their fathers' country, they represent their exile as a privileged marginalization that paradoxically exposes the homogeneity of heterosexual culture, the heterogeneity of homosexual coupling. Together, they draw on the strength of collaboration in much the way Sappho had prayed for an empowering union with Aphrodite:

> Come, then, loose me from cruelties.
> Give my tethered heart its full desire.
> Fulfill, and, come, lock your shield with mine.
> Throughout the siege.[72]

Department of English
Indiana University

70. The anxiety of becoming the other is dramatized in Stein's depression after the popularity of *The Autobiography of Alice B. Toklas* (1933), her fear that the public was more interested in her personality than in her work; on the other hand, in works like "Ada" and "Lifting Belly," she articulates the pleasure and merriment of speaking for and with the other who is the lover.

71. In *Complete Poetical Works* (n. 61 above), pp. 209–18.

72. Sappho's "Ode to Aphrodite," in *Archilocus Sappho Alkman*, trans. Guy Davenport (Berkeley and Los Angeles: University of California Press, 1980), p. 121.

"I go where I love": An Intertextual Study of H. D. and Adrienne Rich

Susan Stanford Friedman

> I go where I love and where I am loved,
> into the snow;
>
> I go to the things I love
> with no thought of duty or pity.
>
> [H. D., Trilogy]

In *The Dream of a Common Language,* Adrienne Rich initiated her quest for the common language of women by quoting these stern lines from H. D.'s *Trilogy,* an epic that presents the poet's search amid the firebombs of World War II for a regenerative love symbolized by the Goddess.[1] Rich's epigraph is an appropriate beginning for her own volume, which names the love between women as the life-force countering patriarchy's death trip. As an important literary foremother, H. D.'s rich presence nourished the evolution of the younger woman's poetic vision toward the woman-identified, gynocentric feminism of *The Dream of a Common Language.* This essay will explore not only the nature of that influence but also the insights gained through the juxtaposition of their lives and texts.

H. D.'s influence on Rich occurs within the larger context of Rich's compassionate and noncompetitive reading, both as poet and as critic, of

A longer version of this essay will appear in *Reading Adrienne Rich: Reviews and Re-Vision, 1951–1981,* ed. Jane Roberta Cooper (Ann Arbor: University of Michigan Press, 1984). For their insightful criticism of drafts I would like to thank Gertrude Hughes, Rachel Blau DuPlessis, Marilyn Arthur, and Cooper.

1. H. D., *Trilogy* (New York: New Directions, 1973), p. 115, hereafter cited as *T.* Hilda Doolittle (1886–1961), pen name H. D., first published the *Trilogy* in three separate volumes, 1944–46. Adrienne Rich, epigraph in *The Dream of a Common Language: Poems, 1974–1977* (New York: W. W. Norton & Co., 1978), hereafter cited as *DCL.*

Reprinted from *Signs: Journal of Women in Culture and Society* 9, no. 2 (Winter 1983): 228–245.

other women writers. Rich's work expresses a feminist theory of reading in which her drive to create a "common language" that connects women intensifies the underlying identification necessary for any literary influence. Like Virginia Woolf's belief that women writing look back through their literary foremothers, Rich's approach to the female literary tradition operates on a family model of influence in which mothers and daughters seek to transcend the divisive attitudes of patriarchy. This desire to recreate a strong mother-daughter bond through her reading reverses Harold Bloom's theory of the oedipal rivalry between literary fathers and sons.[2] Different women writers have come to represent for Rich the variety of strategies by which women have confronted, subverted, transformed, or been silenced by patriarchy. The result has been essays of critical brilliance, which have not only opened up new perspectives on various women writers but also identified the issues undergoing exploration in Rich's own poetic development. Her early essay on Anne Bradstreet, for example, discusses the movement in Bradstreet's poetry from ordinary "public" poems to extraordinary poems "written in response to the simple events in a woman's life." In her own poetry of the sixties, Rich was herself gradually changing from a poet who had erased all traces of gender to one who explored the dailiness of women's lives, who was beginning to see the links between the personal and the political. Rich's subsequent essays on writers like Emily Dickinson, Woolf, and Judy Grahn mirror her own development and consequently help to demonstrate their areas of influence.[3]

The powerful presence of H. D. in *The Dream of a Common Language* and the brilliant reading that stands behind it are a case in point. Rich has written relatively little about H. D.; her occasional discussions do not seem to explain the central position she gave H. D. by opening a major poetic statement of her lesbian-feminist vision with lines from *Trilogy*. However, a closer look demonstrates that Rich connected H. D. particularly with her own lesbian feminism. Rich has seen in H. D.'s work a comprehensive critique of the violence at the core of patriarchy, a quest for the personal and mythic maternal principle to counter the patriarchy, and a desire to strengthen those bonds between women as friends

2. See Virginia Woolf, *A Room of One's Own* (New York: Harcourt, Brace & World, 1957), p. 101; Harold Bloom, *The Anxiety of Influence* (New York: Oxford University Press, 1973); Betsy Erkkila, "Emily Dickinson and Adrienne Rich: Dreaming of a Common Language" (paper delivered at the Modern Language Association Convention, Los Angeles, December 1982). In "When We Dead Awaken: Writing as Re-Vision" (1971), Rich discussed her introduction to the female literary tradition, inspiring a decade of feminist critics; reprinted in Rich, *On Lies, Secrets, and Silence: Selected Prose, 1966–1978* (New York: W. W. Norton & Co., 1979), hereafter cited as *LSS*.

3. See Rich, "The Tensions of Anne Bradstreet" (1966), in *LSS*, "When We Dead Awaken," pp. 44–47, *Snapshots of a Daughter-in-Law* (New York: Harper & Row, 1963), and *Necessities of Life* (New York: W. W. Norton & Co., 1966). All Rich's essays on women writers have their companion poems.

and lovers that support their emotional, intellectual, and erotic lives. These ideas go to the very heart of Rich's feminist theory as it evolved after the publication of *Diving into the Wreck* (1973); they also constitute the recurring themes of *The Dream of a Common Language*. Her interaction with H. D. consequently reveals the larger process of change in Rich's theoretical and poetic formulations of feminism.[4]

Rich's analysis of patriarchal violence and the symbolic primacy of the mother is encoded in H. D.'s epics more fundamentally than in any other poetic foremother. In her essays Rich explains that she had read H. D.'s imagist poems when she was a young woman, but that in college, "we did not read, and courses in modern poetry still do not teach, H. D.'s epic poem, 'Trilogy,' in which she confronted war, nationalist insanity, the ruin of the great cities, not mourning the collapse of western civilization but turning back for her inspiration to prehistory, to a gynocentric tradition" (*LSS*, pp. 208–9). When Rich began reading *Trilogy*, she was at work on an essay entitled "The Anti-feminist Woman," by her own account the seed for *Of Woman Born*. In this essay, she identified patriarchy as an institution not only unjust to women but dangerous to all forms of life. "I am a feminist," she wrote, "because I feel endangered, psychically and physically, by this society, and because I believe that the women's movement is saying . . . that we can no longer afford to keep the female principle enclosed within the confines of the tight little postindustrial family" (*LSS*, pp. 83–84).[5] Motherhood, as both institution and experience, is at the symbolic center of this "female principle" as Rich identified it. Understanding why feminist theory had to begin by "exploring whatever else woman is and might be besides a body with uterus and breasts," Rich nonetheless stated: "I believe that a radical reinterpretation of the concept of motherhood is required which would tell us, among many other things, more about the physical capacity for gestation and nurture as an intellectual and creative force" (*LSS*, p. 77). Rich called for the use of woman's procreative potential as the symbolic paradigm of the life-force that must counter the "death-spiral" of pa-

4. Rich's discussions of H. D. are in "When We Dead Awaken," pp. 39, 40, "Conditions for Work: The Common World of Women (1976), in *LSS*, pp. 208–9, "Power and Danger: Works of a Common Woman," in *LSS*, pp. 247, 256–57. I have stressed the change in Rich's thought, highlighted by her reading of H. D., but for excellent discussions of important continuities in Rich's poetry, see Albert Gelpi, "Adrienne Rich: The Poetics of Change," in *Adrienne Rich's Poetry*, ed. Barbara Charlesworth Gelpi and Albert Gelpi (New York: W. W. Norton & Co., 1975), pp. 130–47; Judith McDaniel, *Reconstituting the World: The Poetry and Vision of Adrienne Rich* (Argyle, N.Y.: Spinsters, Ink, 1978).

5. Rich, *Of Woman Born: Motherhood as Experience and Institution* (New York: Bantam Books, 1977), p. 257. See also Rich, "The Anti-feminist Woman" (1972), "Motherhood in Bondage" (1976), "Husband-Right and Father-Right" (1977), and "Motherhood: The Contemporary Emergency and the Quantum Leap" (1978), all in *LSS*; Wendy Martin, "From Patriarchy to the Female Principle: A Chronological Reading of Adrienne Rich's Poems," in Gelpi and Gelpi, eds. (n. 4 above), pp. 175–88.

triarchy. Seeking images to describe that force led Rich into a revisionist mythmaking; she used traditions of matriarchy, mother-right, and worship of the great goddesses of gynocentric "periods of human culture which have shared certain kinds of woman-centered beliefs."[6] In this feminist enterprise H. D. served as her model: "H. D. insisted that the poet-as-woman should stop pouring her energies into a ground left sterile by the power-mongers and death-cultists: 'Let us leave / the place-of-a-skull / to them that have made it.' . . . What the male poets were mourning and despairing over had never *been* ours, and, as H. D. saw, what we have yet to create does not depend on their institutions; would in fact rather be free of them" (*LSS*, pp. 256–57).

It was not in H. D.'s epic works that Rich first discovered a theory of the interconnections between sexual polarity and war, and the healing potential of a countering female principle. Rather, Rich's own ideas provided the feminist lens through which she could accurately see the presence of these themes in H. D.'s work. The exploration of violence and the vision of Love embodied in the avatars of female divinity form the motivating purpose and symbolic center of both H. D.'s modernist epics of war, *Trilogy* and *Helen in Egypt*. Refusing to escape to the relative safety of the United States, H. D. lived through two world wars in London. She regarded war as the epitome of the forces that shattered the intersecting personal and public domains of history. Like her friends T. S. Eliot, Ezra Pound, and William Carlos Williams, H. D. expressed the despair for the fragmentation of symbolic systems that characterized modernist poetry. For H. D., as for these other modernists, the experience of modern wastelands initiated a quest poetry of epic proportions whose task was to create new meanings that could replace the inadequacies of the old. But in stark contrast to the male modernists, H. D. directly identified violence as the central force motivating and expressing the disintegration of Western civilization. She brought a woman's perspective both to her analysis of modern fragmentation and to her quest for a vision of regeneration.

Trilogy argues fundamentally that a world at war has lost touch with the female forms of divinity and that the search for life amid death is inextricably linked with the recovery of the Goddess. The poet's alchemical purification of language initiates the necessary re-vision of culture that restores to Venus, whose name has come to stand for "venery," her original and ancient power. "Now polish the crucible," the poet says, "and in the bowl distill" the bitter words. "Set the jet of flame," she continues, "till *marah-mar* / are melted." The poet's alchemy transforms the words into the living jewel: "Star of the Sea, / Mother" (*T*, p. 77).

---

6. Rich, *Of Woman Born*, p. 93; see also pp. 84–109, and *LSS*, pp. 75–77, 80. Rich's poetry of the sixties had attacked the atomic bomb, the Cold War, racist violence, and the Vietnam War. By the early seventies, Rich made the theoretical connection between the culture of violence and patriarchy.

Once restored, the Goddess appears in the poet's dream as the central vision of the epic. Garbed in the shining robes of the Lamb in *Revelation,* H. D.'s "Lady" embodies salvation and rebirth. She resembles the madonna of Christian tradition, even the more powerful Isis of Egyptian religion. But she appears without the Child, the male symbol of salvation. Instead, she carries a "book of life," whose pages are blank, waiting to be inscribed anew by the poet. She is "not-fear, she is not-war," and "she carries over the cult / of the *Bona Dea*" (*T,* pp. 103–4). In H. D.'s poetry of survival, the Lady is indeed the embodiment of the "woman-centered beliefs" that Rich would restore to an endangered planet.

Trilogy does not explicitly link war with patriarchy. But in her profoundly antifascist epic *Helen in Egypt*—written between 1952 and 1954 partially in answer to the fascism in Pound's *Cantos*—H. D. returned to the subject of war and directly connected violence with patriarchy.[7] The narrative retells the story of Helen—the Greek Eve, "Helena, hated of all Greece"—from Helen's perspective. At its beginning, Helen has repressed all memory of her escape from a dull marriage for the springtime love of Paris. But in the course of the meditative "Pallinode" (the first of three sections in the epic), she learns to redefine her own and all women's innocence by understanding the sterility and violence at the core of the masculine ethos. The Trojan War, and by mythological extension, war itself, represents the forces of Death in confrontation with the forces of Love. Forms of the Goddess—Thetis, Aphrodite, Isis, and ultimately Helen—are regenerating Love, "a fountain of water / in that desert" where the "purely masculine iron ring" of war "died of thirst" (*HE,* pp. 48, 51, 55). The "Pallinode" presents H. D.'s view of polarized male and female worlds wherein women express the inner, spiritual powers of Eros, while men command state power and weaponry in a cycle of death from father to son.

Both *Trilogy* and *Helen in Egypt* deeply reinforced the direction of Rich's thought and the urgency of finding poetic expression for her feminist vision. In particular, *Trilogy* and *The Dream of a Common Language* are companion volumes whose echoing ideas and language establish reverberating intertextualities. Experimental polarities, particularly the opposition between love and violence, provide the underlying dualistic structure of both volumes. H. D. contrasts the poet's inner visions of a mystical Love with the cataclysmic war whose bombs have destroyed the London neighborhoods through which the poet walks. Rich broadened the "death-spiral" of patriarchy to include the institutions producing the postmodernist wasteland of hunger, atomiza-

---

7. H. D., *Helen in Egypt* (1961; reprint, New York: New Directions, 1974), hereafter cited as *HE.* For extended discussions of H. D.'s epics and their roots in psychoanalysis and hermetic tradition, see Susan Stanford Friedman, *Psyche Reborn: The Emergence of H. D.* (Bloomington: Indiana University Press, 1981). See also Susan Gubar, "The Echoing Spells in H. D.'s *Trilogy,*" *Contemporary Literature* 19, no. 2 (Spring 1978): 196–218.

tion, and alienation. The city, especially Manhattan, frequently serves as her objective correlative for the spiritual state of mind engendered by a world that devalues the "female principle." "Twenty-One Love Poems," the structural center of the volume, counters the hostile world of the city with the transformative private world of the poet and her lover.[8]

Both H. D. and Rich insist on confronting the worst representations of societal disease. Neither seeks escape to a peaceful countryside that obscures the violence dominating Western culture; both are determined to create an alternative in the very heart of destruction. Their tasks take somewhat different forms, but the dynamic of transformation and the polarity out of which it emerges are similar. H. D., much more the traditional mystic, has apocalyptic visions of the forces of life amid death. As she "crossed the charred portico, / passed through a frame— doorless" after a bombing raid, she saw the "sign" of Astoroth, "sealed with the seal of death": "She set a charred tree before us," the may-apple tree still blooming, though "burnt and stricken" (*T,* pp. 82–87). Rich, not interested in the esoteric traditions so central to H. D.'s mythos, nonetheless searches for life in the rubble of destruction: "We want to live like trees, / sycamores blazing through the sulfuric air / . . . / still exuberantly budding, / our animal passion rooted in the city" (*DCL,* p. 25).

Rooted in the city, scarred by war, H. D. and Rich both found evidence of a regenerating life-force within a desecrated "female princi- ple." The structural center of both volumes is love, an Eros whose in- tangible power is the only force strong enough to confront the tangible power of society. Rich's choice of a quotation from *Trilogy*—"I go where I love and where I am loved"—highlights the centrality of a newly defined Eros in both poets' mythmaking. In philosophical and structural func- tion, Rich's "Twenty-One Love Poems" parallels H. D.'s vision of the "Lady."

Both the *Trilogy* and *The Dream of a Common Language* associate the principle of life with images of matriarchal prehistory, in which, as Rich wrote, the mother's "capacity for gestation and nurture" served as an "intellectual and creative force." H. D.'s presentation of her own Atlantis myth in the final volume of the *Trilogy* has its companion in Rich's re- vision of the matriarchy myth in *The Dream of a Common Language*. Rich's epigraph from *Trilogy* comes from a section in which H. D. images her quest as the flight of the wild geese "who still (they say) hover / over the lost island, Atlantis; / seeking what we once knew." These birds abandon the "foolish circling" of the "steel sharpened on the stone." They know "only love is holy and love's ecstasy" (*T,* pp. 117–22). What follows is "the

8. See Rich, "Not Somewhere Else, But Here," "Upper Broadway," and "Nights and Days" in *DCL* (n. 1 above), pp. 39–46, "Teaching Language in Open Admissions," in *LSS* (n. 2 above), p. 54, and "The Stranger," in *Diving into the Wreck* (New York: W. W. Norton & Co., 1973), with its echoes of T. S. Eliot's "The Love Song of J. Alfred Prufrock."

tale of jars," H. D.'s own parable of the dramatic confrontation between an Arab merchant named Kaspar and Mary Magdalene. Kaspar, suddenly interrupted by Mary's "unseemly" appearance in his shop, is offended by the indecency of her unveiled hair, by her refusal to contain this symbol of woman's power. Annoyed when she ignores his repeated rebuffs, Kaspar represents the patriarchal world that tolerates the presence of women only when their power, especially their sexual power, is controlled by men. Suddenly, however, he sees a grain of light in her hair that reveals a vision of Paradise, the Atlantis lost through man's desecration of woman. This revelation converts Kaspar to a worship of Mary, which in turn makes him worthy to bring a gift to the Child in later years. The epic ends with his journey to Bethlehem, where he kneels not before the Child but before Mary, the primal mother who embodies the related principles of love and life. In the iconography of the *Trilogy*, Atlantis regained is not an actual historical era but rather a state of mind symbolized by the matriarchal woman.[9]

Rich's short poem "Mother-Right" evokes the matriarchal concept as one with symbolic importance whether or not it reflects a historical reality. Echoing J. J. Bachofen's *Mother-Right*, the title identifies the tradition of matriarchy as the intellectual subject underlying the poem's flashing succession of condensed images. The man in the poem stands firmly "planted / on the horizon," regarding the earth as property to be measured out in boundaries (*DCL*, p. 59). The woman, in contrast, is a figure of motion, running with her child in a field, "making for the open." She is attuned to the earth—"The grass   the waters underneath   the air"—rather than possessive of it. The poem, however, represents a critical re-vision of the matriarchal myth. Bachofen envisioned the mothers of matriarchy as soft, fecund, and inert. Progress, he believed, was achieved by the aggressive thrust of men, whose creativity is centered in the brain rather than the womb.[10] Rich's poem, in contrast, creates a matriarchal image of freedom, strength, and motion. Evoking prehistory, revised from a feminist perspective, the poem nonetheless ends with a prevision of the future. At the end, the woman

9. In her unpublished "Autobiographical Notes," H. D. jotted down from her reading that "Schleimann said Atlantis is Crete," that "women [are] equal in Crete," and that Cretan religion was "strangely wild, strangely civilized—mother-nature—lady of wild-wood . . . supreme God herself" (p. 46). The manuscript, along with most of H. D.'s unpublished writings, is at the Beinecke Rare Book and Manuscript Library, Yale University, New Haven, Conn. H. D. fused the three Marys of the New Testament to create her own Atlantis myth. See Friedman, pp. 78, 113–15, 306–7. Rich brought this passage vividly to life in her reading of and commentary on *Trilogy* at an evening "Tribute to H. D." at the Manhattan Theatre Club (May 16, 1978).

10. See Rich's discussion of Bachofen, Robert Briffault, and Erich Neumann in *Of Woman Born*, pp. 70–97. Both Rich and H. D. bracketed questions about the historicity of matriarchy and worked with it as a symbolically necessary concept. H. D., like Rich, revised the androcentric myths of matriarchy; see Friedman, pp. 269–72.

has been trapped within man's boundaries and must recapture her freedom: "the woman   eyes sharpened in the light / heart stumbling   making for the open" (*DCL,* p. 59). Just as H. D.'s "tale of jars" bore a message for a modern world consumed in violence, Rich's poem about an imaginary prehistory ends with an omen for the present. The image of the matriarchal mother stands symbolically at the center of both poets' re-vision of culture.

The emphasis on the mother in the poetry of H. D. and Rich led both women to explore the mother-daughter relationship as an essential element in their reconstitution of an authentic female principle. In *Of Woman Born,* Rich outlined the causes of conflict between mothers and daughters in a phallocentric world and insisted that women must find ways to heal these divisions. Her theoretical argument serves admirably as a description of the mother-daughter dynamic in the life and poetry of H. D., as well as in Rich's own. Striking biographical parallels highlight the pattern they share: in each some failure or flaw in the early relationship between mother and daughter creates a strong desire for reunion with the mother, which in turn motivates the poetic creation of potent mother symbols. Both women were the favorites of professor-fathers who encouraged their intellectual development. Both had mothers named Helen, whom they associated with Helen of Troy, particularly as she is described in Poe's famous poem. Both believed that their mothers' own victimization served as barrier between the mother's frustrated nurturance and the gifted daughter's unsatisfied need. Both ultimately broke away from a life built on pleasing their fathers and turned instead to their mothers to create the major symbols of their mythos. As poets, both engaged in a process whereby the daughter-poet gives birth to the potent mother symbol who then nourishes her art. So H. D. writes about the motivating force behind *Helen in Egypt:* "My older brother was my mother's favorite; I, my father's. But the Mother is the Muse, the Creator, and in my case especially, as my mother's name was Helen." So Rich writes in *Of Woman Born:* "There was, is, in most of us, a girl-child still longing for a woman's nurture, tenderness, and approval, a woman's power exerted in our defense . . . ; it is the germ of our desire to create a world in which strong mothers and daughters will be a matter of course."[11]

From her analysis with Sigmund Freud (1933–34), H. D. learned to link the mother of her desire with the mother symbols of mythological and mystical traditions. Helen Doolittle's favoritism toward her son and subservience to her husband had divided mother from daughter. In her epics, H. D. reconstituted the Goddess to represent the potent mother

11. H. D., *Tribute to Freud* (1956; reprint, Boston: David R. Godine, 1974), pp. 43–44, and *End to Torment* (New York: New Directions, 1979), p. 41; Rich, *Of Woman Born,* pp. 219–20.

denied her by patriarchy. H. D.'s Goddess contains a strongly religious component based on a hermetic mysticism largely absent from Rich's poetry,[12] but Rich's feminist reconstitution of a matriarchal mother-daughter bond—especially in poems like "Sibling Mysteries" and "Transcendental Etude"—has striking parallels with H. D.'s mythos. "Sibling Mysteries," whose title evokes the potent mother of the Eleusinian mysteries as well as the prophet-poet of *Trilogy,* begins with a family constellation in which the poet, her sister, and her mother live within and without "the kingdom of the sons." Their relationships to their fathers and later to their husbands have divided the sisters; the poet asks for her sister's help in establishing a reunion of all three women.

Like H. D., Rich uses the personal dynamics of her own family to represent the structure of woman's oppression in patriarchy. The attempt to communicate with her sister is the prototypical task of sisterhood, and the role of the mother in this search suggests the primacy of a reinstated maternal principle. Like H. D., Rich creates overlapping palimpsests of the personal, political, and mythic: "Remind me how we loved our mother's body":

> and how she sent us weeping
> into that law
> how we remet her in our childbirth visions
>
> erect, enthroned, above
> a spiral stair.
>
> [*DCL,* p. 48]

As in so much of H. D.'s work, memory is a potent, transformative force that the poet uses to reconstitute the family. The poem's hypnotic structure—"Remind me" at the beginning of each section—conjures up memories of disparate shared experiences: hikes, pregnancies, and camping trips. The recollections resonate with imagery of nature as symbol and occasion of ritual. Fire, food, clay, water, art, childbirth, and child rearing evoke both the ritual of women's everyday life and their contributions to civilization in the prehistorical period. While rooted in memories of the everyday, the poet superimposes mythic prehistory onto the common life of women. The "spiral stair" of the enthroned mother echoes *Trilogy's* Mary Magdalene and her "message / through spiral upon spiral of the shell / of memory that yet connects us / with the

---

12. For extended discussions of the mother symbol in H. D.'s analysis, hermetic researches, and poetry, see Friedman; Susan Friedman and Rachel Blau DuPlessis, " 'I Had Two Loves Separate': The Sexualities of H. D.'s *Her,*" *Montemora* 8 (1981): 7–30; Susan Gubar, "H. D.'s Revisionary Theology" (paper delivered at the Modern Language Association Convention, Houston, December 1980).

drowned cities of pre-history" (*T*, p. 156).[13] In the "kingdom of the fathers," the power of the mother, of women, has been contained, defiled, or ignored. Both poets seek to unveil that power by returning to the mother as symbol of creative regeneration.

"Sibling Mysteries" contains a lesbian-feminist dimension in its family constellation that appears to separate Rich from H. D. The poem serves as antitext to the anthropological fantasy of Freud's *Totem and Taboo,* in which he posits oedipal male rivalry as the origin of social organization. Transforming Freud, Rich's poem argues implicitly that the institution of heterosexuality results from the patriarchy's success in separating women from their mothers—in making the mother's flesh "taboo to us." Reunion with the mother, the sensuous mother, accomplished symbolically, fuses what has been sundered and allows women to escape "the kingdom of the fathers." Women have never been "true brides" of the father, and in recovering their love of the mother, they become "brides of each other / under a different law."

For Rich, reconstitution of a mother-centered world is inseparable from lesbianism. In "Transcendental Etude," she calls this desire for the mother "homesickness" and connects it to the "homesickness for a woman, for ourselves." Love of the mother, of the woman-lover, of the woman-self represent different forms of the same woman-identified act. A total love of woman—of body, soul, and intellect—brings wholeness as a woman: "A whole new poetry beginning here" (*DCL,* p. 76). The structure of *The Dream of a Common Language,* a volume of separate poems that nonetheless constitute a whole, embodies Rich's theory that authentic women's relationships in a patriarchy are essentially lesbian.

"Twenty-One Love Poems," first published as a separate work, occupies the center of Rich's three-part volume and explores how "two lovers of one gender" attempt to live, love, and work together, an accomplishment "nothing in civilization has made simple" (*DCL,* p. 31). Rich avoids the reduction of lesbianism to sexuality (as suggested in words like "sexual preference" or "sexual orientation") by portraying a range of concerns about life, work, and relationship in a hostile world.

13. The spiral is a frequent image in *Trilogy* and *Helen in Egypt,* as well as in H. D., *Hermetic Definition* (New York: New Directions, 1972), and *Vale Ave, New Directions* 44 (1982): 18–166. See Gubar's superb discussion of the image in "The Echoing Spells of H. D.'s *Trilogy*" (n. 7 above). Rich's echoing of H. D.'s spiral imagery is a small part of the much larger influence H. D.'s lucid, concise language, stanza structure, and imagist craft had on Rich. In " 'Cartographies of Silence': Rich's *Common Language* and the Woman Writer," *Feminist Studies* 6, no. 3 (Fall 1980): 530–46, Joanne Feit Diehl rightly connected the "conversational" language of *The Dream of a Common Language* with the evolution of Rich's feminist perspective. But see the longer version of this essay for a discussion of H. D.'s formalist influence on Rich. For an analysis of how Rich's ongoing dialogue with the male literary tradition pervades even "Twenty-One Love Poems," see Barbara Gelpi, "Is a Common Language Really a Dream?" (paper delivered at the Modern Language Association Convention, Los Angeles, December 1982).

But "(The Floating Poem, Unnumbered)" in its celebration of two women's lovemaking shows how essential the erotic component of lesbian love is to Rich. *The Dream of a Common Language* argues throughout that woman-identified love, ultimately lesbian in its defiance of the laws of the fathers, makes the poet's work possible.[14]

At first glance, it seems as if Rich's identification of mother love with lesbianism separates her from H. D. While the goddesses in H. D.'s epics represent her mother and symbolize the female principle, they coexist with the poet's search for male forms of divinity as well. As a deeply religious poet, H. D. accepted the fundamental premise of hermetic tradition: the existence of an androgynous Divine One transcending all dualisms but manifest sometimes in female, sometimes in male iconography. The narratives of *Helen in Egypt* and *Hermetic Definition* are profoundly heterosexual, and the only relationships between women that H. D. explores are the bonds between Helen and her twin Clytaemnestra, between Helen and the mother goddesses.

However, a close look at H. D.'s life, her analysis with Freud, and her unpublished texts reveals not only her underlying common bond with Rich but also the light which Rich's probing perspective sheds on H. D.'s texts. According to H. D.'s account, Freud said that she "had not made the conventional transference from mother to father," that her dreams and visions represented her desire for reunion with her mother, the "phallic mother" of the preoedipal stage. Freud believed that the lesbian remains fixated in her early love for her mother, which she projects onto the lovers who serve as mother substitutes. Freud's diagnosis of H. D.'s "mother-fixation" connects her desire for her mother (about which H. D. openly wrote) with lesbianism (about which she did not openly write).[15]

H. D. privately ignored the prescriptive norms that pervaded Freud's concepts of sexuality and his judgment that she could never have been "biologically happy" with a woman. But she fully accepted the theory that her unconscious desire for her mother was projected onto her love for women—predominantly upon Frances Josepha Gregg, the woman with whom she first came to London, and later upon Bryher (Winifred Ellerman), with whom she lived on and off for most of her adult life. *HERmione*, a roman à clef by H. D. only recently published,

14. Rich's related prose discussions of a broadly defined lesbianism include, "It Is the Lesbian in Us . . ." (1976), in *LSS* (n. 2 above), pp. 199–202; "The Meaning of Our Love for Women Is What We Have Constantly to Expand" (1977), in *LSS*, pp. 277–80; Preface, *LSS*, p. 17; "Compulsory Heterosexuality and Lesbian Existence," *Signs: Journal of Women in Culture and Society* 5, no. 4 (Summer 1980): 631–60.

15. See H. D., *Tribute to Freud*, p. 136; Sigmund Freud, "The Psychogenesis of a Case of Homosexuality in a Woman" (1920), in *The Standard Edition of the Complete Psychological Works of Sigmund Freud* (London: Hogarth Press, 1950), 2:202–31, and Freud, "Femininity" (1933), in his *New Introductory Lectures*, trans. James Strachey (New York: W. W. Norton & Co., 1965), pp. 112–35. For extended discussion, see Friedman and DuPlessis.

portrays the conflict she felt between her love for Pound, to whom she was engaged in 1910, and her love for Gregg, about whom she wrote three novels that she left unpublished. Her relationship with Bryher, who "seemed to take the place of Frances," began some ten years later after her initially happy marriage to the poet Richard Aldington had dissolved in betrayal and bitterness.[16] By 1918, Aldington's affairs during his wartime leaves led to H. D.'s decision to go to Cornwall with Cecil Gray, where she became pregnant just about the time she met Bryher. Aldington wrote to her that he did not mind lovers, even "girl-lovers," but her pregnancy meant that she now belonged to Gray. H. D. refused to marry Gray, and her steadily growing relationship with Bryher helped to sustain her as she faced a series of traumatic events: the war-related deaths of her father and brother; her near-fatal illness from the influenza of 1919; the birth of Perdita in March; and Aldington's final, brutal rejection in April.[17] Bryher's love and promise of a trip to Greece saved H. D.'s life. Associated with her love for Bryher, H. D.'s occult visions began on the Scilly Isles where they spent an idyllic month together in July 1919. During their voyage to Greece in 1920, the transcendental experiences continued and finally culminated in a series of light-pictures projected onto the hotel wall in Corfu. H. D. believed that this "writing-on-the-wall" contained the secrets of her artistic destiny. Unsatisfied with her own efforts to translate these omens of creativity, H. D. described the light-pictures to Freud some thirteen years later. *Tribute to Freud* presents a portion of their collaborative interpretation, emphasizing the vision's representation of her desire to be a priestess and her wish to be Moses, the founder of a new religion. But only her private letters to Bryher reveal that Freud regarded her occult experiences, her love for Bryher, and her desire for her mother as interconnected symptoms of "mother-fixation," the motivating impulse of her lesbianism.[18]

The "Lady" of *Trilogy*, Mary Magdalene, and the other forms of the Goddess in H. D.'s poetry have their roots in her discussions with Freud about "mother-fixation," lesbian desire, and visionary experience. To Bryher only she reported on one dream she analyzed with Freud whose

16. H. D., *HERmione* (New York: New Directions, 1981), and *Tribute to Freud,* p. 152. H. D.'s other unpublished novels about Gregg are "Paint It Today" (1921) and "Asphodel" (1922) at the Beinecke Rare Book and Manuscript Library (n. 9 above).

17. H. D. named Gray as Perdita's father in her 1937 divorce papers. See letters from Richard Aldington to H. D., summer 1918, at the Beinecke Rare Book and Manuscript Library. For a detailed account of these events, see H. D., *Bid Me to Live (a Madrigal)* (Redding Ridge, Conn.: Black Swann Books, 1983); and Susan Friedman, " 'Remembering Shakespeare always, but remembering him differently': H. D.'s *By Avon River*," *Sagetrieb,* vol. 2, no. 2 (1983).

18. See H. D.'s letters to Bryher written while she was in analysis with Freud, March 1–June 2, 1933, and October 30–December 2, 1934, at the Beinecke Rare Book and Manuscript Library.

symbols were a major source for *Trilogy*. In the dream, she, Bryher, and a young girl went out to the country at night and saw a "giant moon, bigger than the sun." The moon was rainbow colored, gradually projecting the image of a "mystic" woman "draped in flowing rainbow coloured robes, seated like a madonna in a curved frame. But she was not Madonna in that sense, she was Greek, she was Artemis, yet she was pregnant." The dream, which revealed a "band of sisters" worshiping the "mother in heaven," demonstrated that "I had, in the uc-n [unconscious] completely turned about to a homo layer."[19] In a poem she wrote during this period but refused to publish, H. D. further makes the connection between lesbianism and a woman-centered religion necessary for the world's survival. "The Master" begins in worship of Freud, but while she never denies this reverence, the poet explores the dimensions of her "anger with the old man," with his "man-strength" and "mysteries." *"Woman is perfect,"* she announces, not the castrated male of psychoanalytic theory. That perfection, sufficient unto itself, is erotically based and, by extension, serves as the center of a new religion in which a woman named Rhodocleia is "that Lord become woman"—that is, the Divine taking female form. Section 5 of "The Master" parallels Rich's "Floating Poem" in function:

> She is a woman,
> yet beyond woman,
> yet in woman
> her feet are the delicate pulse of the narcissus bud,
>
> . . . .
>
> there is purple flower
> between her marble, her birch-tree white
> thighs,
> or there is a red flower,
> there is a rose flower
> parted wide
> as her limbs fling wide in dance
>
> . . . .
>
> for she needs no man,
> herself
> is that dart and pulse of the male,
> hands, feet, thighs,
> herself perfect.[20]

19. H. D. to Bryher, May 26, 1933, at the Beinecke Rare Book and Manuscript Library.

20. H. D., "The Master," *Feminist Studies* 7, no. 3 (Fall 1981): 407–16, esp. 411–12. For extended discussion, see Rachel Blau DuPlessis and Susan Friedman, " 'Woman Is Perfect': H. D.'s Debate with Freud," *Feminist Studies* 7, no. 3 (Fall 1981): 417–30.

H. D.'s epics are not explicitly lesbian in the way that the poem she suppressed defiantly is. But the goddesses in *Trilogy* and *Helen in Egypt* are encoded versions of H. D.'s exploration of her love for women and her belief that women embody a principle of life which the violent world of patriarchy must learn to absorb and revere. Rich, familiar only with the coded epics, was nonetheless attuned to aspects of H. D.'s work that have become definitively known only after the publication of *The Dream of a Common Language*. It was this sensitivity, I believe, that led Rich to highlight H. D.'s visions of Corfu with Bryher at her side as a model of how women working together empower each other and "give courage at the birth throes of one another's insight."[21]

The aspects of H. D.'s life and work that Rich has rejected reveal as much about Rich's development as the issues to which she was so acutely attuned. Rich concluded her discussion of H. D.'s and Bryher's empowering bond at Corfu with a warning against the trap male mentors pose for women. Such a mentor can give only the "illusion of power," possible success "in the common world of men. But he has no key to the powers she might share with other women" (*LSS*, pp. 209–10). Rich did not explicitly direct her comments to H. D., but given the significance of male mentors and lovers for H. D., Rich certainly might have had her in mind. "The Master," which substitutes H. D.'s own gynocentrism for Freud's androcentrism, nonetheless remains a poem that testifies to his genius and to his continuing importance to her. Other men served as her mentors and companions as well, among them Pound, Aldington, D. H. Lawrence, Gray, and Kenneth Macpherson. Her love for these men often entangled her in an artistic, erotic, and religious intensity that equalled her involvements with women.

She wrote to Bryher that she "was that all-but extinct phenomena [*sic*], the perfect bi-[sexual]," and she was grateful to Freud for teaching her to accept that she "had two loves separate."[22] Rachel Blau DuPlessis has argued convincingly that H. D.'s conflicted relationships with her male lovers and companions vitalized her art, particularly as it was expressed in the long poems of the fifties. Entrapped by "romantic thralldom," the "scripts" of conventional heterosexual romance, H. D. repeatedly experienced her involvements with men as a pattern that began with attraction, moved to a companionship with love and work entwined, and ended with male rejection and betrayal. In her poetry, DuPlessis concludes, H. D. transformed the actual male suitor, whose love had been experienced as an attack, into a spirit twin to her own soul with whom she transcends the patriarchal divisions of male and female, vic-

21. Rich, *LSS* (n. 2 above), pp. 208–9. Among the many critics who have written about H. D.'s Corfu visions, Rich is the only person who has stressed the importance of Bryher's presence.

22. H. D. to Bryher, November 24, 1934, at the Beinecke Rare Book and Manuscript Library; H. D., "The Master," p. 409.

tim and victimizer.[23] Within this context, the poet invokes the protection of the Goddess to fortify herself as she makes her forays into the dangerous territory of heterosexuality.

H. D. never gave up the hope of finding in her life or creating in her art the ideal male companion, converted by her influence to a humanism based in a reverence for life symbolized by the Goddess. In *Helen in Egypt,* the pervasive imagery of twins expresses that desire, as does the transformation of Achilles from a warlord into a worshiper of Eros. The myth of Isis, the goddess with whom Helen most deeply identifies, infuses the human quests of Helen and Achilles. In Egyptian religion, Isis is the twin, lover, and savior of Osiris. After Set dismembers Osiris, Isis travels the world over in search of her lost twin-husband. Her magic revives the scattered limbs of Osiris; her reunion with him results in the birth of Horus and the rule of Isis and Osiris as a single regenerative power. In H. D.'s poetic recapitulation of the myth, Achilles' love for Helen leads to the death of the warlord and the birth of the "new mortal," her Osiris. They come to realize that "it was God's plan / to melt the icy fortress of the soul, / and free the man" (*HE,* pp. 51–52). Reflecting concepts of androgyny H. D. adapted from both esoteric tradition and psychoanalysis, this liberation of Achilles from the masculine ethos and Helen's concurrent quest for wholeness represent H. D.'s desire to transcend all dualisms, especially the polarity of male and female. The birth of their child Euphorian, whose gender is not specified, symbolizes that desire for transcendence. Taken as a whole, the complex epic begins by demonstrating the separation of male and female worlds, moves to an eloquent revaluation of woman as Eros, explores the oppositions of Eros and Thanatos within all individuals, and concludes with symbolic affirmations of transcendence.[24]

Rich has never commented directly on H. D.'s search for an androgynous male lover-companion or her belief in men's potential for transformation. But evidence suggests that Rich carried on a silent debate with H. D. that helped to widen the gap between the feminist humanism of *Diving into the Wreck* and the lesbian feminism of *The Dream of a Common Language.* In the early seventies, Rich used the concept of a feminist androgyny to demonstrate the failure of patriarchy and to envision the transcendence of patriarchal values open to women and men.

23. Rachel Blau DuPlessis, "Romantic Thralldom in H. D.'s *Helen in Egypt,*" *Contemporary Literature* 20, no. 2 (Summer 1979): 178–203, and "Family, Sexes, Psyche: An Essay on H. D. and the Muse of the Woman Writer," *Montemora* 6 (1979): 137–56; Friedman and DuPlessis (n. 12 above). Janice Robinson's theory that H. D. remained obsessed with Lawrence for forty years is not supported by the manuscripts that testify to the importance of many other men in her life (see *H. D.: The Life and Work of an American Poet* [New York: Houghton Mifflin Co., 1982]). For an excellent discussion of the presence of these men in her poetry, see Albert Gelpi, "Hilda in Egypt," *Southern Review* 18, no. 2 (April 1982): 233–50.

24. See Friedman (n. 7 above), pp. 273–96.

"The Stranger" presented the gender-free poet as the "androgyne," "the living mind you fail to describe / in your dead language." The sex of the diver in "Diving into the Wreck" is carefully left unspecified, so that both women and men could identify with the search for the "she-he," the potentially androgynous self wrecked by a sexually polarized world. In "When We Dead Awaken," Rich called eloquently for the birth of woman, but she also envisioned the necessity and the potential for men's transformation: "One thing I am sure of: just as woman is becoming her own midwife, creating herself anew, so man will have to learn to gestate and give birth to his own subjectivity."[25]

By the time *The Dream of a Common Language* took shape, Rich no longer envisioned the transformation of men, much less associated childbirth imagery with their potential changes. In reprinting "When We Dead Awaken" in *On Lies, Secrets, and Silence,* she left out her earlier call for man's rebirth and rewrote her concluding paragraphs to emphasize the continuing sterility of men. Paralleling this change is her repudiation of the concept of androgyny; section 13 of "Natural Resources" opens with the declaration: "There are words I cannot choose again: *humanism   androgyny*" (*DCL,* p. 66). This poem, whose fourteen sections create a symbolic mythos of feminist quest, explores at length her rejection of androgyny and her advocacy of a separatist lesbian feminism. The separatism of *The Dream of a Common Language* is not a simplistic separatism that involves withdrawing "from the immense, burgeoning diversity of the global women's movement," which Rich describes as tempting but ultimately too narrow to accomplish the broader goals of lesbian feminism (*LSS,* p. 227). Rather, it emerges out of Rich's belief that women must devote all their creative energies to one another.[26] Man's all-consuming need, the poem argues, has required "women's blood for life / a woman's breast to lay its nightmare on" and has resulted in "women stooping to half our height" (*DCL,* pp. 63–64). Women must develop the "impatience" of the spider's rebuilding, as they "make and make again" a new way of being. Such impatience characterizes the poet's ironic interchange in section 4 of "Natural Resources" with the insensitive male interviewer (*DCL,* p. 61), and contrasts with the curiosity about masculine consciousness expressed in the early version of "When We Dead Awaken."

The poet's exchange with the interviewer leads her to reflect in the

25. Rich, *Diving into the Wreck* (n. 8 above), pp. 19, 22–24, "When We Dead Awaken," in Gelpi and Gelpi, eds. (n. 4 above), p. 98, and "Toward a Woman-centered University" (1973–74), in *LSS* (n. 2 above), p. 141.

26. "True separatism," Rich wrote, "has yet to be defined" (*LSS,* p. 229). For other discussions of separatism, see *LSS,* pp. 223–30, "Compulsory Heterosexuality" (n. 14 above), and *Of Woman Born* (n. 5 above), pp. 183–217. For Rich's more recent thoughts on separatism, see "Notes for a Magazine: What Does Separatism Mean?" *Sinister Wisdom* 18 (1981): 83–91.

following four sections of the poem on the experiences that have led to her present stance. The argument and imagery of these sections directly echo *Helen in Egypt* and strongly suggest that Rich's silent debate with H. D. was of central importance to her change in perspective. The poet reflects that the main diversion of women's energies from themselves has been their search for "the man-who-would-understand, / the lost brother, the twin." Echoing the image of the twin so central to H. D.'s epic, the poet remembers that "It was never the rapist: / it was the brother, lost, / the comrade / twin whose palm / would bear a lifeline like our own" (*DCL*, p. 62).[27] In other ways as well Rich's imagery carries recollections of Helen's soldier-lover, Achilles, whose motif is the light-ning, whose dangerous "flash" Helen must transform to love (*HE*, p. 100). Rich's "comrade / twin" is "decisive, arrowy, / forked-lightning of insatiate desire," the "fellow-creature / with natural resources like our own" (*DCL*, p. 62). "For him did we leave our mothers, / deny our sisters, over and over?" she asks. "Did we invent him, conjure him?" Rich's question hovers over H. D.'s troubled relationships with men like Pound and Aldington and the brilliant poems she constructed out of those experiences.

* * *

The exchange between Rich and H. D. is a literary dialogue of resonance and dissonance that highlights essential elements of each poet's work. In H. D.'s poetic critique of culture, Rich found confirma-tion for her own growing analysis of the connections between worldwide violence and the oppression of women. H. D.'s matriarchal mythos and her celebration of woman in the form of mother symbols charted for Rich a pathway that connected the female iconographies of tradition and the personal dimensions of women's love for other women. For both poets, the mother as symbol and living presence is central for woman's rebirth and for the regeneration of civilization. Whether highly coded or directly affirmed, love for the mother in both poets is part of a healing self-love and a sustaining lesbian love of other women. Here, however, in the very center of similarity, the two poets part ways.

H. D.'s regeneration of woman as symbol and self took place within a context that included men as mentors, lovers, and companions. She never gave up her search for "the-man-who-would-understand" (*DCL*, p. 62), for the masculine forms of divinity that she balanced with the woman symbols he had resurrected. In contrast, the growth of Rich's lesbian feminism coincided with her abandonment of the radical humanism that pervaded her poetry during the sixties and culminated

27. Rich may also have had in mind Sylvia Plath's lines in "Daddy": "Every woman adores a Fascist, / The boot in the face," *Ariel* (New York: Harper & Row, 1965), p. 50.

in the androgyny of *Diving into the Wreck*. Unlike the Lady's rainbow that affirms the Divine One in H. D.'s *Trilogy*, the rainbow at the conclusion of "Natural Resources" holds out the promise of transformation only in the bonding of women through history: "I have to cast my lot with those / who age after age, perversely, / with no extraordinary power, / reconstitute the world."

Department of English and Women's Studies Program
University of Wisconsin—Madison

Comment on Friedman's " 'I go where I love': An Intertextual Study of H. D. and Adrienne Rich"

Adrienne Rich

A faith in the regenerating possibilities of feminist criticism leads me to respond in this forum to Susan Friedman's essay (pp. 111–28). For my difficulties with it come to more than a personal objection to a particular treatment of my work; they throw light, I believe, on some central problems of feminist criticism, lesbian-feminist writing, and the practice of both in a climate both misogynous and homophobic. Although I am responding to specific elements in Friedman's essay, the overall problems are by no means Friedman's only.

First let me say that I have great respect for Friedman's scholarship and for her sensitively attuned ear for H. D.'s words. But H. D. is dead; there are archives of her work, boxes of notes and letters and unpublished manuscripts, besides the published books, to document the journeys of her mind. One obvious question raised by Friedman's essay is, How does the feminist critic approach the work of a writer who is still alive, able to feel the air on her skin, who continues to argue, experiment, learn, create? How might this be different from the study of someone whose lifework is ended?

Friedman's essay centers on *Dream of a Common Language* ([New York: W. W. Norton & Co., 1978], hereafter cited as *DCL*) because she sees in it the influence of H. D.; her announced intent is to "explore not only the nature of that influence but also the insights gained through the juxtaposition of their lives and texts" (p. 111). To note in *DCL* particular connections with H. D.'s work is certainly appropriate; to write as if it were my last, or even latest book, let alone my final word as a poet, is to encapsulate it and drastically skew its possible meanings, the very nature of its creation. Friedman does not even mention the existence of *A Wild Patience Has Taken Me This Far* (New York: W. W. Norton & Co., 1981)—a book that is both continuous with and in some ways contradictory to *DCL;* I am surprised by this silence.

About the importance of H. D.'s epic poems to me in the period when I was writing *DCL*, there is no question—to me, and to other lesbian-feminist poets, including Judy Grahn, Marilyn Hacker, and Susan Sher-

Reprinted from *Signs: Journal of Women in Culture and Society* 9, no. 4 (Summer 1984): 733–738.

man. As to Friedman's second objective, I believe that her method jeopardizes her insights, leaving the impression of an unstated motivation, a hidden agenda. Her concluding paragraph, for instance, explicitly contrasts "H. D.'s regeneration of woman as symbol and self . . . within a context that included men as mentors, lovers, and companions" with "the growth of Rich's lesbian feminism [as it] coincided with her abandonment of the radical humanism that pervaded her poetry during the sixties and culminated in the androgyny of *Diving into the Wreck*" (pp. 127–28). Friedman then underlines a contrast between "the Lady's rainbow that affirms the Divine One in H. D.'s *Trilogy*" and the rainbow at the conclusion of "Natural Resources" that "holds out the promise of transformation only in the bonding of women" (p. 128).

There is, immediately, a problem of terminology. Like many other feminists, I have, in the poem and elsewhere, questioned the terms "androgyny" and "humanism" and found them inadequate to feminist discourse because of both their history and their false inclusiveness. An entire issue of *Women's Studies* (2, no. 2 [1974]), with articles by Catharine Stimpson, Barbara Charlesworth Gelpi, Cynthia Secor, and others, was devoted to a critique of the concept of androgyny; Gelpi in particular showed its dubious historical provenance. "Humanism" has also been widely criticized as a false universal, one that especially fails to address the racial, sexual, and class differences among humans and the dehumanization of the bearers of those differences in white male Western tradition.[1]

Friedman passes over such discussions and sticks to "androgyny" and "humanism" as positive terms, treating my rejection of them as an individualistic, man-excluding choice deriving from what she calls my "lesbian separatism." In this connection, she footnotes but does not discuss my "Notes" on separatism in *Sinister Wisdom* (18 [1981]: 83–91), nor does she ever define separatism herself. The term, however, given the valances she accords to "androgyny" and "humanism," is clearly negative for her. Whether, and how, it is an accurate term as applied to my work is left unexplored. H. D., because she "never gave up her search for 'the man-who-would-understand'" (p. 127) even at the price of "romantic thralldom" (Rachel DuPlessis's term), scores points over AR, who has abandoned the "transcendent" ideology of "radical humanism." I deplore this sad and truly unnecessary competition and the oversimplifications it induces.

A greater problem, I think, than terminology, is the critic's isolating of the artist from her political and historical matrix. "Natural Resources" is a poem about how you live in the universe of male violence if you are a

---

1. See Marilyn Frye's discussion of "humanism" in *The Politics of Reality: Essays in Feminist Theory* (Trumansburg, N.Y.: Crossing Press, 1983), pp. 43–44, 66 ff.

woman, how this affects your vision of men, what gentleness means in such a world, how you stop being a victim, and how you think about the future—including who your allies will be. The nature of patriarchal violence is indeed a theme that H. D. had pursued long before, and it is absolutely true that her poetry—and her spirit—were with me when I was writing that poem. But I was writing, as H. D. was not, out of a movement that has described and analyzed male violence politically, not only as it expresses itself in war, but also as it is manifested in the bed, the workplace, mental institutions, the international traffic in women, media imagery, sexual surgery, and elsewhere.

Friedman has sensitively overheard the "silent dialogue" I was having with H. D. as I wrote. But the veiled scenario that seems to be her subtext leads to a misreading of the ending of "Natural Resources." Why does she assume that, when describing those with whom I "cast my lot," I mean only women? Does she believe that the mind that has contemplated the range of male violence against women would become inexorable, "close the valves of her attention / like stone," as Dickinson said in another context? But there are surely other possibilities besides "romantic thrall-dom" or the search for a male muse, on the one hand, and the rejection of all men forever simply on biological grounds, on the other. To eschew completely a romantic, mythic, unexamined relation to men is to open oneself, rather, to values that romantic thralldom and unexamined heterosexuality conceal. Placing women at the center allows women for the first time to see "from the center"; this was a necessary aspect of the writing of *DCL* and is a necessary aspect of lesbian feminism. Nonetheless, poems of mine do extend—from a strongly lesbian core—a "silent invitation" to men to participate in transformative action; and there are men who hear it.[2]

From her skewed reading of my work, Friedman derives some mistaken assumptions. It is the lifeline in the palm—male or female—that can be "decisive, arrowy / forked-lightning of insatiate desire," *not* the "comrade-twin" himself. She quotes from my speech at the New York 1977 Gay Pride March (and badly misconstrues what she quotes), then interpolates words from that speech with words from the poem "Natural Resources" as if they were the same kind of work. A political speech is not the same as a poem. It is given for a specific audience, under particular historical pressures. I tried to describe these in the introductory note to that speech

2. There is undoubtedly a real difference between searching for an "ideal male companion" and exchanging certain resources or making common cause with men who also endure stigmatized identities and who are also determined to make the connections. I am indebted to the work of black lesbian feminists, especially Barbara Smith, for the concept of "simultaneity of oppression." See, e.g., Smith's " 'Fractious, Kicking, Messy, Free': Feminist Writers Confront the Nuclear Abyss," *New England Review and Bread Loaf Quarterly* 5, no. 5 (Summer 1983): 582.

when it was reprinted in *On Lies, Secrets, and Silence*.[3] Friedman does not acknowledge any political context for this speech; she wants it to support her reading of "Natural Resources." She does not consider the political context of the poem "Natural Resources" at all; she writes as if "the violence at the core of patriarchy" were an idea in the head of H. D. or AR. She erases—as they are constantly erased—both the social reality of male violence against women and the movement of women that opposes it.

In like manner, she quotes selectively from my prefatory essay to *Working It Out*. Any attention to context should make it obvious that I am speaking of the powerful male professional mentor "who guides and protects his female *student or* colleague";[4] I am extending a caution against tokenization and false assimilation. I am not warning against reading men's books, learning whatever men have to teach, but against the dangers of identifying with the male mentor to the exclusion of other women. I had in mind the many warnings about the limits of male mentoring inscribed throughout that book, not by my hand alone.

To isolate what I write from a context of other women writing and speaking feels like an old, painfully familiar critical strategy. Phallic criticism has always tried to isolate the feminist, package or condemn her as an oddity or a crazy, thus disempowering both the artist and her movement. Feminist criticism cannot afford to imitate this strategy. It has far more radical work to do.

In unified, traditional communities, in which art is an extension of living, there may be no need for criticism. But in a profoundly fragmented society such as capitalist patriarchy, in which diverse ancient communities still exist as residues but in which art and social life are deliberately severed, criticism bears an immense responsibility. Without a criticism that illuminates context, art carries an intolerable burden of self-explication. As I write tonight Ronald Reagan has been saying across the electronic media that motherhood and women's piety are the major source for hope in the world and that prayer in the schools should be the primary focus of the women of America. Art that opposes dominant values, that makes visible what is hidden, that addresses an extreme and usually veiled injustice, deserves the illumination of a criticism that fully reckons with the social factors impinging on both artist and critic. If Susan Friedman feels that my work is narrowed and limited by placing women at the center, that it fails in compassion, that it has become a closed and static

3. Adrienne Rich, "The Meaning of Our Love for Women Is What We Have Constantly to Expand," in *On Lies, Secrets, and Silence: Selected Prose, 1966–1978* (New York: W. W. Norton & Co., 1979), pp. 223–30.

4. Adrienne Rich, "Conditions for Work: The Common World of Women," in *Working It Out*, ed. Pamela Daniels and Sara Ruddick (New York: Pantheon Books, 1977), pp. xiv–xxiv.

system, I think she ought to say so and try to prove it carefully. If she does not, it is important that she make clear what she *is* saying.

With the emergence, in this contemporary wave of feminism, of a greater diversity of women writing than ever before; with the increased visibility particularly of Third World/Jewish-identified/working-class/lesbian writers, in their several ways challenging false universals, more and more is asked of the feminist critic. She is or may be the mediator between the living and the dead, between writers of color and white writers (and their readers), between lesbian writers and heterosexual writers and readers, between writers and readers of the expanding and mixed cultures of a global society. But to fulfill this potential, I think she, like the imaginative writer, will have to recognize the kinds of bias she brings to her task, based on ignorance, old indoctrination, privilege, the limits of her training. She will not posit a world saner and more harmonious than it is. Her work will call her to educate herself not only about the Kaballah or the Gnostic Gospels but also—for example—about South African women's organizations and the system of apartheid that surrounds them; gay history; the connections between militarism and women's oppression. Feminism really means the end of that world in which any poet or critic can draw safe lines within which we will evoke what is already familiar. "She carries a book but it is not / the book of the ancient wisdom." What I said in a speech in 1977, I still believe: "The meaning of our love for women is what we have constantly to expand."[5]

Montague, Massachusetts

5. H. D., *Trilogy* (New York: New Directions, 1973), p. 103; Rich, "The Meaning of Our Love . . . ," p. 230.

Reply to Rich

Susan Stanford Friedman

I am delighted to have Adrienne Rich confirm my central point that H. D.'s epic poems were important to her while she was writing *The Dream of a Common Language*, even that "Natural Resources" contains a "silent dialogue" with H. D. Although I see feminist criticism today as a fertile field, not a dead one in need of regeneration, I welcome Rich's views on future directions because of her vital role in its development. But Rich requires, I believe, a totality of analysis and context that would paralyze a feminist critic into silence, certainly the critic confined to the length of a journal article.

Reprinted from *Signs: Journal of Women in Culture and Society* 9, no. 4 (Summer 1984): 738–740.

First, no single essay can fully reckon with all "the social factors impinging on both artist and critic." Feminist criticism must be able to focus discussion on specific topics without facing an impossible imperative to recreate an entire historical context. A comprehensive understanding should permeate our focused exploration of a given aspect of women's struggles, strategies, and achievements. It was precisely this understanding and my commitment to feminism that led me to see H. D. and Rich as powerful voices identifying violence as the core of patriarchy and posing woman-centered, lesbian visions as alternatives. I chose to focus the article directly on one kind of significant context: the female precursors who provide for women writers a validating family of literary women. I did not isolate Rich from the context of women writing; I celebrated it. I did not erase the social realities of oppression and revolution; I made H. D.'s and Rich's shared views on patriarchy the centerpiece of their literary bond.

Second, Rich demands a comprehensiveness for feminist criticism that may be the objective of critical biographers but is a sheer impossibility for the writer of a critical essay. No article can encompass a writer's entire canon in all its changing vitality, let alone give the feel of the air on a living writer's skin. While focusing on the resonances between H. D.'s *Trilogy* and *The Dream of a Common Language*, I pointed out the dynamic evolution in Rich's work from *Diving into the Wreck* (1973) to *The Dream of a Common Language* (1978), an argument that implicitly suggests a continuance of change, although it was beyond the essay's scope to address her views after 1978. Rich's response, however, testifies to the special vulnerability and courage of the poet—not only because of the raw exposure that art requires (Rich's new volume *Sources* [Woodside, Calif.: Heyeck Press, 1983] is a powerful testament to that) but also because a poem "fixes" a poet in inadequate words that give us the illusion that we know more of the living woman than the partial reflection on the page.

More disturbing than Rich's prescriptions for feminist criticism are her unsupported accusations that I had a "hidden agenda" to set up the two women in a "competition" in which H. D. "scores points" over Rich, whose work is characterized as "narrow" and "limited." I used no such words, made no such judgments, implied no such homophobic "subtexts." I took no sides in favor of "androgyny" or "humanism." I used those terms because Rich herself used them positively in the early seventies and then rejected them in "Natural Resources" and elsewhere. H. D., on the other hand, continued to work with the concept and imagery of androgyny. Rich is correct to insist that her rejection of "androgyny" belongs in the context of the extensive androgyny debate, and I regret that my footnotes to that effect were cut out of the longer version of the essay. But even without the debate noted, I made no suggestion that H. D.'s search for the "comrade-twin" is superior to Rich's lesbian feminism. Indeed, I gave Rich the "last word" in the article and implied that

H. D. might have broken through the cycle of "romantic thralldom" if she had been able to live out her lesbian self more fully. As for not defining "separatism," who has done so satisfactorily to date? Not even Rich herself, whose "Notes for a Magazine: What Does Separatism Mean?" (which appeared after I wrote my essay) is an important series of meditative questions implying but never directly stating that separatism *may* not incorporate a commitment to ending all forms of oppression.

My reading of "Natural Resources" differs from Rich's. In suggesting that this poem holds out a "silent invitation" to men to change, Rich may well be reading the poem through the lens of what lesbian feminism has come to mean to her in recent years. She has, for example, agreed with other lesbian feminists "that women must re-think issues such as racism, class, imperialism, from a lesbian/feminist center."[1] Not only must feminists understand women's diversity, she has argued, but also all forms of oppression should be our concern. I could not agree with Rich more profoundly. While "Hunger" and "IV" in *The Dream of a Common Language* foreshadowed this later concern, I do not think that "Natural Resources" did. This poem about women's spiritual quest for the mother lode in the mines of patriarchy rejects not only the "nightmare" created by violent men but also the "phantom of the man-who-would-understand." There never was such a "comrade-twin," she wrote in 1977, and she "wearily" told the insensitive male interviewer that she could indeed imagine "*a world where men are absent.*" Perhaps from Rich's current lesbian-feminist perspective, she would not change the ending of her essay "When We Dead Awaken," as she did when she reprinted this 1971 essay in 1979. Without notation, she deleted her "curiosity" about men's potential for change and substituted a naming and celebration of women's bonding.[2]

No poem ever produced a "definitive" reading. Although a poet's reading of her poem is always especially welcome, Rich's attack on my reading of "Natural Resources" demonstrates an unwillingness to grant a plurality of interpretations. In spite of her theoretical recognition of women's diversity, she discredits my reading by implying that it is not feminist. Such questioning of a feminist critic's feminism, however indirect, is a kind of tyranny in itself; it is a type of attack that has repeatedly divided feminists at a time when we need to find strength together in the very heart of our diversities.

Department of English and Women's Studies Program
University of Wisconsin—Madison

1. Adrienne Rich, "Notes for a Magazine: What Does Separatism Mean?" *Sinister Wisdom* 18 (1981): 83–91.

2. Adrienne Rich, "When We Dead Awaken: Writing as Re-Vision," in *On Lies, Secrets, and Silence: Selected Prose, 1966–1978* (New York: W. W. Norton & Co., 1979), pp. 33–49.

Displacing the Phallic Subject: Wittig's Lesbian Writing

Namascar Shaktini

Adieu continent noir de misère et de peine adieu villes
anciennes nous nous embarquons pour les îles brillantes
et radieuses pour les vertes Cythères pour les Lesbos
noires et dorées. [MONIQUE WITTIG]
[Farewell black continent of misery and suffering
farewell ancient cities we are embarking for the brilliant
and radiant islands for the green Cytheras for the black
and gilded Lesbian Islands.]

Though Monique Wittig's first two books, *L'opoponax (The Opoponax)* and
Les guérillères (Les Guérillères), have been the focus of considerable attention, her last two, which have the word "lesbian" in the title, have been
relatively ignored. The present essay analyzes one of these neglected
works, *Le corps lesbien,*[1] which I consider an important contribution to the
epistemological revolution now being carried out by feminist thought,
especially the aspect of the revolution that attacks the semiological
problem of "phallogocentrism." Wittig's reorganization of metaphor
around the lesbian body represents an epistemological shift from what
seemed until recently the absolute, central metaphor—the phallus.[2]

1. Monique Wittig, *Le corps lesbien* (Paris: Minuit, 1973), hereafter cited as *Lcl;* the
book appeared in the United States as *The Lesbian Body,* trans. David Le Vay (New York:
Morrow, 1975), hereafter *TLB;* a paperback ed. was published by Avon-Bard in 1976. Also
neglected is the book she coauthored with Sande Zeig, *Brouillon pour un dictionnaire des
amantes* (Paris: Grasset & Fasquelle, 1976); a translation by the authors was entitled *Lesbian
Peoples Material for a Dictionary* (New York: Avon, 1979).
2. See Jacques Derrida's usage of the term "phallogocentrisme" in "Le Facteur de la
vérité," *Poétique* 21 (1975): 96–147. For a discussion of this term, see Namascar Shaktini,
"The Problem of Gender and Subjectivity Posed by the New Subject Pronoun *j/e* in the
Writing of Monique Wittig" (Ph.D. diss., University of California at Santa Cruz, 1981), pp.
1–103.

Reprinted from *Signs: Journal of Women in Culture and Society* 8, no. 1 (Autumn 1982):
29–44.

Phallogocentrism may be described as the current tradition that constitutes a signifying system organized around gender. By "gender," I refer to a binary concept of relation that assumes such dichotomies as male presence/female absence, male word principle *(verbe)*/female verbal object, male center/female margin. I regard gender as the "logical" dichotomizing principle of phallogocentrism. This organizing principle regulates a set of systems that maintain the male-identified subject at the center of words. These signifying systems occur in all the arts and sciences, not just in "belles lettres." Thus the phallus may be regarded as the organizing principle for all standard systems including that of law, since at this time—though, we can hope, not forever—no legal communication can entirely ignore its referential order.[3]

Currently, when we use standard forms of communication, we default to the male-centered, heterosexual point of view. We do so even in the word used to name us as adult, human females: "women." The English word "woman" derives etymologically from the word for "wife"; even today the French word "femme" means both "woman" and "wife." The social idea of "wife" has thus become indistinguishable from the bodily idea of adult, human female, making it impossible for the word "woman" to represent us except as past, present, or future "wives" of men.

What, essentially, is the concept, "wife"? The structuralist answer to this question can be examined in Claude Lévi-Strauss's representation of women-wives as "ball of twine" or "liana." Men, in this view, just as they build a network of roads or thatch a roof from materials, create a communication-exchange network from the females they turn into wives in the act of wife-exchange. In the following passage Lévi-Strauss explains that women are exchanged like money, passing from hand to hand, establishing for the exchangers relations of reciprocity:

> It is the same with women as with the currency the name of which they often bear, and which, according to the admirable native saying, "depicts the action of the needle for sewing roofs, which, weaving in and out, leads backwards and forwards the same liana, holding the straw together."[4]

Note that the phallic subject (Lévi-Strauss's at least, and the subjectivity that presumably produced the "admirable native saying") depicts the

3. The reader who doubts this might recall that legal contracts must be dated in reference to Christ's birth, the point of demarcation between B.C. and A.D. This point functions as absolute origin for our legal time system much as Greenwich, England, functions as absolute origin for our geographical system of longitude.

4. Claude Lévi-Strauss, *The Elementary Structures of Kinship* (Boston: Beacon, 1969), p. 479.

"needle for sewing roofs" as leading the liana (a vine that grows in tropical rain forests), which is itself depicted as led. If we take a close look at this structuralist figuration we see that the action seems to reside in the needle (no doubt an image of the phallus), while the liana seems to be inert. The connecting function of the liana is like the reproductive function of a woman in the view of structuralism. And the straws that need to be united are like men (who, we may note, are distinguished here from the phallus). We may compare this functional image of woman-wife to another that Lévi-Strauss takes from a Kachin myth of creation and uses in a headquote to make vivid his theory of masculine networking:

> The earth, it is true, is in good condition, but roads are yet wanting; Ningkong is going to open them; he takes under his arm his sister, 'Ndin Lakong, a ball of twine, unwinds part of it on China, and re-enters his palace; henceforth there is a fine road to China. He then goes towards the Shan countries, again unwinds his sister, and it is the Shan road. In the same way he opens the Kachin, Burmese and Kala roads.[5]

Here the woman is figured as a ball of twine, as the matter itself from which her brother forms a webbing, a weaving, a network.

This concept of woman-as-wife, we see, is essential for the social contract assumed by structuralist theory, since this theory is developed exclusively from the male, heterosexual point of view. The two-sentence disclaimer on the penultimate page of *The Elementary Structures of Kinship* notwithstanding, Lévi-Strauss systematically reifies women as "signs," only once recognizing "woman . . . as a generator of signs."[6] Wittig dryly points to this contradiction when she says, "Since, as Lévi-Strauss said, we talk, let us say that we break off the heterosexual contract."[7] The result of this break is lesbian writing, an "illicit" poetic method that escapes the centralizing "presence" of wife-exchanging subjectivity. It escapes at the same time the dichotomizing organizational mode of sex-gender itself.[8]

Any pair of concepts, like masculine/feminine or male/female, that signifies sex-gender automatically constitutes a distinction of "marked-ness." It was the "unmarked" status of the masculine that led Simone de Beauvoir in 1949 to identify it as both "neutral" and "positive," while the

5. Ibid., p. 231.

6. Ibid., p. 496.

7. Monique Wittig, "The Straight Mind," *Feminist Issues* 1, no. 1 (Summer 1980): 103–11, esp. 110.

8. See Gayle Rubin's discussion of the term "sex-gender" in her excellent theoretical article, "The Traffic in Women," in *Toward an Anthropology of Women,* ed. Rayna [Rapp] Reiter (New York: Monthly Review Press, 1975), pp. 157–210.

"marked" status of the feminine led her to identify it as "negative." Today, markedness is increasingly recognized as essential to the sex-gender distinction.[9] As the Harvard Linguistics Department has put it, "For people and pronouns in English the masculine is the unmarked and hence is used as a neutral or unspecified term."[10] The unmarked is assumed to be desirable, expected, familiar, while the marked is considered undesirable, unexpected, unfamiliar. The unmarked form is usually shorter and therefore easier to say than the marked; for example, "male" is shorter than "female," and "man" is shorter than "woman." If a person crosses the sex-gender line in occupational roles, the unexpected situation must be "marked" by an additional signifier. Marking may be carried out by suffixes like the "-ess" in "poetess" or by qualifiers such as those in the expressions "woman doctor" and "male secretary." More obvious than the complicated sexism of "markedness" in language is the simple quantitative overrepresentation of male figures in books; according to the computerized study of Alma Graham, seven times as many men as women appeared in children's textbooks in the United States in 1973.[11] It is the trace of this all too ubiquitous masculine "presence" that must be erased from lesbian language. Lesbian metaphor must overwrite phallogocentric metaphor, just as, historically, phallogocentric metaphor had to overwrite an earlier symbolic system. Let us now examine the process of overwriting.

The phallus is not without a token "presence" in Wittig's lesbian book. Placed near the center of the collection of 110 poems, we find in poem 51 the ithyphallic god, Osiris. But he has been lesbianized. If we read the poem in the original French, we see that Osiris has been attributed grammatically feminine gender through the feminine modifiers, "m/a . . . cherie . . . m/a . . . affaiblie . . . m/a . . . belle . . . défaite . . .

9. For a discussion of "markedness," see Herbert H. Clark and Eve V. Clark, *Psychology and Language* (New York: Harcourt Brace Jovanovich, 1977), pp. 426–28, 455–56, 498–99, 513, 523–24, 533–36, 538–39.

10. Quotation of the Harvard Department of Linguistics in Casey Miller and Kate Swift, *Words and Women* (New York: Doubleday/Anchor, 1977), p. 69. For a linguist's analysis of the so-called generic masculine, see Julia Penelope Stanley, "Gender-Marking in American English: Usage and Reference," in *Sexism and Language*, ed. Alleen Pace Nilsen et al. (Urbana, Ill.: National Council of Teachers of English, 1977), pp. 43–74. For a social-psychological analysis of the so-called generic masculine, see Wendy Martyna, "Using and Understanding the Generic Masculine" (Ph.D. diss., Stanford University, 1978). For a comprehensive annotated bibliography of studies on gender and language and selected papers, see Barrie Thorne and Nancy Henley, eds., *Language and Sex: Difference and Dominance* (Rowley, Mass.: Newbury, 1975).

11. "The schoolbook world," according to a computerized study of 5 million words found in a thousand representative books used by children in grades three through nine throughout the United States, is "inhabited by twice as many boys as girls and seven times as many men as women" (Alma Graham, "The Making of a Nonsexist Dictionary," *Ms.* [December 1973], pp. 12–14, 16; reprinted in Thorne and Henley, eds., pp. 57–63).

épuisée." The reader can see that this grammatical feminizing is lost in Le Vay's English translation of the French.

> m/oi Isis la très puissante j/e décrète que comme par le passé tu vis Osiris m/a très cherie m/a très affaiblie j/e dis que comme par le passé nous pourrons faire ensemble les petites filles qui viendront après nous, toi alors m/on Osiris m/a très belle tu m/e souris défaite épuisée. [*Lcl,* poem 51, lines 34–39, p. 87][12]

> [*I* Isis the all-powerful *I* decree that you live as in the past Osiris m/y most cherished m/y most enfeebled *I* say that as in the past we shall succeed together in making the little girls who will come after us, then you m/y Osiris m/y most beautiful you smile at m/e undone exhausted.] [*TLB,* p. 80]

Powerful as a displacer of consciousness, Wittig relocates subjectivity outside the orbit of phallogocentrism. In the passage cited above, she has effeminized the ithyphallic figure, evoking an old tradition of the brother's castration of Osiris. A closer look at this myth, central to Wittig's treatment of death and rebirth, will make clearer the essentially metaphorical nature of the phallus, and the political nature of metaphor.

According to one version of the Isis-Osiris myth, recounted by Esther Harding, "Set . . . tore the body of Osiris to pieces. . . . Isis managed to collect thirteen of the pieces which she welded together by magic. But the phallus was missing. So she made an image of this part and 'consecrated the phallus.' Isis conceived by means of this image and bore a child."[13]

The phallus produced is a simulacrum, an artifact crafted by Isis who then attributes to it sacred meaning. Thus the "phallus" comes into existence according to the wish of the goddess Isis. Harding's research points to both the symbolic nature and social importance of the phallus: "Public rituals of Isis and Osiris were celebrated. . . . The festival culmi-

---

12. Poem numbers refer to the first-line cross-reference index, pp. E-2 and E-3, in the appendices of Shaktini, "The Problem of Gender and Subjectivity" (n. 2 above). Page numbers are cross-referenced for the Minuit French edition and the Morrow (hardcover) and Avon (softcover) English editions (see n. 1 above). There is one error of publication in the English Morrow (hardcover) edition and two in the Avon (softcover) edition concerning the pagination and placement of poems. The Morrow edition prints poem 16 (pp. 32–33, p. 28 in the Minuit edition) as if it were two poems, when in reality the poem is just continued onto the next page in the original French edition. (A translator with full comprehension of the text would not have made this mistake.) This error is repeated in the Avon edition (pp. 30–31). In addition, the Avon edition on p. 77 of its text joins poems 49 and 50 of the original French. The third line from the top, "The bandage keeps m/y eyes closed. *I* am in darkness," is the beginning of poem 50 (p. 84 in the Minuit edition).

13. Esther Harding, *Woman's Mysteries* (San Francisco: Harper & Row, 1971), p. 175.

nated in a procession at the head of which was carried the huge image of the phallus, representing the lost organ of Osiris."[14]

Although Harding refers to the gender symbols "the bowl and the phallus" as "the eternal symbols of generation," the examples she cites show the nature of the phallus to be destructive, not generative, and historical rather than eternal: "We find [the 'eternal' symbols] in primitive rites—the fire stick, which is called the man, and the cup in which it bores, called the woman; the fundus in the earth in the center of the camp into which each Roman soldier threw his spear; the chalice of the Holy Grail into which a spear, perpetually dripping blood, was thrust; the holy font of baptism fertilized by plunging in the lighted candle."[15]

Harding, though contributing much useful research, remains metaphorically within a contradictory position, according to which fire (an agent of destruction) "signifies" fertility. This problematic metaphor may have a traditional root in the concept of the Old Testament god, both fire-god ("logos" as fire speaking out of the burning bush to Moses) and father-god.

Norman O. Brown, who on the penultimate page of *Love's Body* refers to the "Word" (Greek "logos") as "spermatic," has also contributed useful research on the phallus. His report of the "cult" of Hermes, like the myth retold by Harding, emphasizes the magical rather than biological nature of the phallic symbol: "The phallus is so closely identified with magic in Roman religion that the word *fascinum,* meaning 'enchantment,' 'witchcraft' (cf. fascinate), is one of the standard Latin terms for the phallus. . . . When Greek craftsmen [*sic*] hung images of ithyphallic demons over their workshops, it is clear that to them the phallus symbolized not fertility but magic skill at craftsmanship [*sic*]."[16] As is consistent with his phallogocentric view, Brown simply identifies the activity of "crafting" as phallic—crafters for him were "craftsmen," notwithstanding the ancient evidence of female crafters (e.g., Isis as welder in the myth cited above, or females in general identified with the "magic skill" of witchcraft). But most important for feminist thought is Brown's report that historically the phallus is not essentially a signifier of the penis but of craft itself. It alerts us to look for the origins of linguistic sexism in "crafty" and misogynist practices in the crafting of words. By comparing Wittig's recrafting of the phallic figure, Osiris, and Hesiod's recrafting of Pandora, we may better understand the political nature of metaphorical takeover.

The takeover of Pandora, a figure of womankind, is a prime example. She was, as Brown reports, "originally a figure of the earth-goddess

14. Ibid., p. 190.
15. Ibid., p. 190.
16. Norman O. Brown, *Hermes the Thief* (New York: Vintage, 1969), p. 37. I use [*sic*] after certain quoted words to indicate their erroneous "generic" usage of the masculine gender.

type, the original meaning of the name being 'the all-giver.' "[17] But as Hesiod exercises his craft a remodeled Pandora figure emerges typifying woman as "gift," the object of gift-exchange by men.[18] She is brought into existence according to the wish of the Father, made "in the likeness of a decorous young girl, as the son of Kronos had wished it."[19] Like the phallus made by Isis or its extensions—the burning stick or the soldier's spear—she is an artifact, a product of craft. By textually redefining this figure of womankind, Hesiod strips her of subjectivity. Taking as his material the existent earth goddess figure, Pandora, he recrafts her into a man-made Pandora, "modeled . . . of earth."[20]

Transformed by Hesiod's text, the Pandora figure may be read as the product of a displacement of subjectivity, the displacing process itself figured by the author effecting it. Hesiod's text points to a prepatriarchal symbolic order, where the principle of intelligence is embodied in a female-identified figure, Metis, who "knew more than all the gods or mortal people."[21] Zeus, metaphorically described by Hesiod as swallowing Metis, appropriates to his own phallic body two of her subject-signifying attributes—the ability to think and the ability to reproduce parthenogenetically: "Zeus put her [Metis] away inside his own belly so that this goddess should think for him, for good and for evil. . . . Then from his head, by himself, he produced Athene. . . . The father of gods and men gave birth to her."[22] Athena's birth from the brow of the father figure repositions there the point of view of subjectivity, the standard for good and evil. This viewpoint, subsequently absolute, takes over the function of divinity as Roland Barthes has defined it: "Divinity's role is . . . to *mark* one of the two terms of the binary."[23]

According to Hesiod, Athena is born (or more precisely, rebirthed and renamed) "with her panoply of war upon her." As we see from the *Oxford English Dictionary*, Athena's symbol of power is but a "marked" version of the aegis of Zeus: the aegis is "a shield or breastplate emblematic of majesty that was originally associated chiefly with the god Zeus but later, bordered with serpents and set with a Gorgon's head, associated mainly with the goddess Athena."[24] The aegis or shield (and the weapon it implies), a militaristic means of social control, thus ultimately signifies the authority of the father-god.

This aegis figures importantly in the death of Pallas, whose name

17. Ibid., p. 60.
18. Richmond Lattimore, trans., *Hesiod* (Ann Arbor: University of Michigan Press, 1959), "Works and Days," lines 84–85, p. 27.
19. Ibid., lines 70–71, p. 27.
20. Ibid.
21. Ibid., "Theogony," line 887, p. 176.
22. Ibid., lines 892, 924, 929a, pp. 177, 179, 180.
23. Roland Barthes, *Sade/Fourier/Loyola* (Paris: Seuil, 1971), p. 76; the English edition is *Sade/Fourier/Loyola*, trans. Richard Miller (New York: Hill & Wang, 1976), p. 72.
24. *The Compact Edition of the Oxford English Dictionary* (1971), s.v. "aegis."

was to become the "extra name of Athena."[25] As we learn from Jeanette Foster's *Sex Variant Women in Literature*: "The conscientious chronicler Apollodorus reports . . . of Athene and her boon companion, Pallas . . . that in their girlhood they were so equally matched in the practice of arms that Zeus felt obliged one day to interpose his aegis between them lest his daughter be slain. As a result, Athene's thrust killed Pallas, whereupon, overcome by grief, Athene herself fashioned a wooden statue of her friend, wrapped it in the aegis [sometimes described as made of sheepskin], set it up beside that of Zeus, and honored it as she did his image. Hence her later epithet, Pallas-Athene."[26] It is in relation to the father's brow—the epistemological center of Olympian metaphor—that Metis, Pallas, and Athene are related by Hesiod to each other. In one version of Hesiodic text, it was actually Metis who "conceived Pallas Athene, but the father of gods and men gave birth to her."[27] In this version "Metis herself, hidden away under the vitals of Zeus, stayed there; she was Athene's mother. . . . Metis made the armor of Athene, terror of armies, in which Athene was born with her panoply of war upon her."[28]

Athena emerges as the central figure while Metis and Pallas are marginalized. Metis, a figure of generation (the producer of Athena and of her armor), exists from the moment of the swallowing only for Zeus, not for herself. Pallas, a shadowy amazon-lesbian figure, is effectively killed by the authority of Zeus, ambiguously associated with that of Athena. Like Isis, Athena fabricates and consecrates an image of the beloved to replace what has disappeared. Thus only a trace remains of the existence of the amazon-lesbian figure.

Hesiod's story of Zeus' appropriation of Metis and suppression of Pallas figures the displacement and appropriation of a prepatriarchal form of subjectivity by a patriarchal one, the "brow" of the father thereby becoming the figurative center of consciousness for Greek myth. It is in this sense that the "Word" became "spermatic," in Norman O. Brown's phrase, or, as feminists more commonly say today, "male-identified."[29] The shift to the "brow" of Zeus is at once a shift to logocentrism (word centeredness) and phallogocentrism (male-centered word centeredness).

Athena, issuing directly from the divine "brow," may be seen as a figure of the male-identified feminine subject. She then acts as Zeus' agent in the Olympic fabrication of Pandora, male-defined feminine

25. Lattimore, trans., p. 238.

26. Jeanette Foster, *Sex Variant Women in Literature* (1956; reprint ed., Baltimore, Md.: Diana Press, 1975), pp. 25–26.

27. Lattimore, trans., "Theogony," line 929a, p. 180.

28. Ibid.

29. Norman O. Brown, *Love's Body* (New York: Vintage, 1966), p. 265.

object. Athena thus mediates between absolute phallic subject and absolute feminine object. As bearer of the Gorgon-marked aegis, she represents herself as agent—half subject, half object. The mark on her aegis, the head of the Gorgon, may be read as another aspect of herself as goddess figure—that aspect slain and appropriated by Perseus. Identified with the head of Zeus, Athena is marked by a beheaded form of the goddess and effects the veiling (hiding) of the head of Pandora. The Athena figure is thus a triple denial of feminine subjectivity: Herself "born" from the father's brow, she may be considered an extension of it; "marked" by an appropriated image of the goddess, she may be considered an appropriated goddess figure; and finally, "veiling" (hiding) the head, the place of Pandora's logocentric subjectivity, she helps produce the Greek prototype of alienated woman—woman as gift, exchange-object, chattel.

"Woman," then, signifies "gift" for others to give-exchange. Understandably, in a profoundly lesbian gesture, Wittig puts under erasure the concept "woman." At the Simone de Beauvoir Conference of 1979 in New York, delivering a paper titled to echo de Beauvoir's own words, "One is not born a woman," Wittig defines, at least for herself, the concept "lesbian": "Lesbian is the only concept that I know of that is beyond the categories of sex (woman and man) . . . because the designated subject (lesbian) is *not* a woman either economically or politically or ideologically."[30] We see that as defined by Wittig, lesbianism is not just a matter of "sexual preference" but one of class. And it is as a trace of this lesbian class consciousness that we may examine Wittig's modification of the heterosexual metaphors that have provided her with writing material.

By comparing Wittig's recrafting of the phallic figure, Osiris, and Hesiod's recrafting of Pandora, we may see the significance of her transformation of myth for the history of consciousness. As she reidentifies the phallic figure as lesbian, Wittig operates a reversal in the signifying system and a displacement of subjectivity. By producing Olympian metaphor (specifically in metamorphosizing unalienated feminine figures into alienated ones), Hesiod also operates a reversal and displacement. Hesiod historically displaces a prepatriarchal order by emplacing the brow of Zeus (metaphorically the male-identified subject) at the absolute center of his signifying system. In *Le corps lesbien* Wittig displaces this phallic body and subject with the lesbian body and the lesbian subject. (See, for example, her ironic recrafting of Zeus as Zeyna in poem 43.) The reversal operated by both of these crafters of words signifies a shift of the biological body of reference for human consciousness.

30. Monique Wittig, "One Is Not Born a Woman," *Feminist Issues* 1, no. 2 (Winter 1981): 47–54, esp. 53.

By showing her own process of transformation of meaning from that of the current phallogocentric order, Wittig makes visible the earlier process of absorbing and transforming that took place when the idea of mother-goddess was superseded and appropriated (overwritten) by the idea of father-god. Taking the persona of the goddess Isis, "j/e" assumes the subjective posture of the female-identified subject before its il-locutionary power became alienated by that of the phallic Word:

m/oi Isis la trés puissante j/e décrète . . . j/e dis . . . [*Lcl*, poem 51, lines 34–36, p. 87]

[*I* Isis the all-powerful *I* decree . . . *I* say . . .] [*TLB*, p. 80]

Isis, as we learn in the *Egyptian Book of the Dead*, possessed the power of the living Word: "I am Isis the goddess, lady of words of power, worker with words of mighty power, in utterance of speech."[31] Her power must have been greater than that of the divine sun-king, Ra, for she could "make Ra reveal to her his greatest and most secret name."[32] And, as we have noted, it was she who empowered the very phallus of Osiris.

The figure of Isis embodies the power of speech, the power of naming with which we may symbolically fragment and reassemble the world. Although the process of naming is largely unconscious for us, Wittig's frequent use of the word "nom" (name)—which appears twenty-seven times—heightens our consciousness of the power of the illocutionary process while also making us aware that naming implies the point of view of the namer.

It is the displacing process itself that is figured in poem 106 of *Le corps lesbien* on "Archimedea." That is, this poem may be read as a reflection or figuration of "j/e" in its aspect as displacing subject. The first-person singular, present-tense narrator, "j/e," displaces us as readers from the mainland to an island, which serves as image of both the central and marginal position. Central from the point of view of its own center, the island is marginal from the point of view of the body of water that surrounds it. The displacing lesbian subject, "j/e," addresses the beloved as "Archimedea," whose name may be associated with the historical Greek figure credited with the discovery of the principle of displacement. Archimedes, the author of *On Floating Bodies*, a text on hydrostatics, is credited with discovering that "the solid will, when weighed in the fluid, be lighter than its weight in air by the weight of the fluid displaced."[33]

N'y a-t-il pas Archimedea d'autre endroit pour se rencontrer que les bains si parfumés d'eau de Chypre soient-ils? Jamais j/e ne te vois

31. Cited in E. A. Wallis Budge, *The Gods of the Egyptians II* (1904; New York: Dover, 1969), p. 227.

32. Ibid., p. 214.

33. Marshall Clagett, *Greek Science in Antiquity* (New York: Collier, 1963), pp. 97–98.

dans les pinèdes fraîches bleues sombres qui bordent la côte de l'île, là pourtant dans l'obscurité m/es yeux se reposent de l'éclat du jour le poids de m/es bras de m/es jambes ne m//embarrasse plus quand j/e les appuie sur les aiguilles de pin, l'odeur de la résine chaude de la mer mêlées m/e porte à te chercher toute couchée à côté de m/oi. Mais c'est un fait tu es aux bains, c'est là que j/e te rejoins, tu es occupée à flotter tout à plat sur l'eau chaude, j/e te regarde, ton corps se détache au-dessus des mosaïques orange et violettes. [*Lcl*, poem 106, lines 1–13, p. 181]

[(However perfumed with Cyprus water they may be is there no place to meet other than the baths, Archimedea?[34]) *I* never see you in the cool dark-blue pine groves which flank the island shore, but there in the gloom m/y eyes relax from the daylight's dazzle the weight of m/y arms m/y legs burdens m/e no longer when *I* rest them on the pine needles, the mingled odours of the warm resin and the sea lead m/e to seek you lying beside m/e. But in fact you are at the baths, it's there that *I* join you, you are engaged in floating flat on the warm water, *I* look at you, your body stands out against the orange and violet mosaics.] [*TLB*, p. 159]

In the first sentence of this playful passage, the speaker questions whether the only meeting place for the lovers is that place of displacement, the baths. The next two sentences, an interesting example of Wittig's method of displacement, situate the lover and the beloved outside the centristic organizational mode of the phallic subject by placing them outside of the presence/absence and center/margin dichotomies. In the second sentence, an image of absence and marginality is juxtaposed to the image of central presence constituted by the third sentence. The scene of the lover's absence is set on the margin of the island while the scene of the lover's presence is made to seem more central through heightening of the visual foreground/background effect. Yet Wittig gives as much textual development to the beloved's image as absent-marginal as she does to her image as present-central. This juxtaposition of absence with presence has the effect of making relative the otherwise absolute logocentric privilege of presence over absence. Wittig thus deconstructs her own word-centered positionality, situating herself now in the center, now in the margin, signifying now what is present, now what is absent.[35]

These Archimedean baths, perfumed with water from Cyprus, the island reputed to be the birthplace of Aphrodite, are situated on an island—the setting par excellence for lesbianism in *Le corps lesbien*, no doubt because of the historical association with Lesbos, the site of Sappho's lesbian community. "Ile" (island) occurs twenty-nine times in the

34. The translation of the first sentence is mine. Le Vay's translation is incomprehensible: "Is there no Archimedea to be encountered anywhere that the baths are so perfumed with *eau de Chypre*?"

35. For other examples of this type of displacement, see poems 83 and 110.

text as compared with the word "continent" (continent), which occurs only three times.[36]

The epigraph of this essay, taken from the end of poem 11, contains one of these appearances:

> adieu continent noir de misère et de peine adieu villes anciennes nous nous embarquons pour les îles brillantes et radieuses pour les vertes Cythères pour les Lesbos noires et dorées. [*Lcl*, poem 11, lines 30–34, p. 20]

> [farewell black continent of misery and suffering farewell ancient cities we are embarking for the shining radiant isles for the green Cytheras for the dark and gilded Lesbos.][37] [*TLB*, p. 26]

By setting the pluralized *Cythère* and the pluralized *Lesbos* in apposition, Wittig has lesbianized the idea of Watteau's famous painting, *Embarquement pour Cythère,* which portrays heterosexual couples of the French classical period presumably embarking for Cythera, a Greek island known for its magnificent temple of Aphrodite. Since this lesbian poet invokes Sappho—whose name appears twenty-four times—instead of the heterosexual goddess of love, Aphrodite's name never appears in her text, though the names of two pre-Olympic goddesses of love, Isis and Ishtar, do appear (in poems 43, 51, and 61). Wittig's poëms situate lesbianism in relation to islands (on them, in the air above them, in the water around them) and contrast the islands to the "black continent."[38] She evokes the metaphor of embarkation as an image of displacement

36. References to word frequency in this article are based on the "Concordance of *Le corps lesbien*" in the appendices of Shaktini, "The Problem of Subjectivity" (n. 2 above), pp. C1–E663. I wish to thank Sally Douglas for programming this concordance and for lending me her computer, as well as for reading and criticizing this article.

37. In the epigraph, for greater clarity, I have changed Le Vay's translation, which, however, I have cited unchanged above. He correctly renders "les . . . Cythères" as the pluralized "Cytheras," but incorrectly renders "les Lesbos" (also plural in French) as the singular "Lesbos." I have changed the English for "les Lesbos" to "the Lesbian Islands," using the more familiar word for "isle," "island."

38. Wittig has herself made a "journey" of self-definition. In 1970, she participated in the writing of the "Hymne" of the Mouvement de Liberation des Femmes, which begins: "Nous qui sommes sans passé, les femmes, / Nous qui n'avons pas d'histoire / Depuis la nuit des temps, les femmes, / Nous sommes le continent noir. / Levons nous femmes esclaves / Et brisons nos entraves, / Debout!" (We who are without past, women / We who have no history / Since the night of time, women / We are the black continent. / Let's rise up women slaves / And break our chains, / Arise!) [My personal recollection and translation]. Wittig, in composing this with other feminists, speaks as a woman-identified subject. At that time, Wittig and other French feminists said "nous les femmes" (we women) in an effort to avoid the contradictory problem from which Simone de Beauvoir had failed to extricate herself when she referred to "les femmes" (women) as "elles" (they) in her famous book, *Le deuxième sexe (The Second Sex).* By 1973, however, in *Le corps lesbien,* Wittig identifies subjectivity as lesbian. And by 1979, in her paper "One Is Not Born a Woman," Wittig radically puts into question the idea of "woman."

from the "dark continent of femininity which Freud never really penetrated."[39]

Wittig's semiological method does not aim at feminizing meaning, nor does it continue the default situation, which constitutes meaning for the male-identified subject. When, for example, she inserts the name "Medea," known as a figure of prepatriarchal myth, into the name "Archimedea" (and into the name "Ganymedea" in poem 23), Wittig is placing herself neither at the feminine nor at the masculine end of the gender polarity. By introducing a female name into these male names, Wittig mixes gender signifiers, confounding the dichotomizing principle of gender. She positions herself, her text, and her readers outside the system which makes female and male into polar opposites.

Even in reference to time, Wittig has succeeded in situating herself without having recourse to dichotomous, linear, phallogocentric methods. In the dominant, officially Christian society, time is measured in reference to a central metaphor and reference point: the supposed birth of the male Logos, Christ, which divides time absolutely into B.C. and A.D. But this linear, phallogocentric system can be easily displaced by an older, cyclical one, ready at hand.

In poem 36 Wittig marks time in relation to a metaphor that existed prior to words—"la lune" (the moon). The lunar cycle provides a point of reference for marking the months at the "vingt-huitième . . . jour" (twenty-eighth . . . day) (*Lcl*, poem 36, line 2, p. 60; *TLB*, p. 59). From this central point, the four-week month and lunar-centered system of representing time can be constructed. Concomitantly, the Logos-centered system of representing time is deconstructed. In *Le corps lesbien* there are fourteen references to the moon. The birth of Christ is thus displaced as the central reference point for the marking of time and replaced, at least in the context of poem 36, by a central lunar point of reference.

The male Christ, moreover, as a sacrificial figure, is replaced by "Christa la très crucifiée" (Christa the much-crucified) (*Lcl*, poem 17, line 24, p. 30; *TLB*, p. 35). "J/e," in poem 82, one of the most beautifully written in the book, assumes the lesbianized persona of Christ:

> J/e suis au Golgotha par vous toutes abandonée. [*Lcl*, poem 82, line 1, p. 138]

> [Abandoned by you all *I* am at Golgotha.][40] [*TLB*, p. 122]

Displaced by lesbian metaphor, Golgotha is stripped of its phallic signifiers. Wittig's telescoped scene of Gethsemene/Golgotha is peopled

---

39. See Jane Gallop's article on Lacan, "The Ladies' Man," *Diacritics* 6, no. 4 (Winter 1976): 28–34, esp. 29.

40. My translation replaces Le Vay's erroneous: "*I* am at the Golgotha you have all abandoned."

with lesbians. The indefinite "quelqu'une" (grammatically feminine "someone") in a universe with no occurrence of "quelqu'un" (grammatically masculine "someone") takes on a "generic" meaning (*Lcl,* poem 82, line 14, p. 138; *TLB,* p. 123).[41] And the subject addressed is generic feminine, both as the specific "tu" and in the more general context of the plural "vous."

"Tu" is compared to a female figure from a prepatriarchal order of divine power:

> tu ressembles à une des Gorgones terrible puissante rouge de rêve [*Lcl,* poem 82, lines 4–5, p. 138]

> [you resemble one of the Gorgons terrible powerful ruddy in dream] [*TLB,* p. 122]

Similarly, the "generic" use of "une" represents a shift from a phallic to a lesbian assumption concerning human subjectivity:

> pas une de vous ne sait rien de m/on angoisse [*Lcl,* poem 82, lines 8–9, p. 138]

> [not one of you knows anything of m/y anguish] [*TLB,* pp. 138–39]

And when the deity is addressed, it is as mother-goddess rather than as father-god:

> j//implore la grande déesse ma mère et j/e lui dis mère mère pourquoi m//as tu abandonnée [*Lcl,* poem 82, lines 9–11, p. 138]

> [I cry out in m/y distress mother mother why have you forsaken m/e] [*TLB,* p. 123]

By systematically displacing phallic with lesbian linguistic assumptions, Wittig changes meaning itself.

What happens if meaning is for the lesbian rather than the phallic subject? In poem 5, for example, Wittig rewrites a famous heterosexual love story from the lesbian perspective. Though the names "Orphée" and "Eurydice" are not uttered, this poem, in four sentences, appropriates the main structures of the well-known narrative of Orpheus' descent

41. In addition to systematically changing to generic feminine for human reference, Wittig's lesbian writing includes—in one instance at least—the generic feminine "elles" for grammatical reference to words of mixed gender, though in English, a language without grammatical gender, this is lost: "la terre les arbres les eaux les fleuves les rivières les mers les étoiles du ciel ne tremblent-elles pas" [the earth the trees the waters the rivers the torrents the seas the stars of the sky do they not tremble] (*Lcl,* poem 61, lines 9–11, p. 102; *TLB,* p. 93).

into the underworld to save his bride. Here, the speaker assumes the persona of Eurydice:

> J/e dirai seulement comment tu viens m/e chercher jusqu'au fond de l'enfer. . . . Tu chantes sans discontinuer. Les gardiennes des mortes attendries referment leurs gueules béantes. Tu obtiens d'elles de m/e ramener jusqu'à la lumière des vivantes à condition de ne pas te retourner sur m/oi pour m/e regarder. [*Lcl,* poem 5, lines 2–10, p. 11]

> [*I* shall recount only how you come to seek m/e in the very depths of hell. . . . You sing without pause. The female guardians of the dead mollified close their gaping mouths. You obtain their permission to bring m/e back as far as the light of the living on condition that you do not turn round to look at m/e.] [*TLB,* p. 19]

Wittig's lesbianized Orpheus figure, however, unlike the phallic one, triumphs over Eurydice's death through the force of lesbian love:

> Pas une fois tu ne te retournes, pas même quand j/e m/e mets à hurler de désespoir les larmes roulant sur m/es joues rongées à te supplier de m/e laisser dans m/a tombe à te décrire avec brutalité m/a décomposition les purulences de m/es yeux de mon nez de m/a vulve les caries de m/es dents les fermentations de m/es organes essentiels la couleur de m/es muscles blets. Tu m//interromps, tu chantes à voix stridente ta certitude de triompher de m/a mort, tu ne tiens pas compte de m/es sanglots, tu m//entraînes jusqu'à la surface de la terre où le soleil est visible. C'est là seulement là au débouché vers les arbres et la forêt que d'un bond tu m/e fais face et c'est vrai qu'en regardant tes yeux, j/e ressuscite à une vitesse prodigieuse. [*Lcl,* poem 5, lines 36–50, pp. 12–13]

> [Not once do you turn round, not even when *I* begin to howl with despair the tears trickling down m/y gnawed cheeks to beg you to leave m/e in m/y tomb to brutally describe to you m/y decomposition the purulence of m/y eyes m/y nose m/y vulva the caries of m/y teeth the fermentation of m/y vital organs the colour of m/y rotten-ripe muscles. You interrupt m/e, you sing with strident voice your certainty of triumph over m/y death, you do not heed m/y sobs, you drag m/e to the surface of the earth where the sun is visible. Only there at the exit towards the trees and the forest do you turn to face m/e with a bound and it is true that looking into your eyes *I* revive with prodigious speed.] [*TLB,* p. 20]

Wittig's translation of the myth into lesbian terms not only radically improves the outcome of the story for Eurydice—who, we may recall from the heterosexual version, dies on the day she is married—but also changes the meaning by recasting the roles from the traditional active male/passive female figures to active lesbian lovers.

Appropriating from the most central cultural contexts phallocentric, heterosexual metaphor, Wittig has lesbianized it. In *Le corps lesbien* the default, or unmarked, phallic subject has been displaced by the lesbian subject. *Ecriture lesbienne* is a *coup d'écriture*.

Palo Alto, California

Ourself Behind Ourself:
A Theory for Lesbian Readers

Jean E. Kennard

Ourself behind ourself, concealed—
should startle most.

[EMILY DICKINSON]

If feminist criticism has demonstrated anything, it is surely the importance of the reader to what is read. Increasingly, the connections between
reader-response criticism and feminist criticism are becoming more
widely acknowledged, most frequently but not exclusively by feminist
critics. Yet feminists, like all theorists using this approach, face the primary problem of defining their reader.[1] In what sense is it meaningful to
talk about the "woman reader"?

1. For discussions of the relationship between reader-response theory and feminist
criticism, see, for example, Annette Kolodny, "A Map for Rereading; or, Gender and the
Interpretation of Literary Texts," *New Literary History* 11, no. 3 (Spring 1980): 451–67;
Jonathan D. Culler, *On Deconstruction: Theory and Criticism after Structuralism* (Ithaca, N.Y.:
Cornell University Press, 1982), pp. 43–64; Judith Fetterley, *The Resisting Reader: A Feminist
Approach to American Fiction* (Bloomington: Indiana University Press, 1978); Jean E. Ken-
nard, "Convention Coverage or How to Read Your Own Life," *New Literary History* 13, no. 1
(Autumn 1981): 69–88; Elizabeth A. Flynn, "Gender and Reading," *College English* 45, no. 3
(March 1983): 236–51. I am aware that, in contemporary critical theory, feminist and
nonfeminist, the existence of the reader as a "self" is as problematic as the existence of the
text. For the purposes of my discussion here I assume with Elizabeth Flynn that "reading
involves a confrontation between self and 'other.' The self, the reader, encounters the

Reprinted from *Signs: Journal of Women in Culture and Society* 9, no. 4 (Summer 1984):
647–662.

Most feminist scholars have assumed a definition of woman based on biology even though doing so has inevitably led to some questionable generalizations. What does the term "woman reader" signify if it is presumed to include Third World women, Caucasian women, upper-middle-class women, women living below the poverty level, and, my chief concern here, both heterosexual and lesbian women? Can we safely assume that there are no innate differences between the lesbian and the heterosexual woman? If there are, then surely they must be considered in any studies of gender and reading. Even if there were no social or political evils in a denial of lesbian experience, recognition of that experience would remain a necessity unless feminist research is to operate from a limited or inaccurate definition of its terms.

This article assumes that we need at least to ask whether the lesbian reader is not a different reader from the heterosexual woman reader and, if she is, how her lesbianism affects the reading enterprise. It assumes also that, despite an increased awareness of available lesbian material, lesbian students, both inside and outside classrooms, will for the foreseeable future be expected to read the familiar heterosexually biased literature. If as lesbian readers we can appreciate only literature that reflects our own experience, we are likely to be very limited in our reading pleasure.[2] In the background of my discussion, then, are three questions: How do we define "lesbian reader"? Can we reread/rewrite the old canon so that it no longer excludes the lesbian reader? Can we do it in such a way that we do not in the process exclude other readers?

Much of the new lesbian scholarship focuses on the definition of "lesbian." In a recent review article on the history of sexuality Martha Vicinus summarizes the work of recent participants in the debate between those who insist that lesbianism must imply an explicitly erotic component and those who wish to broaden the definition to include all women whose primary emotional bonds are to other women.[3] Vicinus—rightly, to my mind—links self-definition to periodization: those historians interested in the period before 1910 are more likely than modernists to call romantic friendship lesbianism.

This discussion impinges on a definition of the lesbian reader since only if we insist on the erotic nature of a lesbian bond can we consider the

---

'other,' the text, and the nature of that confrontation depends upon the background of the reader as well as upon the text" (p. 236).

2. Although the situation is likely to be worse for the lesbian reader, enjoying literature seemingly antithetical to her beliefs is a problem for any feminist reader. For comments on this problem see Annette Kolodny, "Dancing through the Minefield: Some Observations on the Theory, Practice and Politics of a Feminist Literary Criticism," *Feminist Studies* 6, no. 1 (Spring 1980): 1–25.

3. Martha Vicinus, "Sexuality and Power: A Review of Current Work in the History of Sexuality," *Feminist Studies* 8, no. 1 (Spring 1982): 134–56.

possibility of lesbianism as an innate aspect of sexual identity. Also relevant to a definition of the lesbian reader is the related question of "nature" versus "nurture" that Lillian Faderman outlines in *Surpassing the Love of Men*.[4] Is lesbianism a congenital defect (Krafft-Ebing)? Is it congenital but not necessarily a defect (Hirschfeld)? Is it the result of childhood trauma, that is, an environmental hazard (Freud)?

One of the problems in current writing about lesbianism is that the debate between "nurture" and "nature" has been treated as synonymous with a debate between "choice" and "no choice." Given the historical reasons for resisting the biological argument and the modern predilection for an existentialist construct of self, it is not surprising that most lesbians have opted for "choice." In *Lesbianism and the Women's Movement*, for example, Coletta Reid claims "they could choose to be lesbians, lesbians weren't born, they were made." Similarly, Barbara Solomon states, "Lesbians are not born. We have made a conscious choice to be lesbians." Faderman talks of lesbianism as "a natural impulse and a choice made in a healthy response to one's environment."[5] But lesbian literature—often works by the same authors who talk about choice—also contains an apparently contradictory theme of discovering "one's true self." Many of the women Deborah Wolf interviews in *The Lesbian Community* talk of lesbian experience as fulfilling a need they had always had, as "just seeming right."[6]

Certainly choice is involved. Even if lesbians are born rather than made, one can choose to accept or to deny one's lesbianism, something one cannot yet do so easily with one's gender. But does one choose to *be* a lesbian? What do Faderman's words "natural impulse" imply? Certainly lesbianism is to be found in nature, that is, in female human beings. Then are all women potentially lesbians? Have some more potential than others? What is the lesbian discovering when she feels she is discovering her true self?

4. Lillian Faderman, *Surpassing the Love of Men: Romantic Friendship and Love between Women from the Renaissance to the Present* (New York: William Morrow & Co., 1981). Kinsey researchers concluded recently that, since there is insufficient evidence for any of the suggested "causes" of homosexuality, we should look again at "possible biological bases for homosexuality" (Alan P. Bell, Martin S. Weinberg, and Sue Kiefer Hammersmith, *Sexual Preference: Its Development in Men and Women* [Bloomington: Indiana University Press, 1981], p. 213). For a discussion of medical research on this topic, see Susan W. Baker, "Biological Influences on Human Sex and Gender," *Signs: Journal of Women in Culture and Society* 6, no. 1 (Autumn 1980): 80–96.

5. Coletta Reid, "Coming Out in the Women's Movement," and Barbara Solomon, "Taking the Bullshit by the Horns," in *Lesbianism and the Women's Movement*, ed. Nancy Myron and Charlotte Bunch (Baltimore: Diana Press, 1975), pp. 91–103, and 39–48, esp. pp. 97, 40. Faderman points out the connections between supporting "choice" and opposing the patriarchal definition of lesbianism in entirely sexual terms (p. 323).

6. Deborah Goleman Wolf, *The Lesbian Community* (Berkeley and Los Angeles: University of California Press, 1980), p. 35.

Despite the attractiveness of the idea that a lesbian life-style is a viable option for all women, we put future lesbian scholarship at risk if we ignore the evidence of those who feel as if they, more than others, have lesbian tendencies. We should at least be willing to consider the possibility of a biological predisposition. As Sara Ruddick says in a different context, "Neither our own ambivalence to our women's bodies nor the bigoted, repressive uses which many men, colonizers, and racists have made of biology, should blind us to our body's possibilities."[7] Nor should we feel that to accept the idea of a predisposition toward lesbianism in some women negates the political validity of a choice to *accept* a lesbian identity.

The conflicting views on the nature of lesbianism could make for significant differences to a theory of the lesbian reader. If the lesbian reader has chosen a lesbian identity but has no innate predisposition toward lesbianism, she may respond positively to lesbian characters or experience when either overtly presented or encoded in the text; she may respond negatively to negative portrayals of lesbianism or to the assumption of exclusive heterosexuality.[8] However, if the lesbian reader has an innate predisposition toward lesbianism or if her sexual preference has become mentally coded during her maturation, we may have to ask a different set of questions about her responses. Does the lesbian reader read or the lesbian writer write in ways that are characteristic of her lesbianism but that are not necessarily chosen deliberately or even consciously? Does the lesbian mind produce styles and structures in any way different from those of the heterosexual female mind? Will we eventually be able to define lesbian thinking as, for example, Sara Ruddick has defined maternal thinking?[9]

Further research may one day clarify these questions. In the meantime a useful compromise between the two positions is Ethel Spector Person's theory of sex printing. Arguing for "nurture" over "nature," she nevertheless describes sex printing as a gradual, universal, and inevitable narrowing of sexual potential: "From the subjective point of view the sex print is experienced as sexual 'preference.' Because it is revealed rather than chosen, sexual preference is felt as deep rooted and deriving from one's nature." Person apparently sees determining the cause of sex printing as neither possible nor efficacious—and thus avoids the resurrection of possessive mothers and absent fathers—but she stresses the "relative irreversibility of the sex print," which is nevertheless "learned" behavior.[10]

7. Sara Ruddick, "Maternal Thinking," *Feminist Studies* 6, no. 2 (Summer 1980): 342–67.

8. On encoding lesbian texts as a strategy for survival, see Catharine Stimpson, "Zero Degree Deviancy: The Lesbian Novel in English," *Critical Inquiry* 8, no. 2 (Winter 1981): 363–79, esp. 366 ff.; and Faderman, pp. 400 ff.

9. Recent work on mothers and daughters is also relevant here. See Marianne Hirsch's review essay, "Mothers and Daughters," *Signs* 7, no. 1 (Autumn 1981): 200–22.

10. Ethel Spector Person, "Sexuality as the Mainstay of Identity: Psychoanalytic Perspectives," *Signs* 5, no. 4 (Summer 1980): 605–30.

Person's theory seems to me valuable partly because it appears to describe my own experience. It is useful because it accounts for the most frequent descriptions of lesbian self-awareness and for the difficulties experienced by those who attempt to change a homosexual orientation[11] but does not subscribe to biological determinism. Her interpretation of the term "lesbian" is the one I will use in this discussion. I shall assume, too, that, although we bring to our reading other aspects of our identities, sexual identity is, as Ethel Person claims, uniquely central.

What I wish to suggest here is a theory of reading that will not oversimplify the concept of identification, will not subsume lesbian difference under a universal female, and will be applicable to all texts—including those written by men, heterosexual women, and self-hating lesbians. My purpose is to show how lesbians could reread and write about texts (in-scribe them if you will) rather than to describe lesbian critics' present strategies, though for demonstration purposes I shall draw on such criticism. When consciously employed as a critical method, the theory is applicable to any of the definitions of "lesbian" I have discussed so far; however, if we accept the idea of an innate or imprinted lesbianism, the reading process may not be entirely volitional. As will become apparent, it is a method of reading that necessarily includes the lesbian reader rather than a theory of lesbian reading. Although it can be used by any reader, it is particularly valuable to those readers whose experiences are not frequently reflected in literature.

I am particularly interested in the question of lesbian rereading of the dominant heterosexual tradition, of finding something to do other than substituting "woman" wherever the word "man" appears.[12] Although, as I have argued elsewhere, readers have a different understanding of texts that describe their own experience,[13] most reading involves texts that have a very limited relationship to the reader's life. How can we read alien texts and avoid the schizophrenia (often more severe for a lesbian than for a heterosexual woman) that so many feminists have described as a result of their education in the male tradition?[14]

Psychological theories of identity formation, which underlie the work of Judith Gardiner, Wolfgang Iser, and implicitly that of all reader-response critics, can be helpful here, at least as paradigms. As Norman Holland says, "To go from the text as an object to our experience of it calls for a psychology of some kind."[15] Catharine Stimpson's objection to a

---

11. Ibid., p. 621: "In therapy, change in sexual orientation . . . is achieved only with great difficulty and sometimes not at all."

12. Faderman, p. 357.

13. Jean E. Kennard, "Personally Speaking: Feminist Critics and the Community of Readers," *College English* 43, no. 2 (February 1981): 140–45.

14. See Fetterley (n. 1 above), pp. xx–xxiv, for a good overview of these problems.

15. Judith Kegan Gardiner, "On Female Identity and Writing by Women," *Critical Inquiry* 8, no. 2 (Winter 1981): 347–61; Wolfgang Iser, *The Act of Reading: A Theory of Aesthetic Response* (Baltimore: Johns Hopkins University Press, 1978), esp. p. 28: "Recourse to

psychological approach to literature on the grounds that "psychology hardly defines the totality of our lives" misses the point, I think.[16] Psychology does aim to define the totality of our lives; it is, though, only one of the languages that do so.

The kind of psychology used is the more important issue, for, as feminist scholars have demonstrated, the male bias on which some psychological theory rests essentially invalidates it. Since reading is a process—one that we invariably describe as beneficial to the reader—it would seem sensible to look at a form of therapy that stresses process. Since psychological theories often fail in their generalizations about human nature to distinguish female from male, let alone lesbian from heterosexual female, we also need a theory that at least does not distort lesbian experience by its premises about "human" or even "female" reactions. We need a theory, then, that is client (reader) centered.

I am using Joseph Zinker's views on therapy as outlined in *Creative Process in Gestalt Therapy* because, first, they meet these conditions. Second, I am comfortable with the language in which he talks about therapy because it is frequently the language of literary criticism: "Each therapy session has an intrinsic flow and structure"; "the theme is then elaborated"; "a simple translation of a person's metaphor." Indeed Zinker's descriptions of the therapeutic process can often be transferred verbatim to the reading process: "We must take the risk of projecting the most idiosyncratic, personal imagery upon objects, words and other symbols." However, in borrowing Zinker's ideas, I do not mean to suggest that other theories might not work as well.[17]

The aspect of Zinker's theory most useful to a discussion of reading process begins with his concept of the individual as a composite of "polarities" or opposing characteristics. "In an oversimplified example, we might say that a person has within him [*sic*] the characteristic of kindness and also its polarity of cruelty, the characteristic of hardness and its polarity, softness" (p. 197). Zinker recognizes that all these qualities may, in a given case, generate different opposing characteristics; the polarities are not fixed. On different occasions the opposite of lesbian emotions may be those of a heterosexual female, a homosexual male, or a heterosexual male. In this way the concept of polarities really incorporates a spectrum of differences that under specific circumstances can be defined as opposites.

---

psychology, as a basis for a particular category of reader in whom the responses to literature may be observed, has come about not least because of the desire to escape from the limitations of other categories." Norman Holland, *The Dynamics of Literary Response* (New York: Oxford University Press, 1968), p. xv. See Culler (n. 1 above), p. 225, for a discussion of the possible complexities in the relationship between literature and psychoanalysis.

16. Stimpson, p. 377.

17. Joseph Zinker, *Creative Process in Gestalt Therapy* (New York: Random House, 1977), pp. 18, 9. Further citations of this work will be included parenthetically in the text.

One's inner reality consists of both those qualities in oneself that one finds acceptable and those that are unacceptable and therefore often hidden or denied. Zinker explains, "We often identify ourselves with one characteristic and not its counterpart, e.g. I see myself as peaceful and not aggressive, or stingy and not generous, or honest and not devious" (p. 33). The aspects of ourselves we do not own he calls "dark polarities," those we see as part of ourselves, "light polarities."

The concept of polarities is one of the few premises about human nature that Zinker asks us to accept. It is, perhaps surprisingly, compatible with Ethel Person's theory of sex printing in which there is a narrowing of sexual potential until the individual's sense of her or his own sexual identity finally does not acknowledge the polarity from which it became differentiated. So it is often true, I think, when an aspect of our identity— lesbianism, for example—is claimed in the face of societal opposition, that we stifle the doubts (deny the polarities) all the more forcefully in order to maintain it. Jane Rule, talking about her younger self, says, "I was sexually so hungry, humanly so isolated, psychically so traumatized by social judgment that I required of myself a purity of motive so self-sacrificing, a vision of love so redeeming that to be a lover was an annihilation of all the healthy instincts of self-preservation I had."[18] This reaction explains perhaps why apparently clearly defined personalities so often acknowledge or reveal a chink in the armor of their self-concepts. Who has not known (or been) the intellectual who watches soap operas, the vegetarian who makes an exception of hamburgers, the pacifist who enjoys war movies. The chink acts as a safety valve but also indicates the pressure of the so-called dark polarities.

Of course Zinker is not saying that we are not what we claim to be, that all kind people are really cruel, all lesbians are really heterosexuals. He merely claims that even if we are primarily kind, the impulse toward unkindness is still within us. Indeed his aim in therapy is to strengthen, deepen the original self-concept and to change only those forms of behavior that disturb the client. Health, for Zinker as for all therapists, lies in self-awareness, in letting the light in on the dark polarities. Healthy people may not approve of all their tendencies, but their acknowledgment of them indicates "inner strength" (p. 200).

At the center of gestalt methodology is the experiment, an often playful acting out of new behavior, none of which is necessarily to be incorporated into "real" behavior. "The experiment," says Zinker, "gives us permission to be priest, whore, faggot, holy man, wise witch, magician—all things, beings, notions hidden within us" (p. 18). He could have added, of course, "heterosexual." Particularly relevant to an application to the reading process is the word "notions"; the "things hidden within us" are qualities as much of the imagination as of the self, or, rather, what we

18. Jane Rule, *Outlander* (Tallahassee, Fla.: Naiad Press, 1981), p. 182.

are capable of imagining is given equal weight with our actions. The experiment may involve dramatizing, drawing, writing, talking, and is clearly adaptable to reading if this is seen as incorporating projections of the reader.

What we become, for a time, during the experiment is an extreme form of an aspect of ourselves, often a denied one. Doing so, we act on two premises (the final ones Zinker asks us to accept): first, when we exaggerate ("lean into" is the gestalt jargon) one side of a polarity/aspect of the self, the other side gets "attracted" toward it, pulled as if in a magnetic field; second, the side that gets pulled is deepened and solidified in the process. "My theory of polarities dictates that if I do not allow myself to be unkind, I will never be genuinely kind," explains Zinker. "If I am in touch with my own unkindness and stretch that part of myself, when my kindness emerges it will be richer, fuller, more complete. . . . I call this the 'around the world' phenomenon: If you keep flying north long enough, you'll eventually be heading south" (p. 202). I do not become heterosexual by allowing that part of me to breathe, I become more fully, completely lesbian.

Needed to begin the experiment is a willingness to "lean into" or invade the dark polarities that one finds unacceptable. In the therapeutic process clients may reach part of this hidden side through unstructured activity with an observant therapist who will spot the chinks in the armor. But the process of reading, "of losing oneself in a book," as it was once innocently called, can serve the same purpose.

To read Zinker's ideas as a methodology of reading takes remarkably little translation. As an experiment in reading—a lesbian reading a heterosexual male work, for example—the process might take the following form. Rather than resisting the text, the reader acknowledges one familiar or shared aspect of the male protagonist,[19] for "we *can* only bring another person's thoughts into our foreground if they are in some way related to the virtual background of our own orientations."[20] Using strategies she has been taught so well, she "leans into" the character, identifies with him as fully as possible, in a sort of willing suspension of belief; without fear of experiencing schizophrenia, she allows the polarities to coexist, forcing concentration on the heterosexual until the lesbian in her is pulled forward to the surface of her consciousness. The text or the character is made to signify also what it is not. For example, to be Stephen Dedalus—as most of us educated in British and American English departments have had to be—is to be a heterosexual. The lesbian reader, identifying initially perhaps with Stephen's alienation from his

19. What I am explaining here is perhaps more readily understood if I talk about fictional characters, but it can be applied equally to aspects of texts'/authors' attitudes.

20. Iser, p. 155.

family or with his guilty adolescent sexuality, must finally experience his heterosexual maleness, his sense of the female as other, as symbol. By fully examining this aspect of his character (and its implications) the lesbian reader can make apparent its opposite. Stephen Dedalus is not a homosexual female.

Iser provides an interesting gloss on Zinker as a reading theorist: "Thus there occurs a kind of artificial division as the reader brings into his [*sic*] own foreground something which he is not. This does not mean that his own orientations disappear completely. . . . In reading, then, there are also two levels, and despite the multifarious ways in which they can be related they can never be totally kept apart." Iser claims that "a layer of the reader's personality is brought to light which had hitherto remained hidden in the shadows." The result of the reading process is therapeutic to the reader, for "it enables us to formulate ourselves."[21]

Although Iser acknowledges the necessity of some projection from the reader's past experience in order to enter the text, he puts more emphasis on the effect of text on reader than I intend here. Seeing the reading process as a transaction, he nevertheless stresses the capacity of the text to open up an inner world in the reader of which she or he had not previously been conscious rather than the reader's capacity to deepen the self-concept. As readers we do more than simply repeat ourselves, more than recognize "the already familiar," but I suggest the process is closer to reinforcing than to transforming. We redefine aspects of ourselves through contrast with the opposite aspects in a fictional other that we have temporarily experienced.[22]

It is, I realize, one thing to take the study of literature into the world of psychoanalysis and another to leave it there. The reading process certainly involves more than providing low cost therapy for the individual reader, though it may serve that function. What are the implications of the theory of polar reading to critical methodology? How does a polar reader write about literature? Polar reading/writing is primarily a question of contrast. Just as with a black and white photograph, the intensification of the black means the inevitable intensification of the white, so the

---

21. Ibid., pp. 155, 157, 158.
22. See Holland, p. 101: "One of literature's adaptive functions, then, is that it allows us to loosen boundaries—between self and not self, inner and outer." Iser quotes Edmund Husserl on this subject, p. 157: "We might say that the ego as ego continually develops itself through its original decisions, and at any given time is a pole of multifarious and actual determinations, and a pole of an habitual, radiating system of realizable potentials for positive and negative attitudes." This does not have to mean as David Bleich suggests in his objections to Holland's description of reading as a reiterative process that "the idea of novelty loses its meaning altogether" (*Subjective Criticism* [Baltimore: Johns Hopkins University Press, 1978], p. 111). Each new text calls on slightly different aspects of ourselves and thus strengthens different parts of our identity.

polar reader intensifies the attitude of character or author, embodies it so fully that the contrasting aspects of the reader's own attitudes come into the picture. (The implications of negatives, of backgrounds and fore-grounds, and, considering the earlier discussion, of prints could obvi-ously be developed here. But the process is primarily, to deconstruct my own image, one of overexposure.)

While the work of many critics might no doubt furnish examples of polar reading, two essays by Virginia Woolf and Adrienne Rich are particularly useful: Woolf's reading of *Robinson Crusoe* and Rich's reading of Emily Dickinson's poetry. These two essays illustrate a distinction needed in any discussion of reading theory. Just as "reading as a woman is not necessarily what occurs when a woman reads," so reading as a lesbian is not necessarily what happens when a lesbian reads.[23] Woolf, in one sense a lesbian reader, is not reading as a lesbian in this essay, although the emotions summoned by the reading do not exclude those characteristic of lesbian experience.[24] Rich, on the other hand, is specifically concerned— to adapt Elaine Showalter's comment on the *female* reader—"with the way in which the hypothesis of a *lesbian* reader changes our apprehension of a given text" (emphasis mine).[25]

Much of Woolf's criticism is so marked by an awareness of readers' responses that it provides a link between the affective criticism of the nineteenth century and contemporary reader-response theory. She writes frequently of the influence of the reader on the reading[26] and, like Iser, recognizes two "selves" involved in the process, that other self elicited by the text and the reader's predefined self, which can never be entirely subsumed by the other: "We may stress the value of sympathy; we may try to sink our identity as we read. But we know that we cannot sympathise wholly or immerse ourselves wholly."[27] Although for Woolf both the text and the author are more substantial than they are for many a contemporary critic, she nevertheless writes, perhaps playfully, of read-ers who "know without a word to guide them precisely what he [a charac-ter] thought and felt."[28]

The texture of *Orlando* alone, woven as it is from the opposing tension of male and female selves, from contrasted scenes, from reversed

23. Culler, p. 49.
24. This, of course, raises the question of the definition of "lesbian." Recent bio-graphical work on Woolf demonstrates that she had lesbian sexual experiences; I would argue too that her primary emotional bonds were with women.
25. Quoted in Culler, p. 50.
26. In *Virginia Woolf: The Inward Voyage* (Princeton, N.J.: Princeton University Press, 1970), Harvena Richter points out that Woolf's "vision of the novel . . . implies an unusually close relationship between the reader and the work" (p. 234).
27. Virginia Woolf, "How Should One Read a Book?" in *The Common Reader, Second Series* (London: Hogarth Press, 1932), p. 268.
28. Virginia Woolf, *Orlando* (London: Hogarth Press, 1928), p. 69.

mirror images, invites a consideration of polarities in Woolf's other work. A comment by T. S. Eliot suggests her interest in what is not stated in the text: "Instead of looking for the primitive, she looks rather for the civilized, the highly civilized, where nevertheless something is found to be *left out*. And this something is deliberately left out, by what could be called a moral effort of the will. And, being left out, this something is, in a sense, in a melancholy sense, present."[29] It is precisely this characteristic (one typical of her own work) that she observes in the essay on *Robinson Crusoe*.

The essay begins with a discussion of two possible critical approaches to the text, the historical and the biographical. Her consideration of the historical recognizes the relationship of reader to text: "A middle class had come into existence, able to read and anxious to read ... about themselves."[30] Her consideration of the biographical deals with the relationship of Defoe's "self" to his text. Woolf quickly dismisses both approaches as unlikely to make reading either more pleasurable or more intelligent.

The "book itself remains" (p. 52), says Woolf, and the contemporary critic awaits an argument for a "new critical" reading. But Woolf continues in language that suggests Iser or Holland: "There is a piece of business to be transacted between writer and reader before any further dealings are possible" (p. 52). Thus at the outset she establishes the reading process as an interchange between two entities, the reader and an "other" who is variably Defoe as writer, Defoe as represented by the "perspective" implied in his text, and Defoe as projected on the protagonist of his novel. The first task of the reader is to see the world from Defoe's point of view, to look at things from his perspective: "All alone we must climb upon the novelist's shoulders and gaze through his eyes until we, too, understand in what order he ranges the large common objects upon which novelists are fated to gaze" (p. 52). This is a familiar direction from Woolf: elsewhere she instructs us "to go back three or four hundred years and become in fancy at least an Elizabethan"; she cautions us, "Do not dictate to your author; try to become him."[31] She is not, however, talking loosely of "losing oneself in a book," of escaping. She is fully aware of the difficulties of identification, of participating in the alien world of

29. T. S. Eliot in *Virginia Woolf: The Critical Heritage*, ed. Robin Majumdar and Allen McLaurin (London: Routledge & Kegan Paul, 1975), p. 192.

30. Virginia Woolf, "Robinson Crusoe," in *The Common Reader, Second Series*, p. 51. Further citations of this work will be included parenthetically in the text.

31. Virginia Woolf, "The Strange Elizabethans," in *The Common Reader, Second Series*, p. 9; Woolf, "How Should One Read a Book?" p. 259. Woolf's own intensity of identification with the characters she creates is a relevant parallel here. In "An Unwritten Novel" (in *A Haunted House* [London: Hogarth Press, 1944], pp. 22–23), she talks of a desire "to lodge myself somewhere in the firm flesh . . . or find a foothold on the person, in the soul," in order to feel "the suck and regurgitation of the heart."

the "other"—difficulties perhaps suggested by the impossibility of seeing through the eyes while standing on the shoulders.

If readers could fully participate in the world of a novel, that is, completely lose all sense of self while reading, "the battle" between reader and text would be over. But "we have our own vision of the world," Woolf explains, and are afraid and angry when that is challenged. This "vision of the world" is more than merely a set of opinions, though it may be manifested in that fashion; it is basic to our sense of our selves, "our private harmony" (p. 53). When the perspective of the novel differs from our own, "we are afraid because the old supports are being wrenched from us" (p. 54). So we resist the text. She describes two letter writers to the newspapers: Major Gibbs who objects to Hardy's pessimism and Miss Wiggs who "must protest that though Proust's art is wonderful, the real world, she thanks God, has nothing in common with the distortions of a perverted Frenchman." Both, Woolf explains, "are trying to control the novelist's perspective so that it shall resemble and reinforce their own" (p. 53).[32] Unlike the polar reader, they seek to affirm themselves by a denial of "the other" rather than through a full recognition of it.

Reading begins with our own expectations as readers. We come to *Robinson Crusoe* knowing it is the story of a man shipwrecked on a desert island. We thus expect, says Woolf, sunsets, sunrises, solitude, and soul—in other words, an intense spirituality, an awareness of the mind in isolation. But who is the reader who expects these things? Woolf herself. The expectations she describes are those she satisfies in readers of her own fiction. Isolation, the life of the mind, solitude, and soul are among the most obvious of her own preoccupations, noted and documented by every critic from Winifred Holtby on.

Robinson Crusoe initially resists Woolf, who as reader is "rudely contradicted on every page" (p. 54). Everything is "fact," "substance." "Each sortie of ours in pursuit of information upon these cardinal points of perspective—God, Man, Nature—is snubbed back with ruthless common sense." Reflecting her own attempt to "control the novelist's perspective," she repeats each of her three terms—"God," "Man," and "Nature"—three times within one paragraph. Each is furled, reduced, shriveled, and finally "does not exist." "Nothing exists except an earthenware pot. Finally that is to say, we are forced to drop our own preconceptions and to accept what Defoe himself wishes to give us."

Woolf makes the journey from York to the island sitting on Crusoe's shoulders. She does not tell us exactly what enables her to gain access to his perspective but is "drawn on" by a consideration, a shared knowledge

32. Woolf, however, recognizes as does Iser that readers need some common ground to deal with a text at all, "for what pleasure or amusement can be plucked from a brand new idea" (p. 54).

of the virtues of British middle-class life. Those rarely acknowledged aspects of Woolf, "temperance, moderation, quietness and health" (p. 55), come to the foreground. She "leans into" Crusoe, "his shrewdness, his caution, his love of order and comfort and respectability" until "everything appears as it would appear to that naturally cautious, apprehensive, conventional and solidly matter-of-fact intelligence" (p. 56).

Woolf marks this change in her position as reader by beginning to write from Crusoe's point of view: "He is so busy and has such an eye to the main chance that he notices only a tenth part of what is going on around him. Everything is capable of a rational explanation, he is sure, if only he had time to attend to it. We are much more alarmed by 'the vast creatures' that swim out in the night and surround his boat than he is. . . . He is for ever counting his barrels, and making sensible provisions for his water supply . . . ; the pressure of life when one is fending entirely for oneself alone on a desert island is really no laughing matter. It is no crying one either. A man must have an eye to everything; it is no time for raptures about Nature when the lightning may explode one's gunpowder" (pp. 56–57). Woolf has come as close to participating in Crusoe's emotions as she can. But there is another voice here. She is after all on his shoulders and not in his head: she also sees "what is going on around him." There are two selves present. The reader's own self can play at matter-of-factness, but barrel counting will in time come to feel excessive. Her imaginative pole is drawn forward; she is alarmed where he explains. She knows him well enough to know what he is not and can only know this because of what she is: a woman capable of laughter and tears and raptures about nature.

Woolf attributes to Defoe the capacity to suggest great emotion by describing fact: "Thus Defoe, by reiterating that nothing but a plain earthenware pot stands in the foreground, persuades us to see remote islands and the solitudes of the human soul" (p. 58). But is it Defoe who has done this, or is it Woolf who has revealed to us that pole in herself that this novel with all its matter-of-factness has attracted? By the end of the essay Woolf has found in *Robinson Crusoe* those best aspects of "Man," "Nature," and "God" she initially thought the novel denied. The text has allowed her to affirm herself.

Has Woolf's self—at least the aspect of it attracted to this subject—been affected at all? Has Woolf's capacity for the sublime been changed, reinforced by reading *Robinson Crusoe*? Perhaps. She now describes the beauty of common objects and actions as revelation and asks in a tone of discovery "why," after all, "the perspective that a plain earthenware pot exacts should not satisfy us as completely" as "a background of broken mountains and tumbling oceans with stars flaming in the sky?" (p. 58). She remarks how by mentioning the absence of his companions, visible now only in "three of their hats, one cap, and two shoes that were not fellows,"

Defoe suggests "a sense of desolation and the deaths of many men" (pp. 57–58). And I remember the end of *Jacob's Room* where Jacob's death in war is suggested so powerfully by his empty shoes.[33]

In her preface to the reprinted version of her 1975 essay "Vesuvius at Home: The Power of Emily Dickinson," Adrienne Rich provides a context for it within lesbian-feminist scholarship. Quoting Toni McNaron's call for a lesbian-feminist reading of Dickinson, Rich gives us her view of what that might be: "to 'prove' that a woman of the nineteenth century did or did not sleep with another woman, or women, is beside the point. . . . Such a criticism will ask questions hitherto passed over; will not search obsessively for heterosexual romance as the key to a woman artist's life and work."[34] A lesbian reading, then, will allow for different answers to the questions about Dickinson's life and work, will create "a context in which the importance, and validity, of Dickinson's attachments to women may now, at last, be seen in full" (p. 162).

Unlike Virginia Woolf reading *Robinson Crusoe*, Rich is a self-defined lesbian reader. Her subject, the "other" of her essay, is also on the surface much more similar to her than Defoe is to Woolf; in "Vesuvius at Home" a lesbian poet reads another woman poet she sees as woman identified. The major difference between Rich's essay and Woolf's is this initial distance between reader and text.

Nevertheless Rich's essay as much as Woolf's is an illustration of polar reading. In an earlier essay Rich defines the imagination in terms of polarities in a way surprisingly reminiscent of Zinker: "You have to be free to play around with the notion that day might be night, love might be hate; nothing can be too sacred for the imagination to turn into its opposite or to call experimentally by another name. For writing is renaming."[35] Rich "renames" Dickinson, whom she defines as a composite of polarities: a practical woman seen by others as "partially cracked," a strong woman who emphasized her "littleness," "a creative and powerful" self hidden within a "publicly acceptable persona"—in other words, "Vesuvius at home." The Massachusetts from which Rich writes is composed of polarities also; both "peaceful" and threatened," it is hills and fruit trees contrasted with "ARCO, MacDonald's, shopping plazas."

The structure of Rich's essay, however, differs from that of Woolf's. Rather than moving gradually into identification with a protagonist against whom she finally defines herself, Rich moves toward and away

33. Although *Jacob's Room* precedes the essay on *Robinson Crusoe*, it can be fairly assumed, I think, that Woolf had read Defoe's novel much earlier.

34. Adrienne Rich, "Vesuvius at Home: The Power of Emily Dickinson," in *On Lies, Secrets, and Silence: Selected Prose, 1966–1978* (New York: W. W. Norton & Co., 1979), pp. 157–83, esp. p. 158. Further citations of this work will be included parenthetically in the text.

35. Adrienne Rich, "When We Dead Awaken: Writing as Re-Vision," in *On Lies, Secrets, and Silence*, pp. 33–49, esp. p. 43.

from Dickinson, "leaning into" a point of identification, then clarifying its opposite. The difference in method is, perhaps, the difference between a polar reading of a novel and the polar reading of individual poems.

Rich begins with a Woolfian image, describing herself as an insect hovering for most of her life against the screens of Emily Dickinson's existence. At once she acknowledges their differences: "The methods, the exclusions, of Emily Dickinson's existence could not have been my own." To recapture the time that separates them, Rich, like Woolf, begins with a journey, "traveling at the speed of time along the Massachusetts Turnpike" (p. 158). But as she drives through Northampton, Hadley, Amherst, it is her own past, "college weekends" of her undergraduate days, which are polarized with an unstated present: a heterosexual past with a lesbian present.

In order to broaden her own and our understanding of a Dickinson "reduced to quaintness or spinsterish oddity by many of her commentators," Rich has been "trying to visit, to enter her mind, through her poems and letters" (pp. 159, 160). The tone of Rich's commentary is that of someone who has a special understanding of Dickinson's poetry. She simply tells us what the poems are without arguing for her reading or demonstrating its validity. Again like Woolf, this "inside" position is alternated with a polar position in Rich herself. There are two voices here, too. "I do not pretend to have—I don't even wish to have—explained this poem" (p. 174), Rich says at one point.

In fully experiencing the reasons for Dickinson's seclusion Rich finally understands it as creative freedom. She describes Dickinson deliberately intensifying "the confined space in which the genius of the nineteenth-century mind in America moved" in order to create a language for poetry "more varied, more compressed, more dense with implications, more complete of syntax, than any American poetic language to date" (p. 163). But it is not freedom as Rich defines it in her own life and work. Objecting to the pointless hunt for a secret male lover in Dickinson's life, Rich offers as one possible definition of the masculine element, the "he" of Dickinson's poems, her own power externalized as a "daemon." But, Rich points out, "the archetype of the daemon as masculine is beginning to change" (p. 173). Her discussion of Dickinson "slanting" the truth in order to voice it in her poetry reminds us of the contrasting directness of Rich's own work, of a named lesbianism, of the title of the book in which this essay is reprinted, *On Lies, Secrets, and Silence*. But, Rich reminds us, "the nineteenth-century woman had much to repress" (p. 175). In almost every way the twentieth-century woman has less. In one important respect, however, that is not so: Dickinson's deeply charged relationships with women could be experienced in greater freedom than that available to contemporary women, for "none of this was perceived or condemned as 'lesbianism' " (p. 163).

So Rich's insight into Dickinson allows her to affirm her own values through polarizing aspects of her "real" self. It is not coincidental that Dickinson finally teaches Rich what Rich has taught us: "More than any other poet Emily Dickinson seemed to tell me that the intense inner event, the personal and the psychological, was inseparable from the universal; that there was a range for psychological poetry beyond mere self-expression" (p. 168).

Polar reading permits the participation of any reader in any text and thus opens up the possibility of enjoying the widest range of literary experience. It does not, however, involve the reader's denying herself. The reader redefines herself in opposition to the text; if that self-definition includes lesbianism, this becomes apparent in any commentary she may make on her reading.

Polar reading, then, is not a theory of lesbian reading but a method particularly appropriate to lesbian readers and others whose experience is not frequently reflected in literature. Of course there is much work to do on whether lesbians read and write differently from heterosexual women, on encoding lesbian experience, on specifically lesbian literature. But we also need a way of reading and of writing about any literature that does not reconfirm the universality of heterosexual experience. Because it is based in readers' individual differences, the theory of polar reading must necessarily include us. As individual lesbian readers, our critical work can in this way expose the assumption of universal heterosexuality for what it is—a false assumption.

Department of English
University of New Hampshire

Homosexuality, Homophobia, and Revolution: Notes toward an Understanding of the Cuban Lesbian and Gay Male Experience, Part I

Lourdes Arguelles and B. Ruby Rich

Thousands of homosexual men and women have migrated to the United States and to other capitalist nations since the start of the socialist revolution in Cuba in 1959.[1] This exodus has been interpreted as stemming almost exclusively from the homophobic nature of the Castro regime and a set of repressive policies that have purportedly rendered gay and lesbian expression on the island virtually impossible.[2] At least, such has been the interpretation within North American gay academic and artistic circles and within segments of the Left.[3]

Conventionally accepted factors such as economic incentives and personal troubles, which migration theorists usually point to as powerful stimulators to individual migration, are seldom considered in evaluations

1. Note that the term "homosexual" and not "gay" is used when describing prerevolutionary Cuban society. Both words are used, along with "lesbian," in the discussion of Cuba after 1959. Whether the term "gay" should be applied at all to the style of homosexuality and homosexual identities common in Cuba is arguable, while the term "lesbian" seems less politically specific and hence applicable to different historical periods. But differentiation among these terms is necessarily imprecise, due to the lack of theoretical work on cross-cultural usage.

2. See, e.g., stories on the "gay" Mariel migration in the *Washington Post* (July 7, 1980); *Oakland Tribune* (August 3, 1980); and the *Advocate* (New York; August 21, 1980).

3. See, e.g., Allen Young, *Gays under the Cuban Revolution* (San Francisco: Grey Fox Press, 1981); Dennis Altman, *The Homosexualization of America, the Americanization of the Homosexual* (New York: St. Martin's Press, 1982).

Reprinted from *Signs: Journal of Women in Culture and Society* 9, no. 4 (Summer 1984): 683–699.

of Cuban gays' migratory patterns since the revolution began. The more structuralist explanations for international population movements, which stress the role of capital and of capitalist states in organizing migratory flows from less developed to more developed economies, have yet to be invoked in the interpretation of gay migration from Cuba.[4]

Such reductive interpretation is consistent with the acritical nature of bourgeois thought and its well-known tendency to simplify motivations and homogenize differences among "lesser mortals": Third World peoples, ethnic minorities, the working class, and particularly the gay and female segments within them. It is also consistent with the easy way in which this style of thought validates suspect information; Cuban "refugee" testimony, for example, becomes its main source for evaluation of Cuban gay life, despite knowledge of the pressures on émigrés to testify to political persecution in their country of origin in order to attain the legal and economic advantages of refugee status in their new country.[5]

The success of this interpretation has served anti-Cuban interests, most notably the American state, rather well. First, credibility of the story has neutralized badly needed support for the Cuban revolution among its natural allies (North American progressive lobbies) and legitimated the presence in traditionally liberal circles of some of the more reactionary elements within the Cuban émigré population. Second, it has obscured the changing realities and subtleties of everyday gay life on the island as part of the ongoing revolutionary process itself. Third, it has made the historical legacy of prerevolutionary political economy and homophobia seem immaterial to an understanding of contemporary Cuban gay and lesbian issues. Fourth, it has helped to conceal the oppressive and exploitative features of life for gay men and women in the émigré enclaves. Fifth, it has distanced gay activists in capitalist mainstream culture from minority gays involved in the liberation movements of their respective countries and national communities. Finally, the continual scapegoating of Cuban revolutionary homophobia has made the growing number of progressive gay émigrés who criticize but also support the revolution into living contradictions: invisible to gay liberation forces but easy targets for the homophobic anti-Castro army in exile.

This report is based on research on lesbian and gay male experience conducted between 1979 and 1984 in Cuba and in Cuban émigré enclaves in the United States, Puerto Rico, Mexico, and Spain. The object of the investigation was to begin apprehending the nature and dynamics of

4. See articles on Cuban gay migration in the *Boston Gay Community News* (October 25, 1980); and the *Advocate* (August 21, 1980).

5. For a discussion on the problems of bourgeois interpretations of "refugee" testimony, see Geoffrey Fox, *Working Class Emigres from Cuba* (Palo Alto, Calif.: R & E Associates, 1970), pp. 11–21.

Cuban gay experience so as to provide an adequate context in which contemporary Cuban gay life, migration, and resettlement could be understood. The research was also intended as a preliminary contribution to two areas of inquiry that remain grossly underdeveloped: description of gay and lesbian everyday life in Third World countries and communities and theory on the nature of the relationships between the structures of sexuality and the corresponding structures of socialist organization.[6] The data were obtained through diverse systems of inquiry (historical analysis, along with survey, field, and experiential methods) and interpreted within a theoretical framework drawn from lesbian-feminist and critical gay scholarship and the politicoeconomic and phenomenological study of Cuban social life.

We are aware of the risks incurred by disseminating this study: giving ammunition to anti-Cuban lobbies and to strongly homophobic cliques on the island and risking the enmity of those Cuban émigrés who have long capitalized on this unexamined issue as a condemnation of the revolutionary process. Despite such risks, we and most of the collaborators of the study (the dozens of Cuban gays and lesbians who willingly shared their lives and analyses throughout the investigation) strongly believe that the benefits of initiating an informed discourse on Cuban homosexuality will far outweigh the potential costs—that there is an urgent need for it because of both the ongoing debates regarding sexuality and repression within capitalist and socialist countries and the complexities of gay and lesbian existence in Cuba and abroad.

This report is divided into two parts. Part I deals primarily with prerevolutionary Cuban homosexuality and with lesbian and gay experience in Cuba after the beginning of the revolution. It includes a succinct (given space limitations) analysis of different gay migratory waves. Part II (to be published in an upcoming issue of *Signs*) focuses on gay and lesbian life in the émigré enclaves and on the ways in which the American state and anti-Castro groups have used the Cuban gay issue.

Prerevolutionary Cuba

With the exception of bourgeois homosexuals who spent extended periods of time abroad, most Cubans engaged in homosexual relations (whatever their sexual identity) gravitated toward the capital city of Havana in search of work and a more liberated life-style before the revolution. Job opportunities in the interior of the island were severely limited

---

6. For more information on research method, see Lourdes Arguelles, "The Gay Issue in Cuban and Cuban-American Studies" (paper presented at the Cuban American Studies Conference, Massachusetts Institute of Technology, Cambridge, May 27, 1984).

due to the country's sharply uneven development pattern.[7] Further, Cuba's Afro-Hispanic patriarchal culture, with its emphasis on compulsory heterosexuality, was strongest in rural areas.[8] Also, the very smallness of prerevolutionary villages and cities made life intimate; sexual policing was thus an easy task and an effective deterrent against deviance from the norm. The openly homosexual man or woman who remained in the interior was often ostracized or cast in the role of village queer—the homosexual version of the village idiot.[9]

Even in the Havana of the 1950s, everyday life was not easy for the working-class or petty-bourgeois homosexual. Unemployment was high and had been steadily increasing throughout the decade. The scarcity of productive occupations demanded a strictly closeted occupational life. For all women, and especially for lesbians, employment almost invariably entailed continual sexual harassment. Aida, a lesbian seamstress now living in Miami, remembers: "At work, you had to pretend to have a boyfriend all the time . . . make up stories . . . even get someone to accompany you to work once or twice. . . . If not, you were in trouble. Because they'd be after you every day, every hour, every minute, caressing you, showing off their genitals. It was hell."[10]

The only occupational sector showing substantial growth was that connected to tourism, drug distribution, gambling, and prostitution. This sector was mostly controlled by American organized crime and members of an indigenous bourgeoisie directly linked to Batista's political apparatus.[11] It employed more than two hundred thousand workers as petty traders, casino operators, entertainers, servants, and prostitutes.[12]

During this period of severe sexual repression in advanced capitalist nations, homosexual desire was often channeled into illegal and lucrative offshore markets like the Havana underworld. Not surprisingly, then, Cuban homosexuals had preferential hiring treatment in the Havana tourist sector in order to meet the demands of American visitors and

7. Juan y Verena Martinez Alier, *Cuba: Economia y sociedad* (Paris: Ruedo Iberico, 1972), esp. pp. 26–57.

8. See Fernando Ortiz, *Los Negros Esclavos* (Havana: Revista Bimestre Cubana, 1916); Wyatt MacGaffey and Clifford R. Barnett, *Twentieth-Century Cuba: The Background of the Castro Revolution* (New York: Doubleday & Co., 1965), p. 62.

9. For an analysis of the role of honor and shame in small villages, see J. G. Peristany, "Introduction," in *Honour and Shame: The Values of Mediterranean Society*, ed. J. G. Peristany (London: Penguin Books, 1965). See also M. T. Mulhare, "Sexual Ideology in Pre-Castro Cuba" (Ph.D. diss., University of Pittsburgh, 1969).

10. Personal interview, Miami, June 23, 1982.

11. Fulgencio Batista was the Cuban dictator who assumed power officially for the second time through a military coup on March 10, 1952, and ruled until his overthrow in 1959.

12. The best portraits of fifties Havana are found in the less inhibited guidebooks. See A. Roberts, *Havana: Portrait of a City* (New York: Coward-McCann, 1953).

servicemen for homoerotic experiences. Other buyers of homosexual desire were the fathers and sons of the Cuban bourgeoisie, who felt free to partake of homoerotic practices without being considered homosexual as long as they did not take the passive, so-called female role in sexual relations. Yet another common practice for Cuban heterosexual men was the procurement of a lesbian prostitute's favors for a night.[13]

Apart from employment realities, social pressures made thousands of prerevolutionary homosexuals part of this underworld. Even homosexuals such as students (who were differently placed) were integrated into this subculture through the bars that they frequented: the St. Michel, the Dirty Dick, El Gato Tuerto. Then (as is still today the case in the U.S.) most of these bars were owned and operated by organized crime. Given the sharply stratified nature of prerevolutionary Cuba, working-class heterosexual men in order to make a living were also drawn into this underworld or alternatively into a homosexual underground dominated by the Cuban homosexual bourgeoisie. The bourgeois male homosexual of this era tended out of guilt to avoid same-class liaisons with other homosexuals and was constantly on the lookout for the heterosexual macho from the lower strata of the population. Thus, in many ways prerevolutionary homosexual liaisons in themselves fostered sexual colonialism and exploitation.

The commodification of homosexual desire in the Havana underworld and in the bourgeois homosexual underground during the prerevolutionary era, however, did not produce a significant toleration of homosexual life-styles in the larger social arena. Attitudes in traditional workplaces and within the family involved a combination of ridicule and violence toward the *locas*, or queens, and shame toward the *maricones*, or faggots. *Tortilleras* (or dykes)—considerably less visible owing to the overall repression of female sexuality—were either ignored or made objects of ridicule. If legal sanctions and official harassment were rare, this tolerance was due less to social acceptance than to overriding considerations of profit and the economic interests of the underworld that dominated the Cuban political apparatus.[14]

The consumer structure of the Havana underworld never spawned a "gay culture" or "gay sensibility" even in strictly commercial terms, due to its isolation from the mainstream of social life and the degree of guilt and self-hatred afflicting its members. Homosexual expressions in literature and other arts were few and guarded when compared to the intellectual and artistic achievements of gays in other Latin American countries such

13. Key informant interviews, Havana and Miami, 1982. See also articles in *Bohemia* and *Carteles* magazines during 1957–59.

14. Key informant interviews, Havana, November 14, 1981. For details on the 1939 Cuban Penal Code's specifying of prison sentences for homosexual behavior, see Jose A. Martinez, *Codigo de defensa social* (Havana: Jesus Montero, 1939), esp. articles 384–85.

as Brazil, Mexico, and Argentina. Even sympathetic observers of the homosexual scene frequently derided those engaged in same-sex relationships. When misogyny was added to homophobia, the reactions to lesbians in particular could be vitriolic. The following passage from Guillermo Cabrera Infante's more recent writings is typical of those of the period: "Margarita was under and on top of her . . . as if swimming, indecently rubbing her . . . trying to create for herself the instrument that nature had denied her."[15]

Homosexual challenges to the sexual order of everyday life and its rigid gender identities tended to be private and frequently were projected onto religious practices such as *Santeria*, an Afro-Cuban cult comprised of a syncretism of West African (primarily Yoruban) beliefs and rituals with those of Roman Catholicism. Because the *Santeria* gods "mount" either sex arbitrarily during ceremonies of possession, *Santeria* was and still is a favored form of gender transcendence for many Cuban homosexual men and lesbians.

Thus, in this prerevolutionary setting, discrete lesbian or gay male identities in the modern sense—identities that are based on self-definition and involve emotional as well as physical aspects of same sex relations—were rare.[16] Erotic loyalty (and, in the case of women, subservience) to the opposite sex was assumed as normal even by homosexuals. Hence, for many Cubans of this era, homosexuality was a mere addendum to customary marital roles. Among others, it was just a profitable commodification of sexual fantasy. For the vast majority, homosexuality made life a shameful and guilt-ridden experience. Such was gay Havana in its fabled *avant la guerre* period.

The Revolutionary Era

The revolution of 1959 eradicated the Havana underworld and initiated the development of a productive economy. With the profit motive removed, the superficial tolerance of homosexuality by the strongly homophobic Cuban society quickly eroded. At the same time, the revolutionary leadership rallied against the evils of capitalist vice—which were often associated with homosexuality. The demands of a revolutionary puritanism left few heterosexual escape clauses and no homosexual leeway at all.

Emigration began immediately. The promoters and overlords of the

15. Guillermo Cabrera Infante, *La Habana para un infante difunto* (Barcelona: Seix Barral, 1981), p. 621; our translation.
16. On modern gay identities, see John D'Emilio, "Capitalism and Gay Identity," in *Powers of Desire: The Politics of Sexuality*, ed. Ann Snitow, Christine Stansell, and Sharon Thompson (New York: Monthly Review Press, 1983), esp. p. 104.

Havana underworld along with large numbers of their displaced workers (many of them homosexuals) headed for Miami. Many lesbians who had liaisons with members of the bourgeoisie followed their male protectorate to Miami, as did gay men who had worked for U.S. firms or had done domestic work for the native bourgeoisie. Bourgeois homosexuals, many of whom had lived largely abroad anyway, now moved out permanently.

The exodus and resettlement of so many homosexuals was made possible by an unprecedented legal accommodation: the United States never invoked the Immigration and Naturalization Act of 1952, which authorized the barring and expulsion of "sexually deviant" aliens, against these 1959 immigrants. The Florida Legislative Investigation Committee continued this official blindness when its 1964 report on homosexuality in the state omitted any reference to the influx from Cuba.[17] Coming as it did at the end of a decade of McCarthyism, the Cuban gay immigration posed a difficult contradiction for the U.S. government, pitting its strong desire for a real advantage in the Cold War against its equally strong homophobia. Then, as now, anticommunism won out. Those fleeing the socialist revolution were welcomed despite their frequently open homosexuality.

Back in Cuba, life for homosexuals changed. Some veterans of the old underworld enclave joined counterrevolutionary activities or were pushed into them by the CIA. Other homosexuals, especially those from working-class backgrounds or students from petty-bourgeois families, worked to integrate themselves into the revolution. For the majority this meant going into a more guarded and, it was hoped, temporary closet. For these homosexuals, class and class interests were perceived as more elemental aspects of their identity than homosexual behavior. And the revolution spoke to these interests and this identity.

The limited social outlets still available for homosexuals, however, prolonged the relationship between the declining underworld and more progressive homosexuals, locking the two groups together for sheer companionship and sexual pleasure. Again, given the differences between male and female behavior and sexual rituals, this merging was much truer for homosexual men than for lesbians of the period. Not a few of the progressive homosexuals became implicated by default in counterrevolutionary activities and were even jailed. Young homosexuals seeking contact with "the community" in the bars and famous cruising areas of La Rampa were thus introduced to counterrevolutionary ideology and practice. One example of such a dynamic is the case of Rolando Cubela, a homosexual student leader who fought in the revolutionary army but was later enlisted by the CIA to assassinate Fidel Castro.[18]

17. Florida Legislative Investigation Committee, *Homosexuality and Citizenship in Florida* (Tallahassee: Florida State Legislature, 1964).

18. See Anthony Summers, *Conspiracy* (Paris: Gallancz, 1980), esp. pp. 349–52; Warren Hinckle and William Turner, *The Fish Is Red: The Story of the Secret War against Castro* (New

At the same time, homosexual perspectives on the revolution could shift according to class interests. Petty-bourgeois homosexuals joined the remaining veterans of the underworld in opposing the revolution when their privileges were threatened by the laws of agrarian and urban reform. Pressures escalated. Propaganda campaigns directed by the CIA urging the Cuban people to emigrate were taking their toll on the island's population. The agency saw the potential migration of thousands of Cubans to the United States as an event that would discredit the Cuban revolution internationally, remove its much-needed technical personnel, and score an American Cold War victory. Therefore it used a number of campaigns tailored to appeal to different groups that felt threatened by the revolution.[19]

Meanwhile, the 1961 invasion of Giron (called the Bay of Pigs by the U.S.), systematic commando attacks from Florida bases, and internal CIA-sponsored subversion created in Cuba an increase in militarization, surveillance, and concern over national security. Realistic fears and objective dangers gave rise to paranoia, and (as in the McCarthy years here) anyone who was "different" fell under suspicion. Homosexual bars and La Rampa cruising areas were perceived, in some cases correctly, as centers of counterrevolutionary activities and began to be systematically treated as such.

In keeping with this narrowing of tolerance in the early 1960s, the Committees for the Defense of the Revolution (CDR), established just after the revolution, took on a new significance as watchdogs.[20] Created to meet the internal security needs of the island, the CDRs now expanded into social regulators, policing personal and public life in their neighborhoods with obviously negative implications for lesbians and male homosexuals. In this climate of postinvasion paranoia, private space was invaded as never before. Not surprisingly, deep suspicion came to dominate the everyday life of Cuban lesbians and male homosexuals—a feeling exacerbated by the fact that legal migration to the United States had been halted by new American immigration limitations and quotas. There was no longer any route out, except for risky escape on a small vessel or the

---

York: Harper & Row, 1981), esp. pp. 191–92. Cubela was apparently distraught because he felt that his homosexuality had precluded his receiving a high-level post in the revolutionary government; his thoughts of this period were obtained through interviews with his friends, Madrid, August 1980.

19. For a historical chronology of CIA anti-Cuba campaigns, see Lourdes Arguelles, "The U.S. National Security State: The CIA and Cuban Emigre Terrorism," *Race and Class* 23, no. 4 (Spring 1982): 287–304.

20. See Richard Fagen, "Mass Mobilization in Cuba: The Symbolism of the Struggle," *Journal of International Affairs* 20, no. 2 (1966): 254–71. By 1963, there were already 102,500 Committees for the Defense of the Revolution, with a membership of 1.5 million; it was later calculated that one out of every two adults in Cuba actively participated in a CDR.

long wait for legal migration through a third country (many of which formally or informally excluded homosexuals).

Major ideological changes also were taking place. The influential Popular Socialist Party (PSP) moved to fill an analytical vacuum on homosexuality by lending "scientific" credibility to the antihomosexual harangues of the revolutionary leadership and to the homophobia of the Cuban people. The leaders of the PSP, with an attitude resembling that of Soviet society in the thirties and forties, saw homosexuality as a product of bourgeois decadence. Further, the PSP leaders considered expression of sexuality not a private affair or a personal freedom but a fulfillment of obligation to society.[21]

The lesbian and homosexual male intelligentsia, now concentrated in the Cuban Writers' and Artists' Union (UNEAC), made no public countercritique on the issue of homosexuality. The homosexual resistance and survival strategies of the time were largely private, individual in nature, and lacked effective oppositional qualities. As a result, the silence permitted the PSP analysis to assume undisputed hegemony even in intellectual circles. Among many reasons for the absence of any such public gay countercritique and resistance in this period, three stand out. Foremost was the lack of a tradition of feminist discourse and, thus, of any liberatory and substantive base for discussions of sexual order and gender politics. Another reason lay in the contemporary conception of homosexuality: as a legacy of the prerevolutionary period, homosexuality was still seen, by both the Cuban gay and straight worlds, as something performed in the dark with little or no nonsexual implications. Self-interest dictated the third reason: many closeted intellectuals who were bringing Cuba international recognition feared the loss of their personal privilege—especially the loss of their ability to travel abroad, which allowed so much latitude in their own sexual expression—if they spoke out against the official stand on homosexuality.

The sixties became increasingly difficult for homosexuals (particularly those at the vanguard of intellectual and artistic life). Their sexual practices began to be detailed in public and were invariably linked with bourgeois decadence or counterrevolutionary predispositions.[22] The growing crescendo of antihomosexual rhetoric culminated in 1965 in the establishment of UMAP camps (Military Units for the Aid of Production) aimed at safeguarding the revolution and guaranteeing the public good. Male homosexuals were among those drafted into the camps, while les-

21. See, e.g., Carlos Rafael Rodriguez, *La revolucion rusa y sus consecuencias* (Havana: Fundamentos, 1955), and *Lo que es esencial en las diferencias entre capitalismo y comunismo* (Havana: Fundamentos, 1956).

22. Key informant interviews, Havana, July 1982. See Lisandro Otero, "Para una definicion mejor de Jose Lezama Lima," *Boletin del Circulo de cultura Cubana* (New York; August 9, 1983).

bians, due to their comparative invisibility and the sexism that mandated different treatment for women, were spared. After much international protest and internal denunciation, the camps were closed at the end of the sugar harvest in 1967. Described at length in other sources, the UMAP camps have become permanent symbols of Cuban homophobia. While short-lived and denounced extensively within and outside Cuba ever since their abolition, the camps remain a damnable episode in revolutionary history.[23]

The UMAP years had seen as well such forms of persecution as the forced disbanding of the El Puente Literary Group on the grounds that some of its members were homosexual. In the post-UMAP period, persecution continued in a less overt form. In the absence of a developed gay liberatory consciousness, some Cuban homosexuals retreated further into *Santeria* and various forms of Eastern mysticism. Some migrated to the United States via a third country. Those who remained in Spain or in Mexico for years awaiting the American visa carved out small gay Cuban enclaves there. Homosexuals who chose to stay in Cuba became even more guarded yet continued to believe that the substantial material and emotional benefits they were deriving from the revolution outweighed the pain of repressing or concealing their sexuality.

It was only in the late sixties that a certain relaxation in the parameters of permissible sexual behavior in the international communist world began to filter into official circles in Cuba. In 1968, for instance, East Germany legalized homosexual acts between adults.[24] Cuba's need to relate to progressive political forces emerging in the United States and Western Europe also modified the official rhetoric, which began to describe homosexuals as sexual deviates (not criminals) to be cured (not condemned). While such changes in perspective were slowly occurring in official Cuban circles, everyday life for gays and lesbians began to improve.[25]

Three additional events marked the gradual but continual improvement in life conditions of gay men and lesbians in Cuba during the seventies: the First National Congress on Education and Culture, the promulgation of the Family Code, and the creation of a national group on sexual education. In 1971, the First National Congress delivered a mixed message to gays and the population at large. On the one hand, the customary denunciations of homosexuals as decadent were gone;

23. For a thorough discussion of the camps, the critical literature on them, and persecution of homosexuals in this period, see Jorge Dominguez, *Cuba: Order and Revolution* (Cambridge, Mass.: Belknap Press, 1978), esp. pp. 357, 393.

24. Armando Fluvia, "La represion legal," in *El homosexual ante la sociedad enferma*, ed. Jose R. Enriquez (Barcelona: Tusquets, 1978), pp. 72–93.

25. For an account of lesbian life in this period, see Barbara Coro, "A Cuban Lesbian's Story," *Chicago Gay Life* (March 13, 1981), pp. 17–19.

homosexuality was no longer seen by the revolutionary leadership as a fundamental problem in Cuban society but, rather, viewed as a form of sexual behavior requiring study. And for the first time in an official document, homosexuality was referred to in medical and psychological rather than criminal terms. On the other hand, declarations from the same congress called for the removal of homosexuals from the field of education, thus continuing the view of homosexuality as a contamination of the body politic.[26] Mayra, a lesbian photographer still living in Cuba, described these years: "You were not totally accepted by the revolution and there were positions you could not get if you were open about [being gay] unless you were in the arts. Still . . . there was no persecution unless you were involved in counterrevolutionary activities. Then you were in trouble, and usually it was blamed on the weakness of being a homosexual."[27]

Then in 1976, the celebrated Family Code began to make advances in eradicating sexism and, at least in principle, offered to Cubans for the first time a vision of more fluid gender definitions.[28] However, the code's focus on the nuclear family and its failure to address the compulsory nature of heterosexuality eventually made it less effective than anticipated in obtaining its goals and in reducing the popular homophobia of Cuban society.

In 1977 the Cuban National Group for Sexual Education was established, headed by a Cuban physician, Celestino Lajonchere, and an East German sexologist, Monika Krause. Working primarily with those involved in health and education, the group helped publicize the latest findings on the nature of sexuality and made some progress, despite the resistance Krause credited to Cuba's "cultural heritage," in updating sexual attitudes, including those pertaining to homosexuality.[29] Because of the many gains in conditions for women during the seventies, life for lesbians improved markedly. Ada, a lesbian rural nurse, acknowledged that things were not "perfect" but stated nevertheless, "I remember how it was before [the revolution] and for the first time, I feel I'm a human being."[30]

26. Proceedings of the First National Congress on Education and Culture (Havana, 1972). For documents on the conference, the aftermath, and the relevance of the well-known Heberto Padilla case to issues of homosexuality and intellectual formalism, see Lourdes Casal, *El caso Padilla—literatura y revolucion en Cuba: Documentos* (New York: Ediciones Nueva Atlantida, 1971), and "Homosexuality in Cuba," *Jump Cut: A Review of Contemporary Cinema* 19 (December 1978): 38–39.

27. Personal interview, Havana, August 16, 1981.

28. See *Granma Review*, English ed. (March 3, 1975), pp. 3–5; also Margaret Randall, "La mujer cubana en 1974," *Casa* 15 (March–April 1975): 67–75.

29. Personal interview with Monika Krause, Havana, October 13, 1983.

30. Personal interview, Pinar del Rio, Cuba, July 1, 1982.

Gains and setbacks merge throughout this period. The 1979 Penal Code, for example, was a disappointment to gays because it failed to legalize manifestations of homosexual behavior in the public sphere and left intact antigay laws dating to the Cuban Social Defense Code of 1939. By leaving in place legislation against "public scandal" or "extravagance," the Penal Code continued to provide a rationale for gay paranoia.[31]

Throughout the late sixties and early seventies, Cuban gay men and lesbians continued to migrate in small numbers to the United States via a third country, as direct migration was still prohibited. Class interests and economic incentives were the main influences on their migration. In particular, the promise of unlimited consumption—the most effective propaganda of the capitalist society—remained as important an impetus for gays as for other emigrants. Family reunification was another shared goal. There was, however, a uniquely gay reason for leaving: the age-old, prerevolutionary tradition in which families encouraged gay offspring to emigrate in order to avoid family stigma. Since Havana no longer absorbed the sons and daughters into a homosexual occupational sector, emigration abroad took the place of the journey to the city.

The Mariel Exodus and Present Gay Life in Cuba

The year 1979 was an unsettled one. Even though living conditions were better than in any previous period and compared favorably with those in the rest of the Caribbean, there were serious problems. The economy still suffered from the U.S. blockade; suspicious epidemics afflicting the island's cash-crop harvests raised the specter of biological sabotage; and a productivity drive aimed at reducing *sociolismo* (slacking off) put workers under greater disciplinary pressure. Most critically, there was considerable frustration and unrest sparked by visits (the first since the revolution) of thousands of émigrés who brought gifts as well as tales of comfortable lives in the United States. These visits of "the American cousins" increased consumer envy and added to the effectiveness of counterrevolutionary propaganda.

Lesbians and gay men were particularly vulnerable. The CIA targeted the homosexual intelligentsia and worked to persuade its members to defect, promising generous academic grants and publishing contracts. The more cost-effective ploy of blackmail was also used, especially against those gays less willing to leave, in the hope that political anxiety would force victims into exile. Carlos Alberto Montaner, a Madrid-based anti-Castro writer, for example, published two full pages listing names of

---

31. Codigo Penal de la Republica de Cuba, Havana, March 1, 1979, esp. articles 354, 359, 367.

homosexuals inside Cuba in an attempt to discredit them and to encourage them to migrate.[32] Such cynical "assistance" in coming out continues to be a favored weapon against lesbians and gay men who are well integrated into the revolution.

The visits also provided a context in which Cuban lesbians and gay men could hear of the more open and affluent gay life-styles available in the United States as a benefit of consumer capitalism. Other common reasons for wanting to emigrate included the lack of career mobility in a still underdeveloped economy and, for men, a traditional desire for the adventure of travel that had to focus on emigration since the United States and other capitalist nations deny tourist visas to Cubans. For some Cuban gays (especially for the men), emigration also provided wider sexual parameters than they felt could ever be possible in Cuba. Other Cuban lesbians and gay men, however, steadfastly refused to fulfill their gay identity at the cost of their national and political identities.

In the spring of 1980, through the instigation of the U.S. government, a series of events inside and outside of Cuba culminated in Fidel Castro's opening of the port of Mariel to allow a massive migration, thereby forcing the United States to accept an immigration far in excess of its own quotas. The boats leaving Mariel carried many who had waited years for a visa from the United States: many former political prisoners suffering social ostracism; young men bent on adventure, many with wives and children left behind; and gays, mostly male, opting for the comparatively more open gay life promised in the United States.[33]

Significantly, there were few lesbians in the Mariel exodus. Their small number by comparison with that of gay men points, again, to the fuller integration of women into Cuban society and the increased status and freedom enjoyed by lesbians, as women, under the revolution. For all the gay men and the few lesbians who left, there were many more who chose to stay. Their lives had been constantly improving. The revolution might not yet speak to the homosexual in them, but it continued to address other vital aspects of their being. They, in response, put the revolution—and Cuba—first, and put off sexual politics until later.

Today, life for lesbians and gay men in Cuba is similar, in some senses, to life for gay people in the United States pre-Stonewall, prior to the development of the gay liberation and lesbian-feminist movements and modern identities they produced. In this, its style is not very different from that customary throughout most of Latin America and the Caribbean, where *se dice nada, se hace todo* (say nothing, do every-

32. Carlos Alberto Montaner, *Informes secretos sobre la revolucion cubana* (Madrid: Playor, 1978).

33. See "The Refugee Dilemma," a special issue of *In These Times*, vol. 4, no. 28 (June 18–July 1, 1980), esp. Lee Aitken and Pat Aufderheide, "The Anti-Castro Welcome Wagon," pp. 6–8.

thing) is the rule. It is a closeted life but by no means a secret one. While the homosexuality of many men and women is a matter of common knowledge, it is never a matter of public record. Indeed, it is the complete absence of a public sphere that most clearly distinguishes the life of homosexuals in Cuba from any corresponding life-style in the United States or Western European urban centers.

Most commentary on homosexuality in revolutionary Cuba has concerned itself strictly with legal or occupational prohibitions. However, within the private sphere, there are a clear latitude and range of possibilities for lesbians and gay men that surprise the critical observer. The seeming contradictions in Cuba between homosexual expression and homosexual repression correspond quite clearly to the distinction made between private (expressive) and public (repressive) space. As delineated in a Latin American socialist setting, private space is far wider than in the United States, encompassing virtually all behavior outside the purview of official sanction or attention, while approved policy, published texts, and official stances compose the public sphere.

In the context of this dichotomy, there are two areas of particular concern to any critic of Cuban homophobia. One is the use of the laws governing public display to authorize "street sweeps" of obvious queens or lumpen gay males prior to major public events. Many informants explain that those arrested are gays engaged in black-market activities; others contend that they are engaged in sexual cruising or solicitation; yet others deny that the roundup of gays qua gays even occurs. Given the nature of the public sphere in Cuba, though, the actuality of these sweeps seems likely.[34]

A second area of concern is the effect of material conditions on the latitude of homosexual expression in the seemingly most private of private spheres: the bedroom. Havana's longstanding housing shortage reflects both the limited resources of an underdeveloped nation and the punitive effect of the U.S. blockade. An affliction to the entire urban population, the housing crisis has a special impact on Cuban homosexuals.

Due to the high divorce rate, Havana's housing shortage has forced many no-longer-married people into prolonged cohabitation or a return to the family home during the long wait for a new apartment. One temporary Cuban solution to the housing crisis has been the creation of a new institution, the *posada*—a legitimization of the well-known room-by-the-hour system formerly used by the commercial sex industry, now transformed into respectable rooms for hire for the couple in search of sexual privacy. By necessitating the transfer of the bedroom from the private into the public sphere, the housing crisis has created a situation

34. Key informant interviews, Miami-Havana, June 1982. Denials taken from a personal interview with Dr. J. Vega Vega, vice-president of the Cuban National Association of Jurists, Havana, October 13, 1983.

particularly crippling to lesbian or gay male couples. By all accounts, lesbians and gay men do use the *posadas*. However, the homophobia of the society must make such an option more available to the couple with some special "in" or good connections than to the ordinary pair. The admission to *posadas*, like the ability to book hotel rooms and tables in the most select restaurants, rests on the individual manager's interpretation of official policy and thus frequently entails long waiting periods. The move, then, from private to public space is almost inevitably a movement from freer expression to greater repression for the Cuban homosexual.

Despite such restrictions and despite the fact that Party membership is an impossibility for known gays, homosexuals are nonetheless a visible feature of the Cuban social landscape. They appear at every level of the hierarchy in Cuban society, in government, and of course in the arts. They are no longer confined to an underworld economy or alienated from the mainstream of social life as they were in the prerevolutionary era. Particular individuals are well known and pointed to with pride as evidence of revolutionary nondiscrimination. They may not be "out" in the U.S. sense, in that prominent lesbians and gay men in the worlds of music, poetry, art, film, or literature never make their sexuality the subject of their work. Similarly, the absence of a gay public space means that there are no lesbian or gay bars; yet there is a flourishing homosexual social scene centered around private parties and particular homes. This rich "salon" society, a feature of Havana life in general, is particularly well suited to the expansive private sphere required by homosexuals. Beach resorts, where the zones of tolerance are much wider, offer other escapes from restriction.

While their sexuality may be an open secret inside Cuba, many lesbians and gay males who participate in cultural and academic exchanges with the United States become more guarded when abroad, fearful of how homosexual issues are utilized in the war against the Cuban revolution. But many still take the opportunity to visit lesbian and gay bars and bath houses in New York or San Francisco. Ironically, their own adjustment to a greater social integration in Cuba causes them increasingly to feel out of place in these sites, viewing their sexual consumerism as bizarre. Some, like Jorge, an artist, contend that, "for all the repression, there is more true sexuality for gays in Cuba."[35]

Conclusions

Lacking the necessary understandings or factual bases for their judgments, even progressive gay men and lesbians in the United States assist in perpetuating a dangerously misguided set of criteria by which Cuban

35. Personal interview, New York, 1983.

homosexual issues—and the Cuban revolution, for that matter—are judged and found wanting. Similarly, inside Cuba the lives of homosexuals, in spite of some dramatic improvements, continue to be circumscribed by antiquated conceptions of homosexuality out of place in a modern and humane socialist society in transition.

The need for a distinctively Cuban socialist countercritique on behalf of homosexuality is increasingly evident. It must reconcile lesbian and gay male experiences with the island's realities and offer the international gay community critical insights into the immensely complex, rich, expressive, and problematic nature of those experiences. Until such a countercritique exists, the manipulation of the Cuban gay issue by anti-Cuban interests will remain largely unchallenged, and homosexual experience will continue to be marginalized within Cuban society.

It is obvious, however, that this countercritique is at present inhibited on at least three levels. First, the context today for any work on homosexuality in Cuba is inescapably that of a renewed Cold War, and few people—capable or not—are willing to undertake such a challenge, given the increasing manipulation from abroad to which Cuban gays can be exposed. Second, among gay men and lesbians in Cuba, the traumatic memories of the UMAP are a continued deterrent to public demand or support for such a countercritique. Third, the Cuban leadership has demonstrated a persistent reluctance to test the Cuban people's capacity for change on this subject. Other campaigns on unpopular topics—for example, the Family Code's professed mandate for equality between the sexes within the home—have been initiated, but no such effort has been directed against homophobia.

Recently, however, there are slight changes in official policy, intimations that progay elements inside and outside Cuba are putting moderate pressure on those in positions of influence on the island to consider the human and political costs of homophobia. For example, ICAIC (the Cuban Film Institute) opposed the screening of a gay documentary, *Word Is Out*, in a U.S. section of its 1983 international film festival. At the same festival, however, after an internal debate, ICAIC supported the presentation of a symposium paper—which was subsequently translated into Spanish and distributed to all festival delegates—detailing the politics and aesthetics of U.S. gay cinema.[36] Also significant were both the recent report in a major Cuban newspaper, *Juventud Rebelde*, urging tolerance for homosexuality, and the interested and nonantagonistic reception this article received from Cuban social researchers and university teachers at a conference held in Havana in the autumn of 1983.

36. See B. Ruby Rich, "The Aesthetics of Self-Determination" (paper presented at the Fifth International Film Festival of Latin American Cinema, ICAIC, Havana, 1983). Information drawn from author's meetings with ICAIC, August and December, 1983.

Part II of this report, by focusing on everyday gay life in the émigré enclaves and on the specifics of the contradictory uses of Cuban homophobia by anti-Cuban elements in the United States, is an attempt to develop a countercritique on Cuban homosexuality that will add to and in turn be enriched by that beginning to emerge from our gay male and lesbian *compañeros* in Cuba. To them, the *entendidos*,[37] this part of our report is dedicated in solidarity.

Chicano Studies Research Center
University of California, Los Angeles (Arguelles)

Film Program
New York State Council on the Arts (Rich)

37. *Entendido* is the Cuban subcultural term for "gay."

Discrimination against Lesbians in the Work Force

Martin P. Levine and Robin Leonard

The lesbian and gay movement has long maintained that there is widespread discrimination against lesbians and gay men in the work force.[1] Gay men and lesbians have repeatedly claimed that they were fired, not hired, or not promoted because of their sexual orientation. To redress this wrong, they have turned to employers, legislative bodies, and the courts, demanding laws and personnel policies that bar such discrimination.[2]

This article is a revised version of a paper presented at the seventy-seventh annual meeting of the American Sociological Association in San Francisco. We are grateful to Dr. Barry D. Adam, Dr. Linda Joseph, L. R., and the two anonymous reviewers for their invaluable comments and suggestions.

1. See Sidney Abbott and Barbara Love, "Is Women's Liberation a Lesbian Plot?" in *Women in Sexist Society: Studies in Power and Powerlessness*, ed. Vivian Gornick and Barbara K. Moran (New York: Mentor Books, 1972), pp. 601–21; Carl Wittman, "A Gay Manifesto," in *Out of the Closets: Voices of Gay Liberation*, ed. Karla Jay and Allen Young (New York: Douglas/Links, 1972), pp. 330–45; Dennis Altman, *Homosexual: Oppression and Liberation* (New York: Avon Books, 1971), pp. 45–49; Toby Marotta, *The Politics of Homosexuality* (Boston: Houghton Mifflin Co., 1981).

2. For a review of the pertinent court cases, see Donald C. Knutson, "Job Security for Gays: Legal Aspects," in *Positively Gay*, ed. Betty Berzon and Robert Leighton (Millbrae, Calif.: Celestial Arts, 1979), pp. 171–87; Judith M. Hedgpeth, "Employment Discrimination Law and the Rights of Gay People," *Journal of Homosexuality* 5, nos. 1/2 (Fall–Winter 1979–80): 67–68; E. Carrington Bogan et al., *The Rights of Gay People*, rev. ed. (New York: Bantam Books, 1983), chaps. 2, 3.

Reprinted from *Signs: Journal of Women in Culture and Society* 9, no. 4 (Summer 1984): 700–710.

While this action has met with some success, conservatives and religious fundamentalists have often stymied lesbian and gay men's efforts.[3] The opposition justifies employment discrimination on the basis of biblical teaching and stereotypical misconceptions, arguing that lesbians and gay men are sinners, sufferers of mental illness, and child molesters.[4] In a number of American cities—Miami, Florida; St. Paul, Minnesota; and Eugene, Oregon—citizens convinced by these arguments have voted to overturn local ordinances that banned, among other things, discrimination against gay men and lesbians in the labor force.

Opponents with a more sophisticated approach argue that the evidence supporting lesbian and gay claims of discrimination is not conclusive, consisting mainly of "personal statements by individuals concerning specific cases."[5] Charging that these random instances do not constitute hard evidence or prove widespread discrimination, they conclude that the problem is insignificant and that lesbians and gay men do not require any protection.

While lesbian and gay activists vehemently reject this conclusion, it is true that they lack hard and systematically collected evidence of employment discrimination. Although this problem has been in the national spotlight for over a decade, it has been the subject of only minimal empirical inquiry, and, with one exception, the little data collected have not been assembled and made readily available to those in the gay and lesbian movement.[6] Moreover, researchers who conducted many of the existing studies based their findings on combined samples of lesbians and gay men, making it difficult to determine whether the problem appears differently in the two populations.[7]

This report focuses on employment discrimination against lesbians since no one has yet synthesized what is known about their situation. After a review of the existing literature, we will present new empirical evidence documenting the lesbian and gay movement's claim of job discrimination and will then try to gauge the extent of the problem.

3. For a list of corporations with antidiscrimination policies, see National Gay Task Force, *The NGTF Corporate Survey* (New York: National Gay Task Force, n.d.). For a list of places with antidiscrimination ordinances, see National Gay Task Force, *Gay Rights Protection in the U.S. and Canada* (New York: National Gay Task Force, n.d.). For a review of the favorable court decisions, see Hedgpeth.

4. For an account of the religious/conservative counterattack, see Dennis Altman, *The Homosexualization of America, the Americanization of the Homosexual* (New York: St. Martin's Press, 1982), chap. 4.

5. National Gay Task Force, *Employment Discrimination in New York City* (New York: National Gay Task Force, n.d.), p. 1.

6. The one work reviewing the literature for gay men is Martin P. Levine, "Employment Discrimination against Gay Men," *International Review of Modern Sociology* 9, nos. 5–7 (July–December 1979): 151–63.

7. For reports mixing the two groups, see National Gay Task Force, "Employment Discrimination in New York City"; American Psychological Association, *Removing the Stigma:*

Literature Review

Evidence of employment discrimination to date largely comes from data collected in studies of the psychological and sociological status of lesbians and from personal accounts. There are three main sources for the anecdotal evidence: courtroom testimony by the small number of lesbians who have sued former employers for reinstatement, alleging wrongful termination on account of sexual preference; personal accounts presented before legislative bodies and human rights commissions—often during debates on gay rights bills; and general reports on lesbian life that show that lesbians fear job discrimination and describe how they cope with it.[8] In typically brief discussions of the problem, authors of such reports support their assertions that employment discrimination is common by recounting individual instances of discrimination. According to the authors, most lesbian workers try to avoid discrimination by living a dual life: on the job, they "pass for heterosexual, complete with imaginary boyfriends; during evenings and weekends with homosexual friends, they let their hair down."[9] But this tactic has its costs for these women, for pretending to be heterosexual generates tremendous anxiety over possible sanctions as well as severe strain from pretending to be what they are not.[10]

Although this anecdotal evidence illustrates instances of and responses to employment discrimination against lesbians, isolated personal

Final Report of the Board of Social and Ethical Responsibility for Psychology's Task Force on the State of Lesbian and Gay Male Psychologists (Washington, D.C.: American Psychological Association, 1979); The Norman Human Rights Commission, *Community Attitudes on Homosexuality and about Homosexuals* (Norman, Okla.: Norman Human Rights Commission, 1978); State of Oregon, Department of Human Resources, *Final Report of the Task Force on Sexual Preference* (Portland: State of Oregon, Department of Human Resources, 1978); Jeffrey Escoffier, "Stigmas, Work Environment, and Economic Discrimination against Homosexuals," *Homosexual Counseling Journal* 2, no. 1 (January 1975): 8–17; Joan Huber, chair, "Report of the American Sociological Association's Task Group on Homosexuality," *American Sociologist* 17, no. 3 (August 1982): 164–88.

8. For a review of court cases, see Hedgpeth; Bogan et al., chap. 2. For personal accounts presented to official committees, see Norman Human Rights Commission; and State of Oregon, Department of Human Resources. For general reports, see Del Martin and Phyllis Lyon, *Lesbian/Woman* (New York: Bantam Books, 1972), pp. 207–29; Sidney Abbott and Barbara Love, *Sappho Was a Right-on Woman* (New York: Stein & Day, 1973), pp. 46–51; Dolores Klaich, *Woman + Woman: Attitudes towards Lesbianism* (New York: William Morrow & Co., 1975), p. 225; Sasha Gregory Lewis, *Sunday's Woman: A Report on Lesbian Life Today* (Boston: Beacon Press, 1979), pp. 87–90; Donna M. Tanner, *The Lesbian Couple* (Lexington, Mass.: Lexington Books, 1978), pp. 76–77.

9. Martin and Lyon, p. 207. See also William Simon and John H. Gagnon, "The Lesbians: A Preliminary Overview," in *Sexual Deviance*, ed. John H. Gagnon and William Simon (New York: Harper & Row, 1967), pp. 269–72.

10. Barbara Ponse, *Identities in the Lesbian World: The Social Construction of Self* (Westport, Conn.: Greenwood Press, 1978), chap. 3.

accounts cannot substantiate any assertion that such discrimination is widespread. What is needed to support this claim are systematic data collected from a broader spectrum of the lesbian population.[11]

Five empirical studies of lesbian behavior, which typically ask one or two questions about job discrimination, provide only a small amount of data concerning the extent of this problem.[12] For example, only three out of the 528 questionnaire items in Alan Bell and Martin Weinberg's study—and only one out of fifty-three in Virginia Brooks's research—pertain to employment discrimination.[13] Moreover, researchers apparently added these questions as an afterthought, for none examined employment discrimination in depth: Bell and Weinberg were concerned with social and psychological adjustment of lesbians; Brooks with how stress influenced lesbian behavior; Janet Chafetz and her associates with the social and sexual dimensions of lesbian life; and Marcel Saghir and Eli Robins with lesbian etiology, psychopathology, developmental background, sexual behavior, and sociological concomitants. Only Beth Schneider's study concentrated on labor-force status, but her major concern was with coming out at work.

The picture that emerges from this research is bleak, for even this small amount of data shows that lesbians anticipate and encounter significant employment discrimination. Chafetz and her associates found that most lesbians feared losing their jobs (two-thirds of their sample agreed that their jobs would be in jeopardy if it became known that they were lesbians), while those who did not feel this threat were either self-employed or working in "a small number of occupations, such as the arts or hairstyling, in which homosexuality is tolerated." Brooks reported similar findings; nearly two-thirds of her respondents "could not state with any certainty that they would not lose their jobs if their sociosexual orientation were known." Likewise, about three-quarters of Schneider's sample felt that disclosure of their sexual preference would cost them their jobs or income.[14]

The studies that uncovered actual instances of discrimination demonstrated that such fears were not groundless. In Saghir and Robins's work, 12 percent of the respondents were asked to resign, were fired, or

11. National Gay Task Force, "Employment Discrimination in New York City," p. 1.

12. See Alan P. Bell and Martin S. Weinberg, *Homosexualities: A Study of Diversity among Men and Women* (New York: Simon & Schuster, 1978); Virginia Brooks, *Minority Stress and Lesbian Women* (Lexington, Mass.: Lexington Books, 1981); Marcel T. Saghir and Eli Robins, *Male and Female Homosexuality: A Comprehensive Investigation* (Baltimore: Williams & Wilkins, 1973); Janet S. Chafetz et al., "A Study of Homosexual Women," *Social Work* 19, no. 6 (November 1974): 714–23; Beth E. Schneider, "Coming Out at Work: Detriments and Consequences of Lesbians' Openness at Their Workplaces" (paper delivered at the annual meeting of the Society for the Study of Social Problems, Toronto, August 1981).

13. Bell and Weinberg, pp. 41, 296, 361, 362; Brooks, pp. 63, 206, 210.

14. Chafetz et al., p. 718; Brooks, p. 63; data in Schneider, table 4.

were given warnings after detection of their sexual preference. Bell and Weinberg discovered that 6 percent of their sample lost or almost lost a job and that 1 percent were denied better work assignments due to sexual orientation. In addition, 10 percent of Schneider's lesbian respondents reported "losing a job when their sexual identity became known."[15]

Two of the studies showed that a significant percentage of lesbians believed that their sexual orientation had hurt their careers by making them vulnerable to discrimination. Saghir and Robins found that 12 percent of their sample felt that their lesbianism restricted their choice of work or their career advancement, and almost one-fifth of Bell and Weinberg's respondents felt that their lesbianism had a negative impact on their careers.[16]

Researchers also collected some data on coping strategies among lesbian workers. Bell and Weinberg found that most of their sample hid their sexual identity on the job, with two-thirds concealing it from employers and nearly half concealing it from co-workers. Almost one-third of Schneider's respondents did the same, hiding their lesbianism from all people in their workplaces, while only 16 percent of those she studied were totally open. Schneider's closeted women were extremely uncomfortable with this behavior: 84 percent felt that their only choice was to be closeted; 62 percent felt ill at ease about being secretive; and 42 percent found the anxiety about being discovered paralyzing. Moreover, a little more than one-third of the closeted women put significant energy into maintaining a heterosexual facade.[17]

The studies reported two additional coping tactics without giving any empirical data on their extent: self-employment and "job tracking," that is, working in fields that accept lesbianism.[18] Bell and Weinberg found that a number of women ran their own businesses, typically ones catering to lesbians and gay men, and Chafetz and her associates discovered that the lesbians who did not expect job discrimination were in occupations tolerant of their sexual orientation. Unfortunately, they did not identify what these fields are.[19]

New Empirical Evidence

In 1980 and 1981 we conducted a study in metropolitan New York City designed to explore in depth the factors affecting employment discrimination against lesbians, since previous studies had only reported

15. Saghir and Robins, p. 311; data in Bell and Weinberg, p. 362; Schneider, table 1.
16. Saghir and Robins, p. 311; data in Bell and Weinberg, p. 361.
17. Data in Bell and Weinberg, p. 296; data in Schneider, p. 4.
18. For a discussion of "job tracking," see Escoffier (n. 7 above), pp. 12–13.
19. Bell and Weinberg, pp. 246–47; Chafetz et al., p. 718.

on the discrimination itself. In addition to measuring standard socio-demographics, we examined each worker's job type, work environment, work history, experience with perceived and actual discrimination, and openness about sexual orientation. As far as we know, our study is the first to focus solely on these factors.

The questionnaire contained thirty closed- and open-ended questions, and we recruited the field sample from a range of different gathering places (bars, women's bookstores, a dance), organizations (political groups, professional associations), and social networks. There were 203 women in the sample, and they were primarily white collar, middle class, and highly educated.

The data analyzed support the findings of previous empirical research and indicate that employment discrimination is a serious problem. The lesbians we studied both anticipate and encounter job discrimination.

Anticipated Discrimination

Three-fifths of the women in our study expected discrimination if their sexual orientation were discovered. Most of the remainder worked in fields known to accept gay people or in settings in which their supervisors or a majority of their co-workers were lesbians or gay men.

Three-quarters of the women who feared discrimination anticipated problems with their immediate supervisors; about two-thirds expected to be fired and 13 percent predicted harassment. The prior experience of others in their offices often led to these fears: "I would not come out to my supervisor because there was a woman who did and she went through hell! My supervisor mocked her and abused her and eventually fired her. I know I would be too"; "I know I would be fired. There is a lot of gay-baiting in my office, as well as anti-gay remarks and jokes. One gay man was already fired." Some felt that their supervisors would take punitive actions because of occupational license requirements or the sensitive nature of their work:[20] "My job would most definitely be in jeopardy. I am licensed under the New York State Health code which carries a section under the title of Moral Turpitude, which includes homosexuality as a grounds for dismissal"; "I'm a teacher. In education I would fear not only supervisory but also parental opposition. I can't come out."

Those who feared discrimination also expressed concern about the possible reactions of co-workers. Nine-tenths of these women predicted that their co-workers would harass them with taunts, ostracism, and even violence.

20. For a discussion of occupational licenses, see Bogan et al. (n. 2 above), chap. 3.

Actual Discrimination

Fears of discrimination and harassment were completely warranted. Nearly one-quarter of the women reported actual instances of formal or informal job discrimination. "Formal" discrimination involves the use of institutionalized procedures to restrict officially conferred work rewards, such as promotions, salary increases, or increased job responsibilities. Hiring or firing tactics posed the biggest problem; of the women reporting actual discrimination, 29 percent were not hired for a job, were fired, or were forced to resign: "I used to be a physical education teacher. I was asked to leave because I trained youth"; "My previous employer saw me on the street one weekend evening holding hands with my lover. Two weeks later I was fired. Before seeing my supervisor on the street my work was excellent. After the incident, it was incompetent." The second most common problem was restricted job mobility. Nearly one-tenth of the women who reported discrimination were not promoted or were demoted. The women also experienced problems with pay and work assignments. Four percent of the women were denied raises or restricted in duties: "Most people know I am a lesbian and are basically hostile to the realization. I don't discuss it because I can lose my job if I became vocal. As it is already, I have been removed from some job responsibilities."

"Informal" employment discrimination consists of noninstitutionalized policies that permit harassment and other unofficial actions taken by supervisors or co-workers: "I was harassed at my last job because I had my name on a sign for starting a lesbian support group. My boss said this was bad for the program's image." Verbal harassment was the most common informal discriminatory act. Three-quarters of the women who experienced discrimination reported that they were exposed to gossip, taunts, and ridicule. The second most common type of informal discrimination was nonverbal harassment; a little more than one-third of the women endured hard stares, ostracism, and damages to personal belongings. Finally, about one-tenth faced physical harassment, including violence.

Coping Strategies

To shield themselves from possible discrimination, most women in our study stayed closeted; only 23 percent informed most or all work associates. Almost four-fifths (77 percent) were partially or totally closeted on the job: 29 percent told some friends, 21 percent told only close friends, and 27 percent told no one at all.

But this tactic has its costs. Most women were dissatisfied with passing; slightly less than two-thirds of those who were either completely closeted or out only to close friends were displeased with this situation

Table 1

Satisfaction with Degree of Closetedness at Work (%)

	All or Most Know (N = 47)	Some Know (N = 59)	Close Friends Know (N = 42)	No One Knows (N = 55)
Pleased...........	85	51	40	31
Displeased........	15	49	60	69
Total..........	100	100	100	100

(table 1). As the following comments make amply clear, the mental anguish associated with living a double life is the root of this dissatisfaction: "They do not know the real me and I am always looking over my shoulder"; "I hate lying and making up stories about boyfriends. It hurts"; "I live a dual life. There is pressure to act straight and pretend my lover is a man"; "I do not feel free to share certain aspects—most really— of my life away from the job with my co-workers. This results in my feeling detached and alienated from the people with whom I work"; "I hate hiding. I hate being the brunt of jokes—either directed at me or at 'queers' in general." Women who were either mostly or totally out indicated that they did not feel this psychological stress: "I feel as though I am an integrated part of a bigger reality—and I enjoy it"; "I don't have to worry about being found out or losing my job"; "I expend no energy by having to hide."

Some women who were not out reported being pleased with this decision because it spared them problems on the job. A little less than two-thirds (59 percent) of those who were satisfied with being out to no one or only to close friends liked being closeted because they thereby avoided job discrimination: "I am satisfied being closeted because at the present time, with job situations being very bad, financially this would be a secure thing to do."

Coping strategies other than staying closeted included self-employment and job tracking. Some lesbians stated that they set up their own businesses to sidestep discrimination. "It is very difficult to work where you cannot be yourself. Instead of accepting this compromise, I chose to adjust my career to my life-style. I now own two gay businesses." The owner of a feminist bookstore asserted, "I am the boss in this situation. If someone is not happy with my lesbianism, she doesn't have to work for me." Other women sought jobs in fields that tolerated lesbians, including jobs employing large numbers of gay men (the arts, beauty, fashion) or in firms either that are owned by lesbians, women, or gay men or that serve their communities.

We are still in the process of analyzing the dynamics of employment discrimination. Preliminary study of our data indicates that individual attributes such as age, occupation, education, and income have minimal impact on anticipated and actual discrimination or coping strategies. What does seem to count is the work setting. Women who worked in New York City suburbs were far more likely to expect and encounter discrimination than those who worked in the city itself. In addition, lesbians working in public institutions were far more apt to anticipate discrimination than those in private settings, although the latter in fact experienced discrimination more frequently. Finally, lesbians employed in small enterprises were less likely to anticipate discrimination than those who worked for medium or large institutions.

Extent of Discrimination

While our data indicate that employment discrimination is a significant problem for lesbians, they do not tell us about its extent. We can, however, compute an approximate measure through a secondary analysis of the data from our study and the previous studies, since all posed similar questions to ascertain job discrimination and looked at similar samples.[21] (All of the researchers used nonrepresentative field samples, and all of the samples, except for Schneider's, came from urban areas.)

In determining the overall extent of the discrimination, we defined anticipated discrimination as the expectation that disclosure of sexual identity would jeopardize one's job; actual discrimination as firing, nonhiring, nonpromotion, or harassment; and coping strategies as passing for heterosexual. We calculated the percentages of lesbians who anticipated or experienced discrimination or used coping strategies by dividing the number of respondents in all the studies who asked questions about these factors by the number who answered these questions affirmatively (tables 2, 3, and 4).

Thirty-one percent of the lesbians surveyed anticipated employment discrimination because of sexual orientation, and 13 percent had actually experienced it; 8 percent of the women had lost or had almost lost their jobs because they were lesbians. In order to avoid discrimination, 72 percent of the lesbian community remained at least partially hidden at work, with 28 percent completely closeted on the job.[22] The only comparable estimates for gay men reveal that 29 percent of all gay male workers have had their careers negatively influenced by their sexual orientation,

21. Levine (n. 6 above) used this method for studying employment discrimination against gay men.

22. These figures fail to include the data presented in Bell and Weinberg, p. 296, because they asked about closetedness in a way that was not comparable to our research or Schneider's.

Table 2

Extent of Anticipated Employment Discrimination among Lesbians

Studies	Lesbians Anticipating Discrimination (%)
Chafetz et al. ($N = 51$).....................	67
Brooks ($N = 675$)	5
Schneider ($N = 222$).......................	76
Levine and Leonard ($N = 203$)	60
All four studies ($N = 1,151$)................	31

Sources.—Janet S. Chafetz et al., "A Study of Homosexual Women," *Social Work* 19, no. 6 (November 1974): 714–23; Virginia Brooks, *Minority Stress and Lesbian Women* (Lexington, Mass.: Lexington Books, 1981); Beth E. Schneider, "Coming Out at Work: Detriments and Consequences of Lesbians' Openness at Their Workplaces" (paper delivered at the annual meeting of the Society for the Study of Social Problems, Toronto, August 1981).

Table 3

Extent of Actual Employment Discrimination among Lesbians

Studies	Lesbians Experiencing Discrimination (%)
Saghir and Robins ($N = 57$)................	12
Bell and Weinberg ($N = 287$)...............	7
Schneider ($N = 222$).......................	10
Levine and Leonard ($N = 203$)	24
All four studies ($N = 769$)..................	13

Sources.—Marcel T. Saghir and Eli Robins, *Male and Female Homosexuality: A Comprehensive Investigation* (Baltimore: Williams & Wilkins, 1973); Alan P. Bell and Martin S. Weinberg, *Homosexualities: A Study of Diversity among Men and Women* (New York: Simon & Schuster, 1978); Beth E. Schneider, "Coming Out at Work: Detriments and Consequences of Lesbians' Openness at Their Workplaces" (paper delivered at the annual meeting of the Society for the Study of Social Problems, Toronto, August 1981).

Table 4

Extent of Closetedness among Lesbians in the Workplace

Studies	Totally Open (%)	Totally Closeted (%)
Schneider ($N = 222$).......................	16	29
Levine and Leonard ($N = 203$)	23	27
Both studies ($N = 425$)	20	28

Sources.—Beth E. Schneider, "Coming Out at Work: Detriments and Consequences of Lesbians' Openness at Their Workplaces" (paper delivered at the annual meeting of the Society for the Study of Social Problems, Toronto, August 1981).

and 17 percent have lost or been denied employment because they were gay.[23]

Although undoubtedly impressive, these figures offer only an imprecise gauge of the extent to which lesbians suffer discrimination in the work force and most likely represent a low estimate. First, all the data are based on self-report studies; yet lesbians often experience work-related discrimination without knowing about it. Employers may be worried about negative public reaction or may be too embarrassed to acknowledge that sexual orientation is the reason for dismissing, demoting, or taking other punitive actions against a lesbian. Thus they may hide the true motive for their discriminatory actions by asserting that, for example, a lesbian employee was incompetent or unqualified, or that their business had no openings for a lesbian job applicant. In addition, the figures may be low because most of the research took place in cities, where, a recent Gallup poll reports, residents are far more accepting of homosexuality than are nonurban dwellers.[24] Finally, three of the five studies took place in New York and San Francisco, cities well known for their tolerance of homosexuality.

Conclusion

Whatever the precise statistics may be, the data in this article clearly show that many lesbians anticipate and experience discrimination in the labor force and that the claims made by the lesbian and gay movement about this problem are accurate and valid.

Such discrimination on the grounds of sexual orientation runs counter to American public opinion; a 1982 Gallup poll found that 59 percent of the respondents felt that homosexual men and women should have equal rights regarding job opportunities.[25] It is time that this sentiment became public policy. The enactment of laws barring job discrimination against lesbians and gay men would be a step in this direction and is long overdue.

Department of Sociology
Bloomfield College (Levine)

Cornell University Law School (Leonard)

23. Levine (n. 6 above), p. 160.
24. The Gallup Report, "Homosexuality," *The Gallup Report*, no. 205 (October 1982).
25. Ibid., p. 14.

Sexuality, Class, and Conflict
in a Lesbian Workplace

Kathleen M. Weston and Lisa B. Rofel

Lesbian-feminist discussions of class and conflict have defined class almost exclusively in liberal terms by reducing it to a matter of individual background.[1] "Liberal" in this sense describes not a position on the political spectrum from left to right but a conception of society as a collection of individual actors who make independent choices based on free will alone. These liberal assumptions are not unique to lesbian feminism; indeed, they underlie the dominant world view in American society, with intellectual antecedents far back in the Western tradition.[2] As lesbians concerned about recent conflicts in lesbian institutions, we have found that liberal interpretations leave too many questions unanswered about how class affects the way power and privilege are structured in those institutions. Socialist-feminist and Marxist analyses offer valuable criticism of individualistic approaches to class theory but are of limited use insofar as they ignore debates about sexuality and sexual identity or assume that sexuality and class constitute discrete levels of oppression.[3]

Our thanks to the women of Amazon for their willingness to relive their experiences of the conflict with us; and to Jane Atkinson, Akhil Gupta, Nancy Hartsock, Rebecca Mark, Sabina Mayo-Smith, Kathy Phillips, Renato Rosaldo, the San Francisco Lesbian and Gay History Project, and Anna Tsing for their insights and support.

1. For examples of the interpretation of class as class background within the lesbian-feminist movement, see Charlotte Bunch and Nancy Myron, eds., *Class and Feminism* (Baltimore: Diana Press, 1974); Joan Gibbs and Sara Bennett, eds., *Top Ranking: A Collection of Articles on Racism and Classism in the Lesbian Community* (New York: Come!Unity Press, 1980).

2. See Zillah R. Eisenstein, *The Radical Future of Liberal Feminism* (New York: Longman, Inc., 1981).

3. Christine Riddiough, "Socialism, Feminism, and Gay/Lesbian Liberation," in *Women and Revolution*, ed. Lydia Sargent (Boston: South End Press, 1981).

Reprinted from *Signs: Journal of Women in Culture and Society* 9, no. 4 (Summer 1984): 623–646.

Our intention in this article is to move toward an integrated theory of class and sexuality that views class as the ongoing production of social relations structured through the division of labor, rather than simply as class background, and that also comprehends the significance of lesbian identity as a historical construct affecting social relations in lesbian institutions.

In order to examine these issues in a specific context, we undertook a case study of a recent strike at a lesbian auto-repair shop in a metropolitan area with a sizable lesbian community. The study was based on in-depth interviews with eight of the ten women who worked in the shop at the time of the strike, including the two owners.[4] Although this is just one example of the conflicts that have emerged in lesbian institutions in recent years, its dynamics clarify cultural constructs and material relations that operate in larger social processes.

The women we interviewed constitute a fairly diverse group of self-identified lesbians. The different conceptions they have of their lesbian identity are reflected in the labels they choose to describe themselves—"queer," "gay," "dyke," or "lesbian." Some consider themselves feminists; others do not. Some are in long-term relationships with lovers; some are not. Two co-parent children. They range in age from mid-twenties to late thirties. They locate their class backgrounds along a continuum from working class to upper middle class, with both workers and owners at each end of the spectrum. Everyone is white; two of the women are Jewish. For reasons of space, we are unable in this analysis to explore the interconnections among race, ethnicity, class, and sexuality, a topic we believe is crucial for any comprehensive theory of conflict in lesbian institutions.

Although all the women interviewed were willing to be quoted by name, we have chosen to alter their names as well as the name of the business. This strike has generated a certain amount of controversy, and we want to be able to explore the theoretical issues it raises without reducing those issues to the sum of the personalities involved.

History of the Conflict

Amazon Auto Repair was founded in 1978 by two lesbian auto mechanics, Carol and Lauren, with $1,400 in capital from personal savings. Within the first two years, their financial success led them to hire several more mechanics, who were paid on a commission basis of 50

---

4. One woman had moved out of the area, and we were unable to contact the remaining mechanic.

percent. In the summer of 1981, the owners embarked on a major expansion, raising the total number of employees to eleven. When their clerical worker left in August of that year, both owners went into the office, discontinuing the practice of one owner's supervising on the shop floor at all times.

The first overt incident in the conflict occurred about this time when Mary, the parts runner at the bottom of the job hierarchy, refused to stop working on a car in order to get lunch for everyone, as had been her custom. The owners not only insisted that this task was one of her job responsibilities but also added office filing to her duties, a change she resisted. In Mary's view, they also reneged on their earlier promise to make her an apprentice.

When the owners responded to new problems and pressures associated with expansion by tightening shop discipline, conflicts with other employees seemed to escalate as well. Tensions erupted at Christmas when the owners gave each employee a small gift that included a nailbrush and chocolate-covered almonds. The workers, insulted by what they regarded as insignificant gifts in place of bonuses, presented the owners with a list of issues and demands calling for continued commission with a guaranteed base pay of $200 per week, paid sick leave and a paid vacation, and a salaried shop manager. On February 2, 1982, the owners distributed statements rejecting the employees' demands, accompanied by nonnegotiable job descriptions that put everyone on an hourly wage effective the following week. That Friday, the workers asked the owners to postpone implementation of the descriptions and to meet with them in order to discuss salaries, the apprenticeship promised Mary, and other issues.

At this meeting the owners informed their employees they could no longer work at Amazon if they did not sign the job descriptions by 8 A.M. that day. Employees refused and, claiming they felt sick, left the shop. While the owners insist the employees walked out on their jobs, the workers say they were essentially locked out. The workers promptly filed charges of unfair labor practices with the National Labor Relations Board and set up a picket line, successfully turning away much of Amazon's business.

On February 24, the owners offered immediate and unconditional reinstatement under the old working conditions if the workers would drop all charges. But contrary to their stated intentions, the owners instituted speedups, set up procedures for signing in and out, and fired Mary for refusing to do filing. Two days later the workers went on strike. After picketing for several weeks with no sign of negotiations resuming, the workers reluctantly decided to join the Machinists Union and sought other employment. The owners continue to operate the business with a reduced staff of new employees. Technically the Amazon conflict still has not been resolved, but a year after the strike workers have given up hope of reaching a settlement.

Bridging the Public and Private

The establishment of Amazon as a lesbian workplace challenged one of the deepest cultural divisions in American society: the split between private and public life. The very categories "lesbian" and "work" mirror this dichotomy, since lesbian identity has historically been defined in terms of the sexual and the personal,[5] whereas wage work in a capitalist context constitutes the public activity par excellence. In a homophobic society, any attempt to establish an institution that links lesbian identity and productive activity entails—not as a matter of ideological principle but by definition—a renegotiation of the culturally constructed boundary that differentiates public and private spheres. To the degree that Amazon integrated these spheres by hiring lesbians and bringing them into an environment that encouraged them to be "out" on the job, it not only provided a space sheltered from the heterosexism of the wider society but also undermined the compartmentalization of lives and self characteristic of most workplaces. Out of this radical potential to create a nonalienating work environment emerged an atmosphere of involvement, excitement, and commitment at Amazon during its early years. An analysis of the reconciliation of private and public inherent in the project of a lesbian workplace cannot explain Amazon's ultimate failure to realize this radical potential. But because sexual and class politics meet at the boundary between personal and public life,[6] such an analysis is crucial for understanding aspects of the Amazon case that resemble conflicts in other lesbian institutions and that distinguish it from more traditional labor disputes.

The measure of what made Amazon a specifically lesbian workplace was not the sexuality of individual employees or the women's music played on the shop floor but the extent to which sexual identity received public affirmation in a place where being a lesbian was the rule rather than the exception.[7] Being out at Amazon was different from "coming

5. Regardless of where one stands in the definitional debate on lesbian identity (see Ann Ferguson et al., "On 'Compulsory Heterosexuality and Lesbian Existence': Defining the Issues," *Signs: Journal of Women in Culture and Society* 7, no. 1 [Autumn 1981]: 158–99), it is clear that competing usages of the term "lesbian" all rest on criteria such as friendship, sexuality, and feeling, which historically have been assigned to the realm of the personal.

6. See Annette Kuhn and AnnMarie Wolpe, eds., *Feminism and Materialism: Women and Modes of Production* (London: Routledge & Kegan Paul, 1978); Iris Young, "Beyond the Unhappy Marriage: A Critique of Dual Systems Theory," in Sargent, ed. (n. 3 above), pp. 43–69.

7. Lesbian identity then becomes a defining element of a distinctive type of workplace culture, making Amazon something more than an aggregation of isolated employees who

out" at a straight workplace because, as one mechanic put it, workers "didn't *have* to talk about being dykes. It was pretty obvious!" Yet, as another woman said, "You could go in and when you're sitting around having lunch you could talk about your family, you could talk about your lover, you could talk about what you did last night. It's real nice to get that out and share that." Conversations at work led to friendships that carried over into the evenings and weekends. Women went to flea markets together, carpooled to work, cooked dinner for one another, and attended each other's sporting events. Lovers were treated as members of the extended Amazon "family" and welcomed into the shop during business hours. One woman's lover acknowledged: "There's nothing like walking into a women's[8] business and being able to walk right up to my lover and kiss her and have lunch with her and have my kids behind me, our kids. But you can't do that in the straight world, you know? It was a real valuable place to be." Friendships spanned all levels of the job hierarchy, weaving together employees' lives inside and outside work.

In a sense, Amazon resembled other small and alternative businesses that foster the development of multiplex ties among employees. Although such businesses often promote an integration of personal and work relationships, the size of an enterprise does not necessarily contribute to a breakdown of the private/public split within the self. The compartmentalization of life in Western industrial societies often leads individuals in public situations to withhold full expression of their feelings, sexuality, and other central aspects of identity regarded as private.[9] One decisive difference between Amazon and the "straight" businesses employees mentioned in contrast was the way public and private aspects of the self were united once lesbian identity became linked to productive activity. In attempting to elucidate how lesbian identity shaped social relations at Amazon, we are not asserting that the reconciliation of the cultural dichotomy between public and private is characteristic of lesbian institutions alone. A similar integration may occur in any organization of an oppressed group that explicitly invokes racial, ethnic, gender, or sexual identity to set the institution and its members apart from the dominant society. At the same time, we believe there are factors unique to lesbian institutions that affect the way conflicts are generated and negotiated but that cannot be explored here. These include the effect of same-sex romantic and sexual involvements on work relationships; the possibility that lesbian institutions foster what Audre Lorde calls "the power of

---

"happened" to be lesbians or a repository for the piecemeal importation of artifacts from lesbian feminism.

8. In our heterosexist society, "woman" and "feminist" often function as code words among lesbians for "lesbian" and "lesbian feminist," in much the same way as sexism encourages the substitution of "people" or "men" as generic terms for "women."

9. Nancy Hartsock, "Political Change: Two Perspectives on Power," in *Building Feminist Theory*, ed. Quest Staff (New York: Longman, Inc., 1981), pp. 3–19.

the erotic," which may contribute to the transformation of alienated labor;[10] and the ways in which lesbian-feminist ideology, the organization of production, and systems of meaning originating in the wider lesbian community interact in the formation of lesbian workplace culture.

A principal effect of structuring Amazon so that lesbians could "be themselves" at work was the integration of emotions into workplace dynamics. "There was far more feeling than there ever is when it's just a cold business situation with men," remembered one owner. The reason was not simply, as she surmised, that women are socialized to express their feelings more freely than are men. Most former Amazon employees emphasized that their present work situations in straight businesses are not as emotional for them. But as a lesbian-identified workplace, Amazon encouraged the women who worked there to bring with them onto the shop floor the entire range of emotions and personal attributes associated with identity in American culture.[11]

Despite the lesbian-feminist principles of Amazon's owners, it is important to remember that this integration of public and private was not the product of a shared ideology. The commitment workers felt to Amazon was developed on the job, not brought to the workplace from other contexts. Some started their jobs with a nine-to-five attitude, only to find themselves becoming increasingly involved in what happened during business hours. It would therefore be a mistake to portray the Amazon conflict as a case in which women's unrealistically high expectations for an alternative institution led to disappointment when those expectations could not be met.

When she first came to Amazon from her job in a straight repair shop, one woman said, "I didn't *have* different expectations." But within a month, she was "like a kid in a candy store." It was precisely because working at Amazon had been such a positive, fulfilling experience, said another, that the rift between owners and workers came as such a shock and a loss: "That's why [leaving Amazon] feels like death. It was a part of my life—it was a part of our [family's] life—that would have gone on and on." By December 1981 the excitement of earlier years had given way to feelings of anger and betrayal, feelings so intense that the women involved in the dispute still dream about Amazon a year after the strike. "It hurts more with lesbians," concluded one mechanic, recalling that it had felt as though her whole being were under attack. The hurt was as much a

10. Audre Lorde, *Uses of the Erotic: The Erotic as Power* (New York: Out & Out Books, 1978).

11. The bridging of the private/public split provides a mechanism to explain the high levels of commitment often noted as characteristic of lesbian institutions. See Barbara Ponse, *Identities in the Lesbian World: The Social Construction of Self* (Westport, Conn.: Greenwood Press, 1978). Contrary to Ponse's findings, no significant association between commitment and conformity appeared in the Amazon case.

product of the integration of private and public as the fulfillment that preceded it. In most work situations, the compartmentalization of life and self that accompanies alienation also protects individuals from the destructive effects of fixed power inequities.[12] Without that protection, the women at Amazon found themselves particularly vulnerable as tensions began to explode.

When Mary refused to get the mechanics' lunches, her intention was to defend herself against what she regarded as the owners' arbitrary exercise of power. Because she refused on the grounds that this task was a personal favor rather than a job duty, she tacitly reinvoked the private/public split. As the conflict deepened, attempts to reaffirm this distinction assumed a key position in the strategies of both parties. Workers called for a "businesslike" handling of affairs and tried to put their emotions aside. The owners took steps to distance themselves from workers by curtailing friendships and adopting written rules. By the time women were called back to work the employee phone had been disconnected, giving symbolic emphasis to the new segregation of work from personal life.

Even as Amazon's radical potential to provide a nonalienating work environment was being undermined, its distinctive characteristics as a lesbian workplace continued to shape the course of the conflict by focusing the struggle on the division between the private and the public. But with the reaffirmation of the private/public split, many of the special qualities that distinguished Amazon from straight repair shops seemed to disappear. "I'm not in business to be a machine, to be a man, to be something I don't want to be," protested one owner. "This wasn't what we wanted to create," insisted the other. Both sides were left wondering how the conflict could have escalated so quickly, destroying relationships of trust and cooperation built up over three and one-half years.

The Politics of Trust

In the eyes of everyone who worked there, Amazon was built on trust. The owners trace this trust to their political commitment to lesbian feminism, which fostered a sense that a common lesbian identity would override other differences.[13] Before the February 8 walkout/lockout, neither seriously believed a strike could occur at Amazon. They displayed a similar degree of confidence in each other when they elected to go into

12. Hartsock.
13. An assumption widely criticized in recent years in the discussion on race and difference within the women's community. See Cherríe Moraga and Gloria Anzaldúa, eds., *This Bridge Called My Back: Writings by Radical Women of Color* (Watertown, Mass.: Persephone Press, 1981).

business without a partnership agreement. For the workers, trust was not so much an outgrowth of ideology as a consequence of the multiplex ties that developed in the workplace. Not all employees identified strongly as feminists or saw themselves engaged in the project of creating a feminist business. But for workers and owners alike, trust was underpinned by friendships and the support Amazon provided for being openly and proudly lesbian.

From the beginning Lauren and Carol stressed that they were the owners, that Amazon was not a collective, and that they reserved the right to make all business decisions. Beyond these ground rules, however, they assumed a basic compatibility between their needs and those of their employees. In accordance with a feminist ideology that valued being "nurturing" and "supportive," the owners installed a separate phone for employees' use and agreed to flexible scheduling around women's extra-work commitments. The lack of set policy and formalized rules, combined with the owners' efforts not to "act like bosses," made it easy to believe that everyone was equal at Amazon and that trust grounded in the integration of public and private life would constitute a sufficiently radical solution to the problems of oppression women face in other workplaces. But in the absence of a clearly defined business structure, this trust became politicized when owners and workers had to rely on interpersonal relationships to negotiate labor relations from day to day. The emergence of a politics of trust at Amazon points to a conclusion the owners never reached and the workers only gradually realized: the personal can be political, even among lesbians, whenever the personalization of work relations obscures power differentials structured through property relations and the division of labor.

As managers, the owners had the authority to define and evaluate others' needs, transforming what would otherwise have been examples of mutual agreement into instances of benevolence. Even if they had been able to satisfy every request or concede every point raised by employees, control of the business altered the meaning of their actions. What the owners perceived as gifts or favors the workers often saw as customs or rights. It is not surprising, then, that the owners began to get angry when workers stopped asking permission for routine procedures such as leaving early when work was finished for the day. Conversely, the workers' mistrust for the owners developed when Lauren and Carol chose to assert their covert power—for example, when they forced Mary to get lunches or do filing. For some workers the strike came to be seen as a fight to create a work environment in which the owners "would not have the power to say one thing and do another thing and change things around" when their decisions could have a major impact on employees' livelihoods.

It was not coincidental that the politics of trust fragmented along class lines, pitting owners/managers against workers. But because such a politics was grounded in interpersonal relationships it tended to personalize the issues for the women involved, leading them away from a relationally defined class analysis. The politics of trust, rooted in the liberal conception of autonomous selves interacting on a basis of equality, supported interpretations that reduced the conflict to a matter of individual actions, intentions, and capabilities.

The analysis of the conflict favored by the owners was built on a personality/provocateur theory, which held that the strike was instigated either by chronically dissatisfied workers or by someone in league with outside forces interested in destroying a "growing, thriving lesbian business." The owners alternately portrayed the workers as lazy, irresponsible, resentful because of unrequited love, or consciously determined to undermine the business. Power enters into this analysis only in the owners' focus on the individual psychology of certain employees who allegedly were not comfortable accepting authority and so created a strike situation in order to feel some measure of control.[14]

Explanations that ascribe the conflict to static personality traits fail to account for the workers' movement from enthusiasm to anger over time. The provocateur theory provides no better explanation, since it discounts the solidarity maintained by the workers throughout the struggle.[15] To speak of the "mob mentality" that held workers together, or the weakness of character that prevented individuals from standing apart from the group, implies that the workers followed one another like sheep, without legitimate grievances and a clear understanding of their own actions. The owners' preoccupation with the personality/provocateur theory also draws attention away from the possibility that they too might be implicated in the conflict.

The workers were less inclined to reduce the conflict to personalities, insisting instead that "nobody [at Amazon] was a good guy or a bad guy." They learned to distinguish between an individual's particular attitudes or competencies and her standing in the job hierarchy. Rather than defending Mary's actions, they identified broader problems with training and apprenticeship. Rather than attacking Carol's decision to side with Lauren about the lunches, they criticized the division of labor that induced the owners to take the same position. However, this growing awareness of structural factors underlying the conflict existed alongside, and in contradiction with, a set of liberal presuppositions evident in the

14. Compare Sherry McCoy and Maureen Hicks, "A Psychological Retrospective on Power in the Contemporary Lesbian-Feminist Community," *Frontiers: A Journal of Women Studies* 4, no. 3 (1979): 65–69. Their exclusively personal conception of power ignores the possibility that both power and needs may be shaped by social relations like class that divide the lesbian community.

15. We do not mean to imply that the owners' fears for the survival of lesbian businesses are groundless; we do question the allegation that the workers acted as agents of reactionary forces.

workers' two most popular explanations for the dispute: the miscommunication theory and the mismanagement theory.

The miscommunication theory represents the women of Amazon as
equal, rational, independent individuals who came into conflict only
because they misunderstood one another. Individual interviews clearly
show, however, that both sides in the dispute can accurately reproduce
the other's point of view. In addition, the premises of this theory are
invalidated by the power differential that allowed the owners to set the
terms for communication and to refuse to negotiate with their employees.

The mismanagement theory depicts the owners as incompetent managers; presumably, if Lauren and Carol had taken a few business courses
or had acquired more experience running a shop, the conflict could have
been avoided. Although this analysis recognizes the power differential at
Amazon, it does not call for a redistribution or redefinition of power
because it shares the owners' basic assumption that the needs of employers and employees can always be reconciled. But if we consider needs
as historical products tied to a changing division of labor,[16] it becomes
apparent that merely substituting more competent actors or rectifying
individual "mistakes" would not have been sufficient to prevent these
needs from coming into conflict.

We believe that a class analysis is essential for comprehending the
social, historical, and structural factors shaping the conflict that these
theories ignore. By class we mean the relations of property and production mediated by the division of labor that separated the women of
Amazon into owners/managers and workers, adding a dimension of
power to personal relationships that politicized bonds of mutual trust. In
our view, material factors like ownership, the division of labor, and the
organization of production are dynamically interrelated with the production of needs, culture, perceptions, and feelings. Obviously, then, we
disagree with those who interpret class in a narrowly economistic or
deterministic sense. The way in which the public/private split is bridged
by linking lesbian identity to productive activity demonstrates that class
relations alone cannot explain events at Amazon. But without an understanding of class relations, lesbian feminism remains grounded in the
same liberal, individualistic assumptions that originally led the women of
Amazon to expect the bonds of trust to prevail over any dissension that
could arise.

Class Relations and the Organization of Production

Class relations at Amazon, based on a hierarchical division of labor
that enabled two individuals to own the business and maintain the power

16. Agnes Heller, *The Theory of Need in Marx* (London: Allison & Busby, 1976), p. 25.

to define the conditions under which the others would work, shaped the tensions that eventually led to the strike. From the beginning, these tensions were inherent in the organization of production at Amazon, particularly in four key areas: the commission system, job allocations, apprenticeships, and informal job definitions.[17] They surfaced and became the focus of overt conflict only after the owners decided to expand the business and work in the office, creating a dichotomy between mental and manual labor that sharply distinguished owners from workers. In the face of these changes, Lauren and Carol found themselves struggling to defend their prerogatives as owners as their needs increasingly came into contradiction with the needs of their employees.

Carol and Lauren certainly never aspired to be bosses. In establishing Amazon they were motivated not by the desire for profit or the will to exercise power for power's sake but by the vision of working independently and determining the conditions of their own labor. Like many entrepreneurs who open small businesses, they initially hoped to escape the alienation[18] they had experienced in other work situations: "Do we want to work for those creepy lawyers and doctors for the rest of our lives? [Or] do we want to try to set up something that's ours? It may be a lot of things, but it will at least be ours." The connection Lauren and Carol drew between ownership and self-determination lay behind their insistence on maintaining control as tensions heightened during the months prior to the strike.

When Carol and Lauren first began to hire mechanics to work under them, they decided to pay them by commission rather than salary to ensure that the fledgling business would not go in the red. The commission system allowed mechanics a degree of control over their work, an arrangement that neither owner initially regarded as problematic but that later became a key issue in the struggle. Because mechanics were paid not by the hour but for jobs actually completed, they came to feel, as one mechanic phrased it, that "the time we worked there was our time." Some saw themselves more as subcontractors than employees, insisting, "All we were doing, really, is using [the owners'] space and giving them half the money we made." Workers felt not so much a time obligation to Amazon as an obligation to get the work done.

The commission system also tended to give employees a clearer picture of how Amazon made its profit and how much of that profit came from their labor: "We could see how much money they made off of our

17. On the links between the changing organization of production and class relations under industrial capitalism, see Harry Braverman, *Labor and Monopoly Capital* (New York: Monthly Review Press, 1974); Richard Edwards, *Contested Terrain: The Transformation of the Workplace in the Twentieth Century* (New York: Basic Books, 1979).

18. Bertell Ollman, *Alienation* (London: Cambridge University Press, 1971), pp. 133–34. Following Ollman, we take alienation to mean a separation of the individual from her life activity, the products of her labor, and other human beings within the labor process.

labor. . . . You doubled everybody's wages and they got it, plus the money they made on parts." This perception of the relation between their work and the business's prosperity fed the workers' sense of outrage when the owners refused to negotiate the terms of the February job descriptions.

The owners' control of job allocations constituted another potential source of conflict. A mechanic's commission-based income was contingent on the availability of work and on whether or not she received time-efficient jobs that matched her skill level. Several workers recalled being the "star" or the "fave" when they first arrived at Amazon only to become the recipients of time-consuming "shit jobs" as newer employees were given preferred assignments. Although not all the mechanics at Amazon experienced favoritism, concentration of the power to allocate jobs in the hands of the owners made the workers equally dependent on Carol and Lauren's continued good will.

Training and apprenticeship were vital under commission, since specialization in only a few tasks left an apprentice-level mechanic particularly vulnerable to job-allocation decisions. Without adequate supervision and opportunities to learn new skills, a novice assigned an unfamiliar task—and the more experienced mechanics she turned to for help—lost time and money. At Amazon apprenticeship was not a formal program but a loosely structured arrangement in which employees were told an owner would be available to assist them when necessary. After the owners moved into the office, apprentices were largely left to fend for themselves in what became an increasingly untenable position.

Finally, the informality of job definitions under the politics of trust highlighted the inconsistencies between the owners' feminist ideals and Amazon's actual business structure. The owners promised their parts runner, Mary, that she could become an apprentice as part of their commitment to helping women enter the auto-repair trade. At the same time, however, the owners expected her to continue to make herself generally available to meet their needs because she was the only salaried worker below them in the job hierarchy. Without reorganizing the division of labor, the owners never provided the conditions that would have made it possible for Mary to become a mechanic. Nor were the owners willing to relinquish their control over defining the content of workers' jobs, as Mary discovered when she confronted them on this issue.

Because capitalist culture values conceptual work over the "mere" execution of ideas,[19] the mental/manual division between owners and employees that arose in the late summer of 1981 reinforced the owners' power to set the terms for the other women's labor. In practice, this separation meant that the two owners' needs and perceptions became

19. Karl Marx and Frederick Engels, *The German Ideology* (New York: International Publishers, 1978), pp. 51–52.

more congruent and more opposed to those of their employees. One owner noted, "There's always been a kind of an 'us' and a 'them' between the office and the shop," a division that separated even the two owners when they worked in different spheres. "You're in the shop and you see everything from the mechanics' side. You're in the office and you see everything from the customers' side." For Carol, "the one thing that was a big pull for me about both of us being in [the office] was that we were going to be on the same side."

The way the owners chose to expand the shop and the creation of a mental/manual split deepened class divisions at Amazon and brought underlying tensions to the fore. A heavier work load, tighter scheduling, and a greater number of mechanics meant an increase in work pressures and a decrease in the time available to resolve conflicts as they emerged. As the owners perceived a need to cut overhead and raise productivity, they began to contest accustomed areas of worker self-determination in a general move to tighten up the shop.

Control over mechanics' hours became a matter of controversy once the owners decided to adhere to a strict 8:30 to 5:30 rule. When workers resisted rigid scheduling by arguing that their time was their own under commission, the owners interpreted their defiance as laziness and a lack of commitment to Amazon's success. In their proposed job descriptions, the owners finally decided to replace the commission system with salaries "because that was the only way . . . we could know we were going to get eight hours of work from people." Many mechanics opposed the change because their new salaries were based on individual averages of their previous year's wages, which meant that they would receive the same amount of money annually for working longer hours.

Meanwhile, the owners' preoccupation with office work meant a decline in income for apprentice-level mechanics, who lacked regular supervision. Although the more experienced mechanics were willing to offer their assistance, they nonetheless resented these costly intrusions on their time. The owners rebuffed the workers' suggestion to pay a mechanic to be a lead worker or supervisor, even though the owners previously had compensated themselves for the same responsibility. Problems involving novice mechanics' limited training and narrow specialization were compounded when the owners allocated simple but moneymaking jobs to a new employee hired in the fall of 1981, who turned out to be on an apprentice level. The other less-experienced mechanic in the shop promptly witnessed a sharp drop in her weekly paycheck as she lost most of the jobs she knew how to do well. Such actions incensed many workers, ultimately leading to their demand for a steady base pay.

Carol and Lauren found themselves in the middle of yet another struggle when what they saw as a need for greater efficiency with expansion led them to oppose Mary's efforts to renegotiate the definition of her job to meet her need for an apprenticeship. By insisting Mary get the lunches and do the filing, the owners invoked tasks especially symbolic of female subordination. The other workers, disturbed by the way the owners were "jerking Mary around," made her right to an apprenticeship a major issue as the strike developed.

With tensions mounting, workers saw their Christmas presents as the "last straw." The owners still find it incomprehensible that the workers organized over such a seemingly trivial issue because they fail to recognize the symbolic meaning of those presents. Since Christmas bonuses traditionally serve as a statement of evaluation from employers, these token gifts were taken as a "slap in the face" of the workers' commitment to Amazon. The gifts had economic as well as ideological significance, since they were associated with the owners' decision to close the shop for a week, leaving the workers with no income, no Christmas bonus, and, according to employees, no respect. Because the owners were now so clearly treating the other women not as friends and equals but as employees, the Christmas presents symbolized the demise of the politics of trust by marking the class division that later would separate the two sides in the dispute.

Paradigm Shifting: From the Politics of Trust to the Politics of Contract

As the politics of trust began to disintegrate, the women of Amazon adopted an opposing symbolic paradigm, what we term the politics of contract. It represented an alternative mode of negotiating labor relations in which owners and workers ideally would bargain to agree on a business structure made explicit through written job descriptions and set policies. Although this formulation appears neutral from the standpoint of gender and sexual identity, the women at Amazon came to favor it precisely because the two paradigms of contract and trust were relationally defined by incorporating popular—and opposed—notions of male and female.[20] Although the women at Amazon did not consciously define themselves in relation to men, their understanding of a lesbian business as an "all-giving, all-nurturing, endlessly supportive" institution carried an implicit contrast with the "cold, unfeeling" world of heterosexual male businesses where decisions were held to be determined legalistically with-

20. For cross-cultural discussions of relationally defined gender constructs, see Carol MacCormack and Marilyn Strathern, eds., *Nature, Culture and Gender* (London: Cambridge University Press, 1980); Sherry B. Ortner and Harriet Whitehead, eds., *Sexual Meanings: The Cultural Construction of Gender and Sexuality* (New York: Cambridge University Press, 1981).

out regard for workers' needs.[21] Because the categories female and male exhaust the range of possible gender attributes in American society, the link between these categories and the two contrasting paradigms made those paradigms appear to be the only conceivable options for conducting labor relations. When the politics of trust proved inadequate, the politics of contract provided a readily available model sanctioned by the dominant society for attempting to settle the growing differences between workers and owners.

Both paradigms obscured class relations within Amazon. Under the politics of trust, the owners had asserted that Amazon was a nonoppressive environment by definition because it provided a haven from the "real world" where women have to "put up with crap from men." This belief allowed them to argue that any woman dissatisfied with working conditions should "go be with the boys," which had the double effect of augmenting their power and suppressing worker initiatives for change. At the same time, industry standards implicit in the contrast between Amazon and the straight male business world could be selectively invoked to justify practices such as paying the parts runner a minimal salary.

The owners' shift toward a politics of contract came in the wake of expansion. In light of their new concern with raising productivity and decreasing overhead, the owners began to perceive their employees as taking advantage of Amazon's loose structure. The institution of a written policy in October marked the owners' first attempt to establish a more structured work environment. To the owners, this deliberate decision to "act like bosses" meant abandoning the ideals of nurturance and sensitivity they associated with lesbian-feminist entrepreneurs to assume the straight male-identified role of a "wrist-slapping disciplinarian." By the time they handed out job descriptions in the form of ultimatums, they had come to see themselves as "behaving maybe the way the boys do when . . . they say, 'This is it. Either you do it or you're not here.' "

The workers also came to accept the framework of the politics of contract in their interactions with the owners, but for very different reasons. Workers began to press for job descriptions, monthly shop meetings, and more specific policies in order to protect themselves against what they regarded as arbitrary assertions of managerial power. The formal presentation of a list of issues and demands represented their attempt to "depersonalize [the situation at Amazon] and make it a business thing."

Because the politics of contract was identified with a combination of formality and male gender attributes, the women of Amazon began to

21. On the owners' side this understanding reflected lesbian-feminist ideology, but for most workers it developed through an appeal to notions of gender and sexuality to explain differences in their work experiences at Amazon and at other businesses.

belittle emotional reactions to the growing conflict as responses typical of women but inappropriate to businesslike conduct. In the process, they unknowingly rejected one of the most positive aspects of lesbian workplace culture: the integration of public and private that encourages bringing the whole self, including feelings, into work. Workers criticized the owners for responding "on this real emotional level to our demands, about how we were insulting their intelligence and honor." Meanwhile, the owners dismissed the strike as lacking substantive issues by referring to the emotional weight behind workers' actions. Maintaining the bridge between the private and public would have allowed both sides to acknowledge the intensity of feeling surrounding the dispute without separating emotions from more tangible bread-and-butter issues. Instead, the women at Amazon redrew the private/public boundary by shifting to a paradigm identified solely with the public sphere.

No one at Amazon was satisfied with the character of labor relations under the politics of contract, but the dualistic definition of the two paradigms made contractual relations seem to be the only possible substitute for relations based on friendship and trust. Since both sides viewed the loose structure and informal managerial style associated with the politics of trust as the source of the conflicts at Amazon, both initially expected a shift to a more formalized business structure to solve their differences. While some workers continued to hope for a consensual settlement, others began to understand the conflict as a power struggle rooted in the division of labor that would not be resolved by the establishment of a set policy. Implicit in the struggle over job descriptions was the recognition that measures intended to protect workers could also be used by the owners to maintain control. Workers who once had argued against the commission system opposed conversion to salary on the grounds that an hourly wage would "give [the owners] too much power" by allowing them to regulate employees' hours and subject workers to arbitrary requests.

Despite their growing awareness of the implications of the power differential at Amazon, workers believed the dispute could be resolved within the existing class structure. Yet the issues they raised posed a tacit challenge to relations of production that concentrated decision-making power in the owners' hands. This seeming paradox rests on the fact that, to the degree the workers' stand encompassed a claim to self-determination, their concerns could not have been adequately addressed while class relations at Amazon remained unaltered. Ownership never became an articulated issue largely because the workers were tactically and philosophically committed to a politics of contract that limited their proposals to discrete, point-by-point demands.

Frustration with the restrictions of a bargaining procedure derived from male trade unionism led the workers to search for a "different way" to approach the owners, but their efforts to break through the paradigms that framed their struggle were unsuccessful. They failed in part because the shift from a politics of trust to a politics of contract focused discussions on questions of work discipline and managerial style. The deeper questions concerning ownership and the division of labor at Amazon, which were not mediated by notions of gender and sexual identity, could not be addressed within the terms of either paradigm. The final irony was that the configuration of class relations at the heart of the Amazon conflict was never questioned as being incongruous in a lesbian institution but was instead uncritically adopted from the straight male world.

Lesbian Identity in the Formation of a Workers' Alliance

The radical potential created with the bridging of the private and public was not completely destroyed by the elaboration of class relations and the emergence of open conflict at Amazon. The commitment that accompanied the integration of personal and work life had the radicalizing effect of motivating workers to struggle against what they perceived to be unfair labor practices. The unusually high degree of solidarity maintained by the workers throughout this struggle also had its roots in the kind of workplace Amazon was before the strike. Solidarity among workers was not a deterministic consequence of their being lesbians per se, but an outgrowth of a social context that allowed them to be out on the job in a lesbian-identified institution. Any analysis that reduced events at Amazon to a class conflict without taking these distinguishing features into consideration would miss the dynamics that turned a situation of contention and contradiction into a full-blown labor dispute.

The workers' radicalization was gradual. In the beginning, one mechanic commented, "We weren't a political force; we were just a bunch of women working." Concern about working conditions led them to meet as a group, but class and politics were not explicit topics at these initial meetings. At first women simply compared their reactions to incidents at work, breaking through the silence surrounding grievances that had kept individuals believing they were the only ones angered and confused by the owners' actions. As workers found their personal experiences confirmed by the experiences of others, they began to discuss the possibility of collective action.

Paradoxically, the same bonds of trust and friendship that made it difficult for many workers to break with the owners also stimulated their willingness to challenge the owners' position. Because the politics of trust masked power inequalities at Amazon, it had encouraged workers to consider all points negotiable and to believe they could ask for whatever seemed "fair" and "reasonable" according to their own needs. When the owners met their list of issues with a set of nonnegotiable job descriptions, the workers' fundamental point of unity became an agreement not to accept the job descriptions in the form of ultimatums.

The workers' ability to achieve and maintain such solidarity is all the more remarkable given the diversity of the group and the differences in their politics. But the foundation for the collective structure that enabled them to mediate their disagreements had already been laid by the patterns of cooperation and strong emotional ties the women had developed working together in the shop. Workers referred to this sense of camaraderie and closeness to explain what differentiated Amazon from a shop employing straight women, suggesting that these patterns were a product of lesbian workplace culture rather than a composite of individuated ties: "Everybody was a tight group at Amazon. . . . You've got all these dykes! [The owners] used to be a part of that when we were smaller, but then we started getting bigger and everybody had different needs, and so it was 'us' and 'them.' Unfortunately it had to come to that. But we were all pretty grouped emotionally before this stuff came up, so that we were all grouped in battle."

The workers' alliance was based on the synthesis of lesbian identity and a growing awareness of class divisions tied to the division of labor. On the one hand, the women clearly interpreted the conflict as a labor dispute and took a stand based on their needs as workers. On the other hand, they directed their appeals primarily to other lesbians and selected their tactics with the aim of keeping the struggle within the lesbian community.

Sensitivity to stereotypes about lesbians' pugnacity and women's alleged incompetence in business affairs made the workers deliberately protective of Amazon at the gay/straight boundary. Workers consistently refused to address the general public or what they considered the "straight media." They turned to the National Labor Relations Board as a last resort in order to keep the owners' job proposals from taking effect as contracts. Workers reluctantly agreed to bring in the "big boys" from the union only after they felt they had exhausted alternatives within the lesbian community and faced the possibility of having to abandon the strike effort altogether. Today, the union's failure to make progress toward a settlement seems to confirm the workers' original skepticism about the union's commitment to the Amazon struggle and its ability to comprehend the concerns of a lesbian shop.

Stanley Aronowitz has argued that the most significant innovations in recent social theory have come from movements like feminism that have grown up outside the traditional boundaries of Marxist and trade unionist politics. Because strictly economic disputes appear to have lost their subversive potential under advanced capitalist conditions, Aronowitz predicts that questions raised by what he calls "cultural movements" will become the new focus of historical change.[22] Events at Amazon seem to corroborate both hypotheses. However, Aronowitz's thesis is qualified by the fact that lesbian workplaces represent a historically unprecedented form of organizing productive relations that cannot be adequately comprehended by a notion of culture set apart from economic factors. The culture that has emerged in institutions like Amazon is not a simple reflection of lesbian-feminist principles but results in part from the bridge between the public and private spheres created by bringing together in practice the hitherto ideologically opposed categories of labor and sexuality. In the Amazon case, the development of a lesbian workplace culture united workers in a struggle that encompassed both economic and cultural concerns. In this sense the Amazon conflict challenges socialist-feminist theory to grapple with issues of sexuality, and urges lesbian-feminist theory to move beyond its focus on sexuality and its legacy of liberal assumptions, in order to develop an analysis of class relations in the lesbian context.

Conclusion: Class and Sexuality

Why has a dialogue about class comparable to the current discussion of race and racism failed to emerge within lesbian feminism? The Amazon case draws attention to several contributing factors: (1) the limited interpretation of class as class background favored by lesbian feminists; (2) liberal strains in lesbian-feminist theory that discourage a relational analysis of class focusing on social structure; (3) the institutional hegemony of an entrepreneurial and professional stratum within the lesbian community; and (4) the heterosexual bias of socialist and socialist-feminist approaches to class theory, which limits their applicability to lesbians.

Information on individuals' class backgrounds clearly cannot explain events at Amazon, for women from both middle-class and working-class backgrounds allied on opposite sides of the dispute. "It would be so much easier, in a way," observed the owner who grew up in a working-class household, "if Lauren and I were both upper class and my father gave me $50,000 and her father gave her $60,000, and we plunked it into a bank and started the business. . . . But it's not that simple." To claim that class background does not determine present behavior does not mean it did not influence decisions made and strategies adopted during the conflict. For example, the limited resources available to workers from certain class

---

22. Stanley Aronowitz, *The Crisis in Historical Materialism* (New York: Praeger Publishers, 1981), pp. 105–6, 133.

backgrounds made it more difficult for them to remain out on strike. In general, however, Amazon's employees had a clear sense that their current position in the relations of production outweighed their varied class backgrounds: "We all knew where we came from, but we all were working, and we knew how hard we worked, and we knew how we were getting treated. When you're a worker, you're a worker."

A background interpretation of class has led most lesbian feminists to define class according to individualized criteria like occupation, income level, education, values, attitudes, and other indicators of socioeconomic status. While these attributes may be linked to class, they do not define class, unless one accepts the liberal view of society as an amalgam of autonomous actors fixed in absolute class positions. On the basis of occupation, all the women at Amazon could be labeled working class because of their blue-collar trade. If a combination of income and educational attainment were used as a gauge, some workers might be assigned a higher class position than the owners. Aside from the mutual inconsistency of these evaluations, neither offers any insight into the relations of class and power that actively shaped the Amazon conflict.[23] In contrast, placing the owners within the context of the job hierarchy at Amazon and the division of labor that structures ownership in society at large allowed us to explore the power differential that put Lauren and Carol in a position of dominance over other women working in the shop.

A relational analysis of events at Amazon supports the conclusion that since property relations and the division of labor continuously generate class divisions, tactics of consciousness raising and moral exhortations to eliminate classism will be insufficient to keep conflicts from emerging in lesbian and feminist institutions. The expectation that "feminist morality" or a principled politics can mitigate class differences rests on a notion of politics as an individualized, ideological stance adopted at will, independent of material circumstances and capable of transcending them. But at Amazon, differences in the values and political commitments of the owners did not prevent them from taking the same side in the dispute once lines were drawn. Lauren felt "morally justified" in presenting the workers with nonnegotiable job descriptions, never realizing the extent to which she defined morality and "responsible action" with regard to the needs of the business. Carol, on the other hand, found it "bizarre to be on the side of the owner. It's much easier for me to think of it from the workers' standpoint." Yet she held to her position.

The owners both supported the principle of solving Amazon's problems through dialogue rather than firing dissenting employees, yet in the

---

23. Anthony Giddens, "Class Structuration and Class Consciousness," in *Classes, Power, and Conflict,* ed. Anthony Giddens and David Held (Berkeley and Los Angeles: University of California Press, 1982), p. 158.

end their power as owners and managers allowed them to abandon this ideal. In Carol's words, "Somebody reached the point where they put their foot down and said, 'That's it.' And you can only do that when you are in the powered position, which we were." Both owners admitted having discussed strategy about the possibility of an employee walkout in response to their job descriptions: "We did discuss it. We said, 'If that happens, the two of us built this from nothing. Now we have the books, we have the diagnostic equipment, we have the customers, we got the building, we're way ahead.' "

In the workers' eyes, control of the property associated with the business gave the owners a decisive advantage during the struggle. When economic necessity forced the workers to drop the picket line to look for other jobs, the prospect of negotiation receded as the owners continued production in the building all ten women had shared before the strike. Since the owners established Amazon with minimal capital investment and took out few loans in succeeding years, the property and equipment that helped them win the struggle actually came from surplus value created by the combined efforts of Amazon's employees and nonpartisan support from the women's community. The owners' exclusive claim to this property was based solely on a legal concept of ownership backed by a patriarchal state. The same principle of ownership underpinned the dominant class position that structured the owners' moral stance, neutralized their well-meaning intentions, and superseded their lesbian-feminist politics at the point of conflict.

It is true that Amazon is "not Bechtel"—a major multinational corporation—as the owners were quick to point out, but this fact obviously did not prevent class relations and a class-linked conflict from emerging in the shop. Although the lesbian community lies well outside the mainstream of American capitalism, it does include a stratum of entrepreneurs, professionals, and small capitalists like Carol and Lauren who own or control many of the institutions serving and symbolizing that community. We suggest that in practice such control allows this group of women to maintain an institutional hegemony[24] that mediates the relation of lesbian identity to community in ways that alternately support and oppress lesbians who stand in different relations to the social division of labor.[25]

The concern with self-reliance and independence that originally led Carol and Lauren to become entrepreneurs also informed their argu-

24. On the concept of hegemony, see Antonio Gramsci, *Selections from the Prison Notebooks* (New York: International Publishers, 1980), p. 12; Raymond Williams, *Marxism and Literature* (Oxford: Oxford University Press, 1977), pp. 108–14.

25. Introducing power as a variable challenges Susan Krieger's static view of lesbian communities as either supportive or coercive to individuals ("Lesbian Identity and Community: Recent Social Science Literature" [in this book]).

ment that dissatisfied workers should open their own enterprises rather than challenge the owners' right to make unilateral decisions in matters affecting employees.[26] Yet what might otherwise be dismissed as regressive, petty-bourgeois values in the tradition of nineteenth-century entrepreneurial capitalism has a different meaning, origin, and political significance in this lesbian context. For Lauren and Carol, self-sufficiency represented a liberating ideology that signified autonomy from men in the area of skills, training, and the ability to earn an equitable income. The same ideology became oppressive only when, as owners and employers, they confused self-determination with the need to control the labor of women they hired.

The coincidence of entrepreneurial values with aspects of lesbian identity in the ideology of self-sufficiency is one more example of the recurrent theme in this study: there is no justification at the level of concrete analysis for abstracting class from sexuality or for treating heterosexism and class hegemony as two distinct types of oppression operating along separate axes. The strike at Amazon cannot be analyzed as a textbook labor conflict precisely because the male and heterosexist bias of most scholarly texts renders them incapable of grasping this integration. While a critique of the bias in class theory is beyond the scope of this paper, the Amazon case indicates why such an integration is necessary.

Lesbians are not simply exceptions to the rule who defy categorization as "nonattached" or "single" (but presumably self-supporting) women or as women residing in households with men.[27] Since self-identified lesbians in American society share an ideology of self-sufficiency rather than the ideological expectation not to work traditionally held by many heterosexual women, the question of derived class becomes largely irrelevant in speaking of lesbian relationships.[28] None of the women in the Amazon study even suggested the possibility of defining her class position through her lover, though several were in relationships of long standing. Lesbians also fall outside the theoretical focus of most debates in socialist feminism, which tend to center on the sexual division of labor.[29] Although the sexual division of labor and job segregation by sex

26. Clearly it would be impractical for every lesbian auto mechanic to open her own repair shop. This admonition also avoids dealing with the source of divisions in the lesbian community by deprecating worker struggles and initiatives.

27. Elizabeth Garnsey advances these categories in an attempt to correct the androcentrism of such theories ("Women's Work and Theories of Class and Stratification," *Sociology* 12, no. 2 [1978]: 223–43).

28. Jackie West, "Women, Sex, and Class," in Kuhn and Wolpe, eds. (n. 6 above), pp. 220–53.

29. The isolated attempts to apply socialist-feminist analysis to lesbians ignore class relations within the lesbian community, directing their attention instead to the origins of

influence all women's experience, for most lesbians gender distinctions do not coincide with the split between home and work life or with the allocation of tasks within the home. When the split between personal and work life is linked to sexuality with the bridging of the private/public split in lesbian workplaces, socialist feminism proffers no theory capable of grasping the significance of what happens once lesbian identity is joined to productive activity.

At Amazon we saw how the reconciliation of the public and private created the potential for a nonalienating work environment where women were able to develop close ties with co-workers as well as to bring into the shop emotions and other ostensibly personal aspects of the self. After the walkout/lockout this integration shaped the dispute by placing emotions at the center of the struggle so that at various points the struggle itself involved drawing and redrawing the boundary between elements of public and private life. While the bridging of the private/public split could not defuse class relations at Amazon, it generated the conditions for overcoming class divisions by fostering a lesbian workplace culture that promoted solidarity among the workers and motivated them to defend their needs in a situation where the owners held the balance of power.

One of Amazon's owners ended her interview with a plea that lesbians learn to "put aside personal feelings and vested interests" or risk the destruction of community institutions. A careful analysis of the Amazon dispute points to the importance of taking personal feelings into account rather than putting them aside and remaining within the limitations of the contrasting paradigms of trust and contract. The effect of suppressing or ignoring the personal will be to reinvoke the division between the private and public, when the ability to bridge that gap constitutes one of the greatest strengths of lesbian institutions. In this sense, the experience of the women of Amazon Auto Repair challenges both lesbian feminism and socialist feminism to break through old paradigms, to recognize that separating sexuality and class in theory merely replicates the segregation of the private from the public, and the personal from the political, in the realm of everyday life.

As for vested interests, they cannot simply be discarded at will, since they have material roots in socially constructed needs mediated by property relations and the division of labor. Yet there exist options for restructuring lesbian workplaces that reject ownership while providing leadership roles, job rotation, procedures for delegating responsibility, shared decision-making processes, and a division of labor that does not

---

women's oppression or to relations at the gay/straight boundary. In addition to Riddiough (n. 3 above), see Susan Williams, "Lesbianism: A Socialist Feminist Perspective," in *Pink Triangles: Radical Perspectives on Gay Liberation*, ed. Pam Mitchell (Boston: Alyson Publications, 1980), pp. 107–16.

rest on a fixed power differential. The radical potential for nonalienated labor created in lesbian workplaces invites us to explore these alternatives as a means of redefining power as energy, skill, and capacity rather than as domination.[30] By drawing attention to the ongoing reproduction of class relations within the lesbian community, the struggle at Amazon advances the possibility of self-determination inside and outside the labor process for all lesbians, not just for the few who formally or informally control lesbian institutions.

Department of Anthropology
Stanford University

30. Hartsock (n. 9 above) draws a useful distinction between power understood as domination and power understood as energy, capacity, and initiative.

REVIEW ESSAY

Lesbian Identity and Community: Recent Social Science Literature

Susan Krieger

This article reviews recent social science literature on the relationship between lesbian identity and community. Specifically, it considers how lesbian communities both affirm and challenge the individual lesbian's sense of self. There is much in the autobiographical literature on lesbian experience that makes us aware that lesbian communities enhance that sense of self. These communities provide a haven or home in a hostile or distrusting outside world. They lend support for what is frequently a stigmatized life-style choice. They command recognition of a distinctively lesbian sensibility—a sensibility that is unusual because of the value it places on intimacy between women.

Yet lesbian communities, along with their virtues, also pose crucial identity problems for their members. At times, they seem to threaten as well as affirm individual identity. The problems posed by lesbian communities are similar to those found in many other social groups and especially in minority groups, where efforts to achieve group solidarity and cohesiveness often conflict with efforts to foster individuality and to tolerate internal deviance.

Because much of the popular literature and, indeed, much of the scholarly literature on lesbian communities has not focused on the internal problems of these communities—and in particular on the challenges to individuality that these communities pose—this article takes a different approach. It reviews recent social science literature on lesbian identity and community in order to redirect attention from the issue of

Reprinted from *Signs: Journal of Women in Culture and Society* 8, no. 1 (Autumn 1982): 91–108.

"lesbian identity" to the issue of "individual identity" in the lesbian setting. I take this approach for two reasons. First, I view the recent literature from a sociological perspective—a perspective biased toward investigating the constraints on behavior imposed by social groups. Second, as a lesbian who has studied lesbian communities, I have found that internal complaints of exclusion, alienation, extreme disappointment, and loss of sense of self arise often in these communities. Such complaints are not ideologically popular. They are, however, important to acknowledge and understand. An examination of the lesbian identity–community relationship may help us to this end. What is more, it may help us to identify issues that are central to our "togetherness" not only as lesbians but also, more generally, as women.

In this review I look to recent social science literature for what it tells us about the identity-community relationship in the lesbian setting. I examine work in three disciplines: sociology, social psychology, and clinical psychology. For purposes of the discussion, "identity" and "community" are defined broadly. Identity is used to refer to feelings and ideas an individual has about herself. These feelings and ideas change over time but at any point they have a rough coherence. They are the means by which a person distinguishes the "me" from the "not me," the self from the other or from the web of others who constitute a social world.

The idea of community used in this discussion is also deliberately broad. It refers to the range of social groups in which the lesbian individual may feel a sense of camaraderie with other lesbians, a sense of support, shared understanding, shared vision, shared sense of self "as a lesbian," vis-à-vis the outside world. Some lesbian communities are geographically specific (all the lesbians in Newark, for example); some exist within institutions (e.g., prisons); some exist only in spirit; some are ideological (e.g., lesbian feminist); some, primarily social. All are groups in which an individual may share her distinctively lesbian way of being with other lesbians. There are many differences among lesbian communities and these are extremely important. The concern of the present discussion, however, is with identifying characteristics that the range of lesbian groups may share. (These characteristics may later be used to measure differences between groups.)

The present review begins with a brief summary of the history and scope of recent social science literature on lesbianism. The first section describes a major change in perspective that has occurred in this literature over the last twenty years. An understanding of this change provides the context for considering the work reviewed in the second section, which focuses on nine recent studies that elucidate the identity-community relationship. The final section points to gaps in our existing knowledge and suggests directions for new research.

The Change in Perspective

To speak of the change in perspective that has occurred in the social science literature on lesbianism in the last twenty years is to tell an almost too simple story: "Once we were sick and now we are well," the story goes in its most rudimentary form. All contemporary research discussions reiterate some version of it.[1] Before 1960, they tell us, such meager treatments of lesbianism as existed in the literature were based on medical, psychiatric, or psychoanalytic expertise, and depicted lesbians as pathological: sick, perverted, inverted, fixated, deviant, narcissistic, masochistic, and possibly biologically mutated, at best the daughters of hostile mothers and embarrassingly unassertive fathers. In the early and mid-1960s, beginning even as early as the late 1950s, a small number of sociologists, social psychologists, and psychiatrists began publishing work that took issue with the assumptions of the pathological models.[2] They offered new evidence and corrective interpretations and suggested that lesbianism was neither a sexual nor a social disease but, rather, a life-style choice closely linked with a sense of personal identity. Lesbians, their

1. See, e.g., historical overviews in Barbara Sang, "Lesbian Research: A Critical Evaluation," in *Our Right to Love: A Lesbian Resource Handbook,* ed. Ginny Vida (Englewood Cliffs, N.J.: Prentice-Hall, 1978), pp. 80–87; David H. Rosen, *Lesbianism: A Study of Female Homosexuality* (Springfield, Ill.: Thomas, 1974); Barbara Ponse, *Identities in the Lesbian World: The Social Construction of Self* (Westport, Conn.: Greenwood, 1978); Virginia R. Brooks, *Minority Stress and Lesbian Women* (Lexington, Mass.: Lexington, 1981); Donna M. Tanner, *The Lesbian Couple* (Lexington, Mass.: Lexington, 1978); and Dolores Klaich, *Woman Plus Woman: Attitudes toward Lesbianism* (New York: Morrow, 1974).

2. Results of three of the early studies were first published in *The Ladder,* the magazine of the pioneering homophile organization, the Daughters of Bilitis: Florence Conrad et al., "D.O.B. Questionnaire Reveals Some Facts about Lesbians," *Ladder* 3, no. 12 (1959): 4–26; Suzanne Prosin, "The Concept of the Lesbian: A Minority in Reverse," *Ladder* 6, no. 10 (1962): 5–22; and Ralph Gundlach, "Research Project Report," *Ladder* 11, no. 9 (1967): 2–9. See also Ralph Gundlach, "In Opposition to Drs Walker and Bergler on Homosexuality," *Ladder* 6, no. 4 (1962): 6–9, and "Why Is a Lesbian?" *Ladder* 7, no. 12 (1963): 4–6. Other important early works were Virginia Armon, "Some Variables in Overt Female Homosexuality," *Journal of Projective Techniques and Personality Assessment* 24, no. 3 (1960): 292–309; William Simon and John H. Gagnon, "The Lesbians: A Preliminary Overview," in *Sexual Deviance,* ed. William Simon and John H. Gagnon (New York: Harper & Row, 1967), pp. 247–81; Ralph Gundlach and Bernard F. Reiss, "Self and Sexual Identity in the Female: A Study of Female Homosexuals," in *New Directions in Mental Health,* ed. Bernard F. Reiss (New York: Grune & Stratton, 1968), pp. 205–31; Rita Bass-Hass, "The Lesbian Dyad: Basic Issues and Value Systems," *Journal of Sex Research* 4, no. 2 (1968): 108–26; Mark J. Freedman, "Homosexuality among Women and Psychological Adjustment," *Ladder* 12 (May 1968): 2–3; and June H. Hopkins, "The Lesbian Personality," *British Journal of Psychiatry* 115, no. 529 (1969): 1433–36. The study by Alfred C. Kinsey et al., *Sexual Behavior in the Human Female* (Philadelphia: Saunders, 1953), is also credited with significant influence in encouraging a nonpathological view of lesbianism. See, too, the extension of the Kinsey tradition in Alan P. Bell and Martin S. Weinberg, *Homosexualities: A Study of Diversity among Men and Women* (New York: Simon & Schuster, 1978).

studies suggested, were not nearly as sick, perverted, inverted, fixated, deviant, narcissistic, masochistic, and possibly biologically mutated as were those who had previously written about them.[3]

A small but growing body of literature has come to us out of the tradition spawned in the 1960s and has gone far in achieving a shift toward viewing lesbianism as normal. This work—much of it published since the mid-1970s—has rejected ideas of disease, and a number of other perspectives as well, in favor of more sophisticated approaches.[4]

3. Notable among the offenders were: Frank S. Caprio, *Female Homosexuality: A Psychodynamic Study of Lesbianism* (New York: Citadel, 1954); Edmund Bergler, *Neurotic Counterfeit-Sex: Homosexuality, Impotence, Frigidity* (New York: Grune & Stratton, 1951), and *Homosexuality: Disease or Way of Life?* (New York: Collier, 1956); C. L. Bacon, "A Developmental Theory of Female Homosexuality," in *Perversions: Psychodynamics and Therapy*, ed. S. Lorand (New York: Random House, 1956), pp. 131–59; Sandor Rado, "Fear of Castration in Women," *Psychoanalytic Quarterly* 2 (1933): 425–75; and Helene Deutsch, *The Psychology of Women: A Psychoanalytic Interpretation* (New York: Grune & Stratton, 1944), pp. 325–53. See also their distinguished predecessors: Richard von Krafft-Ebing, *Psychopathia Sexualis*, trans. and ed. F. Rebman (New York: Rebman, 1906); Havelock Ellis, *Studies in the Psychology of Sex* (New York: Random House, 1940), 1:195–263; and Sigmund Freud, "The Psychogenesis of a Case of Homosexuality in a Female" (1920), in *The Collected Papers* (London: Hogarth, 1948), 2:202–31. In addition, it should be noted that the tradition of viewing lesbianism as to some degree pathological or deviant continues. See, e.g., Marcel T. Saghir and Eli Robins, "Clinical Aspects of Female Homosexuality," and Judd Marmor, "Overview: The Multiple Roots of Homosexual Behavior," in *Homosexual Behavior: A Modern Reappraisal*, ed. Judd Marmor (New York: Basic, 1980), pp. 280–95, 3–21 (this volume is an update of Marmor's *Sexual Inversion: The Multiple Roots of Homosexuality* [New York: Basic, 1965]); and Carlos E. Climent et al., "Epidemiological Studies of Female Prisoners. IV. Homosexual Behavior," *Journal of Nervous and Mental Disease* 164, no. 1 (1977): 25–29.

4. In the 1970s, the emergence of this literature was encouraged by the *Journal of Homosexuality*, founded in 1974 by researchers and clinicians at odds with the medical model. (See introductory editorial by Charles Silverstein, *Journal of Homosexuality* 1, no. 1 [1974]: 5–7.) Articles dealing with lesbianism which appeared in the *Journal of Homosexuality* between 1970 and 1980 included: Kenneth L. Nyburg, "Sexual Aspirations and Sexual Behaviors among Homosexually Behaving Males and Females: The Impact of the Gay Community," *Journal of Homosexuality* 2, no. 1 (1976): 29–38; Hilda A. Hidalgo and Elia Hidalgo-Christensen, "The Puerto Rican Lesbian and the Puerto Rican Community," *Journal of Homosexuality* 2, no. 2 (Winter 1976–77): 109–21; Alice M. Propper, "Lesbianism in Female and Coed Correctional Institutions," *Journal of Homosexuality* 3, no. 3 (1978): 265–74; Pat Califia, "Lesbian Sexuality," *Journal of Homosexuality* 4, no. 3 (1979): 255–66; Mary Riege Laner, "Growing Older Female: Heterosexual and Homosexual," *Journal of Homosexuality* 4, no. 3 (1979): 267–75; Joyce C. Albro and Carol Tully, "A Study of Lesbian Lifestyles in the Homosexual Micro-Culture and the Heterosexual Macro-Culture," *Journal of Homosexuality* 4, no. 4 (1979): 331–44; and Eileen Shavelson et al., "Lesbian Women's Perceptions of Their Parent-Child Relationships," *Journal of Homosexuality* 5, no. 3 (1980): 205–14. See also Siegrid Schäfer, "Sexual and Social Problems of Lesbians," *Journal of Sex Research* 12, no. 1 (1976): 50–69, and "Sociosexual Behavior in Male and Female Homosexuals: A Study in Sex Differences," *Archives of Sexual Behavior* 6, no. 5 (1977): 355–64. Standing alone at the start of the decade was Charlotte Wolff's *Love between Women* (New York: St. Martin's, 1971), notable for its explication of changes in Freud's views of female homosexuality as well as its attempt to evolve an original theory emphasizing the "intense emotionality" of lesbian relationships.

The best of the recent studies in this area now view lesbianism as a product of multiple influences rather than as traceable to a single cause. Indeed, they look less at causes than at behaviors and perceptions of experience, and less at how lesbians differ from other people—especially other women—than at how they are similar. These studies increasingly view the lesbian individual in a social context—in terms of her relationships in couples, institutions, communities, and a larger society—rather than in isolated individual terms or in relation to a family of origin. They consider lesbianism to be a matter of total personal identity rather than primarily a sexual condition, and they view it as subject to choice and as changeable in definition rather than as something that is a given. In the broadest sense, then, the shift that has occurred may be described as one that moves us from thinking about lesbianism in terms of deviance, narrowness, simple causation, isolated occurrence, and fixed nature to thinking of it in terms of normality, diversity, multiple influence, social context, choice, and change.

The shift from the earlier view to the present one has been gradual since the early 1960s and has been represented differently in each of the social science disciplines. The sociologists—and sociologically oriented anthropologists and historians—who have contributed to this shift have looked, as a rule, at how lesbianism has been shaped in relation both to the lesbian community and to the norms and experiences of the larger straight society. They have focused on how lesbians have "managed" to have identity—meaning lesbian identity—in a largely hostile world.[5] The social psychologists have looked primarily at individual differences, focusing on how lesbians are or are not like other people, particularly other women. They have dealt mainly with individuals' satisfaction with the lesbian life-style choice and with lesbian couple relationships.[6] The clinical psychologists have been concerned with sources of psychological difficulty experienced by individual lesbians (and lesbian couples) and with appropriate methods of treatment by mental health professionals.[7]

5. See, e.g., Ponse (n. 1 above); Alice E. Moses, *Identity Management in Lesbian Women* (New York: Praeger, 1978); E. M. Ettore, *Lesbians, Women and Society* (London: Routledge & Kegan Paul, 1980); Tanner (n. 1 above); and Simon and Gagnon (n. 2 above). See also a related discussion by Dorothy S. Painter, "Lesbian Humor as a Normalization Device," in *Communication, Language, and Sex: Proceedings from the First Annual Conference,* ed. Virginia A. Eman and Cynthia L. Berryman (Rowley, Mass.: Newbury, 1980), pp. 132–48.

6. For an overview of selected literature in this area, see Letitia Anne Peplau and Hortensia Amaro, "Understanding Lesbian Relationships," in *Homosexuality as a Social Issue,* ed. W. Paul and J. D. Weinrich (Beverly Hills, Calif.: Sage, in press).

7. For recent attitudes in clinical psychology not cited in the second section of this article, see Margaret A. Kingdon, "Lesbians," *Counseling Psychologist* 8, no. 1 (1979): 44–61; Josette Escamilla-Mondanaro, "Lesbians and Therapy," in *Psychotherapy for Women: Treatment toward Equality,* ed. Edna I. Rawlings and Dianne K. Carter (Springfield, Ill.: Thomas, 1977), pp. 256–65; and Nancy Toder, "Sexual Problems of Lesbians," in Vida, ed. (n. 1 above), pp. 105–13. For a related social work perspective, see Sandra J. Potter and Trudy E. Darty, "Social Work and the Invisible Minority: An Exploration of Lesbianism," *Social Work* 26, no. 3 (1981): 187–92.

In each of these areas, the studies have been offered with a strong sense of concern for correcting previous views.

Methodologically, the sociologists have used participant-observation combined with in-depth interviewing and survey research. The social psychologists have relied mainly on survey methodology, sometimes supplemented with in-depth interviewing. The clinical psychologists have used cumulative case experience, often in combination with survey methods and the in-depth interview. Independent of method, the samples obtained in each of these fields have reflected disproportionately the white, well-educated, articulate, youthful, middle-class lesbian who has some commitment to feminist ideology. This has been noted repeatedly in the studies, with due apology.[8] Yet there has been enough representation of other populations in these studies to suggest a broader mapping of lesbian diversity than is usually acknowledged.

The individual researchers in each field have been for the most part nonlesbian. In the days of the pathological models, they were primarily men. Increasingly the studies have been done by women, but only a few very recent studies have been done by women whose lesbianism is either acknowledged or strongly implied.[9] This increase in the number of women researchers has been accompanied by an emphasis on the similarities between lesbians and other women, while the increasing number of lesbian researchers has encouraged an emphasis on the positively valued norms evolving among lesbians with regard to identity, relationships, and community—norms that differ from those of heterosexual culture.[10] Many of the studies report that access to lesbian populations has been affected by whether or not the researcher was a lesbian; access and trust are viewed as problematic because of the secret and

8. Moses offers a typical apology: "It must be stressed that the results of this study have a limited generalizability. The sample is too small and the likelihood of bias too great to allow for assumptions of external validity. At best, therefore, we could hope that the sample is similar to a predominantly white population [of] essentially middle-class California lesbian women and that from it we could make some informed guesses about the population from which it was drawn" (Moses [n. 5 above], p. 31). For a suggestion of class and race differences within the lesbian community, see Joan Gibbs and Sara Bennett, *Top Ranking: A Collection of Articles on Racism and Classism in the Lesbian Community* (New York: February 3rd Press, 1980). See also Bass-Hass (n. 2 above) and J. R. Roberts, comp., *Black Lesbians: An Annotated Bibliography* (Tallahassee, Fla.: Naiad, 1981).

9. Acknowledgment of lesbian identity appears in the work of Moses (n. 5 above) and Ettore (n. 5 above). Assertion of nonlesbian identity appears in Ponse (n. 1 above), Tanner (n. 1 above), and Deborah Goleman Wolf, *The Lesbian Community* (Berkeley and Los Angeles: University of California Press, 1979). In most studies, however, the authors do not state whether or not they are lesbian, and most do not discuss the potential effects of this or any other aspect of their identity on their selection of data and interpretation of results.

10. For a useful discussion of heterosexual bias, see Stephen F. Morin, "Heterosexual Bias in Psychological Research on Lesbianism and Male Homosexuality," *American Psychologist* 32 (1977): 629–37.

stigmatized nature of many lesbian populations.[11] Finally, most of the existing research appears to have been conducted primarily by well-educated, white, middle-class researchers, a fact likely to account for the sample bias.

Despite wide variation in the literature, the subject matter of much of the recent research can be subsumed under the heading "Exploration of Lesbian Identity." Only a small amount of it deals with lesbian community, and of this, only one major study deals explicitly and exclusively with the relationship between lesbian identity and lesbian community.[12] This is, in part, a function of tradition in this area; the study of lesbianism began not as a study of women in relation to each other but as a study of isolated, deviant individuals. It is also, in all likelihood, a function of the self-protectiveness of lesbians in society and of the fact that lesbian communities have only recently emerged in a form that is both accessible to researchers and not easily ignored by them.

The Relationship between Lesbian Identity and Community: A Review of Nine Studies

As might be expected, the studies that throw most light on the relationship between lesbian identity and community are those that have moved farthest away from the pathological, simple-cause model of earlier years and have begun to comprehend lesbian diversity in its own terms. Among these, nine studies stand out as especially insightful.[13] Rather than criticize the methods of these works, the following discussion uses key ideas from each study to begin to piece together a larger picture of the identity-community relationship in the lesbian setting. As

11. See Tanner (n. 1 above), pp. 1–2, 47–49; Moses (n. 5 above), pp. 29–31; Wolf (n. 9 above), pp. 1–12; and esp. Ponse (n. 1 above), pp. 9–22. Joseph Styles, in "Outsider/ Insider: Researching Gay Baths," *Urban Life* 8, no. 2 (1979): 135–52, provides a helpful illustration of the difference "insider" status can make in the homosexual situation. An overview of selected relevant issues appears in Carol A. B. Warren, "Fieldwork in the Gay World: Issues in Phenomenological Research," *Journal of Social Issues* 33, no. 4 (1977): 93–107.

12. Ponse (n. 1 above).

13. Other studies may also be useful, however, including some on gay men's communities. See, e.g., Carol A. B. Warren, *Identity and Community in the Gay World* (New York: Wiley, 1974); Martin Weinberg and Colin Williams, *Male Homosexuals: Their Problems and Adaptations* (New York: Oxford University Press, 1974); and John Alan Lee, "The Gay Connection," *Urban Life* 8, no. 2 (1979): 175–98. The nine works discussed here have been chosen from the broader range, not because they are the only works of value, but because of their particular relevance to the purposes of the present review. Readers familiar with the literature may note the absence of attention to Deborah Wolf's book, *The Lesbian Community* (n. 9 above). This is because Wolf 's study—written like a tourist's guide to the San Francisco lesbian-feminist scene—does not further the kind of understanding this essay seeks to encourage.

noted previously, while this discussion recognizes the important identity-affirmation functions of lesbian communities, it also—and perhaps more importantly—seeks to move us toward acknowledging some of the difficulties in identity that lesbian communities pose for their members.

The first and most pertinent of the recent studies is Barbara Ponse's *Identities in the Lesbian World: The Social Construction of Self.*[14] This is by far the richest study we have with regard to sociological theory. Ponse focuses on the way in which a specifically "lesbian identity" is formed in relation to norms of the lesbian community (defined broadly as "a community of like persons"). She identifies a "gay trajectory" consisting of five elements that function, to some degree, as steps individuals may take toward "the assumption of lesbian identity" within the lesbian world. "When women claim (or are thought to have) attractions to women," says Ponse, when they "have sexual relations with women, or are present in the lesbian community over time, or acknowledge a subjective sense of difference from heterosexual others, then the acceptance and acknowledgment of lesbian identity (at least in the company of other lesbians) are expected to follow."[15]

Essentially, Ponse is telling us about a "coming out" process within the lesbian community that parallels and works in conjunction with coming out to the self and to the outside world. Once having come out within the community, the individual may then receive the protection and validation of that community, both of which are supports for the maintenance of identity and are unavailable elsewhere. While such observations are not surprising, they have not, as a rule, been central in social science inquiries into lesbianism. Ponse's book breaks a long tradition because of its focus on the importance of the lesbian community itself as a norm-setting vehicle for the definition of individual lesbian identity.

Her book also includes a strong discussion of the importance of secretiveness to the existence and cohesiveness of the lesbian community and to its identity functions. It offers both a useful identification of the "hiatus in identity" (or loss of sense of self) that may occur when individuals move from the straight world to the lesbian community and a helpful typification of the variety of "styles of affiliation" and "modes of biographic reconstruction" that occur when individuals view themselves in relation to the community.[16] Ponse's work is based on a definition of lesbian identity as an "essential" identity, rather than a "role" identity, and as much more than a sexual orientation. It refers, she notes, to the

14. Ponse (n. 1 above).
15. Ibid., p. 126.
16. See also Barbara Ponse, "Finding Self in the Lesbian Community," in *Women's Sexual Development: Explorations of "Inner Space,"* ed. Martha Kirkpatrick (New York: Plenum, 1980), pp. 181–200.

"state of *being*" rather than to the "mere *doing*" of an individual. It implies "an expansion of experiences of self and a finding of community" and "is a totality of which sexuality is a mere part."[17]

Ponse introduces her study by describing her experience as a straight researcher attempting to enter the "secretive" lesbian world through a gay social service organization. She found there that she was defined as lesbian according to "the homosexual assumption" characteristically made in the lesbian world, much as "the heterosexual assumption" is made in the straight world. She credits her entry experience for making her aware of the gay trajectory, emphasizing "the pervasiveness of the assumption that persons who are *in* the community are most probably *of* it."[18] In doing so, she points to the tendency of lesbian communities to encourage a high degree of conformity and, often, a high degree of commitment on the part of their members.

This tendency toward conformity is further elaborated in a study of a Portland, Oregon, lesbian-feminist "countercultural" community reported by Elizabeth Barnhart, a social anthropologist.[19] Barnhart's study, although not dealing specifically with the relationship between lesbian identity and lesbian community, provides us with a good example of an extreme case of the coercive, or at least co-optive, aspect of lesbian communities. Barnhart focuses on "the tension between the demands of couple relationship and the demands of Community" and thereby identifies a central mechanism by which conformity and commitment to the community are obtained. This mechanism is the structuring and dissolution of couple relationships within the community that results in what Barnhart, referring to the group she studied, labels "the lesbian shuffle," or the "fairly continual changing of pair relationships."

Reasons for "the lesbian shuffle," Barnhart notes, are multiple, but important among them is the fact that initially the couple relationship is the way an individual becomes tied to the lesbian community in a non-threatening way (nonthreatening to other couples). Later, dissolving the couple relationship is the way the individual remains committed to the community, since the claim of the couple may easily become competitive with that of the group. The individual soon learns, says Barnhart, that "just as 'there will always be an England,' there will always be a Community. Pairs may come and go, change and separate, yet the Community will always maintain itself."[20]

Barnhart, like Ponse, reports on the struggle to maintain community membership that ensues when couples break up. She notes that the

17. Ponse, *Identities*, p. 171.

18. Ibid., pp. 13–17.

19. Elizabeth Barnhart, "Friends and Lovers in a Lesbian Counterculture Community," in *Old Family/New Family*, ed. Nona Glazer-Malbin (New York: Van Nostrand, 1975), pp. 90–115.

20. Ibid., p. 114.

community, like the couple, is a source of crucial rewards for the individual. It provides "intimacy, security, love, affection, and friendship," supporting the individual in ways "denied her in 'straight' society." She also comments on the high degree of "social and ideological integration" in the community and suggests that this produces a group that functions as a kind of "psychological kinship system" for the individual.

In a very different kind of study, Madeleine Davis, Liz Kennedy, and Avra Michelson, examining lesbian bar communities, make some similar points.[21] Using oral history methods, Davis et al. depict patterns of sociability characteristic of bars in Buffalo, New York, from 1930 to 1960. In considering some previously unpublished work, as well as in presenting their own findings, they emphasize the role of the bars as "public gay communities" and, especially prior to the gay movement, as "the central institution responsible for teaching gays the meaning of what a 'homosexual' is."[22] Davis et al. describe the role playing (butch/femme) and the atmosphere of trouble, violence, and fighting that characterized bar sociability during the period they examine; yet they nonetheless conclude that this pattern did not "really undermine the feelings of solidarity" found in the bars—the camaraderie, the cohesion of a society whose members share a commitment to, or need for, places where they can "be together and feel somewhat okay."

Similarly, William Simon and John Gagnon, in one of the first "corrective" sociological treatments of lesbianism to appear in the late 1960s, note that lesbian communities "reinforce a feeling of identity" and provide for the individual homosexual "a way of institutionalizing the experiences, wisdom, and mythology of the collectivity."[23] They note that the lesbian community they have observed—consisting of both bar life and social activity centering around homophile service organizations—"includes a language and an ideology which provide each individual lesbian with already developed attitudes that help her resist the societal claim that she is diseased, depraved, or shameful."[24] Yet they also report that a great many lesbians avoid such community. Among the reasons for avoidance, Simon and Gagnon cite the tendency of lesbian communities "to reinforce lesbian commitments at the expense of greater alienation from conventional society." They use the testimony of one of their interviewees to suggest the possibility of a fear of getting "too involved"—of becoming like the "kids who hang around the bars," for

21. Madeleine Davis, Liz Kennedy, and Avra Michelson, "Buffalo Lesbian Bars: 1930–1960" (paper presented at the Berkshire Conference on Women's History, Vassar College, June 1981).

22. See also Nancy Achilles, "The Development of the Homosexual Bar as an Institution," in *Sexual Deviance*, ed. Simon and Gagnon (n. 2 above); and Ethel Sawyer, "A Study of a Public Lesbian Community" (Ph.D. diss., Washington University, 1965).

23. Simon and Gagnon (n. 2 above).

24. Ibid., p. 262.

whom, "just because they're homosexual, the gay life becomes everything."[25]

A more recent work also emphasizing the potentially overwhelming psychological importance of lesbian communities to their members is Sherry McCoy and Maureen Hicks's "psychological retrospective on power" in a contemporary Los Angeles lesbian-feminist community.[26] McCoy and Hicks are clinical psychologists who analyze how lesbians who do join lesbian communities often bring to them great expectations, looking for "magical fulfillment" of "dreams and hopes" that have been frustrated in the outside world. McCoy and Hicks note the disappointment that often occurs when lesbian communities do not fulfill these expectations and the problem individuals often have of separating self from community—a problem in part bred of difficulties the communities seem to have in tolerating differences. Thus, individuals who "separate," or differ, from the collective ideology become "politically incorrect" and risk loss of much-needed support.

In addition, McCoy and Hicks suggest, especially in the contemporary lesbian-feminist setting, members tend to project their "fondest hopes [and] worst fears" onto the community, conceptualizing the community as a "bastion of omnipotence," for instance, and expecting it to be "a haven or a utopia free of conflict and contradiction." There seems to be a conflict between the strong need for such an all-powerful fantasy community in fulfillment, protection, or extension of the individual on one hand, and the individual's need for separation on the other. How, McCoy and Hicks ask, "do we simultaneously strike a balance between the need to be autonomous as individuals, and political affinity groups, and the need to remain intimate as a community?"[27]

This theme is reiterated in recent work by Letitia Anne Peplau, a social psychologist, and her associates—work that explores characteristics of lesbian couple relationships.[28] In one of these articles, "Loving Women: Attachment and Autonomy in Lesbian Love Relationships," Peplau et al. focus on values associated with "attachment and autonomy" that are held by individuals in lesbian couples. The authors discuss desires for autonomy as influenced by feminism and desires for attachment as influenced by more traditional sex-role socialization and by romanti-

25. Ibid., p. 263.

26. Sherry McCoy and Maureen Hicks, "A Psychological Retrospective on Power in the Contemporary Lesbian-Feminist Community," *Frontiers* 4, no. 3 (1979): 65–69.

27. Ibid., p. 68.

28. Letitia Anne Peplau, Susan Cochran, Karen Rook, and Christine Padesky, "Loving Women: Attachment and Autonomy in Lesbian Relationships," *Journal of Social Issues* 34, no. 3 (1978): 7–27; Letitia Anne Peplau and Susan D. Cochran, "Sex Differences in Values concerning Love Relationships" (paper presented at the annual meeting of the American Psychological Association, Montreal, September 1980); Mayta A. Caldwell and Letitia Anne Peplau, "The Balance of Power in Lesbian Relationships," *Sex Roles: A Journal of Research* (in press); Peplau and Amaro (n. 6 above).

cism. Lesbian couples, they suggest, much like other couples, require a "balancing of the desire for intimacy and the desire for independence."[29] This in itself is not surprising, but that is not the measure of their findings. Peplau's work in social psychology, like that of Ponse in sociology, represents a major breakthrough in her discipline's treatment of lesbians. For Peplau et al., with much methodological care, deal with relationships between lesbians on the basis of values identified as significant by the participants in those relationships. Their assertion of the commonality of the lesbian experience goes against a prior and popular tendency to view lesbian relationships as aberrant and to focus on "issues of etiology and personal adjustment."

In general, Peplau et al. find that lesbian relationships share many dynamics with other close relationships, the attachment/autonomy issue being but one.[30] The balance of power in lesbian relationships, they maintain, affects the degree to which individuals are satisfied with them—women in more equal power relationships report greater satisfaction.[31] Furthermore, the authors note that in their relationships lesbians have values that are more like those of other women than they are like those of men. Lesbians, as women, value equality of power, emotional expressiveness or intimate self-disclosure, and similarity between partners.[32]

Yet Peplau et al. repeatedly mention the potential importance of differences that exist between lesbians and others. They point out that the power balance in lesbian relationships may be affected by the different kinds of resources lesbians bring to and value in their relationships.[33] The lesbians sampled gave more emphasis to their partners having similar attitudes or beliefs than did other women (this, they propose, may be an influence of feminism).[34] In addition, the lesbians sampled, like the gay men, placed a greater value on sexual openness in their relationships than did the heterosexual men and women studied.[35]

Another potentially significant difference between lesbian and nonlesbian relationships appears in the work of two clinical psychologists, Jo-Ann Krestan and Claudia Bepko.[36] In an article focusing on dynamics of fusion in "committed lesbian couple relationships," Krestan and Bepko suggest that "fusion" is more of a problem in lesbian relationships than in either heterosexual or gay male relationships. By fusion they mean a lack of "differentiation" of the individual from the

29. Peplau et al., "Loving Women," p. 8.
30. Peplau and Cochran, "Sex Differences," p. 6.
31. Caldwell and Peplau, "The Balance of Power," p. 20.
32. Peplau and Cochran, "Sex Differences," p. 3.
33. Caldwell and Peplau, "The Balance of Power," pp. 19–20.
34. Peplau and Cochran, "Sex Differences," p. 3.
35. Ibid., p. 5.
36. Jo-Ann Krestan and Claudia S. Bepko, "The Problem of Fusion in the Lesbian Relationship," *Family Process* 19, no. 3 (1980): 277–89.

"relational context," or, in Peplau's terms, a lack of autonomy or independence within the couple. Although their clients came to them for many things, Krestan and Bepko report, the "fusion theme" was recurrent—"the intense anxiety over any desire for separateness or autonomy within the relationship."

The importance of the fusion issue in lesbian relationships has its roots not in flaws or traits of individuals, Krestan and Bepko argue, but in the stressful social situation of the lesbian couple. The fusion results, in part, from attempts by the members of the couple to maintain their relationship, as a subsystem, within a larger system "whose feedback about their relationship would constantly suggest that they dissolve it." In the face of this feedback, the members of the couple adopt a "two against a threatening world" position, which increases the extent to which the relationship becomes a "closed system." This, in turn, increases "the intensity of the fusion between the two partners," that is, the blurring of the boundaries between them as separate individuals.[37]

Krestan and Bepko propose, as well, that the socialization of the members of lesbian couples, as women, significantly contributes to the tendency toward fusion in their relationships, since such socialization does not promote personal differentiation. Rather, it encourages the denial of the self in relationships; women have long been taught to put the needs and feelings of other people ahead of their own. The authors point out that fusion may also be strongly encouraged because members of the lesbian couple are of the same sex. There is therefore a greater possibility that they will identify with each other than there would be if they were of opposite sexes.[38] This identification, Krestan and Bepko suggest, may mask the difficulty of maintaining autonomy in lesbian relationships.

In *Minority Stress and Lesbian Women,* Virginia Brooks further develops ideas about the effects of subgroup stress on lesbian individuals and relationships.[39] Her study, emerging from the field of social welfare, analyzes data from the largest questionnaire survey of lesbians to date—a sample size of 675. Brooks uses a systems framework to identify sources of minority stress in the larger society's "ascription of inferior status" to the lesbian subgroup and to suggest possible "stress mediating responses" available to lesbians, one of which is "positive group identification."

37. Ibid., pp. 278–79.
38. For a related discussion of female-female identification, see Nancy Chodorow on the mother-daughter relationship in *The Reproduction of Mothering: Psychoanalysis and the Sociology of Gender* (Berkeley and Los Angeles: University of California Press, 1978), pp. 92–110. See also the discussions of mirroring in Simone de Beauvoir, *The Second Sex* (New York: Vintage, 1974), pp. 464–65; and in Susan Krieger, *The Mirror Dance: Identity in a Women's Community* (Philadelphia: Temple University Press, in press).
39. Brooks (n. 1 above).

In a chapter on identity conflicts, where she discusses negative effects of stress on self-esteem, Brooks notes a recurrent conflict between "personal" identity and "lesbian" identity among members of the lesbian minority: "Just as a black person may seem to communicate simultaneously 'I'm proud to be black' and 'Can you stop describing me as black?' so lesbian women today may be caught between expressing positive self-identity as lesbian and the desire to be considered uncategorically, that is, as an individual."[40] Brooks views the "minority individual" in relation to the outside world, but her analysis suggests the possibility that such conflict may be found internally, within the lesbian community, as well, where a common "lesbian" identity may represent a fused identity against which "personal" identity must repeatedly be asserted.

Dorothy Riddle and Barbara Sang, two clinical psychologists, also discuss effects of stress on lesbians as members of a stigmatized minority in their article, "Psychotherapy with Lesbians."[41] Their intent is to sensitize therapists to the difference between the problems lesbians have with self-concept and those of heterosexual women, as well as to demonstrate that these problems result largely from the negatively sanctioned, "invisible minority" subgroup status of lesbians, combined with their socialization as women. Female socialization patterns, Riddle and Sang maintain, are major contributors to the stress felt by lesbians—as individuals and in their relationships—because lesbians conflict with the given patterns, and this conflict has a negative effect on individual self-esteem.

In discussing the particular socialization patterns that cause difficulty, Riddle and Sang note that "females are expected to assume a role which includes being emotional, sensitive, supportive, nurturing, and noncompetitive and which excludes being dominant, instrumental, and socially ascendent." In addition they suggest that "external sources of self-definition play a particularly salient role in the personal identity of women." They mention that "women are uniquely socialized to be sensitive to the acceptance and rejection of others and to translate that response into a comment on their own self-worth." And they emphasize that from an early age women "learn to identify their sense of purpose with supportive roles in others' lives, while largely ignoring their own needs."[42]

Riddle and Sang make these points in order to suggest that stress is created when lesbians attempt to diverge from traditional female norms

40. Ibid., p. 136.

41. Dorothy T. Riddle and Barbara Sang, "Psychotherapy with Lesbians," *Journal of Social Issues* 34, no. 3 (1978): 84–100. See also Barbara E. Sang, "Psychotherapy with Lesbians: Some Observations and Tentative Generalizations," in Rawlings and Carter, eds. (n. 7 above), pp. 266–78.

42. Riddle and Sang, pp. 85–86.

in their relationships with the outside world—when they seek "to define themselves independent of others' reactions" or "to ignore or challenge the negative sanctions traditionally placed on inappropriate sex-role behavior."[43] Their argument, however, may be interpreted additionally to extend the hypotheses of Krestan and Bepko, and of Brooks, by suggesting that conflict with sex-role socialization may also contribute to boundary conflict, or stress, within lesbian relationships, whether of couples or communities. This observation extends the original argument beyond its intention, but this is what must often be done in social science to make use of available work for the purpose of understanding the relationship between lesbian identity and community.

Summary and Suggestions for New Research

The nine preceding studies are among the richest in recent social science literature on lesbianism. They contain many themes and concepts that may be useful for analyzing the relationship between lesbian identity and community. Yet except for the work of Ponse, none of the studies deals specifically or explicitly with that relationship; basically we do not know very much, in the social sciences, about lesbian communities or about their interconnection with lesbian identity. The research that we have tells us little about internal structures. For the most part this research looks outward, at external boundaries, defining and explaining lesbian identity in relation to the nonlesbian world—by comparison, in reaction to, as secret from. We have some evidence concerning internal structures, but it is spotty and only suggestive of that particular constellation of attributes that distinguishes lesbian sociability as something different from what may be observed elsewhere. We need to know more about that particular constellation in order to supplement other findings and to develop adequate theories of lesbian identity, indeed, to develop adequate theories of personal identity in lesbian settings.

At present social science suggests, at best, a few basic ideas: that in important ways lesbian communities *define identity* for their members; that they are experienced as extremely *vulnerable* in the larger society; that they are experienced as *demanding conformity and commitment;* that they *require intimacy;* and that they *may threaten as well as support* the development of individual identity. Beyond this it is clear that these communities vary across class and racial lines, from city to city, over time, and according to type (bar communities, for example, differ from political communities, home-based social communities from work-based communities, and each of these from institutional communities such as emerge in boarding schools and prisons). It is also clear that individual

43. Ibid., p. 87.

lesbians stand in very different relations to such communities: some are highly involved, others alienated.

The literature has not yet addressed the variety of lesbian social life, however, or its internal intricacy. For this we must turn to journalism, novels, and personal histories.[44] We do not yet know enough about the different kinds of lesbian communities to gauge their potentially different effects on individual identity or to appreciate the way in which together, in interrelationship, they structure identity options for lesbians and, indeed, for all women. We have been told in the literature more about lesbians as types than about their relationships with one another; we have been told more about the lesbian woman than we have about women who are lesbian.

There are interesting research questions that lie just below the surface in the study of the relationship between lesbian identity and community: What happens to identity when aspirations for community are interlaced with expectations about sexuality, and when this occurs in an atmosphere of intimacy where individuals have difficulty maintaining separate boundaries? What happens when the only protection for the self lies in a group that often exists primarily as a terribly precarious fantasy? What happens to the self in a setting where the crises and traumas of breaking up and coming together are the major facts of life? What happens to female identity in an all-female society or, more broadly, what happens to the individual in a community of likeness?

44. For a sense of the variety suggested by personal histories, see Ruth Baetz, *Lesbian Crossroads: Personal Stories of Lesbian Struggles and Triumphs* (New York: Morrow, 1980); Laurel Galana and Gina Covina, *The New Lesbians: Interviews with Women across the U.S. and Canada* (Berkeley, Calif.: Moon Books, 1977); Tracy Young, *Women Who Love Women* (New York: Pocketbooks, 1977); Margaret Cruikshank, ed., *The Lesbian Path: 37 Lesbian Writers Share Their Personal Experiences, Viewpoints, Traumas and Joys* (Monterey, Calif.: Angel, 1980); and Susan J. Wolfe and Julia Penelope Stanley, eds., *The Coming Out Stories* (Watertown, Mass.: Persephone, 1980). Accounts providing more of an overview—either historical or sociological—include: Del Martin and Phyllis Lyon, *Lesbian/Woman* (San Francisco: Glide, 1972); Sidney Abbott and Barbara Love, *Sappho Was a Right-on Woman: A Liberated View of Lesbianism* (New York: Stein & Day, 1972); Klaich (n. 1 above); and Sasha Gregory Lewis, *Sunday's Women: A Report on Lesbian Life Today* (Boston: Beacon, 1979). See also Jean Weber, "Lesbian Networks," *Christopher Street* (April 1979), pp. 51–54; and, for comparative purposes, Jess Stearn, *The Grapevine* (New York: Macfadden 1965), for an early male reporter's view. Useful guides to fiction may be found in Barbara Grier, also known as Gene Damon, *Lesbiana: Book Reviews from "The Ladder," 1966–72* (Reno, Nev.: Naiad, 1976); Gene Damon, Jan Watson, and Robin Jordan, *The Lesbian In Literature: A Bibliography,* 2d ed. (Reno, Nev.: Naiad, 1976); and Jane Rule, *Lesbian Images* (New York: Doubleday, 1975). For short fiction, nonfiction, poetry, and reviews since 1977, see the lesbian literary magazines: *Conditions, Sinister Wisdom,* and *Common Lives/Lesbian Lives. Matrices: A Lesbian/ Feminist Research Newsletter* is also a useful guide to a broad range of literature (available through the Department of English, University of Nebraska at Lincoln), as is the catalog of the Lesbian-Feminist Study Clearinghouse (available through the Women's Studies Program, University of Pittsburgh).

"Once upon a time," begins a lesbian fable, "Deardra loved Carol. . . ."

Deardra also loved Margo, Toni, and Kathy but was just coming out of a primary relationship with Jan and so didn't want to get into anything heavy with anyone. Carol loved Deardra and also Margo and sometimes Renalda, but she didn't give a hang about Toni and she hated Kathy's guts. Actually, Carol loved Deardra best, but Deardra wasn't into loving anybody best and claimed she was equally non-committed to them all.

Margo loved both Deardra and Carol and although she had once been lovers with Toni, she wasn't anymore. Toni was in a primary relationship with Lally and had once loved Margo too, but had gotten so into Deardra that she couldn't relate to Margo at all and Lally wasn't really interested in any of it.

Kathy was just finding out about loving women but claimed she didn't *really* love women she just loved Deardra. Renalda was hot for Carol's body, but was in a primary relationship with Barbara and although Barbara and Carol had once been lovers, they were now just good friends. Toni and Lally were the only ones who lived together and they had been doing that for at least six weeks so it wasn't any big deal anymore. Jan now lived by herself too, but she's not important in this story anymore so we'll just skip her.

One night Carol just happened to be driving past Deardra's house. . . .[45]

The fable continues, tracing Carol's adventure, and concludes with Carol leaving for South America "to live in a cave with a gay boy who had once been friends with her brother." This fable is about a particular community, but it captures something common to all lesbian communities. It appears in a small book of writings by a woman named Chocolate Waters and is titled "A Lesbian Fable (To Be Read Quickly and without Feeling)." What happens, then, to identity when so much that is consequential is hastened over and merged? And what happens to community, and why? We do not, as yet, have very good answers.

In sum, what exists in the social sciences concerning the relationship between lesbian identity and community is by no means adequate. The literature, however, represents a vast improvement in perspective over what existed just twenty years ago. Lesbians are no longer viewed as pathological, deviant, or irreversibly unhappy, and the best work also recognizes the complexity of lesbian experience. Furthermore, the literature indicates that we are looking at lesbians, not only for what they tell us about themselves, but for what they tell us in general about how things work, and in particular about women and about the desires

---

45. Chocolate Waters, "A Lesbian Fable (To Be Read Quickly and without Feeling)," *Take Me Like a Photograph: Writings by Chocolate Waters* (Denver: Eggplant Press, 1977), p. 15.

women may have for independence, self-fulfillment, and self-acceptance.

Looking at the historical development of research on lesbians and their communities, we learn how new categories of persons and experience get incorporated into social science: first they are not seen; then they are found deviant (and viewed as exotic); then defended; and finally, when perceived as sufficiently ordinary, they are included with the rest of what is partly understood. Thus far studies of lesbians are suggestive; they are also few. The field would clearly benefit if more research were done by lesbians and if less were done by heterosexual men. Up until now much of the work has been done by nonlesbian women. As an insider, the lesbian has an important sensitivity to offer, yet she is also more vulnerable than the nonlesbian researcher, both to pressure from the heterosexual world—that her studies conform to previous works and describe the lesbian reality in terms of its relationship with the outside—and to pressure from the inside, from the lesbian community itself—that her studies mirror not the reality of that community but its self-protective ideology. Lesbian and straight women researchers clearly need each other.

Research on the relationship between lesbian identity and community can be extremely fruitful. It can lead us toward an appreciation of distinctively female aspirations. At the same time it confronts us with the challenge of comprehending and acknowledging the constraints we as women impose on each other. Lesbian communities remain difficult to research because their members feel threatened in society. Yet those of us involved in lesbian communities need to learn more about ourselves in order to handle our particular problems and also to influence broader ideas of self and society.

Department of Sociology
Stanford University

Comment on Krieger's "Lesbian Identity and Community: Recent Social Science Literature"

Chela Sandoval

One must never overlook the courage required for self-critique. Susan Krieger's review essay forthrightly attempts to acknowledge and comprehend the "coercive, or at least co-optive, aspect of lesbian communities" (p. 231) by examining "the constraints we as women impose on each other" (pp. 223–40, esp. p. 240). In other words, Krieger wants to analyze what I call, in harsher terms, the fascism that stubbornly emerges in oppositional movements as surely as it exists within the dominant social order itself.

Many feminist thinkers of the eighties concerned with the oppressive internal dynamics of the U.S. women's movement have turned their attention toward understanding the causes of intramovement conflicts. Krieger's work admirably represents an additional testament—this time from a white feminist and scholar—to the dehumanizing modes of behavior that have been carried into the belly of a putative liberatory movement. As such, her work appears to coincide with those analyses and critiques of the women's movement that have been posited by some U.S. Third World feminist thinkers. Remarkably, and in spite of extensive citations, Krieger's work does not recognize any of their contributions; disillusionment seems to be the only ground these writers share. Thus, Krieger's well-constructed analysis contains a serious blind spot, which is reflected in its basic framework and premises.

Krieger believes that there is a unique set of psychological and social dynamics at work when females come together to form communities in opposition to the dominant society. According to her review, the tie that binds lesbians together with women in general is female sex-role conditioning. The review posits all lesbian communities as intensified microcosms of the female condition, allowing the author conceptually to unite all lesbians into what she calls "*the* lesbian community" (my emphasis), thereby leveling the differences (political, ideological, sexual, social,

Reprinted from *Signs: Journal of Women in Culture and Society* 9, no. 4 (Summer 1984): 725–729.

cultural) that exist between actual communities. My reading of the review essay suggests that this lays the groundwork for Krieger implicitly to identify four essential group dynamics operative within every lesbian community. In order to elucidate these shared characteristics, Krieger reviews nine social science studies. She prefaces them with the following statement: "Independent of method, the samples obtained in each of these fields have reflected disproportionately the white, well-educated, articulate, youthful, middle-class lesbian who has some commitment to feminist ideology. This has been noted repeatedly in the studies, with due apology. Yet there has been enough representation of other populations in these studies to suggest a broader mapping of lesbian diversity than is usually acknowledged" (p. 228). The bias of the studies is thus simultaneously acknowledged and swept away.

Krieger then structures the review in a fashion that carries an implicit thesis regarding the psychological and political motives underlying lesbian identity and community. She is to be commended for attempting to examine the internal policing, the intolerance, the constriction of identity roles, and the complaints of exclusion and alienation that have emerged within politically based feminist and lesbian communities. And lesbians do share female sex-role conditioning with heterosexual women. The review, however, works to anchor the difficulties of the lesbian identity–community relationship within the context of such conditioning as if it can be understood apart from the combined effects of other kinds of social conditioning. But there is no single sex-role socialization that holds constant for all women; class, culture, race, and sex intersect in various ways to produce different kinds of women, lesbians, and lesbian communities.

* * *

The first of the four dynamics implied in Krieger's article has to do with the creation of the lesbian community as a ritual space that requires initiation rites for entry. But this dynamic is certainly not unique to female communities, as any anthropologist who has examined bureaucratic institutions will tell us. The second dynamic involves a demonstration of loyalty to the community. This results in "the lesbian shuffle," a mechanism that works to structure couple relationships, dissolve them, and then restructure new couples out of different individuals, thereby providing a living demonstration that the community is of more importance than the needs of any couple, or any individual, for that matter. This dynamic undoubtedly does exist, and not only among young, Anglo, middle-class coeds experimenting with sex, politics, and lesbianism; it was also a highly valued form of behavior within some leftist, radical, and heterosexual groups of the sixties. Furthermore, it is not clear that the dynamic is universal across all lesbian communities. It is a form of sexual behavior frowned on within many Third World lesbian communities, for example, where monogamy and long-term commitments are highly valued. The third dynamic has to do with attempts by many lesbians to fulfill, within the context of their communities, dreams and hopes frustrated else- where. But are these motivations to be seen as problematic—however disillusioned lesbians may become? How else do people move themselves to action? Utopian visions, fantasies, hopes, desires, dreams—and the formation of communities that share them—can effectively work to push against the current social order.

These three dynamics—the creation and maintenance of a ritual space, the demonstration of loyalty, and the elaboration of utopian hopes and desires—are not unique to female, lesbian, or, for that matter, oppo- sitional groups of other kinds. They are necessary components in any organization or institution that depends on the good faith and agreement of its members; they can be usefully read as dynamics utilized by many politically oppressed groups, whether self-consciously or not, to ensure their survival. But it is the fourth dynamic that retroactively adds new and more profound meanings to the first three and that lays claim to a peculiarly female and lesbian form of community building.

Krieger reports that it is female sex-role conditioning (i.e., the denial of self for others and all other conditioning that works against the de- velopment of clear ego boundaries or of personal differentiation) that can lead to lesbians' anxiety over desires for separateness or autonomy. Thus, according to Krieger, fusion among lesbian couples is more problematic than it is among heterosexual or gay male couples. And because lesbians are subjected to societal pressure, the fusion dynamic in their rela- tionships is intensified, which causes further fusion of identities in the formation of a lesbian community unified in solidarity against a hostile world. The result is the creation of a community of likeness that is incapable of tolerating differences. For Krieger it is especially this fourth dynamic that brings about a peculiarly female form of oppressive be- havior within a putatively political oppositional group. If we follow Krie- ger's analysis, the basis for oppressive behavior within lesbian communi- ties is this tendency to fuse, that is, to universalize identity and level all differences. Ironically, however, that is what Krieger herself ultimately does in the construction of her review. Using female conditioning as the basis of her analysis, she does not flinch in identifying group dynamics that are similar for all lesbians across boundaries of time, class, race, and geography.

* * *

Many U.S. Third World feminists have also been analyzing the elements of oppression that Krieger attempts to examine. Their conclu- sions are not the same as hers, however. Their writings have pointed out that the tendency to erase differences is not a psychological or group dynamic unique to those subject to female sex-role conditioning; it is a form of behavior taught to all people who have been formed within the dominant social order—to all of us. We live within a society that promises us an internally coherent organization by which we can live—rational, sensible, controlled, safe, structured so as to make it necessary to exclude or make invisible that which does not fit. This social order is constantly legitimized in our living of it, and this living of it structures not only our material lives but our very consciousness as well. We are thus encouraged to follow the rules; indeed, we are disciplined daily to conform to the needs of a social order that also excludes us. Is it any wonder that we dream our dreams of liberation on the one hand, while dragging with us our proclivities to cleanse, order, prohibit, freeze, and exclude on the other? Even the most revolutionary communities come to prohibit their members' full participation; every marginalized group that has organized in opposition to the dominant order has imported this same desire to find, name, categorize, and tame reality in a way that ultimately works to create marginalized populations within its own ranks. I would suggest to Krieger that *this* is the dynamic which the lesbian, women's, U.S. Third World, and other oppositional movements are subject to.

United States Third World feminists have recently challenged the meaning of the term "women" by insisting on naming the liberatory movement of the seventies the white women's movement. This renaming teaches us that it is impossible to utter the word "women" as if it holds some common, unified meaning. Every woman is subject to very different desires, values, and meanings that have been shaped—not only by her experience of sexuality and gender—but by her particular experience of the intersections of race, culture, and class. United States Third World feminists are pointing out the differences that exist among all women not in order to fracture any hope of unity among women but to propose a new order—one that provides a new possibility for unity without the erasure of differences. This new order would draw attention to the construction and ideological consequences of every order, of every community, of every identity. It would result in a new form of community building among women of all types (as well as men)—coalition building that bridges individual and group differences. Such activity would challenge the patterns that have organized Western thinking and its cultural manifestations at their very foundations.

Female sex-role conditioning has very different meanings and results as it interacts with race identification, cultural influences, class position, and so on. The four dynamics Krieger's review identifies for us may indeed be typical of some female communities under siege. But, without question, these four dynamics cannot be seen as operative in every lesbian community regardless of race, culture, and class. Krieger is correct in challenging the oppressive behavior imported into a liberatory community. However, the four dynamics implied in her review do not form a typology of peculiarly *female* group behavior, nor can they be generalized across all lesbian communities, nor are they necessarily related phenomena to be classified and judged accordingly. Moreover, it is doubtful that there is a commonly experienced female conditioning at the root of these dynamics.

Krieger's attempt to find the causes of oppressive behavior within a marginalized community is organized in such a way as to silence the very different analyses articulated by women of color, women of various class backgrounds, Jewish women, Catholic women, lesbian sadomasochists, and others. The conceptual framework underlying her review works to perpetuate the same leveling of differences that in turn legitimates the very structures of power the author seeks to challenge. Krieger is a disciple of the social sciences who has written a highly convincing and well-constructed report—a report that nonetheless privileges female conditioning as a universalizing concept and that makes invisible the articulated analyses of the marginalized. It is a report that is as dangerous as it also is helpful.

History of Consciousness—Kresge College
University of California, Santa Cruz

Comment on Krieger's "Lesbian Identity and Community: Recent Social Science Literature"

Ann R. Bristow and Pam Langford Pearn

Because social scientists have ignored (or have not been able to access) lesbian communities, we welcome the appearance of Susan Krieger's review essay "Lesbian Identity and Community: Recent Social Science Literature" (pp. 223–40). We admire Krieger's willingness to address issues, such as internal community complaints, that may not be "ideologically popular" (p. 224). Her treatment of lesbians vis-à-vis their communities will probably stimulate further research along these lines. Her work also allows us to see how social science research has been shaped by (and, it is hoped, shapes) the sociohistorical context in which lesbians and their researchers are situated. The lens through which Krieger reviews studies of lesbian experience, however—"a perspective biased toward investigating the constraints on behavior imposed by social groups" (p. 224)—may obscure cultural factors that bear on lesbians and their communities and negate the affirmation a lesbian finds with other lesbians.

Reprinted from *Signs: Journal of Women in Culture and Society* 9, no. 4 (Summer 1984): 729–732.

Krieger focuses on individual identity rather than lesbian identity, defining identity as the "feelings and ideas an individual has about herself" (p. 224). But if lesbian identity is defined as a lesbian's woman-identified feelings and ideas, why deemphasize it? The only people who stand to gain by the neglect of lesbian identity are men, as such neglect separates women from each other emotionally and intellectually.

The literature Krieger reviews links lesbian identity with lack of autonomy in couple relationships. She discusses this "fusion" in lesbian couples, as referred to by Jo-Ann Krestan and Claudia Bepko, in negative terms, equating it with denial of the self and lack of independence within the couple. We suggest that fusion in a couple context has little to do with lesbian identity; rather, it is a heterosexist, male-defined concept. Fusion more accurately describes male-female relationships, in which part of the patriarchal plan is female subjugation to male identity. There is no need to accept the heterosexist assumption that lesbian women's identification must mirror that of heterosexuals or of gay men. Why is lesbian women's identification viewed as a loss of identity rather than an affirmation of who we are? As Mary Daly suggests, the very bonding of women loving women expresses lesbian identity, "dis-covers it, creates it" (*GynEcology: The Metaethics of Radical Feminism* [Boston: Beacon Press, 1978], p. 373).

Finally, Krieger's comments on lesbian relationship patterns obscure positive aspects of women bonding with each other. The distinction between friends and lovers, for example, is heterosexually inspired and more descriptive of heterosexual than of lesbian relationships. In the lesbian community, boundaries between romantic attachments and friendships are less well defined, affectionate bonding is common and valued, and the challenge of maintaining friendships with ex-lovers is supported. In addition to asking, "What happens . . . to identity when so much that is consequential is hastened over and merged?" (p. 239), we might also ask, What happens to identity when our bonds with other women weather the comings and goings of intimate involvement?

Krieger's conclusions about community are primarily extrapolations from studies that actually focus on individuals. But research conducted with such an individualized focus may not provide an adequate concep-tual framework for understanding community influences. Krieger's cita-tion of the work of Anne Peplau et al. provides an example of this difficulty. Prior to introducing this research, Krieger discusses the theme of individual autonomy in relation to one's community; she cites Peplau et al. as contributing to this theme. But what they actually researched was the relationship between lesbians' political views (traditional vs. feminist) and their desires for autonomy and attachment in couple relationships. It is not clear from Krieger's discussion what this tells us about individual autonomy in relation to the larger community. Had she suggested that community members' political views may be tied to their desires for autonomy and attachment with respect to their community, the addition of Peplau et al. would have been more meaningful.

Krieger's use of studies of lesbian identity to address community may explain the particularly individualistic way in which she conceptualizes community. Because she does not explicitly place the lesbian community in the context of a sexist and heterosexist society, she reproduces at the community level the same model of pathology she deplores at the level of the individual. Just as mental health professionals see lesbians who are uncomfortable with their identity as disordered and in need of therapy rather than seeing the social reality of discrimination and hatred that can make lesbians' lives miserable, so Krieger's view levels blame at the community while giving scant reference to its social context.

We must look at that same social reality as it affects the community. For example, Krieger discusses Barbara Ponse's research as elucidating the "tendency of lesbian communities to encourage a high degree of conformity and, often, a high degree of commitment on the part of their members" (p. 231). These tendencies can be understood in the context of the protectiveness that lesbians feel about their communities, which they rightfully perceive as existing precariously. Conformity and commitment are ways lesbians seek to establish trust, and secretness is embraced for safety. (In our community, which includes an army base, the army frequently and sometimes successfully plants women in lesbian groups in order to secure discharges.) Krieger concludes from social scientists' research that "lesbian communities *define identity* for their members" (p. 237). Unless this observation is situated in an awareness of why lesbian identity is defined at all, it is meaningless: "Lesbianism . . . is a category of behavior possible only in a sexist society characterized by rigid sex roles and dominated by male supremacy" (Radicalesbians, "Woman-identified Women," in *Radical Feminism*, ed. Anne Koedt, Ellen Levine, and Anita Rapone [New York: Quadrangle, 1973], p. 241).

Discussion of the "lesbian shuffle" is similarly informed by a contextual analysis. The "lesbian shuffle," a term coined by Elizabeth Barnhart, refers to the dissolution and establishment of couple relationships within a given community. But such a label dismisses the reality of pain, intensity, and joy found in relationships that break up or begin. Because the language we use structures our conceptualization of reality and because lesbian relationships are already denigrated, we feel that the use of this label reflects an acceptance of the dominant society's view of lesbian couples. Krieger notes that this pattern of relationships is an important mechanism tying the individual to the community. But if this pattern is related to community, the link may be more indirect; it may involve instead the social context of lesbian communities. That is, the community may be the only place where there is support for lesbian identity and lesbian relationships, and if part of lesbians' commitment to their communities is their need for this support, then they will remain in the community.

Krieger's analysis of the dissolution and establishment of relationships in lesbian communities trivializes the investment that a heterosexist society has in seeing lesbian relationships end. Relatives may actively seek their destruction. Holidays can become forced choices between a family of origin and a lover. Legitimization for job searches that include consideration of one's lover is virtually nonexistent. Some hospitals will not allow a woman to stay with her partner who is seriously ill. Those who love lesbian mothers have no socially acceptable role with the children, and the children's discomfort with their mother's lesbian relationship can place strain on that relationship. These seem to be among the critical reasons for any difficulties lesbians may have in forming lasting bonds. The failure to recognize them as important further invalidates the lesbian couple.

Krieger notes that the field of research on lesbians would benefit if less work were done by heterosexual men and more by women. But why lesbian women *or* straight women, as Krieger suggests? Her use of the phrase "lesbian and straight women researchers" sets up a dichotomy that is not helpful. Dividing women into two mutually exclusive categories perpetuates the comparison of deviance and normality. This obfuscates the importance of a feminist analysis that reveals our oppressors as those in whose interests such dichotomies are maintained. Let it suffice to say that all women stand to benefit from more research about lesbians; the knowledge to be gained can only serve to strengthen us in our relationships with each other and, in doing so, deepen in each of us our understanding of lesbian identity.

Department of Psychology
Kansas State University

Reply to Sandoval and Bristow and Pearn

Susan Krieger

I am glad that my article, "Lesbian Identity and Community: Recent Social Science Literature," has stimulated the type of thinking reflected in the comments of Chela Sandoval and Ann Bristow and Pam Pearn. Discussions of differences among lesbian communities and of the variety of possible sources for difficulties within these communities is extremely

Reprinted from *Signs: Journal of Women in Culture and Society* 9, no. 4 (Summer 1984): 732–733.

important. So, too, is an emphasis on the positive identity-affirming aspects of lesbian groups.

I fear that, in places, Sandoval and Bristow and Pearn misinterpret my review essay, setting me up as more of an "enemy" than I am. My essay does not, for instance, as Sandoval suggests, posit "female sex-role conditioning" as the primary cause of the coercive or co-optive tendency of lesbian communities. Nor does it claim that all the characteristics of lesbian groups that it identifies are to be found only in those groups. Also, it does not claim to identify "universal" dynamics—nothing so broad as that. Rather it seeks, from a review of a very limited literature (the social science literature on lesbianism), to identify characteristics that in *varying* degrees *may* contribute to *similar* difficulties in many different kinds of groups.

In response to Bristow and Pearn's critique, I should mention that the review does not "blame" the community. Rather it *focuses* on those aspects of the community that may contribute to identity troubles felt by individuals. Furthermore, it does not seek to minimize the effects of social context. The difficulty, perhaps, is one of emphasis. The review concerns itself primarily with internal dynamics because these are often overlooked in current thinking. Our problems are "blamed" on the outside world, and the contributions of our own internal structures and processes are left unexamined.

Perhaps my article was easy to misread. To subjects such as these, we all bring a great wealth of opinion and feeling. The important thing, though, is that discussion go on. The issues raised in both comments are significant, whatever their relationship to my review essay.

Department of Sociology
Stanford University

Review Essay

The Politics of Transliteration:
Lesbian Personal Narratives

Bonnie Zimmerman

> I am a woman committed to
> a politics
> of transliteration, the methodology
>
> of a mind
> stunned at the suddenly
> possible shifts of meaning—for which
> like amnesiacs
>
> in a world on fire, we must
> find words
> or burn.
>
> [OLGA BROUMAS, "Artemis"]

Between 1977 and 1982, seven anthologies were published consisting exclusively or largely of lesbian first-person narratives.[1] This essay departs somewhat from previous reviews of these collections by evaluating

---

1. These seven anthologies, which will be cited in the text using the abbreviations indicated in brackets, are: Laurel Galana and Gina Covina, eds., *The New Lesbians* (Berkeley: Moon Books, 1977); Angela Stewart-Park and Jules Cassidy, *We're Here: Conversations With Lesbian Women* (London: Quartet Books, 1977); Julia Penelope Stanley and Susan J. Wolfe, eds., *The Coming Out Stories* [*COS*] (Watertown, Mass.: Persephone Press, 1980); Margaret Cruikshank, ed., *The Lesbian Path* [*LP*] (Monterey, Calif.: Angel Press, 1980); Ruth Baetz, *Lesbian Crossroads* (New York: William Morrow & Co., 1980); Cherríe Moraga and Gloria

Reprinted from *Signs: Journal of Women in Culture and Society* 9, no. 4 (Summer 1984): 663–682.

personal narratives of lesbian experience not as literary or sociological but as historical and political texts that are part of the larger body of contemporary lesbian feminist works, which includes poetry, fiction, songs, and theory. Like these other forms, the narratives reveal the centrality of identity to lesbian-feminist politics. They also reveal an ongoing tension between the ideas of unity and community and those of diversity and individuality, a tension that recurs in the literature on lesbian identity.[2] I look first at the origins of the genre of lesbian first-person narratives, then at its early role in community building, and finally at more recent trends toward diversity. I conclude with some thoughts on the contributions and the problems of personal politics, as evidenced in contemporary lesbian feminism.

Personal Politics

Just as the organized lesbian political movement was an outgrowth of the women's liberation and gay liberation movements of the 1960s and 1970s, so collections of personal narratives are an extension of the originating feminist structure—the consciousness-raising, or rap, group. As Sara Evans has observed, "Young women's instinctive sharing of their personal experience soon became a political instrument called 'consciousness-raising.' . . . It evolved into a kind of phenomenological approach to women's liberation. Kathie Sarachild advocated that women should junk all the old theories and start from scratch, relying on their own experience. . . . Thus consciousness-raising became both a method for developing theory and a strategy for building up the new movement."[3]

Anzaldúa, eds., *This Bridge Called My Back: Writings by Radical Women of Color* [*TB*] (Watertown, Mass.: Persephone Press, 1981); and Evelyn Torton Beck, ed., *Nice Jewish Girls: A Lesbian Anthology* [*NJG*] (Watertown, Mass.: Persephone Press, 1982). An eighth book— Tracy Young, *Women Who Love Women* (New York: Pocket Books, 1977)—is mentioned in Susan Krieger, "Lesbian Identity and Community: Recent Social Science Literature" (in this book), but I am unfamiliar with it. Krieger also observes that personal testimony is central to nonfiction books on lesbianism, including Del Martin and Phyllis Lyon, *Lesbian/Woman* (New York: Bantam Books, 1972); and Sidney Abbott and Barbara Love, *Sappho Was a Right-on Woman: A Liberated View of Lesbianism* (New York: Stein & Day, 1972). Personal stories appeared in *The Ladder*, the magazine published by the Daughters of Bilitis (a lesbian organization established in the 1950s), but these stories have never been anthologized or reprinted. Personal narratives can also be found in Margaret Cruikshank, ed., *Lesbian Studies: Present and Future* (Old Westbury, N.Y.: Feminist Press, 1982), esp. pp. 3–21.

2. See, e.g., Krieger; Jane Gurko, "The Shape of Sameness: Contemporary Lesbian Autobiographical Narratives" (paper presented to the Modern Language Association, Houston, December 1980).

3. Sara Evans, *Personal Politics* (New York: Alfred A. Knopf, Inc., 1979), p. 214.

This complex process of movement and theory building came to be encapsulated in the slogan "the personal is the political." A leaflet distributed by the Chicago Women's Liberation Union, for example, claimed that through consciousness raising women "see that 'personal problems' shared by so many others—not being able to get out of the house often enough, becoming exhausted from taking care of the children all day, perhaps feeling trapped—are really *political* problems. Understanding them is the first step toward dealing with them collectively."[4] This concept of "the personal is the political" became a potent tool for rejecting the public/private split in American life that dates from at least the nineteenth century. Activists used it to debunk the Freudian and functionalist myth of the neurotic American housewife by arguing that the private, domestic realm was inherently an arena for political struggle. They further insisted on inserting women's psychological and sexual realities into the mainstream of New Left radicalism.[3] Abortion and birth control, child-care centers, equal pay for equal work, the "double jeopardy" faced by women of color, the need for women's studies, and many other issues leaped to the top of the feminist agenda. As women began to comprehend the institutional barriers to self-determination and the measures necessary to lift them, personal politics provided a solid basis for developing a program for social change.

But ambiguities and contradictions within that handy slogan "the personal is political" soon posed problems for activists. What was the force and meaning of the copulate? How was the personal political—by fiat or by struggle? What if the political became overpersonalized? What if consciousness raising led us too deeply into individualism and self-analysis? In the late 1960s, consciousness raising became one focus of the split between "politicos" and "feminists" within the nascent women's liberation movement. The former tended to distrust consciousness raising, emphasizing instead the importance of organization, theory, and

4. Further discussion of the role of consciousness raising in the early women's liberation movement can be found in Judith Hole and Ellen Levine, *Rebirth of Feminism* (New York: Quadrangle, 1971), pp. 125–35; Leslie B. Tanner, *Voices from Women's Liberation* (New York: Signet Books, 1970), pp. 231–54; Jo Freeman, *The Politics of Women's Liberation* (New York: David McKay Co., 1975), pp. 85–86, 116–19; Joan Cassell, *A Group Called Women* (New York: David McKay Co., 1977); Barbara Deckard, *The Women's Movement* (New York: Harper & Row, 1979), pp. 353–54, 459–61; Pamela Allen, "Free Space," in *Radical Feminism*, ed. Anne Koedt, Ellen Levine, and Anita Rapone (New York: Quadrangle, 1973), pp. 271–79; "Consciousness Raising," in Koedt et al., eds., pp. 280–81.

5. See Pat Mainardi, "The Politics of Housework," reprinted in *Liberation Now!* (New York: Dell Publishing Co., 1971), pp. 110–15; Judy Syfers, "Why I Want a Wife," and Betsy Warrior, "Housework: Slavery or Labor of Love," both reprinted in Koedt et al., eds., pp. 60–62, 208–12. See also Meredith Tax, "Woman and Her Mind," and Anne Koedt, "The Myth of the Vaginal Orgasm," both reprinted in Koedt et al., eds., pp. 23–35, 198–207.

action or "practice."[6] Feminists, particularly those in the well-known New York City groups, continued to concentrate on consciousness raising until the demise of those groups in the early 1970s. They saw consciousness raising as the first step in a woman's path toward political action and political theory and often urged her to take that step as quickly as possible. Politics and personal life turned out to be uneasy bedfellows after all. Barbara Haber, for one, argues that heterosexual feminists retreated from a critique of personal life and a politics based on experience.[7] Instead, throughout the seventies, segments of the women's movement grew either more reformist or more theoretical in their orientations. Their emphases shifted to passing the Equal Rights Amendment, mainstreaming women into political and economic institutions, creating and maintaining self-help projects, or reconciling feminism with socialism. While all these concerns developed from analyses elaborated through consciousness raising, it is fair to say that, by and large, members of the women's liberation movement had grown uneasy about personal politics sometime before International Women's Year in 1975.

This ambivalence can be seen in some of the earliest articulations of lesbian-feminist political theory, following the publication of "The Woman Identified Woman" in 1970 by the activist group Radicalesbians and the appearance of Jill Johnston's *Village Voice* articles (which are, in essence, personal stream-of-consciousness narratives of remarkable political and literary quality).[8] A collective of women who called themselves "The Furies" and who published a newspaper by the same name in 1972 and 1973 took up the task of formulating a consistent lesbian-separatist politics. One of the most powerful political visions produced by the lesbian (or even feminist) movement, separatism asserts in the most literal sense that every personal act is the creation and expression of political ideology, that either of the patriarchy or of lesbian feminism. It views the institution of heterosexuality as a cornerstone of male supremacy, lesbianism as a political choice, and classism and racism as primary divisions that must be overcome if the women's movement is to survive.

6. Criticism of consciousness raising can be found in Carol Williams Payne, "Consciousness Raising: A Dead End?" and Joreen, "The Tyranny of Structurelessness," both reprinted in Koedt et al., eds., pp. 282–99.

7. Barbara Haber, "Is Personal Life Still a Political Issue?" *Feminist Studies* 5, no. 3 (Fall 1979): 417–30. Early examples of this ambivalence about the politics of personal life include Anne Koedt, "Lesbianism and Feminism," reprinted in Koedt et al., eds., pp. 246–58 (a response, in part, to Radicalesbians' "The Woman Identified Woman," reprinted in the same volume, pp. 240–45; and the marvelously titled but never reprinted "I Don't Want to Change My Lifestyle—I Want to Change My Life," by Peggy Hopper and Steve Foldz [Boston: New England Free Press, n.d.]).

8. Radicalesbians (n. 7 above); Jill Johnston, *Lesbian Nation* (New York: Simon & Schuster, 1973).

In the mid-1970s, two collections of articles reprinted from the *Furies* were published: *Class and Feminism* and *Lesbianism and the Women's Movement*. Of the ten articles in the latter, two are personal narratives: "Such a Nice Girl" by Sharon Deevey and "Coming Out in the Women's Movement" by Coletta Reid. In these narratives, personal experience essentially provides political ammunition, for each woman couches her story in political language (or, to the fastidious, rhetoric) identical to that of the theoretical essays in the volume. Each values personal experience especially for the political lessons learned from it, as can be seen by juxtaposing an excerpt from Deevey with one from Charlotte Bunch's theoretical manifesto, "Lesbians in Revolt," in the same collection:[9] "At first I did not push anyone to come out, even as I began to see that lesbianism is a political choice" (Deevey, p. 24); "Woman-identified Lesbianism is, then, more than a sexual preference, it is a political choice" (Bunch, p. 30). Rather than deriving political theory inductively from personal reality, the Furies (who were mostly "new lesbians," i.e., previously heterosexual women who came out partly as a response to feminist ideology) reshaped personal reality in accordance with a rigorously logical political theory.

Bunch, for one, was not unaware of this reconstruction of reality. As she states in another *Furies* article: "While reshaping ourselves as women we must also change the identities we have as part of the male hierarchies."[10] Any personal narration, of course, restructures reality simply through the process of selecting one event over another to narrate. All autobiographical fictions or fictive autobiographies are in some sense an idealization or re-vision of the author's own past, as evidenced in works as different as *The Mill on the Floss*, *The Well of Loneliness*, and *Rubyfruit Jungle*. However, such re-visioning may be particularly essential to the formation of lesbian identity.[11] Popular fiction, psychological texts, and community values all provide models to which the lesbian (whether or not a feminist) is likely to adapt herself. Whether the image is created by Stephen Gordon, Beebo Brinker, or mythic Amazons, the reconstruction of past history is constant. Marilyn Frye, reviewing *The Coming Out Stories*, points out that the "temptation to disown our former selves can encour-

9. Sharon Deevey, "Such a Nice Girl," and Charlotte Bunch, "Lesbians in Revolt," both in *Lesbianism and the Women's Movement*, ed. Nancy Myron and Charlotte Bunch (Baltimore: Diana Press, 1975), pp. 21–28, 29–38; Nancy Myron and Charlotte Bunch, eds., *Class and Feminism* (Baltimore: Diana Press, 1974).

10. Charlotte Bunch, "Perseverance Furthers: Woman's Sense of Self," *Furies* (January–February 1973).

11. Barbara Ponse discusses modes of biographic reconstruction in *Identities in the Lesbian World: The Social Construction of Self* (Westport, Conn.: Greenwood Press, 1978); see also Krieger (n. 1 above), p. 98.

age us to falsify our histories."[12] Many of us would like to believe that we were born lesbian, free from the original sin of heterosexuality. Thus, as the Furies collective demonstrated, lesbians tend to reconstruct personal histories in accordance with norms established by either the dominant culture or the lesbian subculture.

Despite the analytical and rhetorical tone of the *Furies*, lesbian feminism, as it developed over the next decade, remained rooted in personal life and disenchanted with structured organizations and political theorizing. One reason for the different directions taken by the lesbian and heterosexual branches of the women's movement involves the time lag in historical development of lesbian feminism. Another reason for the difference may be that becoming a lesbian requires a continual process of coming out through which identity is claimed and embraced.[13] Finally, many construed the lesbian life-style to be uniquely congruent with feminist ideology. In a male-dominated society, the personal is the political for lesbians in a direct and immediate way. In contrast, heterosexual women have a particular interest in theorizing about how to live in and with the very institutions that one rejects politically. Thus, Haber concludes that "lesbians have maintained to a far greater degree than heterosexual feminists a cohesive, critical view of the family and heterosexuality. As women who have stepped outside the sexual definitions and forms that dominate our society, they have a vantage point that is invaluable in future development of a critical theory of personal life."[14] Some have touted this place on the margins as essential to the lesbian point of view. It is also a source of what is a decidedly antipolitical—as political has been defined in the Western male intellectual tradition—bias to lesbian-feminist theory.[15] If the political too often swallowed up the personal in the women's liberation movement of the 1970s, just the opposite tends to be true of much of the contemporary lesbian-feminist movement, in which politics is thoroughly redefined in terms of the personal.

For all these reasons, then, the lesbian-feminist movement has sustained personal politics. What lesbians have added is a uniquely literary

12. Marilyn Frye, review of *The Coming Out Stories*, ed. Julia Penelope Stanley and Susan J. Wolfe, *Sinister Wisdom* 14 (1980): 97–98, esp. 98.

13. See Karla Jay, "Coming Out as Process," in *Our Right to Love*, ed. Ginny Vida (Englewood Cliffs, N.J.: Prentice-Hall, Inc., 1978), pp. 28–30.

14. Haber (n. 7 above), p. 421. A similar perspective is summarized by Cassell (n. 4 above): "Female bonding is the lesbian's only reality; she loves, understands, and needs women. Not only is she willing, she is almost forced to work with women in building a 'women's world' " (p. 81).

15. On the "lesbian perspective," see Sandy Boucher, "Lesbian Artists," *Heresies 3* (Fall 1977), pp. 47–48, esp. p. 48. On lesbianism and male politics, see Harriet Desmoines, "There Goes the Revolution . . ." *Sinister Wisdom* 9 (Spring 1979): 20–23. It is interesting to compare this piece with Robin Morgan's classic denunciation of New Left politics, "Goodbye to All That," in *Going Too Far* (New York: Vintage Books, 1978), pp. 121–30.

shaping of personal experience. Just as rap groups in the early women's liberation movement created community and politics through the sharing of individual women's lives, so too collecting lesbian coming-out stories, personal narratives, open-ended interviews, and letters has been instrumental in defining contemporary lesbian feminism. The book has become a "free space" for lesbian feminists to develop notions of identity, culture, and community.

Speaking Sameness: The First Collections

By 1977, the lesbian-feminist movement (or "community" as it was and is more commonly called) was a recognizable entity distinct from either the women's movement or the gay rights movement. Both of the latter, of course, continued to attract activist lesbians: ex-Fury Charlotte Bunch, for example, continued to do traditional political work, and other lesbians throughout the 1970s worked on such projects as electoral campaigns and lesbian custody cases. Nevertheless, an increasingly large and visible group of lesbian feminists identified themselves as a cohesive community sharing values based on woman identification, cultural feminism, and separatism. Certainly many lesbians—some socialist feminist, some apolitical, and some nonaligned—did not and do not subscribe to these values. The lesbian community may be thought of as having a center, where much of the culture and vision and some of the theory is created, with ripples flowing outward that enfold many other women wholly or partially. These ripples include journals, bookstores, presses, novels, poetry, recordings, and music festivals; indeed, lesbian energy fuels much of what is labeled "women's culture." For example, several members of the Furies collective moved into aspects of culture building, founding Olivia Records, Diana Press, and Women in Distribution. New journals, such as *Sinister Wisdom* (1976) and *Conditions* (1977), replaced defunct lesbian newspapers, providing a locus for the articulation of lesbian-feminist ideas and creative writing. In 1977, the publication of the first collections of personal stories helped to define and inspire this still amorphous lesbian community.

These personal narratives take a variety of forms: open-ended interviews, coming-out stories, more formal autobiographical pieces, occasionally a personal poem or fiction. The first anthology, *The New Lesbians*, consists of anonymous unstructured interviews, conversational in style, with twenty women across the United States. The editors imposed no structure on either the interviews or the book itself. In contrast, the editors of *We're Here: Conversations with Lesbian Women*, a British collection, challenged and directed their respondents in a more aggressively journalistic style. The result, to this reader, is a rather more complex and interesting revelation of the individual. A third book, *Lesbian Crossroads*, also uses the interview format. Its thematic organization places individual stories in a more sociopolitical context than do the other anthologies. *The Lesbian Path* and *The Coming Out Stories*, both published in 1980, consist of personal narratives written by lesbians: some quite celebrated as writers, musicians, teachers, and activists; many unknown before the publication of their stories. Like *Lesbian Crossroads*, *The Lesbian Path* is structured thematically, although the themes—"Young Lesbians," "Catholic Tales," and so on—do not create a similar sociological whole. The most unified collection is *The Coming Out Stories*. Some of these stories are literary, some like tales told at a slumber party, but each recounts how the writer came out—to herself, to her family and friends, and to society. One general point can be made about most of the collections: the editors provided a minimum of intervention, a politically motivated choice to allow the immediate, personal voices of lesbians to express their own lives and the shape of a growing and changing community.

Laurel Galana and Gina Covina, editors of *The New Lesbians*, described the genesis of their collection as a literal journey: "We saw that this was a marvelous opportunity to really find out the truth about 'lesbian nation.' We had a definite hunch that it wasn't what anyone at that time was purporting it to be. . . . We loaded our van with a dozen jugs of good ol' California wine and we took off for the boondocks. We traveled over 12,000 miles visiting lesbians of every conceivable lifestyle" (pp. 9–10). This journey in search of a lesbian nation was transformed into metaphor in the titles of many of the narrative collections—the *coming out* stories, the lesbian *path*, lesbian *crossroads*, this *bridge* called my back—and in much imaginative literature and theory.[16] These personal narratives chart a process of growth and development, both individual and collective: a metaphoric and mythic movement. In what sense is this journey into lesbian identity and lesbian nation a political journey, and how is it reconciled with the more traditional notion of politics as collective action to change institutional balances of power?

The fact that an extraordinarily high percentage of organizers, theorists, and editors of narrative collections are also writers and teachers of language or literature may explain why the politics of lesbianism as it has evolved is intensely interested in language and consciousness. (Of

16. Barbara Ponse, e.g., uses the phrase "gay trajectory" to chart the process of forming a lesbian identity (Ponse, p. 124). Since so many lesbian coming-out novels are variations on the picaresque, journeying is a central element of their narrative structure. See, e.g., Rita Mae Brown, *Rubyfruit Jungle* (Plainfield, Vt.: Daughters, Inc., 1973); Sharon Isabell, *Yesterday's Lessons* (Oakland, Calif.: Women's Press Collective, 1974); Sheila Ortiz Taylor, *Faultline* (Tallahassee, Fla.: Naiad Press, 1982); Elana Nachmann, *Riverfinger Women* (Plainfield, Vt.: Daughters, Inc., 1974); Valerie Miner, *Movement* (Trumansburg, N.Y.: Crossing Press, 1982).

course, the opposite may be true: because lesbian feminism is so rooted in consciousness and culture, we turn to imaginative writers to find our gurus.) Theorizing by lesbians about lesbianism draws most effectively on words like silence, speech, invisibility, naming, lies, and distortion.[17] Frye draws attention to this theorizing by musing on "the *metaphysics* of being a lesbian." For her, *The Coming Out Stories* "provides a picture of what it is to be something which there is no such thing as."[18] Recent lesbian-feminist theory postulates lesbianism as either an empty category—something invisible and unspeakable—or as an existence veiled in lies and distortions enforced by "experts" and by popular culture. In 1977, Julia Penelope Stanley opened a panel at the Modern Language Association (MLA) meetings with a moving personal testimony:[19]

> Last year at MLA I sat with tears in my eyes listening to an unknown woman object to Adrienne Rich's statement that there "is a Lesbian in every womon," saying that she could not accept the "freudian implications of the word *Lesbian*." I raged in silence, torn, wounded, not knowing how to explain that, although I had loved wimmin, and only wimmin, emotionally, physically, sexually, for 24 years, I had not been able to let the word *Lesbian* pass my lips in all those years; that in 1972, when I first tried to apply that name to myself, I stuttered, I whispered, I choked.

Speaking, especially naming one's self "lesbian," is an act of empowerment. Power, which traditionally is the essence of politics, is connected with the ability to name, to speak, to come out of silence: "I think 'coming out'—that first permission we give ourselves to name our love for women as love, to say, *I am a lesbian*, but also the successive 'comings-out' to the world described in this book by so many writers—is connected with power, connects us with power, and until we believe that we have the right not merely to our love but to our power, we will continue to do harm among ourselves, fearing that power in each other and in ourselves" (*COS*, p. xiii). Powerlessness, on the other hand, is associated with silence and the "speechlessness" that the powerful impose on those dispossessed of language.[20]

In a sense, then, contemporary lesbian feminists postulate lesbian oppression as a mutilation of consciousness curable by language. Lesbians do share the institutional oppression of all women and the denial of civil

---

17. See esp. Adrienne Rich, *On Lies, Secrets, and Silence* (New York: W. W. Norton & Co., 1979).

18. Frye (n. 12 above), p. 97.

19. Julia Penelope Stanley, "The Transformation of Silence into Language and Action," *Sinister Wisdom* 6 (Summer 1978): 4–5.

20. Michelle Cliff, "Notes on Speechlessness," *Sinister Wisdom* 5 (Winter 1978): 5–9.

rights with gay men. But what lesbian feminists identify as the particular, unique oppression of lesbians—rightly or wrongly—is speechlessness, invisibility, and inauthenticity. Lesbian resistance lies in correct naming; thus our power flows from language, vision, and culture. By controlling and defining images and ideas, lesbians are able to "reconstitute the world."[21] Language "is action. To speak words that have been unspoken, to imagine that which is unimaginable, is to create the place in which change (action) occurs."[22] Contemporary lesbian feminism is thus primarily a politics of language and consciousness. We have, indeed, been "stunned at the suddenly / possible shifts of meaning" produced by personal testimony, and these words burn at the heart of lesbian feminism today.

On their path toward personal power—which is one way of redefining politics—lesbian narrators like Stanley must first overcome the negative words, stereotypes, and texts that rise up like Apollyon to bar their journey: "Annie and I find ourselves confronted by what are perhaps the most dreadful and terrifying words we have ever heard in our lives—lesbian, homosexual, queer" (*LP*, p. 18); "I was still unable to conceptualize what being a lesbian meant and I thought the context in which I heard people whisper the words bull dagger, dyke, lesbian, and homosexual was slanderous" (*COS*, p. 54). In such an atmosphere of terror, it is understandable that the "undeclared" lesbian Stanley describes should be paralyzed into speechlessness. Lesbian narrators first discover themselves in such texts as *The Children's Hour*, *The Well of Loneliness*, *Mlle. de Maupin*—all of which project inauthentic images of the lesbian as pseudo-male or pathetic sufferer—and in anonymous clinical books on homosexuality. One political function of the first-person narrative is to debunk so-called expert knowledge, replacing it with an insider's knowledge that not only empowers the speaker but also, when communicated through the text, provides alternative role models for lesbians still speechless and powerless. The introduction to *We're Here: Conversations with Lesbian Women* clearly reflects this missionary purpose: "Both of us wasted a lot of years as isolated lesbians trying unsuccessfully to be straight. If the Women's Movement had been as strong then, we could have found out a lot about ourselves and had the support of other women. If there had been one single book that showed us other lesbians and talked about them and us and about our sexuality, it would have made us feel less alone, less lonely" (pp. 2–3).

Reaching out through storytelling is one of the most consistently repeated motifs in these anthologies. The editors of *The Coming Out Stories* decided to create their book because they believed "it should no longer be

---

21. Adrienne Rich, *The Dream of a Common Language* (New York: W. W. Norton & Co., 1978), p. 67.
22. Judith McDaniel, "Transformation," pp. 15–17, esp. p. 17.

necessary for other wimmin to live so much of their lives in painful silence, thinking either that they are 'the only one in the world,' or that their love for wimmin is an abominable perversion" (p. xv). A contributor to *The Lesbian Path* adds a further educational motivation: "I write because I want to ease the suffering of other lesbians and gay men and because I want heterosexuals to understand" (p. 24). Another writer comments wryly that she feels "very inadequate, because I am not well able to make a strong and articulate political statement, and raise pertinent, well-defined questions that will be a source of inspiration to other wimmin who are in the process of coming out" (*COS*, p. 135). Personal narratives are exuberant and unabashed political propaganda, much like Cuban murals or the plays of Brecht. If they are also less artistic, they nonetheless provide a model for contemporary lesbian-feminist fictions, many of which are extremely personal coming-out narratives, or *Bildungsromane*.[23]

As these writers know, personal narratives have been and continue to be instrumental in creating networks and community, a process that constitutes "an essential step in building our movement."[24] As the editor of *Lesbian Crossroads* succinctly states, "How would I find others like myself if I didn't say ['I am a lesbian'] out loud?" (p. 18). Lesbians have molded and shaped their community and culture out of what they perceive to be common experiences (love and sexuality between women; oppression and suffering caused by heterosexism; shared visions, beliefs, and ideals), all of these expressed through stories:

> The stories themselves become part of every woman's coming out process, building a network of connections among wimmin. Many of the writers have since shared their coming out stories with wimmin who were involved in events in their past, and the letters move back and forth among them, a dialogue of each woman's understanding. Once on paper, each story has at least two realities: it exists as an artifact, as words on paper, and as oral culture, as a recounting of past experiences. Thus it enters the world again on two levels, continuing the process of recreating reality and creating a continuum of wimmin's culture and community; connections are made among wimmin in the present, and a record of the past becomes available to the wimmin of the future. These coming out stories are the foundation of our lives as Lesbians, as real to ourselves; as such, our sharing of them defines us as participants in Lesbian culture, as members of a community. [*COS*, p. xxi]

23. See my essay, "Exiting from Patriarchy: The Lesbian Novel of Development," in *The Voyage In: Fictions of Female Development*, ed. Elizabeth Abel, Marianne Hirsch, and Elizabeth Langland (Hanover and London: New England University Press, 1983), pp. 244–57.

24. Barbara Smith and Beverly Smith, "I Am Not Meant to Be Alone and without You Who Understand: Letters from Black Feminists, 1972–1978," *Conditions: 4* 2, no. 1 (Winter 1979): 62–77, esp. 71.

The personal narrative, particularly the coming-out story, forms our "tribal" lore, our myth of origins. Lesbian imagination is profoundly captivated by the vision of female warriors empowered by language, realized in such works as the amazonian poems of Audre Lorde and the stories of the hill women in Sally Gearhart's *The Wanderground*.[25] It is notable that Adrienne Rich's foreword to *The Coming Out Stories* evokes this tribal notion of the "mædenhēap" and that the last three stories in *The Lesbian Path* realize a similar vision of returning to the land in search of self and community.[26] For many lesbians, the political path that begins with telling one's story does lead, in fantasy if not always in reality, to country retreats, immersion in lesbian-feminist culture, and matriarchal religions. Recently intense debates have raged within the community over this aspect of the journey. In particular, many have questioned whether or not lesbian separatism is a white middle-class luxury, especially when it incorporates a retreat from society.[27] Such debates are to be expected since a politics rooted in the articulation of personal experience can lead logically to a reliance on personal, individualized solutions to oppression, even if the personal is extended to include one's friends and community. Tempting as this dream of free lesbian tribes may be, we must consider that tribal cultures have fared poorly under the onslaught of advanced capitalism and imperialism. Some lesbians may be modeling themselves after an ahistorical, apolitical, and ultimately nostalgic vision of what may never have existed and certainly can exist no longer.

25. Audre Lorde, *The Black Unicorn* (New York: W. W. Norton & Co., 1978), esp. "125th Street and Abomey," "The Women of Dan Dance with Swords in Their Hands . . . ," "Harriet," and "For Assata"; Sally Gearhart, *The Wanderground* (Watertown, Mass.: Persephone Press, 1978). For another amazonian fantasy that expresses the values of some lesbian feminists, see Donna J. Young, *Retreat! As It Was* (Weatherby Lake, Mo.: Naiad Press, 1979).

26. "Mædenhēap" is an Old English word meaning "a band of female warriors" (*COS*, p. xii). The final three stories in *The Lesbian Path* are "O! We Are Just Begun" by Barbara Lightner (a lesbian couple's adventures down on the farm); "Remember the Future" by Rosemary Curb (on the Michigan Womyn's Music Festival); and "Hudson Bay Journal" by Judith Niemi (a quest/journey via canoe).

27. For various perspectives on lesbian separatism, see Marilyn Frye, "Some Notes on Separatism and Power," *Sinister Wisdom* 6 (Summer 1978): 30–39; Adrienne Rich, "Some Notes for a Magazine: What Does Separatism Mean?" *Sinister Wisdom* 18 (1981): 83–91; responses by Barbara Smith and Sidney Spinster, *Sinister Wisdom* 20 (1982): 100–105; Pamela Culbreth, "A Personal Reading of *This Bridge Called My Back*," *Sinister Wisdom* 21 (1982): 15–28; Lois Anne Addison, "Separatism Revisited," *Sinister Wisdom* 21 (1982): 29–34; and Barbara Smith and Beverly Smith, "Across the Kitchen Table: A Sister-to-Sister Dialogue" (*TB*, pp. 120–23). A very good early analysis of the pros and cons of separatism can be found in Charlotte Bunch, "Perseverance Furthers: Separatism and Our Future," *Furies* (Fall 1972).

Speaking Difference: Identity and Diversity

I have been arguing that lesbian politics, as it developed in the late 1970s, attempted to draw on shared personal experience in order to create a vision and, when possible, a reality of community. Thus, its emphasis was on the sameness, the commonality, of all lesbian stories. Its dominant political mode was separatism, but a separatism different from that of the Furies. Rather than focusing on a critique of heterosexuality as an institution, this new separatism was visionary and idealistic, suggesting that lesbians create outposts of a lesbian nation now, rather than struggle collectively to transform the social and political structures of a capitalist patriarchy. United around the single issue and image of lesbian identity, women-identified women would create a new Jerusalem.

But this political ideal, seemingly based on concrete lived experience, soon was attacked for being naive, theoretical, and exclusionary. In "La Güera," one of the finest selections from *The Coming Out Stories*, Cherríe Moraga Lawrence opens with a quotation from Emma Goldman that points out one limitation of the personalization that is the essence of the volume as a whole: "It requires something more than personal experience to gain a philosophy or point of view from any specific event. It is the quality of our response to the event and our capacity to enter into the lives of others that help us to make their lives and experiences our own" (*COS*, p. 187). "The lives of others": immediately on publication of *The Coming Out Stories* and *The Lesbian Path*, reviewers criticized the predominance within these texts of stories by white, mostly young, middle-class, university-educated women. Indeed, the editors decried this bias within their own books.[28] The issue is not only that such bias falsifies the impression given of the lesbian subculture. Equally important, no adequate politics can be drawn from the experience of one segment of the community alone, especially when that segment belongs to dominant racial and class groups. Despite the Furies' warning that race and class differences cross-cut simple (and simplistic) notions of lesbian unity, the fervor and excitement of building lesbian culture through the 1970s led many to believe that the commonality of our lesbianism would provide an adequate medium for the growth of a politics and a community. But in this we were guilty of the very theorizing that personal politics was supposed to replace.

---

28. See, e.g., Cruikshank in *The Lesbian Path* (n. 1 above): "White women and middle-class women are over-represented here, as well as academics and former nuns" (p. 8); Stanley and Wolfe in *The Coming Out Stories* (n. 1 above): "We wanted to have stories from Black and third world Lesbians, but we didn't hear from them" (p. xxiv). It is a marked sign of change that such a passive approach is no longer acceptable in the lesbian community.

Women óf color, in particular, have pointed out that the notion of lesbian nation or lesbian tribalism is a white women's dream and that an effective lesbian politics will have to be based on diversity and multiplicity, not on a sameness that melts all women down into one mold.[29] Nevertheless, Moraga insists that the personalizing of politics must continue and even expand. It is not enough to assert the identity of "lesbian"; there are also racial, class, ethnic, and religious identities: "In this country, lesbianism is a poverty—as is being brown, as is being a woman, as is being just plain poor. The danger lies in ranking the oppressions. *The danger lies in failing to acknowledge the specificity of the oppression.* The danger lies in attempting to deal with oppression purely from a theoretical base. Without an emotional, heartfelt grappling with the source of our own oppression, without naming the enemy within ourselves and outside of us, no authentic, nonhierarchical connection among oppressed groups can take place" (*COS*, p. 189). Here is a political insufficiency that is being at least partially countered in a manner characteristic of the lesbian-feminist movement: with the production of new texts, and through them, the production of a new, more inclusive, and more accurate politics.[30]

Two recent anthologies contain a significant number of narratives that address the connections between lesbian identity and ethnic or racial identity. *Nice Jewish Girls* includes narratives as well as essays, poetry, and fiction by Jewish lesbians. *This Bridge Called My Back*, edited by Moraga and Gloria Anzaldúa, both prominent lesbian writers and activists, collects writings by women of color, lesbian and heterosexual, including at least eight that are personal narratives (depending on one's definition) by self-identified lesbians. Although the *Furies* and other lesbian papers of the early seventies, such as *Ain't I a Woman*, made a special point of raising the issue of classism within the women's movement, no anthology of writings by working-class lesbians has been published. Indeed, no systematic theory of class and sexuality has emerged to accompany the focused attack on racism and the articulation of a Third World feminism developed by women of color.

---

29. For an analysis of separatism and racism, see Smith and Smith, "Across the Kitchen Table" (n. 27 above). For an articulation of the relation between difference and power, see selections by Audre Lorde in *This Bridge*, esp. her speech to "The Personal Is Political" panel ("The Second Sex—Thirty Years Later: A Commemorative Conference on Feminist Theory," New York City, September 1979), p. 101.

30. Consider, e.g., a number of imaginative personal narratives recently published: Audre Lorde, *Zami: A New Spelling of My Name* (Trumansburg, N.Y.: Crossing Press, 1983); Michelle Cliff, *Claiming an Identity They Taught Me to Despise* (Watertown, Mass.: Persephone Press, 1980); Anita Cornwall's *Black Lesbian in White America*, which includes "First Love and Other Sorrows: Six Pieces from an Autobiography" (Tallahassee, Fla.: Naiad Press, 1983); Cherríe Moraga, *Loving in the War Years* (Boston: South End Press, 1983). See also forthcoming autobiographical works by Gloria Anzaldúa and Paula Gunn Allen, and narrative selections in Elly Bulkin, ed., *Lesbian Fiction* (Watertown, Mass.: Persephone Press, 1981).

Both *Nice Jewish Girls* and *This Bridge* are much more political in tone than *The Coming Out Stories*, *The Lesbian Path*, or even *Lesbian Crossroads* (which is notable for its relatively large number of narratives by women of color). No doubt this is because the history and personal experience of oppression and violence is more deeply felt by women of color and Jewish women. But, also, both volumes were partly motivated by experiences of discrimination and invisibility specifically within the lesbian and women's movements. Both adopt the explicitly political agenda of challenging racism and anti-Semitism within the women's movement as well as of proudly affirming racial or ethnic identities. Each insists on extending the empirical basis of lesbian politics to encompass the personal realities not just of lesbians per se but of black lesbians, Chicana lesbians, Japanese-American lesbians, Sephardic or Ashkenazi Jewish lesbians. Any other foundation renders a politics incomplete, false, and dangerous.

Claiming a lesbian identity that is also a racial or ethnic identity is at once exhilarating and threatening to the self and to society. Evelyn Beck writes of the disbelief and veiled hostility she encountered on telling people she was working on a book about Jewish lesbians: "My answer was met with startled laughter and unmasked surprise bordering on disbelief, 'Are there *many*?'—as if the juxtaposition Jewish/lesbian were just too much. . . . If you tried to claim both identities—publicly and politically—you were exceeding the limits of what was permitted to the marginal. You were in danger of being perceived as ridiculous—and threatening" (*NJG*, p. xiii). Assertion of a multiply marginal identity strains the limits of liberalism and therefore can be a politically radical weapon. Yet it can also be misunderstood, ignored, or angrily dismissed even by other activists. This is the message of the stories in the sections "And When You Leave, Take Your Pictures with You" (*TB*) and "If I Am Not for Myself, Who Will Be?" (*NJG*). Before we dare name ourselves a movement or a community, these narratives assert, the inbred racist and anti-Semitic attitudes of lesbians and feminists must be eradicated.

But it is the intensity and power of self-affirmation that dominates these volumes. Their themes are similar to those of the earlier anthologies: silence, language, naming, and power. Beck points to the gaps in Jewish history that these stories must fill, while Gloria Greenfield calls for a collective voice to empower Jewish lesbian resistance: "Resistance cannot be a solo act. The individual voices—particularly those of Jewish lesbians—are creating a powerful force. Together, from many corners of the world, we are demanding an end to this hatred and violence. No. We will not remain silent. *Never again*" (*NJG*, p. 25). Throughout the preface to *This Bridge*, Moraga uses the ubiquitous metaphor of the journey through consciousness to politics: "But the passage is *through*, not over, not by, not around, but through. This book, as long as I see it for myself as a passage through, I hope will function for others, colored or white, in the same way. How do we develop a movement that can live with the fact of the loves and lives of these women in this book?" (p. xiv). One answer is through language, for in this book as in the others, words are championed as instruments of power (without, however, losing sight of the material basis of oppression and revolution). Of all the collections, *This Bridge* argues most consistently for the connection between personal life and political ideology—what the editors call "theory in the flesh" (p. 23):

> A theory in the flesh means one where the physical realities of our lives—our skin color, the land or concrete we grew up in, our sexual longings—all fuse to create a politic born of necessity. Here, we attempt to bridge the contradictions in our experience:
> We are the colored in a white feminist movement.
> We are the feminists among the people of our culture.
> We are often the lesbians among the straight.
> We do this bridging by naming our selves and by telling our stories in our own words.

Although this bridging is still embryonic in form, the book of personal narratives is, once again, the free space that nurtures political vision and political change: "We see the book as a revolutionary tool falling into the hands of people of all colors. Just as we have been radicalized in the process of compiling this book, we hope it will radicalize others into action" (*TB*, p. xxvi).

It is the nature of the radicalization proceeding from consciousness raising that continues to be at the heart of debate in the lesbian community. Basically, this debate swirls around questions of separation (or autonomy) and unity. Personal politics historically has led to greater and greater fragmentation within the movement: women separating from men (as blacks separated from whites in the civil rights struggle), lesbians from heterosexuals, lesbians of color from white lesbians, and so on. The editors of *This Bridge* discern a dialectic between these splits and the emergence of a unified political vision and strategy: "Here we begin to fill in the spaces of silence between us. For it is between these seemingly irreconcilable lines—the class lines, the politically correct lines, the daily lines we run down to each other to keep difference and desire at a distance—that the truth of our connection lies" (p. 106). The final section of the anthology offers the inspirational image of *el mundo zurdo*, the left-handed world of "the colored, the queer, the poor, the female, the physically challenged. From our blood and spirit connections with these groups, we women on the bottom throughout the world can form an international feminism" (p. 196). As autonomy—a word used in the early women's liberation movement—replaces separatism, the ultimate theory in the flesh grows out of self-defined groups coalescing to produce both material and psychic change.

The distinction between autonomy and separatism is a delicate one, however, and one that the lesbian and feminist movements have not always been able to keep clear. As personal politics creates more and more specialized groups, the tendency toward fragmentation grows. In one of the finest narratives in *Nice Jewish Girls*, Elana Dykewomon, a prominent separatist, writes about this tension between unity and fragmentation (p. 159):

> Yet she does not want to say she is a jewish lesbian separatist because that means she will only be with other jewish lesbians, which is not what she means. She has spent many years listening, hearing, the stories of what it means, how it feels, to be italian catholic in boston, working class irish in new york, dirt poor protestant in maine, middle class chicana in new orleans, catholic puertoriqueña, black atlanta baptist, hopi, navajo, hindu womon trying to make it in a white sorority at oregon state, she is glad to hear these stories, she wants more, she does not want to waste a single flavor, she wants to agree together on what is bitter and imposed, on what is essential, and what is unique. She wants pride in her own story, possibility to see what it means, to have the acknowledgment, the expansion, of other jewish dykes in this chapter. She believes it helps her listen to the other lesbians' stories with cleaner ears.
>   But she is not sure. . . .

Essentially, Dykewomon accepts the vision of *el mundo zurdo*, but her conclusion is less confident. Is there somehow a transcendent lesbian identity, or only particularized identities? If the latter, what is the basis for unity among lesbians (or women, or, for that matter, the human race)? In the end, "she is not sure." Nor, I think, is the movement today.

Creating a Body Politic

In *Personal Politics*, Evans recalls one critical weakness that developed during the early years of the women's liberation movement: "A preoccupation with internal process—the effort to live out the revolutionary values of egalitarianism and cooperation within the movement itself—took precedence over program or effectiveness." Partly as a result, the movement lost its initial unity: "The rage, the sensitivity, and the overwhelming, omnipresent nature of 'the enemy' drove parts of the women's movement into ideological rigidities, and the movement splintered as it grew."[31] Any fair assessment would have to conclude that similar problems now exist within the lesbian community. On the positive side, I hope this essay has indicated how important the emphasis on personal experience and individual reality has been to the development of a lesbian-

31. Evans (n. 3 above), pp. 222–23, 225.

feminist world view and value system. This emphasis has led to the establishment of an authentic, empirical lesbian voice, or voices, and debunked the so-called expert knowledge that previously defined lesbian experience. It has empowered women through speaking and naming, ending years of silence. It has helped create community through shared storytelling. And, most recently, it has expanded the boundaries of articulated lesbian identity. But there is a price to pay for a politics rooted so strongly in consciousness and identity. The power of diversity has as its mirror image and companion the powerlessness of fragmentation. Small autonomous groups can also be ineffectual groups, especially when, as is true today, they are fraught with division and mistrust. Since the lesbian subculture privileges personal experience, and since most lesbians' lives have encompassed fear, anger, hurt, and pain, it is inevitable that sharp antagonisms should plague the public community.[32] The call for unity is as yet but a hope and a promise. It is certainly true that "our diversity is our strength," as a popular phrase has it. But the community must also work out ways to avoid the fate indicated by a more famous slogan: "We must all hang together, or assuredly we shall all hang separately."

That antagonisms continue to wrack the lesbian community may be substantiated by examining briefly the issue of sexuality, a subject central both to lesbian identity and to recent lesbian debate. Ironically, the personal narratives I have been discussing are sexually quite reticent, although they are deeply romantic, emotional, and sensual. The authors may have wished to dispel the patriarchal myth of insatiable lesbian sexuality; it is also possible that lesbians have internalized the social constraints on women writing about sexuality that Virginia Woolf described in *A Room of One's Own* and *Orlando*, or that some experience lesbian sexuality as more romantic than carnal. Failure to explore the full meaning of eroticism in lesbian lives has led to yet another extension of

32. One place to observe these antagonisms and divisions is in the letter section of *off our backs*. Although this newspaper is not exclusively lesbian, it does accurately reflect the issues and attitudes of the lesbian-feminist political community. Over the years I have noted an increasingly sharp and personal tone taken by the criticisms and comments. The raging battles of the past year or two, in particular, have focused around issues of personal identity: Jewish women and anti-Semitism, lesbian sadomasochism and butch-femme role playing, lesbian mothers of boy children, fat women, disabled women, and so on. To adopt a politically incorrect line on any one of these issues is to bring down on oneself an accusation of personal invalidation. To give one example (and many others could be recounted), as part of a debate concerning access for disabled women at the Michigan Womyn's Music Festival (ironically, the most politically correct of all festivals), a letter from a disabled activist was titled (by the *off our backs* collective, but accurately quoting her letter), "Response: Invalidated Again" (March 1983). What is at stake in so many of these exchanges are not issues and ideas, but identity. The typical tone taken by the writers is one of outrage and indignation, with advocates defending their respective territories in ways that preclude the initiation of meaningful dialogue.

"the personal is political," this time embracing the sexual testimony of lesbians engaged in sadomasochism and, to a lesser extent, in butch-femme role playing.[33] The writings of the former have, in turn, spawned an antisadomasochism position that also relies on personal testimonies, often those of women who adopted and then abandoned sadomasochism.[34] As with most other issues current in the community, this "debate" is couched in personal attacks as well as in political analysis. Supporters of sadomasochism are labeled fascists, racists, woman haters, and perverts; opponents are called sexual fascists, vanilla lesbians, and hysterics. Both sides agree that the practice of lesbian sadomasochism raises crucial questions about the sociopolitical construction of psychosexual identity. What they disagree on are the nature, ethics, and consequences of that construction. And as long as lesbian sadomasochism, or any other personal practice or identity, is considered to be evidence of virtue or vice, it is unlikely that we will be able to listen very carefully to one another.[35]

Thus, to the extent that the movement remains focused on internal process, it is in danger of being insular and solipsistic. Absorbed as we are in self-examination, self-definition, and self-criticism, lesbians (like most radicals) have failed to organize politically in response to the extreme right-wing backlash against gay rights, feminism, and social democracy, as well as the economic distress disproportionately affecting women, minorities, and the poor. Some activists and theorists argue that this is precisely what is necessary to create a movement capable of, in Audre Lorde's words, dismantling the master's house without using the master's tools (*TB*, p. 99). One important lesson we have learned from past decades is that issues postponed are issues forgotten. But how, pragmatically, do we forge a politics of coalition to replace the intense, visionary idealism that characterizes lesbian feminism—before it all becomes an academic question?

33. *Coming to Power: Writings and Graphics on Lesbian S/M*, edited by members of SAMOIS, a lesbian-feminist sadomasochistic organization (Boston: Alyson Publications, 1982), includes personal narratives as well as stories and political analyses. See also personal testimonies in *Heresies 12: Sex Issue*, vol. 3, no. 4 (1981), and the controversial coverage of the equally controversial Barnard conference, "Towards a Politics of Sexuality," *off our backs* (June 1982).

34. Robin Ruth Linden et al., eds., *Against Sadomasochism: A Radical Feminist Analysis* (East Palo Alto, Calif.: Frog in the Well Press, 1982) includes personal testimony, interviews, and analytical essays.

35. A reasoned and aptly titled review of *Against Sadomasochism*, "Polarized Debate" by Muriel Dimen, appears in *New Directions for Women*, March–April 1983. An example of what I am talking about occurred at the National Women's Studies Association meetings in Arcata, California, June 1982. At the panel "Sexuality and Politics: History and Theory," Nancy Hartsock presented a careful analysis of SAMOIS's literature. In the ensuing discussion, her analysis was virtually ignored in favor of deeply felt testimonies about the evils of sadomasochism and pornography.

If lesbian feminism is to remain vigorous through the 1980s, it is essential that the observations and analyses derived from personal narratives of all persuasions as well as from activism be incorporated into a political theory and strategy that can transform both material and psychological structures. Power in this era is at once public and private, centralized and decentralized. In the early 1970s, the Furies placed lesbians as lesbians at the center of the movement for social change. If they were correct, then lesbian feminism can provide strategies for transforming power relations at both levels. But to do so, I believe we must abandon or modify a politics based so strongly on personal identity. Although lesbian feminism evolved during the 1970s as a politics of transliteration, this power of the word has been used primarily to name, and thereby control, individual and group identity. Perhaps we need to refocus our attention on the connecting exchange of language, rather than on the isolating structure of identity, allowing our political language to derive richness and variety from its many dialects, idioms, and even ungrammatical idiosyncrasies. To quote Luce Irigaray's poetic vision of communication, "We must learn how to speak to each other so that we can embrace across distances. Surely, when I touch myself, I remember you. But so much is said, and said of us, that separates us. / Let's quickly invent our own phrases, so that everywhere and always, we continue to embrace."[36] It seems to me that the lesbian-feminist movement must avoid the Scylla of impersonal intellectualism and the Charybdis of solipsism. Our ultimate challenge may be to inscribe personal experience onto a body politic that can then take part in reconstructing the public and private institutions that presently control our lives.

Women's Studies Department
San Diego State University

---

36. Luce Irigaray, "When Our Lips Speak Together," trans. Carolyn Burke, *Signs* 6, no. 1 (Autumn 1980): 69–79, esp. 77.

ARCHIVES

Lesbian Sexuality in Renaissance Italy: The Case of Sister Benedetta Carlini

Judith C. Brown

The archival discovery of an ecclesiastical investigation containing what is probably the earliest detailed account of a sexual relationship between two nuns is a tale of serendipity. Several years ago, when I was revising a book manuscript on the economic and social history of Renaissance Pescia,[1] I looked through the inventory of a collection entitled *Miscellanea Medicea* at the Archivio di Stato of Florence. One entry in the inventory immediately caught my eye. It read: "The case of a nun from Pescia who claimed to be the object of miraculous events but who upon further investigation turned out to be a woman of ill repute."[2] I thought the case would probably involve the sexual affairs of a nun with some of the local priests. There are hundreds of such documented examples. Renaissance convents were notorious for their loose moral standards and their sexual license, which is not surprising since they were largely warehouses for middle- and upper-class women sent there by parents who were unwilling or unable to raise a dowry large enough to find a suitable husband.[3]

What I found instead was much more interesting. The document, consisting of roughly one hundred unnumbered pages, included a de-

1. Judith C. Brown, *In the Shadow of Florence: Provincial Society in Renaissance Pescia* (New York: Oxford University Press, 1982).

2. Florence, Archivio di Stato, *Miscellanea Medicea*, 376, ins. 28. The translation of this material is mine.

3. Brown, pp. 42–43. The moral problems of Renaissance convents and other religious institutions are outlined in Arnaldo D'Addario, *Aspetti della controriforma a Firenze* (Rome: Pubblicazioni degli Archivi di Stato, 1972), pp. 107–14.

Reprinted from *Signs: Journal of Women in Culture and Society* 9, no. 4 (Summer 1984): 751–758.

tailed account of the sexual relationship between two nuns. What I originally thought might be a footnote in a larger history has now developed
into a separate book on a woman whose sexual, emotional, and intellectual experiences shed new light on the life of women in early modern
times.[4]

The ecclesiastical investigation into the case of Benedetta Carlini,
Abbess of the Convent of the Mother of God, dates from the years
1619–23. The records of the inquiry tell of the tragic life of a woman
whose parents brought her to the convent in 1599, at age nine, to fulfill a
vow they made at her birth. Since information about her early years is
scant, her social background, relationship to her family, and adjustment
to convent life can be reconstructed only with slow and painstaking care.
Benedetta belonged to a relatively well-to-do family in a small mountain
town near Pescia. She appears to have had a close relationship with her
father. She was literate and obviously very intelligent and persuasive—so
much so that she became an abbess before she reached the age of thirty
and was able to convince many both inside and outside her convent that
she was the recipient of special divine favors. She asserted, among other
things, that Christ and several male angels spoke through her and that she
had received the stigmata. These extraordinary mystical claims brought
her to the attention of the authorities, who launched an investigation. The
details of her sexual life that were brought to light during the inquiry
make the document unique for this period.

Among the hundreds if not thousands of cases of homosexuality
tried by lay and ecclesiastical authorities in medieval and early modern
Europe, there are almost none involving sexual relations between
women.[5] The Venetian archives, for instance, which are replete with
prosecutions against clergy and laymen for sodomy as well as for sexual
relations with nuns, have not turned up a single case of sexual relations
between women.[6] Thus far records from Spain have also yielded little.
One ambiguous reference by the sixteenth-century jurist Antonio Gomez
discusses two nuns who were burned for using "material instruments."
Another report on prison conditions states that some female inmates are
tough and manly and make artificial male genitalia. In France, four cases
are mentioned by various sixteenth-century writers, but two of these
ended in acquittal for insufficient evidence and the other two are simply
mentioned in passing by authors who did not dwell on the details.[7] The

    4. A more detailed account than that provided here will appear in my forthcoming
book (New York: Oxford University Press, in press.)
    5. John Boswell points out the absence of women in many legal sources concerned
with homosexuality in *Christianity, Social Tolerance, and Homosexuality: Gay People in Western
Europe from the Beginning of the Christian Era to the Fourteenth Century* (Chicago: University of
Chicago Press, 1980), p. 290.
    6. I would like to thank Carlo Ginzburg and Guido Ruggiero, both of whom have had
extensive experience with the inquisitorial and criminal records of Venice, for informing me
of this. See Guido Ruggiero, "Sexual Criminality in the Early Renaissance: Venice 1338–
1358," *Journal of Social History* 8 (Summer 1975): 18–37.
    7. Cited in Louis Crompton, "The Myth of Lesbian Impunity: Capital Laws from 1270
to 1791," *Journal of Homosexuality*, no. 1–2 (Fall 1980–Winter 1981): 17–20; also Mary

first record for Germany dates to 1721.[8] And Swiss sources reveal one case in sixteenth-century Geneva in which the rarity of the accusation is underscored both by the authorities' appeal to the well-known jurist Germain Colladon for advice on how to proceed and by the secrecy with which the case was disposed. In the opinion of the authorities, "A crime so horrible and against nature is so detestable and because of the horror of it, it cannot be named."[9]

Crimes that cannot be named, not surprisingly, leave few traces in the historical records. While this enhances the importance of the document that describes Benedetta's sexual relations with another nun, it also raises a number of difficult historical problems, some of which I would briefly like to discuss here.

First, when such records do turn up, they are usually judicial or inquisitorial documents of some sort. This means that they often veil the truth in various ways. What is said and what is recorded will have been filtered through the minds of the authorities, always male, who conduct the proceedings. Moreover, those accused of sexual crimes are likely to say things in ways that minimized or excused their own misconduct. Both of these factors enter into the record of Benedetta's relationship. The information is circumscribed by the questions asked, most of which do not survive and must be surmised from the answers. The responses are also conditioned by what the witnesses believed the male judges wanted to hear and by what they thought would be least damaging to themselves. Hence, for example, the account of Benedetta's sexual acts is related by her lover as if the lover had been an unwilling participant who was forced into the relationship. The historian's task is to disentangle the complex web of motives that influenced the form of the narrative. This can be accomplished by cultivating an awareness of the circumstances that led to the creation of the historical record and by conducting a close and sensitive reading of the documents themselves. As any lawyer knows, it is very difficult for witnesses to sustain a lengthy fiction without falling into contradictions. Sometimes the truth is revealed by an unguarded word spoken in a different context.

A second problem facing the historian involves determining the extent of sexual relations between women. How common were they? Is the paucity of historical evidence related to the ways in which the male world dealt with such relations? Or did women engage less extensively then men in sexual activities with one another? Satisfactory answers are difficult to come by, although a number of reasonable observations can be

---

Elizabeth Perry, *Crime and Society in Early Modern Seville* (Hanover, N.H.: University Press of New England, 1980), p. 84.

8. Brigitte Erikson, "A Lesbian Execution in Germany, 1721: The Trial Records," *Journal of Homosexuality*, no. 1–2 (Fall 1980–Winter 1981), pp. 27–40.

9. E. William Monter, "La Sodomie à l'époque moderne en Suisse romande," *Annales: Economies, Sociétés, Civilisations* 29 (1974): 1023–33. The nineteenth-century court case of two Scottish school mistresses accused of sexual relations reveals a similar concern about not divulging the details of the case for fear of giving ideas to otherwise innocent female minds. See Lillian Faderman, *Scotch Verdict* (New York: William Morrow & Co., 1983).

made. Undoubtedly, sexual relations between women existed in medieval and Renaissance Europe, especially, though not exclusively, within the world of the convent. It was there, where at times close to 10 percent of the adult female population lived, that such relations had the most opportunity to flourish. To imagine that sexual relationships were absent from these all-female communities strains the limits of credulity. But to move from the probable to the realm of evidence, the discussion in several medieval and Renaissance penitentials of penances for women who engaged in "vice against nature" implicitly acknowledges that such relations existed.[10] The paucity of historical evidence regarding these relations must therefore be related in some measure to the ways in which the masculine world perceived the bonds between women.

Although medieval theologians and other learned men were not totally unaware of sexual relations between women, they for the most part ignored them. The world of the Middle Ages and the Renaissance was not prudish. It was a world that was fully cognizant of human sexuality, but it was also phallocentric. The thought that women could bring sexual pleasure to each other without the aid of a man occurred to very few theologians and physicians. For the millennium that followed the decline of Rome, many laws and commentaries that deal with male homosexuality survive; only a handful, however, mention sexual relations between women. So little was written on the subject that the few authors who discussed it were often uninformed about what others had written and therefore disagreed on what this "unnatural" vice was and how it should be punished. Ignorance about sexual relations between women was so pervasive that one Italian cleric in the eighteenth century, Lodovico Maria Sinistrari, decided to write a treatise on "female sodomy." While moralists claimed that sodomy among women existed, none, he lamented, explained how such a thing could occur. After exploring the subject at great length, he concluded that, except in rare instances, it could not.[11]

What women did with each other is precisely the topic that the document appended below illuminated for Benedetta's male superiors. Yet because they lacked an imaginative schema to incorporate the sexual behavior described, they had a rather difficult time assimilating the account. So disturbed was the scribe writing down what had been said that the heretofore neat and legible handwriting of the report totally breaks down in the section covering Benedetta's sexual relations with another nun. The words are illegible, crossed out, and rewritten.

If the scribe had difficulties comprehending what was taking place, he was not the only one. That Benedetta herself could not easily fit her

10. Some of these penitentials and other medieval literature dealing with lesbianism are cited in Derrick S. Bailey, *Homosexuality and the Western Christian Tradition* (London: Longmans, Green & Co., 1955); Boswell; and Crompton.

11. Lodovico Maria Sinistrari, *De sodomia: Tractatus in quo exponitur doctrina nova de sodomia foeminarum a tribadismo distincta* (Paris, 1843), excerpted from his larger work, *De delictis et poenis* (Rome, 1700). This conclusion had to do with Sinistrari's narrow definition of sodomy rather than the belief, more common in the nineteenth century (see Faderman), that women had no sexual desires.

sexual behavior into a mold that was acceptable to her raises the larger issue of labeling and sexual identity. Do the terms "lesbian" and "lesbianism" best describe the person and activities outlined in the investigators' report? Recent studies of sexual identity and sexual preference have stressed the difficulties inherent in definitions. Human sexual behavior, like other aspects of human activity, defies easy or stereotypical categorizations. Women who have had fulfilling sexual and emotional relationships with other women do not necessarily view themselves as lesbian. Conversely, there are those who have never had sexual relationships with other women who consider themselves lesbians nonetheless. The range of sexual experience and self-identification is immensely varied and operates to a large extent within socially defined categories that influence both identity and behavior.[12]

This problem of labeling becomes particularly acute when dealing with sexual behavior and identity in past times. Although considerable legislation and concern about homosexual practices arose prior to the nineteenth century, the concept of the homosexual, as we know it today, did not exist.[13] This was all the more true for the notion of the lesbian.[14] Adrienne Rich has attempted to surmount this difficulty by positing a lesbian continuum in which lesbian identity is tied not so much to a self-conscious identity or even to sexual relations or attractions as to the emotional bonds that emerge between women in the midst of patriarchal society. While such an approach has the merit of emphasizing the complexity of ties among women and the resistance to oppression implicit in so many of their actions, it is also too encompassing and at heart ahistorical. Closer to the mark is Ann Ferguson's argument that, while some women can be described as sexually deviant in that they departed from the norm, the term "lesbian" cannot accurately be applied to women who

12. See, among others, Allan P. Bell, Martin S. Weinberg, and Sue K. Hammersmith, *Sexual Preference: Its Development in Men and Women* (Bloomington: Indiana University Press, 1981); Sherry Ortner and Harriet Whitehead, eds., *Sexual Meanings* (Cambridge: Cambridge University Press, 1981).

13. There has been considerable debate about whether the category of homosexual can be applied to premodern periods. Among the most clearly articulated arguments against employing the category anachronistically are those of Jeffrey Weeks in *Coming Out: Homosexual Politics in Britain from the Nineteenth Century to the Present* (London: Quartet Books, 1977). Opposing this view is John Boswell, "Towards the Long View: Revolutions, Universals and Sexual Categories," *Salmagundi*, no. 58–59 (Fall 1982–Winter 1981), pp. 89–113. There is even disagreement over when the homosexual role emerged within the modern period. While Mary McIntosh argues for the late seventeenth century, Jeffrey Weeks and John Marshall, among others, favor the late nineteenth century. See their respective essays in Kenneth Plummer, ed., *The Making of the Modern Homosexual* (London: Hutchinson Publishing Group, 1981).

14. Even if there is some merit to Boswell's argument that the concept of the homosexual, albeit in altered form, existed prior to the modern age, his claim cannot readily be extended to the concept of the lesbian since women's restricted cultural and social roles precluded the development of the types of communities that he analyzes for males. For a discussion of some of these problems, see Annabel Faraday, "Liberating Lesbian Research," in Plummer, ed., pp. 112–32.

lived before its emergence as a cultural category in the late nineteenth century.[15]

Benedetta Carlini's case illustrates the complexity of these issues. Benedetta engaged in sexual acts that today would be labeled lesbian. Furthermore, she entered into a sexual relationship with another female even though she could have secured male partners without much difficulty. Her apparent preference for a relationship with a woman is not, however, indicative of a clearly articulated choice. When she made love to Bartolomea Crivelli, she imagined herself to be a male angel. Her voice and even her appearance became more like a man's when she assumed the guise of the angel Splendidiello. Since male-female sexual relations were the only ones she seemed to recognize, her male identity allowed her to have sexual and emotional relations that she could not conceive between women. Attaining the object of her sexual desires required a complete reversal of her own gender and sexual roles.[16] But because Benedetta was a nun for whom *all* sexual activities were prohibited, she could not pass for an ordinary male; she required an angelic disguise to preclude the possibility of sin. In this double role, as male and as angel, Benedetta absolved herself from any possible wrongdoing.

Equally important, the ecclesiastical authorities who heard the case also lacked the terms of sexual identification that would be used in a twentieth-century context. Although an extended discussion of medieval and Renaissance notions of female sexuality is not feasible within the narrow confines of an archival note, suffice it to say that on a scale of sinful sexual acts Benedetta's behavior at worst would have been labeled sodomy (that is, engaging in coitus in an unnatural vessel), which was punishable by burning at the stake. Some theologians and lawyers of her time, however, might have viewed her actions merely as pollution brought on by the rubbing together of the pudenda. Still others might have called them mutual masturbation. Both of these sinful acts were of a lesser degree than sodomy. But no matter how grave the sin or the secular crime that her contemporaries thought Benedetta had committed, they would not have applied the term "lesbian" as a discrete category of female sexual identification. This is not to argue that Benedetta's relationship with her lover was not emotionally or sexually fulfilling but simply to say what is after all rather obvious: sexuality and culture are intertwined, and Benedetta's and the authorities' interpretations of her behavior while different from each other are also necessarily different from our own.

15. Adrienne Rich, "Compulsory Heterosexuality and Lesbian Existence," *Signs: Journal of Women in Culture and Society* 5, no. 4 (Summer 1980): 631–60; Ann Ferguson, "Patriarchy, Sexual Identity, and the Sexual Revolution," *Signs* 7, no. 1 (Autumn 1981): 158–66.

16. In this respect, Benedetta's perceptions coincide with Victorian notions of sexual inversion even though the latter originated in quite different conceptions of female gender and sexuality. See George Chauncey, Jr., "From Sexual Inversion to Homosexuality: Medicine and the Changing Conceptualization of Female Deviance," *Salmagundi*, no. 58–59 (Fall 1982–Winter 1983), pp. 114–45.

How the authorities ultimately disposed of the case is a complex story that cannot be recounted here. The immediate task of the investigators was simply to ascertain the facts and if need be to restore order by their very presence. Having accomplished this to their satisfaction after the initial stages of the investigation, they refrained for the moment from taking any other action. For all their measured and deliberate procedures, however, the investigators' horror at what they heard of the relationship between Benedetta and Bartolomea comes through very clearly in the following account. Yet theirs is not the only voice that emerges from the text. Though refracted through the perceptions of other participants—the clerics, who wrote down what they heard or thought they heard, and Bartolomea, who told them what happened or what she thought would implicate her the least—the voice and the longings of Benedetta Carlini can still be heard.

Department of History
Stanford University

* * *

For two continuous years, two or three times a week, in the evening after disrobing and going to bed and waiting for her companion, who serves her, to disrobe also, she would force her into the bed, and kissing her as if she were a man she would stir herself on top of her so much that both of them corrupted themselves because she held her by force sometimes for one, sometimes for two, sometimes for three hours. And [she did these things] during the most solemn hours, especially in the morning, at dawn. Pretending that she had some need, she would call her, and taking her by force she sinned with her as was said above. Benedetta, in order to have greater pleasure, put her face between the other's breasts and kissed them, and wanted always to be thus on her. And six or eight times, when the other nun did not want to sleep with her in order to avoid sin, Benedetta went to find her in her bed and, climbing on top, sinned with her by force. Also at that time, during the day, pretending to be sick and showing that she had some need, she grabbed her companion's hand by force, and putting it under herself, she would have her put her finger in her genitals, and holding it there she stirred herself so much that she corrupted herself. And she would kiss her and also by force would put her own hand under her companion and her finger into her genitals and corrupted her. And when the latter would flee, she would do the same with her own hands. Many times she locked her companion in the study, and making her sit down in front of her, by force she put her hands under her and corrupted her; she wanted her companion to do the same to her, and while she was doing this she would kiss her. She always appeared to be in a trance while doing this. Her Angel, Splendidiello, did these things, appearing as a boy of eight or nine years of age. This Angel Splendidiello, through the mouth and hands of Benedetta, taught her companion to read and write, making her be near her on her knees and kissing her and putting her hands on her breasts. . . .

This Splendidiello called her his beloved; he asked her to swear to be his beloved always and promised that after Benedetta's death he would always be with her and would make himself visible. He said I want you to promise me not to confess these things that we do together, I assure you that there is no sin in it; and while we did these things he said many times: give yourself to me with all your heart and soul and then let me do as I wish. . . .

The same Angel managed it so that neither Benedetta nor her companion did the usual [spiritual] exercises that the nuns did prior to general confession. He made the sign of the cross all over his companion's body after having committed with her many dishonest acts; [he also said] many words that she couldn't understand and when she asked him why he was doing this, he said that he did this for her own good. Jesus spoke to her companion [through Benedetta] three times, twice before doing these dishonest things. The first time he said he wanted her to be his bride and he was content that she give him her hand, and she did this thinking it was Jesus. The second time it was in the choir at 40 hours, holding her hands together and telling her that he forgave her all her sins. The third time it was after she was disturbed by these affairs and he told her that there was no sin involved whatsoever and that Benedetta while doing these things had no awareness of them. All these things her companion confessed with very great shame.

Archives

The Military and Lesbians during the McCarthy Years

Allan Bérubé and John D'Emilio

The following documents shed light on a little-known area of women's history: the policy of the U.S. military toward lesbian personnel during the McCarthy Era and its impact on women serving in the armed forces. The first three documents—indoctrination lectures on homosexuality designed for WAVE (Navy) recruits in 1952—both articulate the military's implicit ideology concerning lesbians and demonstrate the means by which the military implemented its policy. The second set of documents—1951 correspondence between the ACLU (American Civil Liberties Union) and lesbians being purged from the WAF (Air Force)—records the effects of military policy on individual women in the Air Force.

These letters and lectures are evidence of the "homosexual scare" of the 1950s, which was a side effect of Cold War tensions and American fears about national security. Early in 1950, a State Department official testified before the Senate that several dozen employees had been dismissed on charges of homosexuality. The revelation provoked an uproar, and for the remainder of the year Republican leaders exploited the homosexual issue as a means of discrediting the Truman administration's national security policy. A Senate investigation into the employment of "homosexuals and other sex perverts" painted a menacing picture of the infiltration of the federal government by "sexual deviates" whose presence allegedly threatened the moral welfare of the nation.[1] The popular

1. Senate Committee on Expenditures in Executive Departments, *Employment of Homosexuals and Other Sex Perverts in Government*, 81st Cong., 2d sess., 1950. For a discussion

Reprinted from *Signs: Journal of Women in Culture and Society* 9, no. 4 (Summer 1984): 759–775.

press kept the homosexual issue alive with reports of dismissals from government service and exposés of alleged homosexual "rings." Scandal writers in stories with such titles as "Lesbians Prey on Weak Women" charged that there were cells of lesbians in the schools and in the military bent on seducing the innocent.[2]

Rhetoric portraying sexual deviance as a threat to national security had its analogue in more repressive policies. During the early 1950s the government explicitly excluded homosexuals and lesbians from all federal jobs; many private employers, particularly those under government contract, followed suit.[3] The military's response to the "homosexual menace" was especially severe. By the end of the 1940s, the military was discharging about a thousand men and women per year on charges of homosexuality. But as the campaign against sexual deviance intensified in the 1950s, the number discharged rose to over two thousand per year.[4]

Women in the military were particularly vulnerable to these anti-homosexual policies. A secret investigative board noted in 1957 that the rate of detection for homosexual activity in the Navy had been "much higher for the female than the male" even though "homosexual activity in the female is difficult to detect."[5] As unmarried female volunteers in an intensely masculine institution, women in the military constituted a socially deviant group that too easily fit the popular stereotype of lesbians. Their deviation from the norms of female behavior was especially highlighted by the reassertion of traditional gender roles in the postwar years. By contrast, during World War II, the demands of massive mobilization had allowed large numbers of American women to step temporarily outside their usual roles not only to enlist in the military but also to work in heavy industry, to live away from husbands and other kin, and to look to each other for companionship. After the war, these options faded rapidly.[6]

---

of the "homosexual scare" during the McCarthy Era, see John D'Emilio, *Sexual Politics, Sexual Communities: The Making of a Homosexual Minority in the United States, 1940–1970* (Chicago: University of Chicago Press, 1983), pp. 40–53.

2. Headline reprinted in *ONE Magazine* (April 1954), pp. 16–17. See also Lee Mortimer, *Washington Confidential Today* (New York: Crown Publishers, 1952); Jack Lait and Lee Mortimer, *U.S.A. Confidential* (New York: Crown Publishers, 1952).

3. Exclusion of homosexuals and lesbians from all government jobs was specified in Eisenhower's Executive Order 10450, issued on April 27, 1953, printed in the *New York Times* (April 28, 1953), p. 20. For a detailed analysis of federal policies, see John D'Emilio, "The Evolution and Impact of Federal Antihomosexual Policies during the 1950s" (report prepared for the National Gay Task Force, New York, 1983).

4. Statistics on military discharges on grounds of homosexuality may be found in Colin J. Williams and Martin S. Weinberg, *Homosexuals and the Military* (New York: Harper & Row, 1971), pp. 31–36, 45–47, 53. The statistics are not broken down by gender.

5. Navy, *Report of the Board Appointed to Prepare and Submit Recommendations to the Secretary of the Navy for the Revision of Policies, Procedures and Directives Dealing with Homosexuals, 21 December 1956–15 March 1957* (hereafter cited as Crittenden Report), Captain S. H. Crittenden, Jr., chairman, Board Report, pp. 40–41.

6. On women during World War II and after, see Karen Anderson, *Wartime Women: Sex Roles, Family Relations, and the Status of Women during World War II* (Westport, Conn.:

The contrast between wartime and postwar attitudes toward women is revealed by comparing military policy toward lesbian personnel during and after the war. In 1943, the Women's Army Auxiliary Corps (WAAC), the largest women's branch of the military with nearly 150,000 women in its ranks, prepared a series of sex hygiene lectures aimed at officer candidates.[7] The lecture on homosexuality detailed wartime policy toward lesbian personnel, explaining that "more consciousness of sex and more difficulties concerning it are to be expected in times of war than in times of peace. Whenever individuals are removed from their homes, their communities, and their social groups, they may be thrown into different and often exacting situations." The lectures recognized the value of friendship between women who had left home to serve in the corps: "This can be one of the finest relationships in companionship and working together. Sometimes it can become an intimacy that may eventually take some form of sexual expression." The lectures minimized the differences between women who participated in homosexual expression and "normal" women, stating that the former "are exactly as you and I, except that they participate in sexual gratification with members of their own sex."

The wartime lectures explicitly warned against antilesbian witch hunts. "You, as officers, will find it necessary to keep the problem at the back of your mind, not indulging in witch hunting or speculating. . . . Above all, you must approach the problem with an attitude of fairness and tolerance to assure that no one is accused unjustly." The unusual circumstances of military life could encourage women to have their first homosexual experiences, the lecture continued. "It may appear that, almost spontaneously, such a relationship has sprung up between two women, neither of whom is a confirmed, active homosexual." In the event that an officer discovered a woman in her outfit had "gravitated toward homosexual practices," the lecture advised one of four possible solutions: guidance, using a "reasonable and unscornful approach"; supervision, "such as the shifting of rooms"; transfer, "when it seems likely that a change of environment might help to eliminate the cause"; or, as a last resort, discharge. Only the most overt, disruptive, and intransigent lesbian "addicts" who jeopardized the efficiency and morale of the unit were to be discharged. But "any officer," warned the lecture, "bringing an unjust or unprovable charge against a woman in this regard will be severely reprimanded."[8]

Greenwood Press, 1981); William H. Chafe, *The American Woman* (New York: Oxford University Press, 1972), chaps. 6–8; and Mary P. Ryan, *Womanhood in America*, 2d ed. (New York: New Viewpoints, 1979), chaps. 5–6.

7. "Sex Hygiene Course, Officers and Officer Candidates, Women's Army Auxiliary Corps, May 27, 1943," War Department Pamphlet no. 35-1 (Washington, D.C.: Government Printing Office, 1943). Quotations are from "Lecture I: Introduction," pp. 3–4; and "Lecture V: Homosexuality," pp. 24–29.

8. On lesbians in the U.S. military during World War II, see Allan Bérubé, "Gays at War," *Mother Jones* 8, no. 11 (February/March 1983): 23–29, 45, and "Marching to a Different Drummer," *Advocate*, no. 328 (October 15, 1981), pp. 20–25, reprinted in *Powers of*

These guidelines were not always followed. Branches of the military did at times search for and harass lesbian personnel, and some women were discharged from the service. But the demands of war placed constraints on the military, and instances of harassment coexisted with the relatively tolerant approach suggested by these lectures.

This wartime policy gave way to a more repressive policy toward lesbian personnel in the 1950s, as the Navy lectures reprinted below illustrate.[9] In 1952, teams of naval officers were told to implement a "program for the indoctrination of naval personnel at Naval Training Centers on the subject of homosexuality."[10] Guidelines instructed the indoctrination teams to characterize homosexuality as "one of the very bad things in life." "In training of personnel," program guidelines explained, "emphasis upon homosexuality becomes necessary because there are few other means for obtaining information about it. Information about narcotics, stealing, lying and other crimes flows continuously to people through the press, radio, and institutions of learning. . . . During this period emphasis is going to be placed on another very bad thing that exists in life but about which the majority of people know little or nothing." Naval officers were not to "dress up" the subject in "high flown technical language. Homosexuality is wrong, it is evil, and it is to be branded as such," the guidelines insisted. "No pulling of punches or inferences that the matter is not serious. . . . Homosexuality . . . is an offense to all decent and law-abiding people, and it is not to be condoned on grounds of 'mental illness' any more than other crime such as theft, homicide, or criminal assault."[11]

The 1952 program included three lectures on homosexuality, specifically designed for WAVE recruits, that reflect the era's tightening strictures against homosexuality as well as against women who deviated from social norms. The lectures explicitly reject the guidance and counseling suggested to Army officer candidates during World War II. Instead, the postwar policy considered "first-timers" as guilty as the "practicing homosexual" and subject to immediate discharge. No penalties for false accusations were mentioned. Rather, this Cold War policy instituted a system of sexual surveillance that encouraged WAVEs to

---

Desire: The Politics of Sexuality, ed. Ann Snitow, Christine Stansell, and Sharon Thompson (New York: Monthly Review Press, 1983), pp. 88–99.

9. Lectures are from the Crittenden Report, vol. A, app. 23, "Samples of Standard Indoctrination Lectures."

10. Crittenden Report, Board Report, pp. 42–43. These pages of the Board Report include a chronology of events that led to the implementation of the indoctrination program on the subject of homosexuality.

11. Program guidelines are from Bureau of Naval Personnel, "Proposed Modifications to Recruit Training Curriculum," and "Proposed Procedure for Implementing Program of Indoctrination of Naval Personnel at Naval Training Centers as to Subject of Homosexuality," approved for implementation in Secretary of the Navy to Chief of Naval Personnel, November 14, 1952, all included in Crittenden Report, vol. A, app. 22, "Instructions for Committee on Indoctrination and Education."

inform on each other. Although each lecture advised WAVEs to talk over their personal problems with an officer, the primary duty of chaplains and psychiatrists, as naval officers, was to protect the Navy by detecting and discharging homosexual personnel. Thus, a WAVE who confided in her officer could unknowingly initiate an antilesbian purge. The 1952 lectures did recognize the value of female friendship in the Navy but warned that friendships that became too involved might lead to sexual activity. Antihomosexual rhetoric is used throughout the lectures to warn women recruits that sex must take place only within the institution of marriage, to bolster the traditional role as wife and mother, and to ensure that women in the military, despite their socially deviant status, adhere to the norms of feminine behavior. The lectures project a stereotype of lesbians as sexual vampires: manipulative, dominant perverts who greedily seduce young and innocent women into experimenting with homosexual practices that, like narcotics, inevitably lead to a downward spiral of addiction, degeneracy, loneliness, and even murder and suicide.

The experiences detailed in the set of correspondence below document how this more repressive Cold War policy affected individual women who enlisted in the Air Force.[12] According to one of the letter writers, the implementation of this policy amounted to "psychological warfare" in the relentless search for lesbians. Investigating officers extracted confessions with promises of speedy discharge, and then used the self-incriminating statements to pressure women into naming names. The Air Force had the option of discharging an accused woman administratively rather than acceding to her demand for a trial by court martial. Thus, women lacked the power to meet their accusers, to examine and to refute the evidence, and to cross-examine witnesses.[13] When a female officer intervened to inform women under her command of their rights in an investigation, she was relieved of her command. The authors of the letters express a sense of helplessness in the face of orders that emanated from a remote and powerful Washington.

The targeting of women who stepped beyond the boundaries of heterosexuality had devastating effects. In the purge detailed here, at least two of the accused women committed suicide. But, even for the survivors, a military discharge on grounds of homosexuality represented a lifelong stigma. Besides the trauma of the experience, such a discharge during the 1950s precluded civilian employment with the government as well as in a wide range of other jobs. Many women enlisted in the military for the mobility it promised—the opportunity to leave home and travel, to gain job skills, and to enter nontraditional occupations. The disgrace attached to expulsion for lesbianism dashed these expectations.

12. The letters are from General Correspondence, vol. 16, 1951, ACLU Papers, Princeton University.

13. On the military's use of administrative discharges, see Clifford A. Dougherty and Norman B. Lynch, "The Administrative Discharge: Military Justice?" *George Washington Law Review* 33 (1964): 498–528; and Jerome A. Susskind, "Military Administrative Discharge Boards: The Right to Confrontation and Cross-Examination," *Michigan State Bar Journal* 46 (1965): 25–32.

Despite the grim picture that the letters paint, they are also portents of the future. The authors are, after all, writing to the American Civil Liberties Union for help, and both women display a clearly articulated sense of outrage and injustice. In this instance their request for help was denied because at the time the ACLU held that homosexuality was relevant to an individual's military service.[14] But the letter writers were not alone in their search for recourse. Heightened concern about homosexuality during the 1950s and the intensification of penalties against lesbians and gay men propelled some of them to take action on their own behalf. By the mid-1950s, a lesbian rights organization, the Daughters of Bilitis (DOB), formed in San Francisco, with branches opening later in other cities. In the succeeding years, DOB, along with male homosexual organizations, targeted the antihomosexual policies of the military and civilian agencies of the federal government that had intensified during the 1950s.[15]

San Francisco, California (Bérubé)

Department of History
University of North Carolina, Greensboro (D'Emilio)

* * *

Indoctrination of WAVE Recruits on Subject of Homosexuality [1952]

Line Officer's [Presentation]

Good morning/afternoon! I am ———. The officer on my right/left is Dr. ———. The officer on my left/right is Chaplain ———. We would like to speak to you today about a subject with which, very likely, many of you have never been confronted and on which most of you, perhaps, have never heard a formal discussion. The subject is homosexuality. . . . I shall speak to you as a woman officer because there are some things about homosexuality that concern us as women in the service. This presentation is to tell you the facts concerning homosexuality and most important of all, how to avoid becoming involved with homosexuals. . . .

My purpose today is to: (1) warn you that there are homosexuals[;] (2) inform you why the Navy doesn't tolerate homosexuals in the Naval

14. On the position of the ACLU concerning homosexuality and civil liberties, see Herbert Levy to William Klausner, April 17, 1953, and Levy to Mrs. Thomas Manly Dillingham, Sept. 20, 1955, General Correspondence, vol. 55, 1953, and vol. 27, 1955, respectively, ACLU Papers, Princeton University. The text of the statement, "Homosexuality and Civil Liberties," adopted by the ACLU board of directors on Jan. 7, 1957, may be found in *Civil Liberties* (March 1957).

15. For more information on the DOB, see Del Martin and Phyllis Lyon, *Lesbian/ Woman* (San Francisco: Glide Urban Center Publications, 1972); and D'Emilio, *Sexual Politics, Sexual Communities* (n. 1 above).

service[;] (3) tell you what can happen if you are foolish enough to commit a homosexual act[;] (4) and most important of all, to show how any one of you may become involved in a homosexual act unless you understand the circumstances under which the homosexual may make an approach to you.

Let us first review the definition of homosexuality. It is sexual gratification of an individual through physical contact with another person of the same sex. A homosexual, then, is one who gratifies her sex desires by being sexually intimate with another woman.

You may ask, how can a young woman who has always led a wholesome life become involved? There are several techniques which may be used by the practicing homosexual to lure you into involvement in a homosexual act.

One of the most commonly used techniques is for the practicing homosexual to use friendship as a means to secure for herself a partner in her homosexual acts. . . . The practicing homosexual may begin her approach to you as a sympathetic, understanding and motherly person. At first she will present the same appearance as many of your friends. She will have many interests in common with you, but as time progresses you will be aware that she is developing this friendship as much as possible along emotional lines. This person may begin to demand all of your time, and to shower you with expensive gifts, and to pay all the expenses when you are out together. Even though you may never have indulged in alcohol, she may initiate you into the "art of social drinking." She may plan activities that will end in parties where heavy drinking is being done. She may plan more and more time for the two of you to be alone . . . late rides in her car, intimate conversations between the two of you, and physical advances such as embraces. As time goes by, she may propose that you take a week-end trip with her to a near-by city, to sightsee or take in a show. This trip will involve sharing a hotel or motel room. When you are alone . . . she orders drinks . . . , and more and more alcohol is consumed. Then follow the improper physical advances and a homosexual act is committed. . . .

A woman homosexual may use a technique that is opposite to the one of kindliness, protective sympathy, and understanding. Her approach may be signalled by domineering, severely bossy, mentally cruel or bossy conduct toward the individual approached. This technique is to secure the domination of the sought individual, and to gain mastery and control over her. Just how this dominance is secured, whether through timidity or fear does not matter . . . ; it may lead to seduction.

The "Come-on-and-no-risk" approach is still another technique that may be used, and it fits into the battle against boredom. Navy women may be propositioned to indulge, just a little bit, in homosexuality, "because you can have a lot of fun with no after effects." Frankly, what is being said is that you can experience sexual stimulation and sexual satisfaction in a homosexual act without risk of pregnancy. . . .

It is important that you understand the Navy's policy toward homosexuality. The policy of the Navy is quite positive in that all persons found guilty of so much as one single homosexual act while in the Naval service must be eliminated from the service. The "first timer" or experimenter is just as liable to separation as the confirmed homosexual. A woman is not tried for being a homosexual, she is tried for committing a homosexual act. One thing is certain, she is going out of the Navy and fast. Under certain circumstances she will be given an undesirable discharge, commonly called a U.D. It means she has been discharged from the Navy as an undesirable, and her discharge papers will state that it is under conditions other than honorable and without satisfactory service. In certain circumstances she may face trial by General Court-Martial.

Answer these questions for yourselves . . . if you were discharged from the Navy for committing a homosexual act . . . , what kind of a job would you be able to get? The person hiring you would investigate and find out that you were not the type of person who would be a good risk as an employee. Government employment is impossible. You may lose virtually all rights as a veteran under both Federal and State legislation. You would probably be reduced to getting a job of such low level and so undesirable that your employer wouldn't bother to investigate.

What would you tell your family and friends? Or the man you hope someday to marry? Could you tell them that you were discharged from the Navy as an undesirable, or were Court-Martialed for abnormal sex practices? These facts have an unpleasant way of coming out, no matter how much you try to hide them.

The families, parents, and friends of women who have been discharged from the Navy for homosexual acts, write tearful letters to the Navy Department in Washington, D.C., begging for relief from the type of discharge they have received. They claim the Navy has branded them as homosexuals, and because of this they find it difficult to earn a living, or find an acceptable young man for dating, companionship, or possible marriage. Actually, the Navy has not branded these women. They have branded and disgraced themselves, and no relief is possible. Women who engage in homosexual acts cannot and will not be tolerated by the United States Navy. . . .

If a homosexual makes an approach to you . . . , stay away from her. If you have evidence of homosexual acts report them to the proper authorities. . . .

Remember, the fine friendships between normal, decent women is not the thing I'm referring to today. The many wholesome friendships formed in the Naval service are one of the finest influences in barracks and social life. These friendships are of great value to the Navy woman, both while in the service and in civilian life when she has returned to her home. The annual reunion celebration of Navy women throughout the United States every year gives some concept of the importance of such friendships. It is good for young women coming into the service to use their petty officers as guides and models of service life. Be wise in your choice of friends. Be alert and avoid emotional pitfalls.

Finally, all of us should be very proud to be women serving in the United States Navy, but let us be sure that we retain as much of our basic femininity as possible. We are not competing with the men . . . , we are supplementing and complementing them. We must take pride in the kind of things women do well . . . , that of setting a high standard of conduct by living in accord with the moral beliefs of our society.

May I now present Doctor ———, Medical Corps, U.S. Navy, who will speak to you on the medical aspects of homosexuality.

Medical Officer's Presentation (WAVE Recruits)

The medical officer, particularly one that specializes in psychiatry, is interested in homosexuality as an abnormal form of human behavior. . . .

Generally speaking, homosexual activity is the manifestation of failure on the part of the individual to grow up sexually, which leads to personality disorders in adult life. This is true whether the individual be exclusively homosexual or only a "dabbler." . . . What you have done in your younger and developing life is *not* to be taken as placing you in a position of the person under discussion today, or to be in a position of danger. To draw a comparison, it is not that you wet the bed as a child but do you wet the bed today.

By virtue of the fact that you are now in the Navy, you are considered grown-up and adult behavior is expected of you. If such behavior is not forthcoming, you will be held accountable. . . .

Several common misconceptions exist about homosexuality and it is these misconceptions which lead people into trouble. One such misconception is that it is easy to identify a practicing female homosexual by her masculine mannerisms and characteristics. This is not true. Many practicing female homosexuals are quite feminine in appearance and some are outstandingly so. There are probably more female homosexuals who are completely feminine in appearance than there are female homosexuals who are masculine in appearance.

Another common misconception is that those who engage in homosexuality are safe from acquiring venereal disease. This also is not true, as both gonorrhea and syphilis can be readily contracted through sexual relations with females as well as through sexual relations with males. Reports from various clinics reveal one out of every four male and female patients admitted with syphilis acknowledged homosexual contacts as the source of their infection. Practicing homosexuals are notoriously promiscuous and not very particular in whom they pick up, infected or otherwise.

A third misconception is that homosexuals are born and not made. This idea leads to the beliefs, first, that an individual who is not born a homosexual can participate in homosexual acts without danger and, second, that nothing can be done medically for the confirmed homosexual. Neither of these beliefs is true. Treatment is available for even the confirmed homosexual but this is not an obligation of the Navy Medical Corps. As to the other belief, repeated dabbling in homosexuality in late adolescence as well as in adulthood can and frequently does constitute the making of a homosexual. Some who start as "dabblers" or "experimenters" progress steadily to become exclusively homosexual in their behavior. Experimentation, therefore, aside from being an infringement on social as well as Navy standards, is dangerous in its own right.

In this entire problem, the medical officer has a two-fold interest: first, and uppermost, he is a naval officer and has an interest in the Navy as a whole. It is his duty to help eliminate disturbing and undesirable factors from the Naval service, such as confirmed homosexuals. In the second place, as a physician and a psychiatrist, he offers his experience and knowledge of behavior disorders in helping those who are concerned about this problem. In this latter capacity, he maintains an open door attitude to all, and he is available for interview at your request.

May I now present Chaplain ———— who will speak to you on the social, moral and spiritual aspects of homosexuality.

Chaplain's Presentation (WAVE Recruits)

The Chaplain's primary concern with the problem of homosexuality is its relationship to the individual's social, moral and spiritual life. . . .

Homosexuality Destroys a Woman's Social Status and Her Social Future

I do not feel I have to emphasize to you how delicate a structure is a woman's good name, or how easy it is to tarnish or destroy it.

A single act, or an association, may brand a woman as a sexual pervert. Society allows women more emotional demonstrations in public than it allows men. Women friends may embrace and kiss each other as they meet in public without causing suspicion or starting a whispering campaign. Such displays of emotion and friendship, however, must always be within good taste.

By her conduct a Navy woman may ruin her chances for a happy marriage. Friends should be chosen with great care. Friendships are best when they are carefully formed on the basis of similar ages and interests. . . .

To get entangled with homosexuality means three things: (1) The woman gambles with the possible destruction of her social life and future marriage[;] (2) She will become the target of other homosexuals[;] (3) All normal, decent people who know, or even who strongly suspect the facts will have nothing to do with her.

Homosexuality Destroys a Woman's Character

Homosexuality is a social offense, and is named a felony by law. . . .

People who engage in homosexuality fear exposure for there is always a witness (the other person). It is not possible to live under constant tension and fear, without seriously weakening one's moral fiber, mental and emotional stability.

Homosexuality destroys a woman's personal integrity. Little by little, the individual becomes more deeply entangled in the homosexual web. At first she wonders how it all happened. She reacts with confusion, shame and fear. She rationalizes that she was only a passive partner; that she really did not *do* anything. But she knows better. Then she faces the possibility of blackmail. She finds it easier to submit to homosexuality than to fight against it.

Experience indicates that the odds are heavy against her ever quitting. She slowly deteriorates in character, losing her power of will, and her integrity. Thus the deterioration and destruction of character and integrity are the end results of homosexuality. Even such gross crimes as robbery, suicide and murder often grow out of homosexuality.

Homosexuality Destroys a Woman's Spiritual Values and Her Spiritual Life

Moral and ethical codes reaching far back into history are against any form of homosexuality. It is universally condemned by all religions. All nations who have given way to the practice of homosexuality have fallen and it is against the law of all civilized nations. The guilt associated with homosexuality is a barrier between the individual and God.

The Creator has endowed the bodies of women with the noble mission of motherhood and the bringing of human life into the world. Any woman who violates this great trust by participating in homosexuality not only degrades herself socially but also destroys the purpose for which God created her.

In Conclusion

Let me emphasize the following:

It is important to recognize danger. It is foolish to expose yourself. Good sportsmanship and courage are never proved by taking unnecessary risks, flirting with danger, or "taking a chance!" Homosexuality is dangerous in all of its phases. The woman who takes any chances with it demonstrates only her own stupidity, never her courage or smartness.

We do not wish to alarm you about homosexuality, nor do we intend anything that we say in this lecture to lead you to believe that an unmarried woman who does not engage in sexual practices with men is homosexual. She is, on the contrary, a sensible person. Sex was created for the married state and true happiness can best be found through marriage and a home. We are confident that you will go on through life using common sense and self-discipline.

We would also like to emphasize again the need of avoiding vicious gossip and rumors accusing or implying that someone is a homosexual or engaging in homosexual acts. Before engaging in such talk or spreading such dastardly gossip about anyone, I would suggest that you think of two things. First, think of the terrible harm that may come to this girl and her family because of you. And secondly, ask yourself—How would I feel if someone were to spread such vicious rumors about me?

If you are actually approached by one of these people or if you strongly suspect something that is out of line, talk the matter over with someone who can do something about it without harming someone who may be innocent. Your WAVE officer, your Medical officer and Chaplain are always available for personal counsel. If you wish to discuss this presentation just given, please feel free to contact any of us who have given it or any of the above mentioned officers. Thank you for your attention.

* * *

[*Letters from Lesbian WAFs to American Civil Liberties Union, 1951*]

Feb 15, 1951

Dear Sir,

I'm not sure whether the following is included in the absence of Civil Liberties but if it isn't I think it should be. I recently joined your organization not consciously connecting it with my predicament at the time, but when I saw inked in at the bottom of your "welcome to membership" note the statement that you were glad to have an Air Force girl with you I couldn't resist telling you about this situation—I would like any comments or suggestions you have to offer.

I enlisted in the Air Force in [the summer] of '49 and am about to receive an Undesirable Discharge. Seems I am guilty of lewed [*sic*] and lacivious [*sic*] behavior—this constitutes homosexuality in their eyes—they have been having a housecleaning and work thusly: Down at Keesler about 11 girls were called in and questioned as to their alleged homosexuality by the OSI—Office of Special Investigation—the girls being sick of the worry and strain of being under suspicion and being promised by a very likable chap Capt ——— of the OSI that they would receive General Discharges if they confessed all proceeded to do so and after confessing were informed that it wasn't enough to incriminate only themselves—they must write down also someone else with whom they had homosexual relations—this done they waited and at the end of January they were all out with Undesirables—I was named in one of these statements and when the records got up here was called in by the OSI. Before I said anything I was read the 24th Article of War—where you don't have to testify against yourself and told also that I might have an attorney with me during this questioning—that seems fair enough but their scare technique is such that you don't quite believe what you hear—he tells you that you don't have to say anything, but does it in such a way that you are sure if you don't the consequences will be little short of fatal.

As far as the attorney is concerned—who could afford a civilian one and I didn't know until it was too late that I had a officer on the base at my disposal—so I stupidly went ahead and made a statement to the effect that I had had such relations with this individual—that the relationship had ended and that never before or since had anything of that nature occurred. If I had been aware of the base attorney at my disposal I would of course been advised to say nothing and they would have had to prove every allegation—as it was I just hung myself out of fear. The papers then went to the Judge Advocates office where he reviewed them and recommended an Undesirable Discharge which I was asked to sign a request for and refused—I requested a courts martial but am not very hopeful of that.

My objections to this whole procedure are many—first of all in the recruiting office no indication is given that lesbians are undesirable or considered so to the service—their job is to fill a quota and that's all they do. This alone would have saved many people a good deal of heartbreak. Once in and aware of the govt attitude in this regard there is no way out except that of having your reputation ruined and the chances of a future job nil—if you were to go and confess the type of discharge would be the same. No consideration is given to your quality of work or dependability—whether you seduce every girl in sight or whether you were once seduced and have since been dating and staying far away from the whole business. The OSI encourages you to spy on the other girls and to list girls who are friends and who *might* be engaging in homosexual relations—and they say they want facts! No consideration is given to the vast amounts of money expended on outfitting and training girls for work only to be discharged at great financial loss to the govt. The Air Force Regulation on this matter AFR 35-66 is the strictest ever and contains such gems as . . . if it is thought that a conviction by courts martial cannot be obtained then Washington shall direct the discharge—it provides that anyone with homosexual tendencies may be discharged—and who among us is without such? For every 10 girls they are discharging they recruit 20 more who will be put through basic and through tech school and then discharged and over and over again.

There seems to be no way to fight this thing—those who decide your fate are in Washington and never see you—if they knew the cost in morale of their troops—the nervous wear and tear on the individual—I wonder if they would think twice. A big wheel comes to visit the base and turns in a good report—how does he know the great percentage of airmen living in fear—waiting from day to day for the call from the OSI. I don't mean to sound childishly dramatic—perhaps it's my own amazement that such a situation exists in this country—this wasn't what we learned in school— our govt tells us how well she has done by the Indian and the foreign nation, but where is one speck of regard for the individual govt employee? No doubt you have had experience with this situation when it came up in the State Dept—here was the last place I expected a rotten deal—I am furious at my ineptness at fighting this thing—somehow I should have been aware of the resources at my disposal—but I am more angry that they should be necessary—that such an unreasonable and unrealistic attitude should prevail—the personal heartbreak where my parents are concerned coupled with the job prejudice in civilian life adds up to one hell of a mess. They have discharged married girls for this also—frankly I'm at my wits end and am writing this in the hope that you will have some suggestion or thought on the matter. Have you any info on what kind of jobs those so branded can obtain? I understand Russia has started rejecting homosexuals for military service—is this a clue?

Thank you for your time spent in reading this.

Sincerely,

———

———————

16 Mar. '51

Dear Sirs,

A friend of mine, Cpl. ———, has been telling me a lot about your organization and your continual and magnificent fights for justice in this country. I would very much like to be a part of such a group. Perhaps my interest is greater right at this time than it would have been previously because I have just been separated from the United States Air Force in a manner that I personally feel to have been less than legal. If I may take a few minutes leeway, I'd like to explain the situation to you.

I enlisted in the WAF [in early] 1949. I took my basic training at Lackland AFB. While I was there, I met a girl with whom I became very friendly, and our friendship continued during our basic training. After graduating from basic, we had a party in San Antonio, and it was at this time that I first realized that the girl with whom I'd been associating was a homosexual. For reasons too numerous to state here, this knowledge did *not* terminate our friendship. We were both shipped to Keesler AFB, Biloxi, Miss. where our relationship, which was of a homosexual nature, continued. Because of strong guilt feelings, and various other psychological repercussions, I broke off our friendship in the Thanksgiving season of that year. (1949). I was attending Radio Operator's school there in Biloxi and remained there until the following March, when I graduated with a Superior rating from aforementioned school. From Thanksgiving 1949 until March 1950, I had no further contact with this girl.

I was sent to Wright-Patterson AFB in March, '50. As soon as I was settled in my job, I started seeing the base psychiatrist, Capt. ———, in an effort to get my mental set straightened out. He, very obligingly, took me on as a patient.

Sometime in December, 1950, I received a letter from this homosexual girl, saying that she had been questioned by the O.S.I. (Office of Special Investigation), and had signed a statement to the effect that she had had homosexual relationships with me "several times." I had an opportunity to read her statement later, and most of what she said was true. Her sins were those of ommission [*sic*]; she neglected to state that she had had relations with two other girls after I "walked out" on her. Another [In other] words, she had a grudge to pay back. I was very much worried about this letter and took it in to Capt. ——— [the base psychiatrist]. He told me not to bother about it, because his word meant a lot more than that of a disgruntled lesbian.

I was called in by the OSI office in our base about two weeks later. I explained to them truthfully what had happened, and thought that would be the end of it. Such was not the case.

I was called in by our Troop Commandant about the middle of February and he asked me if I wanted to request an Undesirable discharge—(it seems that this saves the AF a lot of money.) I refused to sign the request and asked for a court-martial.

My squadron called me the 23rd of February and told me to start clearing the base—I was to be discharged the following week. My appeal for a trial had been refused under the following section of AFR 35-66—

(Regulation concerning discharge of homosexuals)—"when conviction by courts-martial is *unlikely*, the Secretary of the Air Force may direct discharge administratively." I was given a General Discharge from the AF February 28, 1950 [1951]. This discharge, under honorable conditions, simply means that I am refused forever the right to wear the uniform of my country; that I may never hold a position of trust in this country because I am a "bad security-risk." Anytime I want to apply for a Civil Service job, it will be right there. With a little less honesty, with a little less integrity, I could have bluffed my way through it!

I was the fourth girl to be discharged thusly on Wright-Patterson, there were eleven at Keesler and I can't get the figures from Lackland.

It's too late to help me at all in this mess, but there are about twenty girls left there at Wright-Patterson who live in constant terror of the telephone. Their's is no small problem. If we were given any consideration as individuals, it would be a different matter. But nobody asked my Squadron Commander about my character, nobody asked my work unit if I did my work well. (They, by the way, when I asked them for a recommendation for a civilian job, told me to write my own if I was in any way displeased with their's—they recommended me without qualification)[.] To all this no attention was paid. To Washington, I was a nonentity with a homosexual contact. I ask you, for all those girls left, is this fair?—is it in keeping with the principles we shout so loud? How efficient can our armed forces be, with this sort of psychological warfare raging within? As an individual, I'm powerless; as an organization, can you help them?

Sorry to have sputtered on so long. I'm still rather incensed at the situation.

Thanks for your attention,

———

San Francisco, Calif.

———————

April 4, 1951

Dear Miss ———:
I can well sympathize with your plight, but unfortunately, there is no violation of civil liberties involved in the policy of the Army that homosexuals of either sex must be discharged from the Army.
So you see, there is really nothing we can do about whether the Army is sensibly handling the matter or whether they could more sensibly handle

it by furnishing medical treatment to the parties concerned, is not for us to say.

Your friend Corporal ———— wrote us about the same problem in a letter dated February 15th. . . . The only suggestion that I can have on this matter is a purely practical one—doubtless social stigma will follow both of you if the present situation continues; the only way of alleviating it that I can think of is to submit yourself to medical treatment if you really desire to abandon homosexual relations.

Sincerely yours,

————

Staff Counsel

————————

April 23, 1951

Dear Mr. ————,

Received your letter dated April 4, and wish to thank you so much for your attention. Believe me, I fully understand that you are unable to help in straightening out our situation. The cause of homosexuals is a decidedly unpopular one. My letter to the ACLU was merely a shot in the dark. I am one of the luckier ones, with an understanding family, but two of the girls discharged for homosexuality have committed suicide and one other has disappeared completely. These girls, you understand, are all girls who never ran into homosexuality until they entered the service.

I was able . . . to influence our Commanding officer to hold a squadron meeting and explain to the girls their rights under the Articles of War. She was shortly thereafter relieved of her position. Maybe it's a coincidence.

I've written to ex-corporal ———— and sent her your letter. I know full well that my grateful thanks may be extended from both of us. We are both proud to be members of the ACLU and wish you continued success in your very fine work.

Very sincerely yours,

————

Index

Abbot, Berenice, as a second-generation New Woman, 12
Abott, Sidney, *Sappho Was a Right-On Woman*, 92
ACLU. *See* American Civil Liberties Union
Acts d'entr'actes (Barney), 96
Addams, Jane, as a first-generation New Woman, 11
Adolescent crushes, 43–65
Ain't I a Woman (newspaper), 264
Air Force. *See* U.S. Air Force
Akins, Zoe, Cather's letters to, 69n
Aldington, Richard, and H. D., 104, 105, 122, 124, 127
Alexander's Bridge (Cather), 81
Allen, Pamela Gunn, on Native American lesbians, 39
Allenswood (school), 55n, 59
American Civil Liberties Union (ACLU): correspondence with lesbians in the military, 279, 283–84, 290–95; on homosexuality and military service, 284, 294–95
Anderson, Margaret, as a second-generation New Woman, 12
Androgyny: Friedman on, 134; Rich on, 125–26, 127, 128; 130
Annas, Pamela, on Vivien, 98
Anthropologists: on Native American cross-gender roles, 40–42; and research on lesbians, 231–32
"Anti-feminist Woman, The" (Rich), 113
Anxiety of Influence, The (Bloom), 95, 108, 112
Anzaldúa, Gloria, *This Bridge Called My Back*, 264–66
Aphrodite: Sappho and, 105; Wittig and, 148
Aphrodite (Louÿs), 96
Arapahos, on the role of cross-gender females in the Lakota tribe, 38–39
Archimedes, Wittig's recrafting of, 146–49
Army. *See* U.S. Army
Aronowitz, Stanley, on social theory, 216–17
Ashmore, Ruth, on romantic friendships, 77
Athena, Hesiod on, 143–45
Atlantis, H. D. on, 116–17